Story

Hier findest du lustige und spannende Texte über die *friends* in Greenwich.

Action UK!

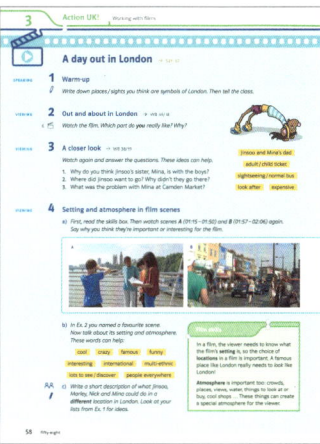

Und hier gibt es tolle Filme aus Greenwich!

Across cultures

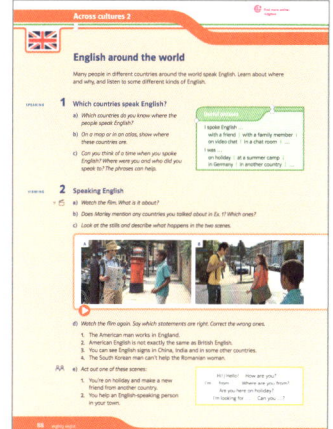

Vergleiche auf diesen Seiten deinen Alltag mit der Alltagskultur und der Geschichte Großbritanniens.

Diff pool

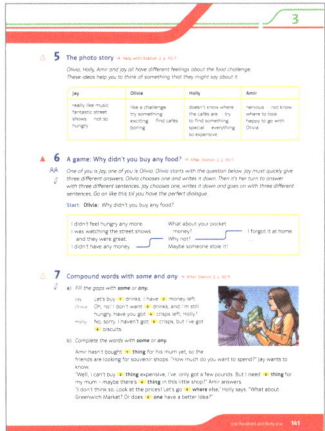

Skills

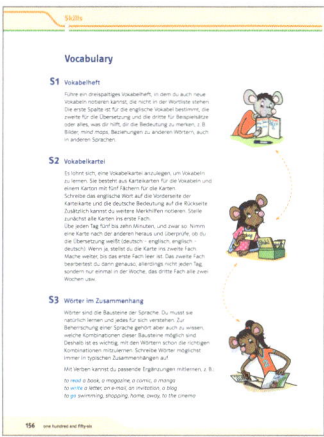

Grammar, Vocabulary

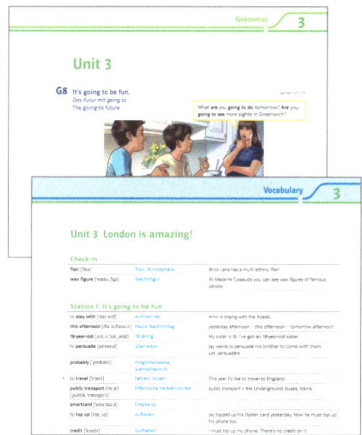

Im hinteren Buchteil stehen dir hilfreiche Anhänge zur Verfügung. *Diff pool*, *Grammar* und *Vocabulary* kennst du schon aus dem letzten Jahr. Neu ab Green Line 2 ist der *Skills*-Anhang. Hier findest du zu den Lernbereichen *Reading*, *Writing*, *Speaking*, *Listening*, *Viewing*, *Mediation* und *Vocabulary* allerlei Lernhilfen und Methodentipps. Die gelben Verweise → S17 bei den Unit-Aufgaben sagen dir, dass es sich lohnt, dort nachzuschlagen!

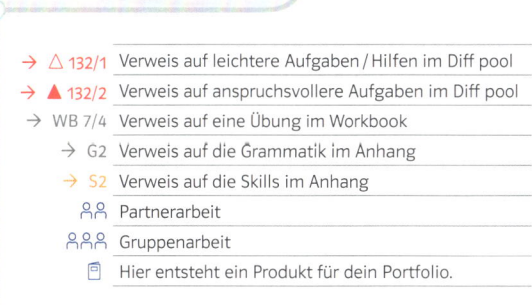

→ △ 132/1	Verweis auf leichtere Aufgaben / Hilfen im Diff pool	
→ ▲ 132/2	Verweis auf anspruchsvollere Aufgaben im Diff pool	
→ WB 7/4	Verweis auf eine Übung im Workbook	
→ G2	Verweis auf die Grammatik im Anhang	
→ S2	Verweis auf die Skills im Anhang	
👥	Partnerarbeit	
👥👤	Gruppenarbeit	
📱	Hier entsteht ein Produkt für dein Portfolio.	

✎	Schreiben (geschlossen / einfach)
✐	Schreiben (offen / kreativ)
S 1/14 ◉	Verweis auf die Schüler-CDs im Workbook (Audio)
L 1/19 ◉	Verweis auf die Lehrer-CDs (Audio)
🎬	Verweis auf die Lehrer-DVD (Film)
🌐	Code auf www.klett.de eingeben und Zusatzmaterial nutzen
🔊 2	Übungen, die die Unit task besonders vorbereiten
🇬🇧	Across cultures

Green Line 2 für Klasse 6 an Gymnasien

Herausgeber: Harald Weisshaar, Bisingen

Autorinnen und Autoren: Marion Horner, Ipswich; Carolyn Jones, Beckenham; Jon Marks, Ventnor; Alison Wooder, Ventnor sowie Paul Dennis, Lahnstein; Barbara Greive, Dortmund; Cornelia Kaminski, Fulda unter Mitwirkung von Manuela Brumme, Stuttgart; Monique Kunhar, Schwaikheim

Beratung: Paul Dennis, Lahnstein; Cornelia Kaminski, Fulda; Nilgül Karabulut, Aachen; Hartmut Klose, Seevetal; Antje Körber, Merseburg; Jörg Nieswand, Berlin; Jörg Schulze, Dresden

Für besondere Unterstützung danken wir herzlich Ms Susan Bolton von der **Thomas Tallis School**, London.

Zusatzmaterial für Schülerinnen und Schüler zu diesem Band:

Workbook + Audio-CD + Übungssoftware	978-3-12-834228-3
Workbook + Audio-CD	978-3-12-834225-2
Fit für Tests und Klassenarbeiten mit Lösungsheft und Audio-CD	978-3-12-834227-6
Das Trainingsbuch mit Audio-CD	978-3-12-834302-0
Vokabellernheft	978-3-12-834282-5
Vokabeltraining aktiv	978-3-12-834332-7

sowie eine Reihe von abgestimmten *English Readers*

1. Auflage

1   12 11 10 9 8 | 27 26 25 24 23

Alle Drucke dieser Auflage sind unverändert und können im Unterricht nebeneinander verwendet werden. Die letzte Zahl bezeichnet das Jahr des Druckes.

Redaktion: Michael Mattison; Anette Dangelmaier; Lektorat editoria: Cornelia Schaller, Fellbach
Herstellung: Anita Bauch

Gestaltung: Petra Michel, Essen
Umschlaggestaltung: know idea, Freiburg; Koma Amok, Stuttgart
Illustrationen: Peer Kramer, Düsseldorf; jani lunablau, Barcelona *(Maskottchen und Story)* sowie Christian Dekelver, Weinstadt *(Karten)*
Satz: Satzkiste GmbH, Stuttgart; Mediengestaltung Elke Kurz, Waiblingen
Reproduktion: Schwaben-Repro, Stuttgart
Druck: Mohn Media Mohndruck GmbH, Gütersloh

Printed in Germany
ISBN 978-3-12-834220-7 (fester Einband)
ISBN 978-3-12-834221-4 (flexibler Einband)

Green Line 2

von
Marion Horner
Carolyn Jones
Jon Marks
Alison Wooder
Paul Dennis
Barbara Greive
Cornelia Kaminski

herausgegeben von
Harald Weisshaar

Ernst Klett Verlag
Stuttgart · Leipzig

Inhalt

Legende

L	Listening	**w**	Writing	**voc**	Vocabulary	🇬🇧	Across cultures
s	Speaking	**m**	Mediation	**sk**	Skills	⟨⟩	Fakultativ
R	Reading	**v**	Viewing	🧩	Kompetenzaufgabe	**R**	Revision

Inhalt

Unit 3: London is amazing!

Inhalt

 Find more online:
ny827k

Unit 1

My friends and I

*Your classmates —
CAUGHT ON CAMERA!*

A

Jay, don't you know that embarrassing outfits always end up in the yearbook? LOL! ☺

B

Dave, Olivia and Luke after a round of boxing. Ouch, those red noses! Oh, wait – it's Red Nose Day, of course! (Nice cake, mmm…)

SPEAKING

1 Talk about the yearbook photos

What can you see? Where are the girls and boys? What do you think they're doing or saying?

LISTENING

2 Caught on camera

L 1/1 ◉ **a)** *Listen to the dialogues. Which photo are the characters talking about? (There is no dialogue for one of the photos.)*

→ S18–20 **b)** *Listen again and then answer the questions.*

1. How does Jay feel about the photo of himself and Holly? 2. Which two characters are on the yearbook team? 3. Who is doing which pages in the yearbook? 4. Why does Holly like the photo of the three boys?

In Unit 1 you learn

… how to talk about special activities in the past and how to give information about places. You learn:

- words about feelings
- the simple past
- words and phrases that describe and compare

C

The eyes say it all for lovebirds Holly and Jay. (The camera never lies!)

D

Luke, Dave and Jay are practising for the class trip. Hey guys, we know that you're funny – but now we know that you're silly too!

SPEAKING **3 Feelings** → WB 2/1–2

 a) *Take turns to act different feelings. Can the others guess your word?*

 b) *Look at the photos again. Say how you think the characters feel and why.*

Example: Photo D: I think Dave feels happy because he's having fun with his friends.

→ △ 132/1 **c)** *Make a mind map for 'feelings'. Add new words to your personal vocabulary.*

happy   shy   excited   embarrassed   proud

Across cultures

Yearbooks are an American tradition, but now they are popular in British schools too. Students on a yearbook team work together to make a fun book for their class, with photos of students and reports about activities during the school year. How do you collect the highlights in the school year?

L 1/2 ⊙   # I love Red Nose Day

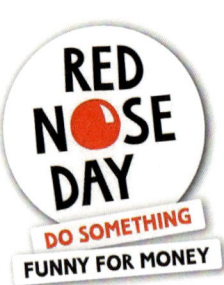

YES, IT'S RED NOSE TIME AGAIN!

RED NOSE DAY

DO SOMETHING FUNNY FOR MONEY

Here at TTS we always do our best for COMIC RELIEF. Two years ago we raised lots of money, but this year let's raise even more! Check the TTS website for more information.

COMIC RELIEF is a great charity. It helps people in need in Africa and also the UK. The comedian Lenny Henry started Comic Relief – that's how it got its name – and on the first Red Nose Day in 1988 people wore red noses, did fun activities to raise money and watched a big comedy show on TV. That was many years ago, but today we still do the same things!

I love Red Nose Day. So when I saw the poster on the school noticeboard last month I felt really excited. My friends and I had lots of crazy ideas about how to raise money. In the end we made and sold cakes with funny faces. After school we went into Greenwich and did our own comedy show in the street. Luke's dog Sherlock was a real star, and lots of people gave us money for the TTS collection. It was great fun! I can't wait till next time.

Olivia Fraser

READING

1   **Charity work: Olivia and her friends**

→ 🔺 132/2   *Look at what Olivia writes about Red Nose Day. What things sound fun to you?*

> **Across cultures**
>
> People in the UK often help **charities**. What charities in Germany do you know about?

LANGUAGE

 **2**   **Irregular simple past forms** → WB 3/3 → G1

> There are no rules for irregular past forms. You must learn them by heart.

 **a)** *Look again at Olivia's text and find the past forms of these verbs. Make a list.*

be ✔	do ✔	feel	get
give	go	have	make
see	sell	wear	

Verb	Past form
be	was / were
do	did
feel	…

→ 🔺 132/3   **b)** *Put in the correct past forms. (The list of irregular verbs on page 284 can help you.)*

Two years ago the students **1** (do) fun activities and **2** (get) money for Comic Relief. They **3** (bring) the money to school. Then the school **4** (put) all the money together and **5** (give) it to the charity. Red Nose Day **6** (be) a non-uniform day, so everyone **7** (come) to school in different clothes. But they all **8** (wear) something red. Of course they all **9** (have) red noses too. Some students **10** (take) funny photos for the school website.

LANGUAGE

3 Find the rule: Regular simple past forms

a) *Look at the example. Find the rule for regular past forms and write it down.*

Example: Lenny Henry **started** Comic Relief in 1988. Last time we **raised** lots of money. In the evening we **watched** the big TV show.

L 1/4

→ △ 133/4

→ S14

b) *Be careful how you say* **-ed***. There are three different sounds. Listen and say:*

1. [d] Two years ago we organis**ed** a great Red Nose Day. I lov**ed** it. We plann**ed** lots of activities.
2. [t] First we help**ed** to raise money. Then we watch**ed** TV. I lik**ed** Lenny Henry's jokes!
3. [ɪd] I want**ed** to look funny so I paint**ed** my face. I need**ed** a red nose too, of course.

LANGUAGE

4 The friends' comedy show → WB 3/4–5

Look at the picture and write 5–6 sentences about the comedy show. Choose from these verbs and use the simple past.

Example: The friends did the comedy show after school.

play   do ✔

chase   watch   collect

dance   laugh   act

LANGUAGE

5 The star of the show → WB 4/6, 5/7

→ △ 133/5

What does Sherlock tell his dog friends the next day?
Write the text again in his words, with the verbs in the simple past.
Check if the forms are regular or irregular.

Start: I **did** lots of great tricks in the comedy show yesterday.

Sherlock *does* lots of great tricks in the comedy show. First he *jumps* over a big box. Then he *runs* around and *chases* his tail. After that he *dances* on a skateboard, and when Olivia *starts* to play the sax he also *sings*. The people *love* it. They *laugh* and *clap* and *give* lots of money for Comic Relief. Luke and his friends *try* to do their best too but everyone's eyes *are* on Sherlock. He *feels* happy and proud – he *is* the real star of the show!

Look at G1 on page 170. You must be careful with the spelling of some regular forms.

SPEAKING

6 Play a game: Something funny for money

People often pay money when you do funny or hard activities for charity. Take turns to say what you did on Red Nose Day. Roll two dice, for an activity and a comment.

Example: **2** + **5** I went everywhere in pyjamas. I enjoyed the day.

Activities
1 turn off my phone for the day
2 go everywhere in pyjamas
3 swim for 30 minutes
4 eat baby food
5 try not to laugh all day
6 speak in a funny voice

Comments
1 have lots of fun
2 find that hard
3 feel great
4 do my best
5 enjoy the day
6 raise lots of money

> If you like, you can think of new ideas for activities and comments.

WRITING

7 Your turn: A report about a special activity

→ △ 133/6

Write a report about an activity that you did with your friends or family. Write 6–8 sentences.

Example: Last year my friends and I helped to tidy a park. We …

Useful phrases	
When?	Last week / A month ago / In July / …
Who?	My friends and I / My dad / …
What?	We did a project / show … | We organised a … / made … / helped …
Feelings?	It was fun / I felt happy / nervous / proud / …

MEDIATION

8 A flyer in a German classroom

→ S17

Answer a British student's questions.

1. I know 'groß', so I can see this flyer is about something big. But what is it?
2. Who wants to sell cakes? And why?
3. Is the sale here in the school building?
4. 10th October – that's the date of your sale, right?
5. What's this about Africa?

> **Mediation skills**
>
> A **quick answer** helps to keep the conversation going.
>
> Don't worry **if the answer isn't in the text**. Just say there's no information.

GROSSER KUCHENVERKAUF

++ Wichtige Ankündigung! ++

Wir brauchen noch Geld für unsere Klassenfahrt. Deshalb planen wir einen großen Kuchenverkauf. (Erinnert ihr euch? Letztes Jahr haben wir auf diese Weise viel Geld für eine Schule in Afrika gesammelt.) Lasst uns also bald wieder in der Küche fleißig werden und viele leckere Kuchen backen!
Um zu besprechen, wann unser Kuchenverkauf stattfindet und wer was macht, treffen wir uns am 10. Oktober in der ersten Unterrichtsstunde. Merkt euch bitte dieses Datum – und bringt viele Ideen mit!

L1/5 # How did they know?

Luke: Only ten days till our class trip! I can't wait!

Dave: Sit down and help us, Luke! It's our group's job to think of games to play on the coach.

Luke: Hey, what about puzzle stories?

5 Holly: I don't know that game. How do you play it?

Dave: I know it! Great idea, Luke. Someone tells a little story with missing information. Then the others ask questions to try and find the solution. Here's a puzzle story for you …

10 After an anonymous phone call the police went to an address to arrest a dangerous man. They didn't know what the man looked like. They only knew that his name was John and that he was at that address. When they got to the house they found four people at a table in the kitchen:

15 a taxi driver, a mechanic, a farmer and a postman. The police didn't ask any questions and the other people didn't say anything, but right away the police arrested the postman. How did they know that they had the right person? Why were they so sure?

Luke: Did the police really arrest the right person?	Dave: Yes, they did.
20 Luke: Were there any photos of the man?	Dave: No, there weren't.
Holly: Did the postman try to run away?	Dave: No, he didn't.
Luke: Did the other people help the police?	Dave: No, they didn't.
Holly: Was it the man's home?	Dave: I don't know.
	But that isn't important.
25 Luke: Was the man's name a clue?	Dave: Yes, it was.

→ Solution on p. 15

SPEAKING ## 9 Talk about games

Do you like guessing games? What ideas have you got for games on a coach trip?

LANGUAGE ## 10 Ask and answer questions about the puzzle story → WB 5/8   → G2–3

1. Did the phone call help the police?
2. Was the man's name Peter?
3. Did the police ask any questions?
4. Was the man dangerous?
5. Were the four people in the kitchen?
6. Were the other people postmen too?

Yes,	he it they	was. were. did.
No,		wasn't. weren't. didn't.

LANGUAGE **11** ## Find the rule: Differences between present and past → G2-3

*Look at the sentences in the present and the past. What are the differences for **questions** and **negative sentences**? Write down the rule.*

Simple present	Simple past
Do you like the story?	Did you like the story?
What does she say?	What did she say?
I don't know the game.	I didn't know the game.
He doesn't want to play.	He didn't want to play.

LANGUAGE **12** ## Guess what we did

→ △ 134/7
→ ▲ 134/8

Think of a fun activity that you and a friend did on a coach. (It needn't be true.) Your partner guesses what you did.

I spy with my little eye …

Example:
Did you tell puzzle stories? – No, we didn't.
Did you count all the red cars? – No, we didn't.
Did you send funny texts? – Yes, we did!

LANGUAGE **13** ## Problems on the coach → WB 5/9

*Complete the sentences. Use **didn't**.*

Example: I felt hungry but I (not have any food) → … but I didn't have any food.

1. I wasn't happy because my best friend (not sit next to me)
2. I helped a girl with her bag but she (not say thank you)
3. It was very loud on the coach so some people (not hear our puzzle stories)
4. The driver was friendly but he (not speak much English)
5. I needed the toilet but the coach (not stop)
6. The coach was slow so we (not get there till late)

LANGUAGE **14** ## Make fun questions and answers → WB 6/10–11 → G2

a) *Work in groups of three or four. Think of six fun questions. Start with question words and use the simple past. Write each question on a piece of paper.*

How?	Why?	What?	Where?

Who?	laugh?	get?	see?

be?	meet?	…?

Examples:
What did you find in your schoolbag?
Why were you in a tree all day?

b) *Swap questions with another group and write funny answers to their questions.*

c) *With the other group, look at all the questions and answers. Choose the three best ideas and read them to the class.*

SPEAKING

15 Revision: Who am I? → WB 7/12

Think of a famous person. It can be a real person (e.g. singer, sports star) or a character from a film or book. Your partner must guess who you are.

Example:

Are you a real person? – No, I'm not.
Can I see you in a film? – Yes, you can.
Is the film a comedy? – No, it isn't.
Do you do dangerous things? – Yes, I do.
Does Daniel Craig act your role? – Yes, he does.
I know! You're James Bond. – Yes, that's right.

> You can only ask questions
> with yes/no answers.
> Are you …? Have you got …?
> Do/Does …? Is …? …?

LISTENING

16 Luke's dream

L 1/6 ⊙
→ S18–20

a) *Listen and find five pictures that go with Luke's dream.*
(One picture is wrong.) Put the five pictures in the correct order.

b) *Listen again and answer the questions.*

1. What was Luke's problem with Sherlock?   2. How did Luke feel when the coach went without him?   3. Who did Luke ask for help first?   4. Why were the police suddenly too busy to help Luke?   5. Why didn't Luke stay on the train?   6. What did Luke find out about the horse in the past?   7. Why didn't Luke find out the end of his dream?

WRITING

17 Your turn: Your puzzle story

Write your own short puzzle story (5–6 sentences).
You can use your own idea or maybe you already know a story like this.
Can your friends guess the solution?

Solution to the puzzle story on page 13: There was only one man in
the house – the postman. The other people were all women.

L 1/7 ◎ # Everyone can enjoy a challenge

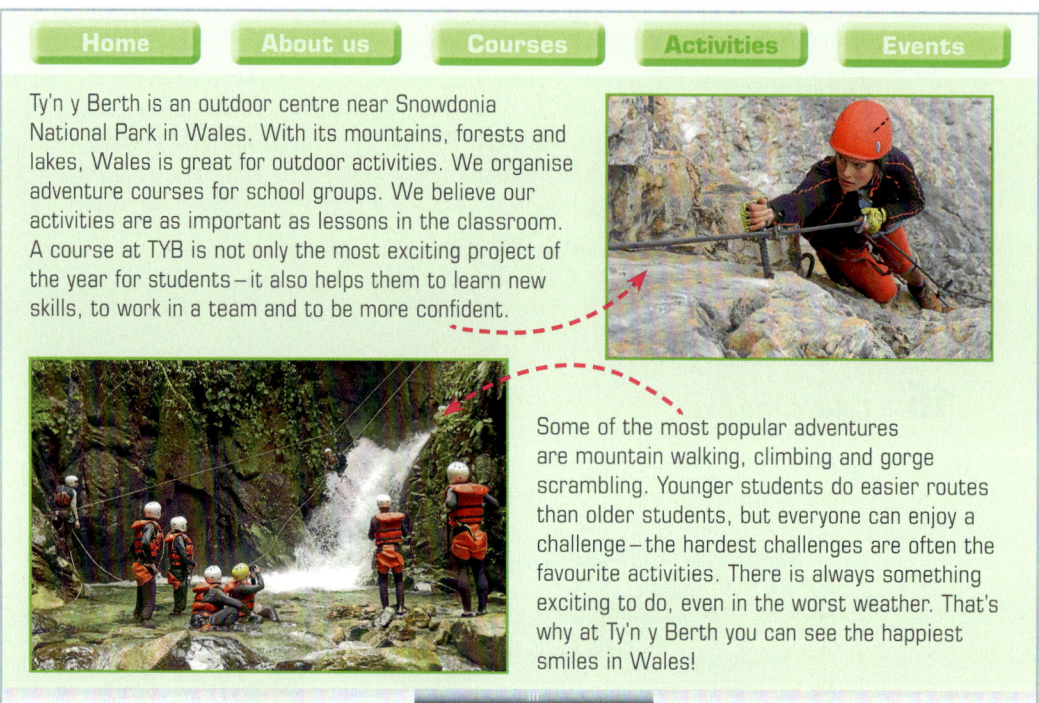

Home | About us | Courses | Activities | Events

Ty'n y Berth is an outdoor centre near Snowdonia National Park in Wales. With its mountains, forests and lakes, Wales is great for outdoor activities. We organise adventure courses for school groups. We believe our activities are as important as lessons in the classroom. A course at TYB is not only the most exciting project of the year for students – it also helps them to learn new skills, to work in a team and to be more confident.

Some of the most popular adventures are mountain walking, climbing and gorge scrambling. Younger students do easier routes than older students, but everyone can enjoy a challenge – the hardest challenges are often the favourite activities. There is always something exciting to do, even in the worst weather. That's why at Ty'n y Berth you can see the happiest smiles in Wales!

SPEAKING **18** ## Talk about the outdoor centre

a) *Close your books. Say what you remember about Wales and the outdoor centre.*

b) *Would you like to go there? What looks fun or interesting to you?*

c) *Your turn: Tell the class about a challenge that you had.*

Across cultures

Wales is an important part of the UK, but it's also a separate country with its own Celtic culture. Many people there speak two languages, English and Welsh. Ty'n y Berth is a Welsh name. You say it like this: [ti:n̩ə 'bɜːθ]

LANGUAGE **19** ## Find the rule: Comparative and superlative forms → G4

a) *Copy and complete the grid. Look in the text for the missing forms.*

b) *Collect more examples from the text and add them to the grid.*

c) *Write down the rule for comparative and superlative forms of adjectives.*

adjective	comparative	superlative
hard	harder	...
big	...	biggest
easy	...	easiest
popular	more popular	...
confident	...	most confident
bad	worse	...
...	...	...

LANGUAGE **20** **Practise the new forms**

a) *Say the comparative and superlative forms of these adjectives.*

proud   good   interesting   funny

dangerous   quiet   brave   excited

→ △ 134/9 **b)** *What do you think about these things? Compare your ideas.*

Example: A: I think mountain walking is the **most exciting** outdoor activity.
B: Oh, I think climbing is **more exciting than** mountain walking.

exciting outdoor activity   good place for a holiday   interesting hobby   (any more ideas?)

LANGUAGE **21** **Say it in different words** → WB 7/13, 8/14–15 → G5

→ △ 135/10 *Use a different adjective and a different form.*

Example: 1. Wales is **smaller than** England.

1. Wales isn't as big as England. (small)
2. The weather today isn't as good as yesterday. (bad)
3. Route A is harder than route B. (easy)
4. The courses are cheaper than most people think. (expensive)
5. I'm more confident than I was about new challenges. (nervous)

> Be careful with **than** and **as**.
> When do you use which word?
> younger **than** = **not as** old **as**

OCABULARY **22** **Find adjectives to describe what you can see** → WB 8/16

Take turns to describe. Use comparative or superlative forms or '(not) as … as …'

→ △ 135/11
→ ▲ 135/12

fast   small   low   big   slow   tall   high

S1/3–7
L1/9–13 ⊙

It was amazing

1 Before you read

→ S5–6, 8

Look only at the words in blue *in part A of the text.*
What do you think the text is about? Collect ideas.

This text and the
exercises help with the
Unit task on pages 22–23.

Dave Preston's report for the class yearbook:

A It was a trip to a different planet! We came
from a place with busy streets and shops
and lots of people, but in this new place
5 there were only mountains and lakes and
lots of sheep …
   Everyone on the coach was excited
when we started our class trip to the
Ty'n y Berth Outdoor Centre that
10 Saturday morning. Even our teacher
Mr Swindon was excited . "Who wants
to go to Wales?" he shouted. "We all do!"
we shouted back.
   It was a long way from Greenwich,
15 but we played games and ate our
sandwiches, and when at last we saw the
big sign "Croeso i Gymru" we all clapped.
Now the roads were quieter. Everything
looked green and the villages and farms
20 had strange Welsh names. Soon we were
in the mountains.

B At last the coach stopped in front of an
old grey building next to fields and trees.
Lots of the buildings in Wales are grey.
25 A man with a friendly face met us at
the door of the building. "Welcome to
Ty'n y Berth, everyone!" he said with a
smile. "I'm Will, one of the instructors at
the centre. And this is your home for
30 the next few days."
   Years ago it was a village school. But
now it's all different inside. The biggest
room is for meals and free time activities,
and most of the smaller rooms are
35 bedrooms for people on courses at the
centre.
   I was in a bedroom with five other
boys. Right away there was a problem

because Luke and Jay wanted the same
bed near the window. "Maybe you can 40
take turns," I said. They thought that was
a good solution, and Luke slept in the bed
first. For all of us that night it felt a bit
strange to be in a new place without our
families. 45

C Most of the time at Ty'n y Berth we
were too busy to think of home. Every
morning and afternoon there were new
and exciting activities to try. Then in the
evening we usually played games. 50
   Everyone loved gorge scrambling.
It was funny when Olivia, Holly and
I tried to help each other to get across
a little river. In the end we just helped
each other to fall *into* it. The water in 55
mountain rivers is very cold!
   We all found some activities harder
than others. For me, climbing was the
greatest challenge. But our instructor
Ceri was great. She gave me lots of tips, 60
and then I felt more confident.
   Late one evening there was a surprise.
Will gave everyone a torch and we went
for a walk in the dark. "Don't talk, just
listen," Will said. So we listened and it 65
was amazing because it was so very quiet.
In Greenwich there's always noise, even
at night. Then we all turned off our
torches and that was amazing too.
It was much darker than 70
in London so the stars
looked much bigger and
clearer.

D Too soon it was the last day, but when
75 we went to bed Luke whispered to me,
"I've got a torch so let's go for a night walk
again. Just you, Jay and me." We knew it
was against the rules, but we wanted one
last adventure. We waited till the others
80 were asleep. Then, as quiet as mice, we
tiptoed from the bedroom.

It was very dark outside, but with
Luke's torch we found our way across a
field and through some trees. Then Luke
85 turned off the torch. Well, I thought he
did, and I didn't know why. "Er, Luke –
it's a cloudy night so we can't look at the
stars, you know. I can't even see you," Jay
said. "I know," Luke's voice answered.
90 "The torch needs a new battery."

Oh no! Now we had a problem. The
night was as black as – well, as black as
night. We tried to be cool but we didn't
feel it. Which was the way back to the
95 centre? We had no idea. We started to
walk. We just hoped it was the right way.
Then suddenly – "Hoo-hoo!" What was
that? The strange noise made us nervous.
"Hoo-hoo!" It was nearer now. What was
100 it? We started to run, but in the dark it
was dangerous. Jay fell over something.
"Help! It's moving! It's a monster!" he

shouted. We tried to run away together.
Something awful hit my face and I
shouted too. We were really scared. 105
It was crazy. I don't know how we got
back to the centre again. We were so
happy to see that old grey building. We
tiptoed to the door and – oh no, the door
was locked! What now? We didn't want 110
trouble, but we needed to get back to our
beds. How did we do it? That's a secret.

E Early the next morning the coach came
to take us back to Greenwich. We were
sad to say goodbye to Wales, but we've all 115
got great memories of our amazing class
trip. (And now everyone knows why Luke,
Jay and I were tired and slept all the way
home!)

READING

2 **Questions about the text** → WB 9/17–18

a) *Take turns to ask and answer questions about Dave's report.*

Example: Where did the students go for their class trip? – They went to Wales.

What …?	the students / go for their class trip	Dave / find the hardest challenge
Why …?	everyone / get to Ty'n y Berth	the stars / look so big and clear
Where …?	the girls and boys / eat their meals	the three boys / go for a night walk
How …?	Luke and Jay / want the same bed	Luke's torch / need?
When …?	the students / do on the course	(*your own idea for questions?*)

b) *Something to think about:* What do you think these things were?

1. the "hoo-hoo" noise (line 97)   2. the monster (line 102)   3. something awful (line 104)

SPEAKING **3** **The secret** → WB 9/19

a) *In the report Dave doesn't say how he, Luke and Jay got back to their beds. How do you think they did this? What ideas have you got?*

> Maybe they found an open window.

> Maybe they …

→ S16  **b)** *Role play: Work in groups. Think of an ending and write a short scene. Act your scene for the class.*

→ △ 135/13

WRITING **4** **How to: Plan a travel report**

→ S7 **a)** *In one or two sentences say what each of the five parts of the report (A–E) is about.*

Start: Part A is about how the students got from Greenwich to Wales.

b) *Find two or three key phrases in each part that can make good headings for that part.*

Example: Part A: Our class trip – A long way from Greenwich – Croeso i Gymru

→ S10–13 **c)** *Use your ideas from a) and b) to make Dave's plan for his report. Use a grid to show the five parts and the main ideas in each part.*

Part	Main ideas
A	class trip – from Greenwich to Wales – long way
B	

Writing skills

Always **make a plan** for a text. A good plan shows how many **parts** the text has got and also the main ideas in each part.

Try to **make your text interesting** for the reader. Think of a special way to start the text. Choose good words and phrases that help the reader to see and feel what you describe.

VOCABULARY **5** **How to: Make a travel report interesting**

 a) *Talk about the first sentence of Dave's report. Do you think this is a good way to start a travel report? Why / why not?*

→ S13

b) *A travel report needs different kinds of words and phrases. Look at the lists below and find more examples in Dave's report. (Some examples can go in more than one list.)*

1. words that explain 'when': that Saturday morning (line 9) – at last (line 22) – …
2. words that describe places: everything looked green (line 18) – busy streets (line 3) – …
3. words that show feelings: excited (line 11) – we all clapped (line 17) – …
4. words that make a text exciting: a different planet! (line 2) – Oh no! (line 91) – …

How to use a dictionary

> Think! Do you really need a dictionary? What do you do first when you see a new English word? What do you do if you don't know how to translate a German word into English?

1 Talk about different kinds of dictionaries

a) *Match A–E to the right kind of dictionary. (Some sentences are correct for all three kinds.)*

<mark>Online …</mark>   <mark>In a book …</mark>   <mark>In an electronic dictionary …</mark>

A. the words are in a list in alphabetical order.
B. you write in the search box to look up a word.
C. you can see the different meanings of the word.
D. you can hear the word's pronunciation.
E. there are two parts: first words in one language and then words in the other language.

b) *What other information do the different dictionaries give?*

c) *Which kind of dictionary do **you** like to use? Explain why.*

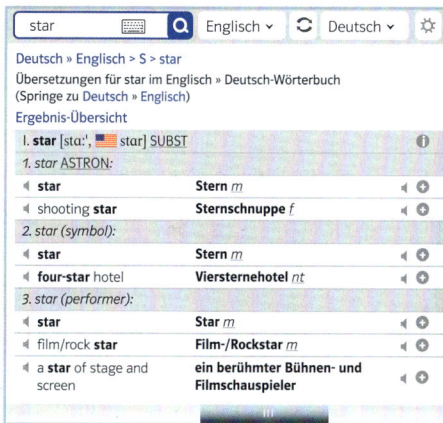

2 Practise with the alphabet → WB 10/20–21

a) *Revision: Take turns to say the alphabet in English.*

b) *Work with the first sentence in part C of Dave's report on page 18. Put all the words in the sentence in alphabetical order. (Be careful with words that start with the same letter – look at the next letters too.) Then check with your partner. Is the order correct?*

3 Find the correct meaning → WB 10/22

a) *English → German: When you find more than one meaning for a word, choose the right meaning for the sentence. Look up the words in* blue *and translate them into German.*

1. Take the second street on the right . That's the right way for the station.
2. I haven't got time to sit and chat today. We can chat when I come next time .
3. This is a very small room . There's room for only one bed.

b) *German → English: Sometimes you need different English words for the same German word. Look up the German words and complete the sentences.*

1. ***tragen***: a) The students … a blue uniform.
   b) They … their books to school in a bag.
2. ***treffen***: a) I often … my friends in the park.
   b) Try to … that tree with your ball.
3. ***Karte***: a) Can you find Wales on the …?
   b) Look at the … for our special lunch.

Our travel report

For your yearbook, work in groups of four and write a short travel report about a class trip. It can be a real trip – or a fantasy trip! It needn't be as long as Dave's report on pages 18–19, but it's important to make it interesting for your readers.

pages 18–19

Step 1

Choose an idea for your trip → WB 11/24

a) *What kind of class trip can your group write about? Do you want to use one of these photos? Or have you got your own great idea? Discuss different ideas and then choose **one** idea for your travel report.*

1

2

3

1. rafting | paddle | current | to capsize
2. science fiction | aliens | planet | spaceship
3. sightseeing | youth hostel | party | trouble

b) *Work with a placemat to collect ideas for your report. You each think about one of the four topics below. Write down ideas in your part of the placemat.*

1. The place: How did you get there?
2. The people: Who is in the report?
3. Typical activities: What did you do or see during the first part of your trip?
4. A special adventure (e.g. problem, surprise): What happened? What did you do?

c) *Choose which ideas you want to use and write them down in the middle of the placemat.*

> For help with questions in the simple past, look back at **Station 2**.
>
> For help with new words, look at the **Skills page**.
>
> For help with placemats look at page 167 in the **Skills section**.

look at page 167 in the Skills section

---

rafting [ˈrɑːftɪŋ] Schlauchbootfahren | **paddle** [ˈpædl] Paddel | **current** [ˈkʌrnt] Strömung | **to capsize** [kæpˈsaɪz] kentern | **to go sightseeing** [ˈsaɪtˌsiːɪŋ] eine Besichtigungstour machen | **youth hostel** [ˈjuːθ ˌhɒstl] Jugendherberge

Step 2

Plan your travel report → WB 11/25

For help with how to write a plan, look at the **Story** again.

a) *Your report has got four parts.*
Together, write a plan that shows the key ideas in each part.

Part 1: **The beginning:** Here you describe how you got to the place.
Part 2: **The first day(s):** Here you describe typical activities for this kind of trip.
Part 3: **The special adventure:** Say what happened, but don't tell the whole story.
This part of the report finishes with a problem or an exciting situation.
Part 4: **The ending:** Explain how the adventure finished; find a good ending.

b) *Decide who writes which part of the report.*

Step 3

Do you remember the four kinds of words for travel reports? Look back at the **Story** exercises.

For help with the simple past, look at **Station 1** and **Station 2** again.

Station 3 helps you with adjectives.

Write your part of the travel report

a) *Work with the plan from Step 2 and make notes about the information in your part. Don't write sentences – just important words and phrases.*

b) *Read through your notes. Have you got interesting ideas and words?*

c) *Now write your part of the report. Don't forget to use the simple past.*

Step 4

Improve your part of the report → WB 12/26

Work with a partner from your group. Check each other's texts. Help each other to improve the texts.

Look at page 161 in the **Skills section** for tips on how to check texts.

Step 5

Finish your travel report → WB 12/27

a) *Put the four parts together and read the whole report. Are you happy with it? If not, discuss it and improve it.*

b) *Now think of the best way to present your report. Use photos or pictures too.*

The new boy → S21–22

VIEWING

1 Film scenes → WB 13/28

1 **a)** *Watch (00:00-03:01). Look at the headings for Scene A and B and at the phrases in the box. Match the phrases with the right scene.*

Scene A: After school   **Scene B:** The new boy

> sneaking around   a bad day?
>
> friends again   why lemons?
>
> trouble (between friends)

b) *Jinsoo and Marley want to know why Nick is buying all those things. What do **you** think Nick is up to? What happens next? Talk about your ideas and then watch the last part of the film (03:02-04:45).*

c) *Do you like the film's ending? Explain why / why not. Write two or three sentences.*

Example: I think the ending is nice / funny / surprising / boring / … because …

VIEWING

2 Film and music

a) *Before you read the box on the right, watch (01:58-04:45) again and listen to the music in the different scenes. What can you say about the music? Why do you think the filmmakers use music that way?*

b) *Now read the box. Then look at the photo. Which adjectives describe the mood and the feelings in the scene? What kind of music would **you** use for the scene?*

> ### Film skills
>
> Films don't work the same way as texts. A film tells a story with words – *and* with **pictures**, **sounds** and **music** too. So you have the story in a film, and you have different ways to tell that story. These are called the audio-visual effects of a film.
>
> **Examples:** If you want to show that a person is sad, you can use slow and sad music. For an action scene, you can use loud and fast music.

Mood / Feelings:

excited   sad   tired   happy

angry   unfriendly   hurt   silly

…

Music:

funny   slow   loud   aggressive

sad   fast   sweet   happy   cool

scary   …

→ Solutions p. 286

Can you ...

1. talk about activities that you did?	I went to … | We played / sold …
2. find out what happened?	Did you see …? | Why was he …? | How did she …?
3. say how you felt?	I was / felt embarrassed/… | It was exciting / …
4. compare things?	It's bigger than / as big as … | It's the most exciting …

LANGUAGE

1 The yearbook team

Look at the list of jobs for the yearbook team. Write down what they did yesterday. Make sentences with the correct past forms.

Start: They talked about … They …

- talk about the 'dreams' page
- put the sports pages together
- look at Jay's ideas for the music pages
- collect ideas for the puzzles page
- take a photo of the yearbook team
- make a list of jobs for next week

LANGUAGE

2 Put in the correct past forms

Holly: I **1** (go) swimming in the sea at Southend yesterday.

Dave: Wow! **2** (be) it your mum's idea to go to Southend?

Holly: No, it **3** (not be). Olivia's family **4** (invite) me.

Dave: Lucky you! **5** (you go) on the train?

Holly: Yes, we **6** (do).

Dave: You **7** (be) brave to go in the sea at this time of the year! **8** (be) the water cold?

Holly: Yes, it **9** (be). So we **10** (not stay) in the water for more than a few minutes.

LANGUAGE

3 What are the questions?

Olivia calls home from Ty'n y Berth. Her dad wants to know more. What does he ask?

1. Olivia: We *got up* early this morning.
   Dad: When did you …?
2. Olivia: We *went* for a long walk.
   Dad: Where …?
3. Olivia: We *saw* lots of interesting things.
   Dad: What …?
4. Olivia: My classmates *laughed* at me.
   Dad: Why …?

LANGUAGE

4 Comparative and superlative forms: Pet profiles for the yearbook

1. Luke's dog Sherlock is the (crazy) animal in England. There's nothing (funny) than when he chases his tail. It's always (fast) than he is!
2. The (cute) pets for Holly are her two guinea pigs. Mr Fluff likes to explore. He thinks a trip in a bag is (interesting) than a game on the floor! Honey isn't as (brave) as Mr Fluff.
3. Cats are the (popular) pets in the class. Dave's cat Sid brings presents for the family. Some presents are (good) than others. The (bad) thing for Dave is a mouse in his bed!

S1/8–12
L1/14–18 ⊙

Middle school: How I got lost[1] in London

Rafe Khatchadorian is not very popular with his classmates, and his best friend Leo only exists in Rafe's imagination. A lot of things go wrong for Rafe, especially on a school trip to London to study Living History (when you visit special museums where they show how people lived in the past). When they
5 go to see a famous London wax museum, he makes some silly mistakes, and his popularity score – a sign of how much the others like him – falls and falls.

The big event of the day was a tour around Madame Fifi's House of Wax. Now, of course we were excited about seeing the
10 main attractions – Will and Kate! David Beckham! Rihanna! – but we were *really* excited about the basement[2]. Because in the basement was Madame Fifi's Temple of Terrors, where you could see beheadings[3],
15 people on spikes and other horrible things. In other words, all the blood[4].

Yeah, yeah, we saw all the famous people. But do you *really* want to stand eye to eye with Tom Cruise? *You do?*
20 Not me. I wanted stuff from *my* world. So I stayed longest at Henry VIII (he had six wives[5] and beheaded two of them!), Winston Churchill (he said "We shall never surrender"[6] to Adolf Hitler!), Charles

Darwin (it's thanks to him we know that
25 we come from monkeys[7]!), Guy Fawkes (he tried to blow up[8] Parliament … Wait: should[9] we like him or not?)

I was sad to leave the upper floors. And also …
30
"Scared …?" Leo whispered.

"No, of course I'm not scared," I said.

"Frightened?"

"Frightened is the same as scared," I told him. "And no, I'm not frightened."
35
But, let me tell you a secret: I *was* nervous.

"Is everyone ready?" Gordon, our tour guide, asked.

"Yeah," we all replied.
40
I remembered my popularity score today (-11) and decided to be brave, so my "Yeah" was the loudest. "YEAH!"

"Right, then, let's go," Gordon said. He opened the door but then stopped. "Does
45 anybody in the group have a weak heart[10]?" he asked.

"No," we replied.

"NO!" came my voice, the loudest.

"And everyone knows about the
50 haunting[11]?"

"YEAH!" I shouted, really enjoying myself.

Everyone looked at me – Gordon too.

"What is your name, young man?" he
55 asked.

---

1 to get lost [gɛt ˈlɒst] verschwinden; verloren gehen | **2 basement** [ˈbeɪsmənt] Keller | **3 beheading** [bɪˈhedɪŋ] Enthauptung | **4 blood** [blʌd] Blut | **5 wives** [waɪvz] Ehefrauen | **6 we shall never surrender** [wi ʃæl ˌnevə srˈendə] wir werden uns nie ergeben | **7 monkey** [ˈmʌŋki] Affe | **8 to blow up** [bləʊˌˈʌp] in die Luft sprengen | **9 should** [ʃʊd] sollten | **10 weak heart** [wiːk ˈhɑːt] schwaches Herz | **11 haunting** [ˈhɔːntɪŋ] Spuk

"Rafe," I said in a very small voice.

"And you know about the haunting, do you, Rafe?"

60 "Yes," I said in an even smaller voice.

"You read about it on the Madame Fifi's website?" he asked, with a strange smile.

"Yes, sir," I replied.

Everyone looked at me. They all
65 really wanted to hear the story about the haunting but thanks to me, they didn't get the chance. Gordon just said: "Excellent. Let's go!" – and my popularity score went down again, to -22.

70 He opened the door and we saw the stone steps that went down into the dark. Down and down we went. At the bottom we heard a loud noise. One of the girls cried out[12] but Gordon told her it was just a
75 passing[13] London Underground train. (OK, it wasn't "one of the girls" who cried out, it was me. Like I say, it was dark …)

Slowly, we started to see the wax figures.

80 "Cool," we said when we saw the heads on spikes, the murderers[14], the blood … Really scary stuff. Stuff that had *actually happened*[15].

"Now, Rafe …" Gordon said. "I'm sure
85 you can tell us about the famous Temple of Terrors story?"

NO WAY. I shook my head "no". Gordon smiled. "Well, let me tell you then …"

"Over a hundred years ago, two gentlemen
90 are taking a tour around the famous Madame Fifi's House of Wax. With them is a lady and they both want to impress[16] her.

"Do you know this Temple of Terrors?" the first one says. "They say it's very scary."

95 "Oh yes, very scary," the second man says.

Eleanor (the lady) says: "Oh, Cedric, it sounds terrible."

Both men see their chance to impress their lady friend. 100

"But I don't believe it," William says.

"Well, William," Cedric says, "let's go down and find out just how scary it is."

And the two men take the stone steps down into the Temple of Terrors. 105

"Well," William says. He looks around in the dark at the scary wax figures and feels very nervous. "I'm not frightened at all!"

"Frightened? Not me!" Cedric says, when he suddenly needs to use the bathroom. 110

"So, let's spend[17] the night here!" William says.

"Good idea!" Cedric says.

And so, because the men badly[18] want to impress Eleanor, they both agree[19] to spend 115
the night …

"They couldn't stay the whole night," Gordon continued. "They soon ran out screaming[20], their eyes wide with terror. And the next day, someone found both 120 men at their homes …"

We looked at Gordon in complete silence. "Dead[21]."

From: *Middle School: How I Got Lost in London* by James Patterson

→ WB 15/1–4

12 **to cry out** [kraɪ 'aʊt] aufschreien | 13 **passing** ['pɑːsɪŋ] vorbeifahrend | 14 **murderer** ['mɜːdrə] Mörder | 15 **stuff that had actually happened** [stʌf ðæt həd ˌæktʃuəli 'hæpnd] Dinge, die tatsächlich passiert sind | 16 **to impress sb** [ɪm'pres] jmdn. beeindrucken | 17 **to spend** [spend] verbringen | 18 **badly** ['bædli] unbedingt | 19 **to agree** [ə'griː] einwilligen | 20 **screaming** [skriːmɪŋ] schreiend | 21 **dead** [ded] tot

Find more online:
c543nu

Unit 2

Let's discover TTS!

1 | Basketball Club

2 | Dance class

3 | Sign Language Club

4 | A wall painting in the school building

SPEAKING

1 What you can do at TTS

a) *Look at the quotes in the speech bubbles on page 29. What are they about? Match them to the photos.*

b) *Read the box on the right and then talk about what you can see in the pictures. What is the same or different at your school?*

c) *Your turn: What pictures can you use to present your school?*

Across cultures

Some **subjects** are different in the UK. At TTS, for example, you can take exams in Dance, Drama, Film Studies or Fashion.

But at British schools there's more than just lessons. In the afternoons, clubs offer **additional activities** like sports, birdwatching, cooking or games like chess. Where can you participate in activities like these in Germany?

A   We start school with our tutor at 8:30. Or sometimes we go to the hall for Assembly.

B   We love competitions against other schools – well, we love winning.

C   Everyone is special and everyone belongs here. We all try to help students with special needs.

D   This school is full of art!

E   We practise a lot and we sometimes do shows.

Assembly

LISTENING **2 This is a fantastic school!** → WB 16/1–2

L 1/19

→ △ 136/1
→ S18–20

a) *Who is Olivia talking to? Take notes about the different parts of her presentation and say what each part is about.*

b) *Choose one of the quotes from A–E. Listen again. What reactions are there from the listeners after the part with that quote?*

SPEAKING **3 How to: Talk about a presentation**

You're one of the listeners at Olivia's presentation. What positive feedback can you give her?

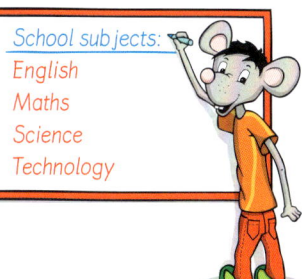

School subjects:
English
Maths
Science
Technology

Useful phrases

I liked your introduction.
Your presentation was nice / lively / …
First you … / Then you talked about …
That was interesting / surprising / …

L 1/20 ⊙ # The queen who loved parties

Luke and Dave are at Luke's house. Luke is telling Dave about his History presentation.

Luke: Listen to this. My presentation is about two queens that lived in Greenwich. Once, there was a queen
5 who loved parties and music and dancing. Her name was Anne. In 1616, her husband, King James, gave her a very special present: a house for her parties! The house had a beautiful
10 view of the Thames. Anne's friends loved to visit her there. The parties which they celebrated were very loud. People say there are ghosts in the house today.
15 Dave: Anne and her friends?
Luke: Maybe … But the ghosts who live in the house don't come out often.
Dave: And is this the building which they used as a hospital later?
20 Luke: No, that's a different story. Later, Queen Mary lived in Anne's house.

She loved the sea and boats and wanted to build a hospital for sailors. The architect whose design she chose was Christopher Wren. That was in 25 1692.
Dave: I know that story! When Wren showed her his plans for the first time, she was very upset. The hospital that he wanted to build was between her 30 house and the river. She wanted to see the river and the boats, not a big building!
Luke: That's right! And in those days angry queens cut people's heads off! That's 35 why Wren needed a quick idea. The idea he had was to cut the hospital in half. And he left a space in the middle so the queen kept her view of the river and Wren kept his head! 40

READING ## **1** Correct the sentences

Example: The queen who loved parties was Mary.
→ The queen who loved parties was Anne.

1. The parties which they celebrated were quiet.
2. The ghosts who live in the house come out every day.
3. The architect whose design she chose was Christopher Wright.
4. The hospital that he wanted to build was next to her house.

LANGUAGE   **2** **Find the rule** → G6

a) *Look at the text again. Collect the nouns in front of the relative pronouns* **who**, **which**, **that** *and* **whose**.

b) *Check if the nouns are people or things. When do you use which relative pronoun?*

LANGUAGE   **3** **Match the sentence parts** → WB 17/3–4

→ △ 136/2   **Example:** The king who / that gave his wife a very special present was James.

1. The king
2. The building ⎤ who / that
3. The queen
4. The river   which / that
5. The house   whose
6. The people

a) runs through Greenwich is the Thames.
b) went to Anne's parties had a lot of fun.
c) name was Mary loved the sea.
d) ghosts are quiet is a museum now.
e) is by the river was a hospital.
f) gave his wife a very special present was James.

LANGUAGE   **4** **Contact clauses** → G6

a) *Look at the sentences. Is the relative pronoun the subject or the object of the clause?*

1. There are museums **which** have special events for children.
2. It's an event **which** everyone finds exciting.

If the relative pronoun is the object, you don't need it!

> If the word after the relative pronoun is a verb, the relative pronoun must be the subject: S–V–O!

→ △ 136/3   **b)** *Check the sentences. Say where you don't need the relative pronoun.*

1. Children that are interested in history must go there!
2. There are many things that you can do.
3. People who like music can learn songs from Old England.
4. The costumes which you can try on are really cool.
5. And you can make jewellery which they sell at the museum shop later.

LANGUAGE   **5** **Make one sentence from two** → WB 18/5

→ △ 137/4
→ ▲ 137/5

Example: History is a school subject. I really like it.
→ History is a school subject which I really like. /
   History is a school subject I really like.

1. Last lesson we talked about a famous person. We all know him.
2. First, we looked at a picture. We found it on the school's website.
3. Then we listened to music. He wrote it for Queen Elizabeth I.
4. Finally, we designed a poster. We called it "Meet Thomas Tallis!"

WRITING

6 How to: Write prompt cards

→ △ 137/6
→ S11

Read the skills box. Then look at the text on page 30 again. Add more key words to the prompt card below. Then make a second prompt card about Queen Mary and Christopher Wren.

Who: Anne, …
What: house, …
Where: Thames, …
When: 1616

Writing skills

In a presentation, don't read whole sentences from the page. Use **prompt cards**. On these cards, you write **key words** to help you to remember the main ideas in your presentation. Write important people, events, places, and dates under the headings: **Who** | **What** | **Where** | **When**

LISTENING

7 Gwen's timetable

L 1/22
→ △ 138/7

a) *Gwen is a new girl at TTS. She's partially sighted. Listen to her conversation with Holly and Olivia. Why does Gwen need their help?*

b) *Listen again. Which subjects do they talk about? How can teachers and other students help Gwen?*

VOCABULARY

8 School subjects → WB 18/6

→ △ 138/8

a) *Look at Gwen's timetable. Compare it with your timetable.*

Time	Monday	Tuesday	Wednesday	Thursday	Friday
08:30	Registration				
08:50	Technology	Science	Maths	RE	English
09:50	Technology	Science	Maths	French	French
10:50	Break				
11:10	Maths	Art	Science	English	Humanities
12:10	English	Music	Technology	Humanities	Humanities
13:10	Lunch				
14:00	Dance	English	PE	Maths	Dance
15:00	Registration in tutor group / Assembly				
15:10	Home / After-school clubs				

b) *Write your own timetable in English.*

→ ▲ 138/9

L 1/23 ◉

Everyone was doing a really great job!

Holly wants to join the Eco Club at Thomas Tallis School. On the TTS website, she finds an article about a project the club did last year.

Home	About	New	Clubs	Community	Links	Contact	Search

Eco Club

The Wildlife Garden project

It was a beautiful morning, the first day of our Wildlife Garden project, and everyone was really excited to get started. The sun was shining, the birds were singing and the bees were humming. So even the animals were already looking forward to their new home!

It was great to have so much help; the list of jobs was a bit long: put up a sign (Henry), make a bee hotel (Jack), dig a hole (Kate and Filip), take photos (Alice and Rose) …

And everyone was doing a really great job! But then it happened: Sally fell into the pond while she was hanging up a bird house. That's when things started to go wrong. It was one of our funniest projects ever. Just look …!

SPEAKING **9** **What were they doing when Sally fell into the pond?** → G7

→ △ 138/10
→ ▲ 139/11

Look at the text and say what the other members of the Eco Club were doing when Sally fell into the pond.

Start like this: Henry **was putting** up a sign.
Alice and Rose **were** …

Do you remember how to make the progressive form of a verb? For the past progressive, look at G7 in the Grammar.

LANGUAGE **10** **Match the parts** → WB 19/7 → G7

→ △ 139/12
→ ▲ 139/13

Now look at the picture on page 33 again. What happened to the other Eco Club members while they were working on the Wildlife Garden?

1. Henry was putting up a sign
2. Sally fell into the pond
3. Filip and Kate hit a water pipe
4. Alice and Rose were taking photos
5. Jack was making a bee hotel

when

while

a) they were digging a hole.
b) he fell off the ladder.
c) he hit his thumb with the hammer.
d) a fox stole their lunch.
e) she was hanging up a bird house.

We mice were having a picnic **when** a fox **came** round the corner.
We ran into the school **while** the fox **was looking** for food.

SPEAKING **11** **A game: What were you doing when …?** → WB 19/8, 20/9

a) *Work with a partner. Think of funny things that you did in your last holidays. (They needn't be true!) Write six sentences in the past progressive and six sentences in the simple past. Number the sentences from 1–6.*

b) *Take turns and throw the dice twice. Choose the sentences that match the numbers on the dice – one sentence in the past progressive and one sentence in the simple past. Then make one sentence with the two and use **while** or **when**.*

MEDIATION **12** **A club at a German school** → WB 20/10

→ S17

Pia finds a club at her school really interesting and wants to tell Olivia about it. But she doesn't know all the words in English. Help her to describe in her own words what the club is about.

> **Mediation skills**
>
> If you don't know a word in English, try to **describe it in other words** you already know. **Relative clauses** can also help you to describe words!
>
> **Example:**
> "*Hausmeister* – It's a person who looks after the school."

Streitschlichter-AG
Mach dich und
andere stark!

In unserer AG lernst du, wie du bei einem Streit zwischen Schülern vermitteln kannst.
Als Streitschlichter hilfst du den Streitparteien, gemeinsam nach einer Lösung zu suchen. Es geht darum, Konflikte durch Reden – und nicht durch Gewalt! – zu lösen.
Lass dich zum Streitschlichter ausbilden und trage zu einem freundlichen Miteinander an unserer Schule bei!

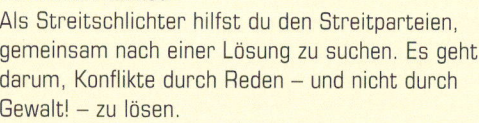

WRITING

13 How to: Write a flyer

→ S11 **a)** *Look at the flyer from the TTS Eco Club. Would you like to join the club? Say why or why not.*

b) *Now read the skills box. Choose **one** of the clubs on the right. Write and design a flyer for it.*

Maths Club   Singing Club

Tallis TV   Football Club   Science Club

c) *Exchange your flyers with another pair of students and peer-edit each other's work.*

Writing skills

When you write a flyer make sure
- it's easy to read
- it has all the important information about your club:
  the **name** of the club
  what you do
  when you meet (day and time)
  where you meet
  why people should join your club
- you welcome people with a special **welcome message** and a **slogan**!

The TTS Eco Club
When?   Tuesdays at 3:15
Where?   Room G23 & The Wildlife Garden
What?   Work on our Wildlife Garden or our Green Classroom projects
Why?   We want to find ways to

Love and protect nature!   Think green!   Recycle!

Save energy!   Stop pollution!

Come and join us –
EVERYONE CAN MAKE A DIFFERENCE!

LISTENING

14 ‹ A song: What a wonderful world › Louis Armstrong

L 1/26 ⊙ **a)** *Listen to the song and look at the pictures. What is the song about?*

b) *Your turn: What are **your** ideas for a wonderful world?*

to protect [prəˈtekt] schützen | **nature** [ˈneɪtʃə] Natur | **to recycle** [ˌriːˈsaɪkl] recyceln; wiederverwerten |
to save [seɪv] sparen | **pollution** [pəˈluːʃn] Verschmutzung | **to make a difference** [ˌmeɪk ə ˈdɪfrns] etwas ändern; etwas bewegen

The film star → S21–22

SPEAKING

1 **Your turn: One day I want to be a/an ...**

a) *What is your 'dream job'? Why is it so great?*
b) *Talk about the pros and cons of the jobs on the right.*

actor	dancer	pilot
police officer		vet

VIEWING

2 **Laura's problem** → WB 21/11

2 ▣ *Watch the film. What is Laura's dream job? But what is her problem?*

VIEWING

3 **Good advice?** → WB 21/12

a) *Watch (01:38–04:00) again. What advice do people give Laura? Take notes.*

b) *Talk about the advice for Laura. Here are some ideas:*

A: Polly is a star, so she knows best!
B: Well Marley isn't a star and *his* advice is great too: "Believe in yourself".

c) *Look at the still on the right (04:35). What is Laura thinking at this moment in the film? Look at the phrases.*

d) *Now watch the rest of the film. Why does Laura thank Polly?*

Useful phrases

Don't panic! | Don't be nervous! |
Just relax! | I'm sure you're good at ... |
You're always so confident. | Try again. |
Take a deep breath. | Believe in yourself!

SPEAKING

4 **What a great film!**

*In groups of 3–4, talk about something **you** saw at the cinema – or want to see. These phrases from the film can give you ideas.*

Useful phrases

That was such a great film!
I'm / I was really impressed with ...
I just love ... He's / She's my favourite actor.
I can't wait for ... | I really want to ...

How to give a good presentation → S14–16

1 What makes a presentation good?

Copy the grid. Then put the tips and phrases from the box under the right headings.

What you talk about	How you present it	How you organise things	What you say
Give facts. ...	...	...	...

"It's fantastic / really interesting / so much fun because …" | Smile. | Give facts. | Be on time. |
"We really want to see you!" | Don't just read from your notes. | "Let's take a look at …" | Add a personal story that is connected to the topic. | Make eye contact with your audience. | "Today, I'd like to …" | Know your facts. | Speak clearly! | "First …, second …, third …" | Introduce yourself. | Don't forget your flyers. | "Do you enjoy / love / want …?" | Give the most important information. | "Hello and welcome to …!"

2 Two presentations → WB 22/14

3–4   **a)** *Watch two presentations. What are they about? Which presentation do you like better?*

b) *Work in groups of four. Each of you chooses one of the headings in Ex. 1. Then watch the presentations again. Focus on your heading and take notes for each film. Add things from each presentation and note down what is missing.*

c) *Talk about your notes. Discuss what makes the presentations good / not so good.*

3 Make a good presentation

Improve Lou's presentation text on the right. You can think of facts that aren't in the text. Then practise your presentation and read it out loud several times.

Er – OK, I'm from Drama Club. We meet every week. I wanted to give you a flyer, but – sorry, I forgot it at home. Oh, and what else did I want to tell you? I can't remember …

Hello and welcome to the Drama Club's presentation! Do you enjoy …?

Join our club!

In this task, work in groups of four. Each group is a school club. At a 'club market', each group does a short presentation (3–5 minutes) about its club. Why is it special? Why is it the best club? You want as many classmates as possible to join **your** club! Each person in your group has a different job to make your presentation great.

Step 1

Which club? → WB 23/16

a) First, decide together which club your group wants to be. Here are some ideas; maybe you've got ideas of your own.

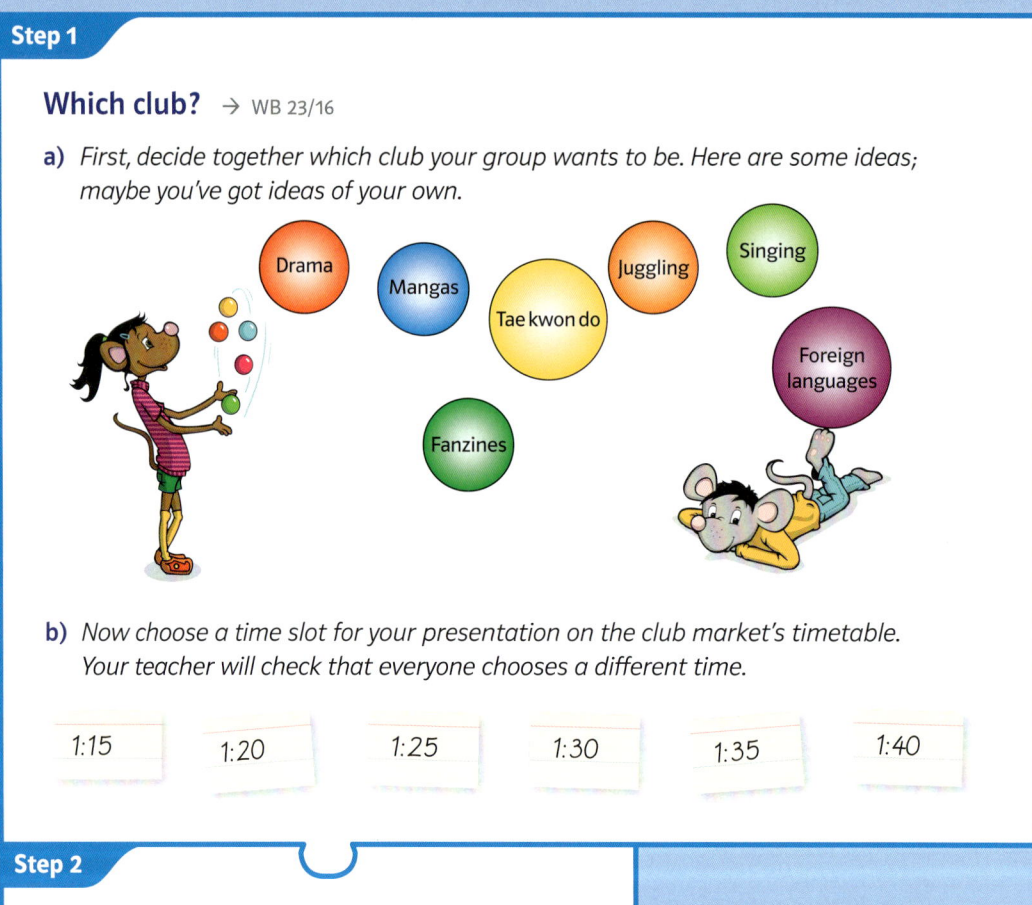

Drama
Mangas
Tae kwon do
Juggling
Singing
Foreign languages
Fanzines

b) Now choose a time slot for your presentation on the club market's timetable. Your teacher will check that everyone chooses a different time.

1:15	1:20	1:25	1:30	1:35	1:40

Step 2

Think of ideas for your club → WB 23/17

a) What's important to know about your club? What do you do when you meet? Collect information and facts that can interest new members. Answer these questions:
What | When | Where | Why | Who | ...

b) Now talk about what makes your club special, what makes it better than the other clubs. Remember, you want new members!

> What makes the Cheese Club special? Well, there's always free cheese at the cheese shop! Mmm …

Step 3

Make your club sound great → WB 24/18

a) *Collect words and phrases which can make your club sound great. Write sentences with them.*

b) *Now think of a slogan for your club.*

Example:
Drama Club: "Once a week you need some drama in your life!"

> Look back at the **Skills page** for phrases to make your club sound interesting.

> Look back at the **Skills page** for help with presentation skills. **Station 1** is the place to look for help with prompt cards.

Step 4

Pair A: Write your flyer

One pair in your group writes the flyer for your club. Give important information on it, and make it easy to read.

Pair B: Write your prompt cards

The other pair decides what needs to go on the prompt cards for the presentation. Write your prompt cards.

> For help with a flyer, look at **Station 2** again.

Step 5

Peer-edit each other's work → WB 24/19

The pair that wrote the prompt cards now checks the flyer; the pair that wrote the flyer checks the prompt cards. Talk about changes in your group.

Step 6

You're on!

a) *Decide together who in your group gives the presentation, and then practise together. Give him / her tips!*

b) *Now give your presentation. Don't forget the flyer!*

Step 7

Which club do YOU want to join? → WB 24/20

a) *As a class, talk about the different presentations.*

b) *Decide for yourself which club **you** want to join.*

c) *Class activity: Put a flyer for each club on a different table. Then each student goes to the table of the club he / she wants to join. Which club has the most new members?*

> Look at **Check-in** and the **Skills page** for giving feedback on a presentation.

S 1/17–22
L 1/28–33 ⊙

What a wonderful world

A "Big news today!" Holly said as she walked home from school with Luke and Jay. "Friends of the Earth are having a poster competition and the prize
5 is a day out in London at the Natural History Museum!"

"Cool – they have dinosaurs!" Luke said. "What do you have to do?"

"Design a poster called 'What a
10 Wonderful World' – just listen to the song for ideas," Holly answered.

Luke was excited. "Why don't we do a poster together, Jay?" he asked.

"Maybe …" Jay said, but he wasn't
15 sure. "I know that song," he thought, "and we can make an amazing poster!" But something felt wrong … He really didn't want to share his ideas with anyone else.

When he was home again, he phoned
20 Luke. "I want to enter the competition," he said, "but not together. I want to try on my own."

Luke was very surprised, but he didn't want to show it. "Cool," he said. "Me too!
25 And I'm sure I can win!" Then, after the phone call, he thought to himself: "Just you wait, Jay Azad!"

B That evening, Jay talked to himself while he was writing and drawing his first ideas.

30 "OK, so on the left side, there's a dirty street with lots of cars and rubbish everywhere, and on the other side we can see the 'wonderful world' with no cars, birds in the trees, flowers everywhere …"

35 He stopped. It was a bit boring. "I need a big idea to make it more fun," he thought. Suddenly, he noticed a manga magazine which was lying on his bedroom floor.

40 "Mangas!" he shouted. "That's it!" He was very good at art and started to do some cool manga drawings. But how could he use them on his poster?

C While Jay was drawing, Luke was at home working on his own ideas. He felt
45 very confident. "OK, Jay", he thought. "If you don't want to work with me, fine – because I know I can win!"

"Hey, Irina!" he shouted. "Imagine this … my poster is a manga world. Each
50 character has a different job and they all work together to make the world a cleaner, better place. They have special costumes and names that start with letters that show what they do – Rokuro
55 does recycling, Tomoko looks after the trees, Satoshi cleans the streets … What do you think?"

Irina was quiet for a moment. "It's *great!*" she said finally. "You can win!"
60

D The next day, Luke and Jay sat together in their Maths class, but they weren't thinking about Maths at all. Luke smiled to himself – he was proud of his brilliant idea! But Jay wasn't happy at all.
65

When it was time for break, Luke got up and went to get a drink. He left his bag on the table with his exercise book on top. Jay looked at it quickly – and he couldn't believe his eyes! There were little
70 pictures all over it … Mangas!

Jay looked again and laughed – Luke's drawings were really bad! But then he noticed some words too … Bunko – bees,

75 Fumio – flowers … "That's so clever!" he thought. "That's the big idea I need for my poster – and I'm much better at drawing than Luke!"

E After school, the friends were walking
80 home together when Luke decided to make Jay feel nervous.

"My poster is amazing!" he said. "I can't wait to get home and do some more work on it. Is yours finished?"

85 "Nearly," said Jay. "I just need a bit more time to think of some cool names for my mang…" He stopped. What was he saying?

"No! Not mangas! That's my idea –
90 you can't steal it!" Luke shouted.

"Calm down!" said Olivia. "It's only a competition."

"Yes, a competition which Jay wanted to enter alone!" Luke shouted. He was
95 very angry now. "When he didn't have good ideas, he stole mine!"

"I didn't – I had my own ideas!"

"Did you look in my bag at break time?" Luke asked as he pushed Jay.
100 Jay turned round and hit Luke's arm.

"Stop!" Dave shouted. He stood between the boys and tried to stop the fight. "Are you crazy?! I thought you were friends!"

105 "But Jay can't just steal my ideas!"

Jay was upset now. "I can't talk to you for another minute," he said. "You idiot!"

Stop and think:
Is Luke right to be angry with Jay? What should Jay do now?

F Dave tried again. "Stop, Jay! Listen, Luke – why don't you help each other?"

"I wanted to work together, but he 110 didn't," Luke answered.

Jay turned back. "You can't draw!"

"So what? You think you're special just because you're good at art!" Luke answered. "But where's your big idea? You 115 haven't got one!"

Jay didn't answer. Nobody spoke for a long time. Then at last Jay opened his bag and took out some papers. "I'm sorry!" he said. "Look, I always planned to use 120 mangas. These are the ones I drew during break, after I saw yours. I just didn't have any good ideas, and your idea with the names was so cool. – Come on, let's do a poster together, like you said yesterday." 125

"I'm not sure," Luke said. He wasn't ready to be friends again and he wanted Jay to know how it felt when your friend didn't want to work with you!

Jay stood next to Luke and gave him 130 his papers. Luke looked at them and saw Tomoko in the trees and Fumio planting flowers – his ideas. But the drawings were just fantastic!

"OK," Luke said at last, "let's try and 135 work together."

"Cool!" Jay answered. "Let's show everyone what a real manga story is!"

SPEAKING

1 Friends? → WB 25/21

a) *Talk about what Jay did and what you think of it. Do you know situations like that?*

b) *Do you like the ending? Say why/why not.*

c) *Say what is good or bad about working together with somebody.*

READING

2 Looking at the story → WB 25/22

→ S7–8 **a)** *Usually a story has three main parts: beginning, middle and end.*
Match the parts (A–F) of the story with the three main parts. Which main part says what the story is about? Which part is about a problem? Which part is about the solution?

b) *Sum up what happens in each part. Use a grid like this for your answers.*

Main part	Letters A–F	What happens?
Beginning: what the story is about	A	…
Middle: …	…	Jay and Luke try to find ideas. …
End: …	…	…

VOCABULARY

3 Inside – outside

a) *In this story we don't only learn what the characters say to other characters, but also what they think or say when they're alone. Go through the story and look for examples. How did you find them? Where did you find the most examples?*

b) *Read the skills box before you look at the story again. Where does the story use language for stronger feelings?*

c) *Now collect different words/phrases for stronger feelings in a mind map.*

→ ▲ 139/14
→ S3

Example: A: What's your favourite club?
B: Drama Club. I **love** acting.

A: Do you like school?
B: I **really like** Maths, but I **absolutely hate** PE.

Vocabulary skills

When you want to **show stronger feelings**, there are special words and phrases you can use like 'really' or 'amazing'. (You can also show stronger feelings when you say things in a **louder voice**.)

fantastic
very
language for stronger feelings
really
absolutely
so
That's it!

Can you ...

1. give more information about people / things? ....   The man who / that ... | The school which / that ... | The queen whose house we visited ...
2. say what was happening in the past?   She was eating lunch when her sister called. | They fell over Sherlock while they were playing in the park.
3. talk about lessons and school clubs? ....   It's really interesting / so much fun because ...

LANGUAGE

1 Relative clauses and contact clauses

a) *Which relative pronoun do you need here?*   who / that   which / that   whose

1. Do you like the poster **1** I designed for the competition?
2. I love films **2** are about nature and animals.
3. New students often make friends with people **3** they meet at clubs.
4. There's the teacher **4** lessons I like best.
5. Jamie is a student **5** is really good at sports.

b) *When is a contact clause possible in the sentences in a)?*

LANGUAGE

2 Past progressive or simple past?

Example: sleep | when | alarm clock ring
→ Dave **was sleeping** when the alarm clock **rang**.

1. wash his face | when | Sid come into bathroom
2. send Jay a text | while | mother make breakfast
3. get his bike | when | father leave the house
4. arrive at school | while | Luke still sleep

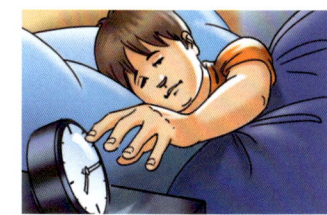

WRITING

3 School subjects

a) *Look at the pictures. What are the school subjects?*

1   2   3   4   5

b) *Which subjects in a) do you like best? Why? Write what is great / interesting / ... about it.*

S 1/23–27
L 1/34–38 ⊙

Horrid[1] Henry's Christmas play[2]

Henry is about 10 years old. He is not a very nice child, so people call him
Horrid Henry. Henry doesn't like school, but he has a dream: He wants to be
really famous one day. When his teacher tells the class about her plans for
a new Christmas play, Henry sees his chance to play the lead[3] – Joseph.
5 But the teacher knows Henry really well and already has other plans …

Horrid Henry sat low down in his chair
and watched the clock – it was moving *so*
slowly! "Please go faster!" he thought. Only
five more minutes until he could go home!
10 Already Henry could taste the crisps that
were waiting for him in his bag outside.
　　Miss Battle-Axe[4] talked on and on about
school dinners (yuck[5]), the new drinking
fountain blah blah blah, Maths homework
15 blah blah blah, the school Christmas play
blah blah … what? Did Miss Battle-Axe
say … Christmas play? Horrid Henry sat
up.
　　"This is a new play with singing and
20 dancing," Miss Battle-Axe continued[6]. "And
both the older and the younger children
are taking part[7] this year."

Singing! Dancing! Showing off[8] in front
of the whole school! Years ago, when Henry
was still at primary school, he played   25
eighth sheep in the Christmas play and
he took the baby from the manger[9] and
didn't want to give him back. Henry hoped
Miss Battle-Axe didn't remember. Because
Henry needed to play the lead this time.   30
Who else could be an all-singing, all-
dancing Joseph?
　　"I want to be Mary!" all the girls
shouted.
　　"I want to be a wise man[10]!" Rude Ralph   35
shouted.
　　"I want to be a sheep!" Anxious Andrew
shouted.
　　"I want to be Joseph!" Horrid Henry
shouted.   40
　　"No, me!" Jazzy Jim shouted.
　　"Me!" Brainy Brian shouted.
　　"Quiet!" Miss Battle-Axe shouted. "*I'm*
the director[11], and *I* decide about who can
act each part. Margaret. You are Mary." She 45
gave her a thick[12] script.
　　Moody Margaret shouted: "I'm so
happy! I'm so happy!" All the other girls
looked at her angrily.
　　"Susan, Linda – you're the donkey[13];   50
cows[14], Fiona and Clare. Blades of grass[15]
…" Miss Battle-Axe continued through her
list.
　　"Choose me for Joseph, choose me for
Joseph," Horrid Henry prayed[16]. Of course, 55

1 **horrid** [ˈhɒrɪd] gemein | 2 **Christmas play** [ˈkrɪsməs pleɪ] Krippenspiel | 3 **the lead** [liːd] Hauptrolle |
4 **Miss Battle-Axe** [mɪs ˈbætlæks] Fräulein Streitaxt | 5 **yuck** [jʌk] igitt | 6 **to continue** [kənˈtɪnjuː] fortfahren |
7 **to take part** [teɪk ˈpɑːt] teilnehmen | 8 **to show off** [ʃəʊ ˈɒf] angeben | 9 **manger** [ˈmeɪndʒə] Krippe | 10 **wise man**
[ˈwaɪz mæn] einer der Heiligen Drei Könige | 11 **director** [dɪˈrektə] Regisseur | 12 **thick** [θɪk] dick | 13 **donkey** [ˈdɒŋki]
Esel | 14 **cow** [kaʊ] Kuh | 15 **blade of grass** [ˌbleɪd əv ˈɡrɑːs] Grashalm | 16 **to pray** [preɪ] beten

the best actor in the school always gets the star part. And the best actor was Henry, wasn't he?

"I'm a sheep, I'm a sheep, I'm a
60 beautiful sheep!" Singing Soraya sang.

"I'm a shepherd[17]!" Jolly Josh smiled.

"I'm an angel[18]," Magic Martha whispered.

"I'm a blade of grass," Weepy William
65 cried[19].

"And Joseph is …"

"Me!" Henry shouted.

"Me!" New Nick, Greedy Graham, Dizzy Dave and Aerobic Al shouted.

70 "… Peter," Miss Battle-Axe said. "From Miss Lovely's class."

Horrid Henry felt sick[20]. Perfect Peter? His *younger* brother? Perfect Peter gets the star part?

75 "It's not fair!" Horrid Henry cried.

Miss Battle-Axe looked at him angrily. "Henry, you're …" Miss Battle-Axe looked at her list.

"Please not a blade of grass, please not a blade of grass," Horrid Henry prayed. 80 Miss Battle-Axe always knew how to make him feel *really* silly and small.

"… the innkeeper[21]."

The innkeeper! Horrid Henry sat up and smiled. How silly he was! Of course, 85 the innkeeper was the star part! He already imagined the scene: Henry the innkeeper is washing glasses and pouring out big drinks to all his happy customers[22] and singing a song. He has a nice long 90 argument[23] about why there is no room at the inn, and finally, he has the chance to close the door in Moody Margaret's face. Wow! Maybe he can even sing a second song like 'Ten Green Bottles'. He can sing 95 and dance and his less talented classmates can play the bottles who he can knock off[24] the wall, one by one. What fun!

Miss Battle-Axe gave a page to Henry. "Your script," she said. 100

From: *Horrid Henry Rules the World*
by Francesca Simon　　　　→ WB 27/1–4

17 **shepherd** [ˈʃepəd] Hirte | 18 **angel** [ˈeɪndʒl] Engel | 19 **to cry** [kraɪ] weinen | 20 **He felt sick.** [felt ˈsɪk] Ihm war schlecht. | 21 **innkeeper** [ˈɪnkiːpə] Herbergswirt | 22 **customer** [ˈkʌstəmə] Kunde/Kundin | 23 **argument** [ˈɑːgjəmənt] Streit | 24 **to knock off** [nɒk ˈɒf] herunterstoßen

LISTENING

1 **Mr Preston's scary story** → WB 28/1

L 1/39 ◎ **a)** *When Mr Preston reads Dave's travel report, he remembers his own class trip to Wales a long time ago. Listen to the story about Mt Snowdon, a castle¹ and ghosts …*

1. **When** did Mr Preston see the ghosts?
2. **Who** were they?
3. **What** did the ghosts do – or not do?
4. **What** does Dave think about the story?

b) *In class, compare Dave's trip to Wales in Unit 1 with his dad's trip. Which trip is more interesting to you? Say why. (Think of the different activities, different feelings, …)*

c) *Choose one of the two 'ghost scenes' you see in the pictures.*
Write 6–8 sentences about the ghost in your scene. What do you think is his/her story?

LANGUAGE

2 **Olivia's dream**

Last night Olivia had a strange dream. Read her e-mail to Holly. What verbs are missing?
Sometimes there's more than one possible answer. Use the simple past.

> Holly – I **1** a really strange dream last night …
> I **2** at school and **3** the classroom door. But nobody **4** there. Suddenly,
> I **5** a strange noise outside. So I **6** out to the playground. That's when I **7**
> something in the air: a UFO! Holly, I **8** sooooo scared! The UFO **9** closer and
> closer. Then, someone **10** the UFO's door and a green alien **11** out. "Hello Olivia!"
> he **12** . "But, how do you know my name?!" I **13** . "Oh, it's me. Jay," he said.
> "I always go to school by UFO." Wasn't that a strange dream? Then, when I **14** to
> school this morning, Jay **15** the first person I **16** ! And: He was wearing a GREEN
> shirt!
> xoxo, Olivia 💗

1 **castle** ['kɑːsl] Burg; Schloss

SPEAKING

3 At Greenwich Market → WB 28/2, 29/5

a) *Talk about the scene at Greenwich Market. What was everybody doing? Be creative!*

b) *Use different adjectives to talk about the scene. Here are some ideas:*

funny   good   happy   angry   jealous   tired

bored   boring   interesting   typical   big

Examples: A: The boy's ice cream isn't as big as the girl's.
B: I think the scene with the bird is the funniest! What do you think?

VOCABULARY

4 A flyer for Drama Club → WB 29/6

a) *Which words can you think of for the gaps? Sometimes there's more than one possible answer.*

b) *Do you think the brochure is a good example for this kind of project? Why / Why not? Find five things you can do differently with this flyer.*

We invite all students `1` love theatre to `2` the TTS Drama Club! We `3` every Wednesday at 3:30 in Room 0.4.04. Our next play[2] is William Shakespeare's Romeo

and Juliet – and Shakespeare is of course Britain's most `4` writer[3]! But this isn't just a play: This is a musical of 'R&J', so we `5` LOTS of boys and girls `6` can act and `7` ! And this isn't a historical 'R&J'! No, we `8` to show the London of TODAY! So, forget `9` costumes like in Shakespeare's days. You can wear your own cool `10` ! Also, we always need people who can `11` posters, sell tickets or `12` with the sound. For more `13` , just ask Mr Gibbons `14` teaches Drama in Years 7 and 9.

2 play [pleɪ] Theaterstück | **3 writer** [ˈraɪtə] Schriftsteller

Find more online:
k298fe

London: A special city

London is a huge city, and Greenwich is only a small part of it. On these two pages you can learn more about the British capital and find out what makes it so special.

SPEAKING

1 First facts about London → WB 30/1

a) *What can you find out from the photos? The words on the right can help.*

multi-ethnic city   famous / historical sights

green spaces   royal family   river

underground trains   busy streets

festivals

Example: 1. The Thames goes through the centre of London. It's a big, busy river. You can see famous …

1 The Thames, Big Ben and the London Eye

2 Oxford Street

3 The Tube

4 The Notting Hill Carnival

5 Buckingham Palace

6 Hyde Park

b) *Match the sentence parts to find out more facts about London.*

1. London was originally a Roman town
2. Today London is the
3. It's the capital city of
4. Over eight million people
5. The students in London's schools speak
6. London has got five

a) England and of the UK.
b) international airports.
c) more than 300 different languages.
d) third largest city in Europe.
e) with the name 'Londinium'.
f) live in London.

c) *Take turns to tell your partner as much as you can about London in one minute.*

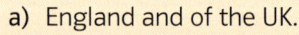

The Tube is over 150 years old. It's the world's oldest underground.

And did you know Big Ben is the name of the clock's bell, and **not** the clock?

VIEWING

2 Royal London → WB 30/2

5

a) *Before you watch: What can you say about the things that Laura is wearing?*

b) *Now watch and choose the correct endings.*

1. Laura's clothes
   a) are for a party.
   b) celebrate royal events.
   c) show what the royal family wear.

2. The Changing of the Guards takes place
   a) in front of Buckingham Palace.
   b) at the Tower of London.
   c) in Hyde Park.

3. Prince Albert was
   a) Queen Victoria's brother.
   b) British.
   c) from Germany.

4. The Royals are part of the British identity
   a) for everyone in the UK.
   b) for some people in the UK.
   c) only for older people.

c) *Your turn: What do you think about royal families? Explain your opinion.*

LISTENING

3 Young Londoners → WB 30/3

L2/1

a) *A class in London is doing a project about their city. While you listen, work in groups of three. Each group takes different notes under one of these headings.*

b) *Share the information you collected in a) with the other groups with the same question.*

| What is good in London?
 – exciting things to do
 – ... | What is not so good?
 – expensive
 – ... | How is London different?
 – bigger than other cities
 – ... |

WRITING

4 What makes London special?

Talk about what you think makes London a special city. Write your ideas in a mind map.

SPEAKING

5 Your turn: Cities in Germany

Talk about German cities. Compare them with London. What is similar and what is different?

Useful phrases

It's also a Roman town / a capital city / ...
It isn't as big / ... as London.
There aren't as many ...
It has / hasn't got famous sights / a river / ...

Find more online:
i9c4u3

Unit 3

London is amazing!

A   Famous sights: the Houses of Parliament and Big Ben

SPEAKING   **1**   **Talk about places in London**

Describe the places in the photos. Say what you can see or do there.
Find the places on the map at the back of your book.

LISTENING   **2**   **A video chat with Amir**

L 2/2 

→ S18–20

a) *Jay is having a video chat with Amir, his cousin. Amir lives in Bradford*
and has plans to see London with Jay. Listen, and say what kind of things
each boy is interested in.

b) *Listen again and take notes*
about these places.

Covent Garden   the British Museum   Brick Lane

the London Wall   Shakespeare's Globe

In Unit 3 you learn

… how to discuss plans and how to describe the way people do things. You learn:

• words for things to do and see in London
• the language of plans (*going-to future*)
• word-building with *some, any, every, no*
• words to describe actions (*adverbs*)

B Brick Lane: multi-ethnic flair and street art

C The wax figures at Madame Tussauds

D Londoners and tourists at Covent Garden

E The Horse Guards at Whitehall

SPEAKING **3** **Your turn: Choose your London** → WB 31/1

→ △ 140/1

Think about what you already know about London. In groups, take turns to tell each other two things that you would really like to see or do there. Explain why. Use your notes from Ex. 2.

VOCABULARY **4** **London vocabulary** → WB 31/2

Collect words and names that are useful for your personal vocabulary. Add more words while you work through Unit 3.

I'm into street art. And great food! So I'd like to see Brick Lane.

It must be fun to walk around Madame Tussauds and see all the famous 'people'!

L 2/3   # It's going to be fun

"It was amazing," Amir tells his aunt. He's staying with the Azads and earlier today Jay took him to the Royal Observatory.

"Good. And what are you two going to do tomorrow?" Mrs Azad asks. "Are you going to see more sights in Greenwich?"

"No, we aren't. We're going to visit the British Museum with Olivia and Holly," Jay tells her. "We met them in Greenwich Park this afternoon, and Olivia is like Amir – she loves museums." 10

Mrs Azad's face shows that she isn't happy with this plan. But Jay can think fast. "Don't worry," he says. "We aren't going to go alone. Shahid is going to take us." His 15 18-year-old brother isn't at home at the moment, so Jay must try to persuade him later.

"Oh, is Shahid going to look after you? That's OK then," says Mrs Azad. 20

"Yes, it's going to be fun. But there's just one thing. The museum is free, but I'm not sure where I'm going to get money for our Oyster cards or for our lunch."

Mrs Azad smiles. "Probably the same 25 place where you *always* get money."

READING

1 What do you think? → WB 32/3

1. What is Mrs Azad's problem with the boys' plan?
2. What is Jay's solution to that problem?
3. Where is Jay going to get money?

LANGUAGE

2 Find the rule for *going to* → WB 32/4, 33/5 → G8

a) *Find phrases with* **going to** *in the text. Which part of the time line are they about?*

 b) *How do you make* **going to** *forms? Write the rule and put it in your folder.*

LANGUAGE

**3** Your turn: What are you going to do?

→ △ 140/2
→ S24

a) *First, write down three sentences about your weekend. Walk around and ask a few classmates about their plans.*

b) *Take turns to say what you found out about your classmates' plans.*

Across cultures 🇬🇧

The cheapest way to travel by public transport in London is with an **Oyster card**. This is a smartcard you can top up with credit. What's the cheapest way to travel where you live?

← yesterday ← today → tomorrow →

What are you going to do next weekend?

On Sunday I'm going to visit my grandma.

→ △ 140/3

LANGUAGE

4 What's going to happen? → WB 33/6

Write about the people in the picture. Find your own verbs.

Start: 1. The old man and woman **are going to sit down.**
2. The man in the wheelchair **is going to** …

SPEAKING

5 Play a game: Guess my plans for tomorrow

→ △ 140/4

Think of a place in London but don't say what it is. Your partner must ask questions and guess the activity. Start the questions with "Are you going to …?"

Example: A: Are you going to listen to music?
B: No, I'm not.
A: Are you going to look at animals?
B: Yes, I am.
A: Are you going to visit London Zoo?
B: Yes, I am. That's right.

look at pictures / …

watch football / street shows / …

visit a historical building / …

listen to street musicians

LISTENING

6 How to: Get around by Tube → WB 34/7

L 2/5 ⊙
→ S18–20

a) *Work with the Tube map on the 'Transport for London' website. A tourist is at Elephant & Castle station and wants to get to Buckingham Palace. Listen to the dialogue. Which route do you think is best – the man's or the woman's? Why?*

b) *Take turns to describe the routes to the other places above. You can start at Elephant & Castle or go from one sight to another.*

Place / Sight	Station
Buckingham Palace	Victoria
Oxford Street	Oxford Circus
Tower of London	Tower Hill
Transport Museum	Covent Garden
Mudchute Farm	Crossharbour

Useful phrases

You take the … line to … | You change onto the … line. | You go north / south / east / west to … | It's three stops to … | You get off at …

L 2/6 ◉ **Good idea!**

After the visit to the British Museum the friends and Shahid are at Covent Garden ...

1 I need to deal with this – it's something important. You four can stay here alone for a little while.

2 'Something important', ha – ha. He means some**one** important. His girlfriend!

What can we do for lunch? Are there any cafés anywhere?

What about a food challenge? Everybody takes some money and we see who can get the most food! – Back here in 15 minutes, OK?

3 Maybe I can find a souvenir here.

OK, but let's have lunch first. I'm hungry.

I bet nobody can beat *these* sandwiches! Nice big ones. – But wait: Where's Jay?

4 I've got no idea where to go!

Follow me, there's a great place around the corner here.

5 15 minutes later ...

6 There's Jay. And he hasn't got anything for the food challenge!

And *he* was the hungry one!

SPEAKING **7** **The photo story** → WB 34/8

→ △ 141/5
→ ▲ 141/6

*Imagine you're **one** of the people in the story. What can he/she say about it?*

Example: (Jay) *I was really hungry. Olivia had a great idea. But then I saw …*

LANGUAGE **8** **Revision: Comparison of adjectives**

*What kind of a food challenge would be the best for **you**? Why? Write about it in 5–6 sentences with different forms of adjectives. The examples can help you.*

Examples: I think the **most important thing** is to find **the best food**!
Healthy food is **better than** … food, but **not as** … **as** …

LANGUAGE **9** **Compound words with *some* and *any*** → G9

a) *Match the parts.*

1. I'm hungry. I need   a) anything expensive.
2. I've only got £1. I can't buy   b) some good tricks.
3. Are there public toilets   c) any more time.
4. Let's watch this guy. He's doing   d) something to eat.
5. I can't see the show – I'm behind e) anyone know?
6. We must go now. We haven't got   f) someone very tall!
7. Where's the Tube station? Does   g) anywhere here?

→ △ 141/7
→ ▲ 142/8

b) *Do you remember the rule for **some** and **any** from last year? Explain it.*

LANGUAGE **10** **Complete the words** → WB 35/9–10, 36/11 → G9   some   any   every   no

→ △ 142/9

Holly: What can we do till we meet Shahid later? Has **1** *body* got a good suggestion?
Jay: It must be **2** *thing* that costs **3** *thing* – we haven't got any money left.
Olivia: Let's just walk around. I'm sure that's fun for **4** *one* new in London like Amir. There are lots of interesting things to see **5** *where* you look. What do you think, Amir?
Amir: Well, if **6** *body* wants to make a different suggestion – yes, I'd like that.
Holly: Is there **7** *where* special you'd like to go or **8** *thing* special you'd like to see?
Amir: Well, **9** *thing* is special for me – it's all amazing. But I'd love to walk near the river.
Jay: Is that OK with **10** *body*? – Great, come on, let's go and find the Thames!

SPEAKING **11** **Your turn: Visitors** → WB 36/12–13

a) *With a partner, think of where you can go or what you can do with young visitors where you live. Make a list of 4–5 different ideas.*

b) *Present your 'Top 3' to the class.*

> **Useful phrases**
>
> **Pros:** good for someone who likes history / … | doesn't cost anything | easy to get there by public transport | something everyone enjoys
>
> **Cons:** (very) expensive | not everyone is into … | boring | too far away | not good in bad weather

L 2/8 ◎ # They can bite *very* hard

If you don't know London well, a bus tour with a guide can be a good idea. You can see and learn a lot much faster and more easily than if you explore the city alone.

"Now we're going slowly past the Tower of London, one of the city's must-see sights –
5 you can see it clearly on the left. William the Conqueror built the Tower when he became king of England in 1066. In the past it was a castle, a prison and even a royal zoo with big animals like lions and bears! Today
10 it's a must-see sight. Many people come specially to see the Crown Jewels, but the Beefeaters give fantastic tours of the whole Tower – they know its history better than anyone! The Raven Master is a Beefeater
15 too. His job is to look after the ravens

carefully and to make sure they stay happily and safely in their home at the Tower. If you visit the Tower, don't go too close to the ravens. They don't always like that – and they can bite *very* hard!"
20

Across cultures

William the Conqueror and his people came from Normandy in France, so after 1066 many French words became part of the English language. Can you give some examples?

SPEAKING **12** ## A must-see sight for you too?

Would you like to visit the Tower? Why or why not?

LISTENING **13** ## Rocky's audio tour

L 2/9–11 ◎ **a)** *Listen once. Who is Rocky? What three topics does he tell you about?*

✏ **b)** *Listen again. What does Rocky say about* **food**, **treasure** *and* **ghosts**? *Take notes.*
→ S18–20

→ S17 **c)** *Mediation: There's no 'Rocky' audio tour in German, and a young German tourist who doesn't speak English wants to know what Rocky says. Give the main information in German.*

Listening skills

When you listen to information, first just try to understand the **gist** (main ideas). Then listen again for **more information**. Collect **key words and phrases** that help you to remember.

LANGUAGE 14 Find the rule for adverbs → G10–11

a) *What do **adjectives** (slow, clear) describe?*
*What do **adverbs** (slowly, clearly) describe?*
How do you make adverbs?

b) *Find adverbs in the text for these adjectives.*
What can you say about the spelling?

easy – special – careful – happy

The bus is **slow**. It's going **slowly**.
It's a **clear** view. You can see it **clearly**.

A few adverbs are irregular.

good → well
fast → fast
hard → hard

LANGUAGE 15 Talk about the people in the pictures → WB 36/14

→ △ 142/10
→ △ 143/11

What are they doing, and how are they doing it? What do you think the situation is?

angry | excited | nervous ✔ | happy

loud | aggressive | fast | …

Example: 1. He's jumping back **nervously**.
Maybe he's scared.

LANGUAGE 16 Adjective or adverb? → WB 37/15

Complete these online comments about two tours in London.

→ △ 143/12
→ ▲ 143/13

A. "It was a `1` (fantastic) tour of the Tower. The Beefeater explained everything `2` (clear) and told us lots of `3` (exciting) stories. After the tour he also gave us some `4` (good) tips about where to eat `5` (good) and `6` (cheap) near the Tower."

B. "I checked the website `7` (careful) and it looked like the `8` (perfect) bus tour. But I was very `9` (disappointed). Most guides work `10` (hard) for their money and are very `11` (nice)! Not our guide. He spoke to us so `12` (rude)! And, the bus went past all the sights *much* too `13` (quick)!"

WRITING 17 Your turn: Write about a sight / a special place in London → WB 37/16–17

In 6–8 sentences, say what the sight is and where it is. Describe it and say why it's special.

A day out in London → S21–22

SPEAKING

1 Warm-up

Write down places / sights you think are symbols of London. Then tell the class.

VIEWING

2 Out and about in London → WB 38/18

6 *Watch the film. Which part do **you** really like? Why?*

VIEWING

3 A closer look → WB 38/19

Watch again and answer the questions. These ideas can help.

1. Why do you think Jinsoo's sister, Mina, is with the boys?
2. Where did Jinsoo want to go? Why didn't they go there?
3. What was the problem with Mina at Camden Market?

Jinsoo and Mina's dad

adult / child ticket

sightseeing / normal bus

look after   expensive

VIEWING

4 Setting and atmosphere in film scenes

a) *First, read the skills box. Then watch scenes **A** (01:15 – 01:50) and **B** (01:57 – 02:06) again. Say why you think they're important or interesting for the film.*

b) *In Ex. 2 you named a favourite scene. Now talk about its setting and atmosphere. These words can help:*

cool   crazy   famous   funny

interesting   international   multi-ethnic

lots to see / discover   people everywhere

c) *Write a short description of what Jinsoo, Marley, Nick and Mina could do in a **different** location in London. Look at your lists from Ex. 1 for ideas.*

Film skills

In a film, the viewer needs to know what the film's **setting** is, so the choice of **locations** in a film is important. A famous place like London really needs to *look* like London!

Atmosphere is important too: crowds, places, views, water, things to look at or buy, cool shops … These things can create a special atmosphere for the viewer.

How to find information on the internet → S5, 9

1 Start with the homepage of a famous attraction's website

Most homepages give basic information and also useful links to other pages. Try to answer these questions with the help of the homepage for the Natural History Museum in London. If the answer is not on the page, which 'quick link' do you think can help?

1. Where is the museum?
2. How do I get there?
3. Is it open every day?
4. Are there any special displays at the moment?
5. Must I pay to visit the museum?

N NATURAL HISTORY MUSEUM

| **Home** | Visit us | Nature online | Education | Support us | Buy online |

Cromwell Road London SW7 5BD UK
Open Monday to Sunday from
  10:00 – 17:50
  except 24 – 26 December.
Last admission 17:30

Entry is free
There is a charge for some exhibitions.

Quick links:
■ Getting here
■ Book tickets
■ Gallery announcements
■ Sign up for news
■ Dino Directory

2 Skim and scan internet texts → WB 39/21

a) *Skim the text on the right for the* **gist**. *What is it about? How can the information help visitors?*

b) *Now scan the text for* **details** *about animals. Make notes.*

Try to guess new words. Don't worry about words that aren't important.

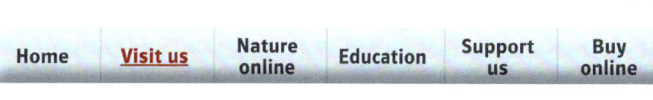

| Home | **Visit us** | Nature online | Education | Support us | Buy online |

The Galleries at the **Natural History Museum** are in four zones. The **Blue Zone** shows you the amazing diversity of life on Earth, from the smallest to the largest animals. This is also where you can find the popular Dinosaurs gallery. In the **Green Zone** you learn about Earth's ecology and how you can help to look after the planet. Visit the **Red Zone** to go back to the beginning of time and find out how and why our planet changes. Also see the minerals and treasures the Earth gives us. In the **Orange Zone** you can explore nature in the Wildlife Garden, which features over 2,000 species. Also, see science in action in the spectacular Darwin Centre.

3 Practise with different websites

Partner A: *Choose a sight in London (an idea from Unit 3 or your own idea).*
Partner B: *Find useful or interesting information about your partner's sight and tell him / her about it.*

Our London tour

For this task, work in small groups. Each group is going to plan and present a different sightseeing tour for a class trip to London. There are three different tour choices:

| a tour by bus and boat | a tour by Tube | a tour on foot |

Step 1

Tour rules → WB 40/23

a) First, read the rules in class. Then form groups of 4–5 and choose a tour. Try to have **two** groups for each tour.

b) The map below can help you to plan your tour and to get a feeling for distances before you use other maps.

Rules

- *Your tour starts at* **Green Park**.
- *There must be* **enough time** *(morning till late afternoon) for everything that you plan to do.*
- *Only* **one** *stop on your tour costs money. The other sights must be* **free**.
- *You've got sandwiches for* **lunch**, *so you must plan when and where you can eat them.*

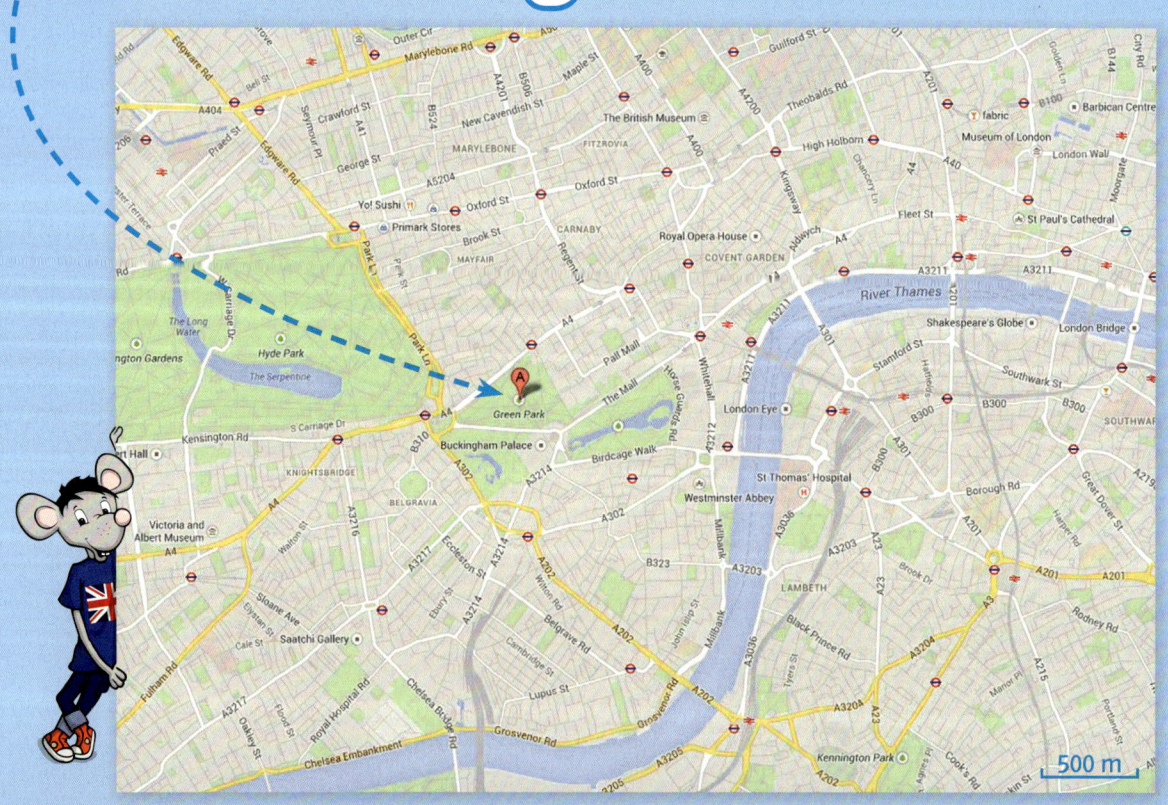

Step 2

Choose the sights on your tour → WB 40/24, 41/25

a) *First think alone for a few minutes about what sights you can visit. Write down your ideas. Then tick (✔) the ones you'd like to visit in one day.*

b) *Share your ideas. What are your group's favourites? Make your decision about the sights. Look at the map again. Are your plans realistic for the time you have and the distance between activities?*

    Start: Good idea – but isn't it a bit far / expensive?
              I think we've got enough time / money for …

> For help with things to do and see in London, look back at **Across Cultures 1**, at pages 50–58 of **Unit 3** and at your **Workbook**.
>
> For help with how to make and discuss suggestions, look again at **Station 2**.

Step 3

Collect information and write a plan

a) *Collect useful information about each of the sights on your list and work out the best route for your tour. Look up the information that you need and make notes.*

b) *Use the information to write a plan for the tour (morning → lunch → afternoon). Make sure it's clear where you're going to go and how you're going to get there.*

Step 4

Prepare your presentation

Decide who is going to talk about what. Think what you want to say and make prompt cards. Also prepare some material about your tour. Maybe these ideas can help:

– a poster of the whole tour
– a tour timetable
– a map with your route / sights

> Has your tour got a special name? I call my tour 'Tony's Top Tube Tour'. That's a tongue-twister (*Zungenbrecher*). Try it!

Step 5

> For help with how to find information on the internet, look at the **Skills page** again.
>
> For help with routes on the Tube, look back at **Station 1**.

Present your tour in class → WB 41/26

a) *Take turns to present your tours.*

> **Useful phrases**
>
> We'd like to tell you about …
> First we're going to …
> Then … / After that …
> We're / You're going to see / visit …
> We can get there easily on foot / by …
> It's a fantastic / an amazing …

h) *Take turns to vote for the best tour. Say why you liked that tour best.*

> Look back at the **Skills page** in **Unit 2** for help with the presentations.

S1/31–35
L 2/12–16

I'm a mudlark

Across cultures

Many London visitors don't know that **the Thames** is a river with two faces – one at high tide, one at low tide. Sometimes, it flows out into the sea like a normal river. But every day at high tide, it flows back towards central London. In the heart of the city there can be a difference of seven metres between high and low tides! At low tide, you can see the muddy banks of the river.

A "Number three is the Wobbly Bridge," Jay told his cousin Amir. The four friends were enjoying their own tour of bridges across the Thames. Now they
5 were walking across their third one, the Millennium Footbridge.

"It isn't wobbly any more. That was just a problem when it was new, but people still use the name," explained
10 Olivia.

Before they got very far, Holly noticed Amir's silver bracelet. "Ooh, that's nice!"

"Yeah, let *me* try it on," Jay said.
15 "Sure, no problem," Amir said. Jay quickly grabbed his cousin's wrist to take the bracelet off. But he wasn't careful enough, dropped it, and the bracelet rolled off the bridge and down
20 into the Thames!

"Jay!" Amir shouted angrily. "That bracelet really meant something to me. And now it's gone!" They all looked down from the bridge. They were lucky.
25 The tide was out and the bracelet was in the mud between the water and the wall.

"Look, there are steps down to the shore," Olivia said. "Come on, let's go
30 and get it. But hm, should we take off our shoes? It's very muddy."

Stop and think:
What could happen next, and why?

B Down on the shore, they found that the mud was very wet. They weren't wearing the right kind of shoes so they needed to walk carefully. They didn't want to fall. 35

"Hi. Are you looking for this?"

The voice came from a man under the bridge.

"Oh, we didn't see you! Yes, that's my bracelet. Thanks! I'm so happy to get it 40 back," Amir told him.

"No problem," the man smiled. "I didn't think it was a present for me! Nice to meet you all. My name is Mike."

Olivia looked at the bucket and trowel 45 which Mike had with him. "Excuse me, but can you please tell us what you're doing here?" she asked politely.

"I'm a mudlark," he said.

C The friends didn't know about mudlarks, 50 so Mike explained. "In the 19th century many children or old people tried to make a little money from things that fell into the Thames. You know – from boats and ships." 55

"And bridges too!" Jay added.

"Yes, from bridges too," Mike laughed. "Anyway, when the tide went out the mudlarks looked on the shore for things to sell. They got their name because they 60 worked in the mud. And at that time, the river was *very* dirty, full of all kinds of pollution. Or worse."

"Worse?" Amir wanted to know.

"Well, dead animals washed up all the 65 time. Human bodies too."

"Yuck!" Holly said. "It's nice to know I've got shoes on my feet!"

"Oh, times are different now – don't
70 worry," Mike explained.

"So you're looking for things to sell?" Holly wanted to know.

"No, no. Mudlarks are different now. We look for history in the mud. Just for
75 fun. There are things in the Thames that go back to Roman times, you know."

"Wow, amazing! Listen to that, Olivia!" said Amir. He knew she loved history too.

"Most things aren't as old as that,"
80 Mike told them. "But look at this glass in my bucket. OK, it's broken, so it doesn't look very good any more. But it's over 100 years old! And when I hold it in my hand I like to think of the story behind it. Who
85 drank from it? How did it get here?"

Mike also showed the friends the other things in his bucket: an old green bottle, a piece of an 18th-century clay pipe, and part of a lucky-charm bracelet. The
90 friends had no idea there was treasure like this in the Thames! They all wanted to help Mike to look for more things. "OK, but please stay near me," he said.

D At first the four new mudlarks found it
95 hard to see anything in the mud, but Mike showed them the best places to look and they started to notice things more easily. Olivia found a euro coin, Amir found an old key, and Holly found a shoe.
100 And then she found something awful, with hair on it.

"Ugh, a HEAD!!!" she screamed.

Mike laughed. "Well, a head from across the sea!" he laughed, as he pulled a coconut from the mud. Then he said, 105 "Sorry, guys, time to go now. The tide is coming in fast and – hey, where's your friend?"

Suddenly they saw that Jay wasn't with them. He wasn't far away, but the water 110 between them was already near the wall.

"Jay! Look, you're going to be cut off!" Mike shouted. "Come on – quick! We need to get to the steps!"

> **Stop and think:**
> What is Jay's problem?
> What could happen next?

E After a few dramatic minutes that felt 115 like *hours*, they all got safely to the top of the steps. The friends said thank you and goodbye to Mike. Then it was time to walk along the south side of the river to the London Eye to meet Shahid. 120

"Mum isn't going to be very happy when she sees our dirty shoes," Jay said to Amir. "Hey, where are you going? That isn't the way to the London Eye!"

Jay, Olivia and Holly watched as Amir 125 ran quickly back onto the bridge and threw something into the river.

"But – that's his bracelet!" Holly said. Jay was surprised too. "The crazy idiot! Why did he do that?" 130

Olivia just smiled. She understood.

SPEAKING

1 Your reaction → WB 42/27

Talk about what you found interesting about the story: the people, the history, the things in the river?

READING

2 Understanding the text → WB 42/28

a) *Explain the difference between mudlarks in the 19th century and modern mudlarks.*

b) *Why do you think Amir threw his bracelet back into the Thames?*

WRITING

3 One story, three different perspectives

a) *Work in groups of three. In your group, each of you (A, B and C) writes about the main ideas of the story in three different ways:*

    A. *Find 6–8 **key words / phrases** from the text. Write down why they're important.*
    B. *Tell the **main ideas** of the story in 6–8 sentences.*
    C. *In 6–8 sentences, talk about **your reaction** to the story.*

b) *Now tell each other your ideas. What ideas are the same or different?*

WRITING

4 What's the story behind it? → WB 42/29

→ ▲ 143/14
→ S10–13

*Choose **one** thing from Mike's bucket and create a little story about its history.
Who did it belong to? How long ago? How did it get into the Thames?
Write at least six sentences.*

Useful phrases

The … belonged to a girl / sailor / tourist / …
He / She lived in the 18th / … century.
He / She visited London last year / …
It was for wine / a treasure box / …
It was his / her favourite …
He / She threw it into the river because …
They / … didn't want it any more because …
It broke (into pieces) when …
One day it fell into the river while …

7 🎬
Mehr zum
Thema Thames

Example:

The wine glass

The wine glass belonged to a family over a hundred years ago. They lived in a house next to the Thames. One day …

Can you ...

1. talk about your plans? — I'm / We're going to visit London.
2. use compound words with *some* and *any*? — I need something to eat. |
   Has anybody got anything nice?
3. make adverbs to say how you do things? — You walk very quickly! I can't walk so fast.

LANGUAGE

1 What are they going to do tomorrow?

Use the clues in the pictures and make sentences about their plans.

Start: 1. The Frasers are going to have …

1 The Frasers

2 Luke and Sherlock

3 Mr and Mrs Azad

4 Holly

5 Amir

6 Shahid

LANGUAGE

2 What do these sellers at Camden Market say?

Put in the correct words.

Does **1** want to buy a cool hat? What about you, young man? I can see you're **2** who likes to look cool.

A book about London in German? I'm sure I've got one **5** . Yes, here you are. Look, **6** is in German.

Come on, **3** ! If you want **4** good to eat, this is the place to get it!

Great souvenirs! You can't find cheaper ones **7** in London – **8** costs more than £1!

everything

anybody

something

someone

anywhere

somewhere

nothing

everybody

LANGUAGE

3 Complete the text with the correct adverb forms

The big car takes the star of the new film **1** (fast) and **2** (comfortable) to the cinema in Leicester Square. The people outside the cinema scream **3** (excited) when they see him. He walks **4** (slow) along the red carpet so that everyone can see him **5** (clear) and take photos. Then he stops for an interview. "Where did you learn to act so **6** (good)?" But the film star never answers the question because suddenly the alarm clock rings **7** (loud). Jay sees **8** (sad) that he isn't on the red carpet – he's in bed at home! It was only a dream.

S 1/36–39
L 2/17–20 ◉

The copper[1] treasure

Jamie, Ten Tons and Davies are young mudlarks who live in London in the
1850s. One day, they climb aboard a big ship in the River Thames and start to
look for things which they can take away and sell for food; they're all hungry.
With them is Patty, a woman who doesn't like Ten Tons very much. This is when
5 they find a real treasure … the copper treasure.

We were moving carefully across the decks
and looking for bits and pieces. But there
wasn't much so we followed Patty down
and started to look for spoons[2] and knives[3]
10 and stuff in the cabins.

I could hear Ten Tons two cabins away.
He was talking and shouting to himself as
usual. Then I saw Patty at the end of the
corridor. She was doing well. You could
15 hear the sound of metal things under her
skirts[4]. She looked annoyed[5] when she
heard Ten Tons, but I didn't say anything.
Yes, Ten Tons was a crazy man, but he was
our crazy man.

I was crazy too – why was I stealing
like this? Davies and Ten Tons didn't have
parents – they needed to do this to live. But
I had a mother and father and a home. I
didn't need to do this. The others laughed
each time I looked to check that everything
was OK. But it was a good thing I checked
so often: I looked up again and … and I
saw the dock. It was floating past[6].

I thought … what? There was a man
with some cows on the river bank … we
were on the other side of the river now!
He pointed at us and shouted. The ship
started to circle and I suddenly understood
… Oh no! The anchor[7] was broken and we
were floating away[8] from the bank.

"Davies, Tens!" I screamed. "We're
moving!"

Ten Tons was up on deck right away.
"My God, I've stolen[9] a whole ship this
time!" he shouted. Like a captain, he
started to march up and down the decks
and to give orders[10] to no one. It was so
funny! He was very short and he was going
up and down the deck like a crazy little
engine[11].

Davies came up too. He looked over the
side.

"We should[12] get …" he started to say.

Then everything moved. We floated
sideways across the river and hit a
tugboat[13]. Our ship went up and down and
we all fell to the deck floor.

---

1 copper [ˈkɒpə] Kupfer | **2 spoon** [spuːn] Löffel | **3 knife** [naɪf] Messer | **4 skirt** [skɜːt] Rock | **5 annoyed** [əˈnɔɪd]
verärgert | **6 to float past** [fləʊt ˈpɑːst] vorbeitreiben | **7 anchor** [ˈæŋkə] Anker | **8 to float away** [fləʊt əˈweɪ]
wegtreiben, abtreiben | **9 I've stolen** [aɪv ˈstəʊlən] ich habe gestohlen | **10 order** [ˈɔːdə] Befehl | **11 engine** [ˈendʒɪn]
Lokomotive; Motor | **12 should** [ʃʊd] sollten | **13 tugboat** [ˈtʌɡbəʊt] Schlepper (*Schiff*)

Davies almost[14] fell into the river. I saw Ten Tons – he was sliding along on his
55 bum[15] and shouting 'Whhhhhooooah!' I held on to the rail[16]. And then we heard a strange sound, like music. I looked along the deck and saw …

The copper! What a sight! It was rolling
60 along the deck and opening itself up into a shining red sheet. It was like a magician[17] who was slowly opening his cape. The ship moved again and the deck turned to one side. The copper was moving faster and faster … and then it crashed into the 65 rail. The rails broke and the copper hung for a moment, right on the edge[18] of the deck. Then there was another movement. It caught[19] the sun, flashed[20] red-golden light[21] at me, went over the edge … and 70 dropped.

I watched it go down. It hummed as it fell. It flashed again in the evening sun and sent a bright[22] red light across the river. Then it hit the water. It was so bright 75 it looked red hot[23]. I was waiting for it to hiss[24]. There was a huge splash in the water … and it was gone. Half a ton or more of new copper, down under the water and lost forever[25]. 80

From: *The Copper Treasure* by Melvin Burgess

→ WB 44/1–3

14 **almost** [ˈɔːlməʊst] fast | 15 **bum** [bʌm] Hintern | 16 **rail** [reɪl] Reling | 17 **magician** [məˈdʒɪʃn] Zauberer | 18 **edge** [edʒ] Rand | 19 **to catch** [kætʃ] einfangen | 20 **to flash** [flæʃ] blitzen | 21 **light** [laɪt] Licht | 22 **bright** [braɪt] leuchtend | 23 **red hot** [red ˈhɒt] glühend heiß | 24 **to hiss** [hɪs] zischen | 25 **lost forever** [lɒst fəˈrevə] für immer verloren

Find more online:
34q3y3

Unit 4

Sport is good for you!

A | Camel racing

B | Marathon

C | BMX

D | Rugby

LISTENING  **1** **On the radio**

L 2/21 ⊙
→ S18–20

Gwen is preparing for the TTS sports and health project week. She's listening to sports programmes on the radio. Which sports? Three of them are in the photos; which ones?

SPEAKING **2** **Talk about sports**

→ S4
a) *Use the word cloud from Ex. 1 to describe the sports in the photos. Where and why are these sports popular?*

→ △ 144/1
b) *Your turn: Talk about sports you like.*

Vocabulary skills

You can use **word clouds** to show how often a word is in a text. The more often a word is in the text, the bigger it is. You can make word clouds on your computer.

In Unit 4 you learn

… how to talk about sports, about your experiences in the past, and about things which have just happened and are still important now. You learn:

- words for sports
- words for health and accidents
- the language of news reports
- the present perfect

Wheelchair basketball

LISTENING

3 **TTS sport and health projects**

L 2/22

a) *Now Olivia is talking to Gwen. Say which sports they're going to use for their projects and why they chose them.*

b) *Make a list of other sports they talk about.*

c) *Why is sport good for your health?*

Across cultures

The **number one sport** in Britain is football, rugby is number two. Other popular team sports in Britain are cricket and hockey. What team sports are popular in Germany and what do you know about them?

CABULARY

4 **Sports words** → WB 45/1–2

Make a grid with words and phrases for the sports you're interested in. (Use a dictionary for help.) Use these four headings:

Sport | Place | Equipment | Team / Individual sport

L 2/23 ⊙ **Have you ever run in a marathon?**

"Have you ever seen the London Marathon?" Gwen asked.

"Of course we have!" Holly said. "It starts right here in Greenwich Park."

5 "I want to run in it," Luke said. "But I've checked: You can't until you're 18."

"But haven't you heard of the *mini* marathon?" Gwen asked.

"No, I haven't," Jay said. "What's that?"

10 "It's for 11- to 17-year-olds," Gwen explained. "It's just the last part of the race, and it's before the *real* marathon."

"Are you going to run in it?" Olivia asked Gwen. "I know you like running."

"It isn't that easy," Gwen said. "There are 15 teams for different parts of London, and there are trials to find the fastest runners."

"Where are the trials?" Dave asked.

"For the Greenwich team, here in the park, next Saturday," Gwen said. 20

"Let's do it!" Olivia said. "Who's in?"

"Me," said Gwen. "It was my idea, remember?"

"I'm in too!" Luke said.

Nobody said a word. Then Jay said, "No 25 thanks, I'm out. I've never enjoyed running much. It isn't cool. And Dave has never run in a race. Right, Dave?"

"I've run in races before, but not in a big one like that," Dave said. 30

Holly said, "I've only ever run in short races too, and I'm not very good at running. But I've got an idea: Why don't you run for charity? People often do charity runs to raise money." 35

"That's great," Olivia said. "We can ask our parents, teachers and friends to give money. So it's Gwen, Luke and me."

"Er … just one thing," Gwen said. "Can we run together? You know, my eyes …" 40

"Of course," Olivia said.

"Yeah," Luke said, "we'll be Team Thomas Tallis! The fastest, coolest team in Greenwich. No, in *London*! Look out, here we come!" 45

1 Are you going to run in it?

a) *Would you like to run in a marathon? Why / Why not?*

b) *Answer these questions:*

1. Say who likes / doesn't like running.
2. What's Holly's idea?
3. Who isn't going to run in the trials for the mini marathon?

Across cultures

The **London Marathon** is one of the world's biggest races, with over 35,000 runners. It starts in Greenwich Park and finishes at Buckingham Palace. Have you ever watched a marathon? What running events are there in your area?

ANGUAGE

2 Find the rule → WB 46/3–4 → G12

a) *There are examples of a new tense in the text, the present perfect.*
Look at these sentences and the verb forms in the box.
*What is different between verbs like **see** and verbs like **check**?*

I have run in a race before.
Have you ever watched a marathon?

There's a list of irregular verbs on page 284.

Infinitive	– Past participle
see	– **seen**
check	– **checked**
hear	– **heard**
enjoy	– **enjoyed**
run	– **run**

b) *Now make two sentences like this about Dave.*

He … … . | … he ever … ?

c) *Write down how you make and answer questions in the present perfect.*

LANGUAGE

3 Say who has done what → WB 47/5

→ ▲ 144/2

… you ever **1** (be) to London? – No, I …, but my sister **2** (be) there.
… you **3** (hear) of the London Marathon? – Yes, I …, I **4** (watch) it three times.
… your parents ever **5** (run) in a marathon? – No, they …, but my dad **6** (play) in an international tennis match.
… your little brother ever **7** (prepare) a meal? – Yes, he … He always helps in the kitchen.
… your grandma ever **8** (give) you extra pocket money? – No, she …

SPEAKING

4 Your turn: Find somebody who … → WB 47/6, 48/7

→ S24

a) *Write at least three questions for your classmates with **Have you ever …?** The words on the right can help.*

Examples:
Have you ever seen …?
Have you ever been to …?
Have you ever eaten …?

b) *Ask some of your classmates the questions you wrote.*

c) *Write down what you've found out and tell the class.*

Example: Nicolas and Maria have been to Austria, but Tom and Lara haven't.

Have you ever been to Austria?
No, I haven't.

L 2/26 ⊙ # Have you been to the doctor's yet?

Gwen:	Hi Olivia. Are you still at home?
Olivia:	Hi Gwen. Yes, I'm at home. I haven't left for school yet.
Gwen:	Good. I've just had an idea. Let's train for the marathon trials. Do you want to go for a run in the park after school today?

5

Olivia:	Great idea, but I've hurt my foot! I think I've twisted my ankle.	
Gwen:	Oh no! Have you been to the doctor's yet?	10
Olivia:	No, I haven't. I hope it isn't serious. But it hurts when I walk, and I can't run on Saturday with pain like this.	
Gwen:	But you've already prepared for the trials!	15
Olivia:	I know, it's so unfair! I've done everything I can! I've bought new running shoes, I've stopped eating chocolate, I've found information on the internet about the *best* way to run, I've –	20
Gwen:	Listen, don't worry. I can train with Luke today, and maybe you can join us tomorrow.	25
Olivia:	OK. Have you already asked Luke?	
Gwen:	No, not yet. I can ask him at school today. See you there.	
Olivia:	Yeah, see you later. Bye!	

READING **5** ## Questions on the text

1. Why does Gwen call Olivia?
2. What's Olivia's problem?
3. What has Olivia done to prepare for the marathon trials?

LANGUAGE **6** ## The checklist → G12

👥 *Ask and answer questions about what the friends have done or haven't done.*

Example: **Has** Gwen **called** Olivia **yet**? – Yes, she **has**.

Things to do	Who?	Done?
1. call Olivia	Gwen	✔
2. make a poster for the charity run	Holly	✘
3. run three miles	Luke	✔
4. read a book about running	Olivia	✔
5. write a chant to cheer the runners	Jay	✘
6. find a good place to watch the marathon	Dave	✘
7. tell their parents about the marathon	Gwen, Luke, Olivia	✔

 **7** **What has just happened?**

→ △ 144/3
→ ▲ 145/4

Example: Mrs Elliot has just cleaned the windows.

Mrs Elliot – clean ✓

Mr Azad – finish

Luke – come back

Jamie – fall off

Amber – buy

Olivia – tidy

Shahid – write

Lucy – go to

---

8 **At the doctor's** → WB 48/8–9, 49/10

Read Olivia's dialogue with the doctor.
Practise your own dialogues with the ideas
in the box.

→ S9

Doctor: So, what's the problem today?
Olivia: I've had an accident and hurt
my foot.
Doctor: Can you walk on it?
Olivia: No, I can't.
Doctor: Let me have a look. – Oh yes,
you've twisted your ankle.
Olivia: Is it serious, Doctor?
Doctor: No, it isn't. But you need to walk
very carefully for a couple of days.

> **Useful phrases**
>
> I've hurt my hand / foot / arm / head /
> shoulder. | I've got a headache /
> backache / stomachache. | I feel bad /
> sick and I can't … | I've got a cold / a
> cough / a fever. | You need to … | You
> shouldn't … | You can take pills / …

Olivia: Oh no, so I can't run in the
marathon trials on Saturday …
Doctor: No, you really shouldn't. Here's a
prescription for an ointment.
You can put it on your ankle to stop
the pain.

---

9 **Children and accidents** → WB 49/11, 50/12

→ △ 145/5
→ S17

Pia has found a German
survey on the internet
that Olivia could use for
her project. What does the
introduction say about
German children's health?
Tell a partner in English.

> Obwohl sie zum größten Teil vermeidbar wären, zählen Unfallver-
> letzungen zu den häufigsten gesundheitlichen Beeinträchtigungen
> von Kindern und Jugendlichen. Pro Jahr erleiden etwa 15 Prozent
> der Kinder und Jugendlichen mindestens eine behandlungsbedürf-
> tige Unfallverletzung; Jungen sind öfter betroffen als Mädchen.
> Kleinkinder verletzen sich am häufigsten zu Hause. Ältere Kinder
> und Jugendliche erleiden Unfälle insbesondere beim Sport und in
> der Freizeit sowie in der Schule.

L 2/28 ◉ **An interview with Ayla**

Dave and Holly have interviewed Ayla Bayram, a Year 12 student at TTS and the school's best runner.

Dave:	Hi Ayla. How are you?
5 Ayla:	I'm fine, thanks.
Holly:	Thanks for your time.
Ayla:	No problem!
Dave:	Er, you had the fastest time in the mini marathon last year. But have
10	you ever run in a *real* marathon?
Ayla:	I've never run in a real marathon, no. But two months ago I ran in a half marathon. It was great!
Holly:	Are you going to run in this year's
15	mini marathon?
Ayla:	I haven't decided yet. But I'm still 17 *this* year, so maybe I should run! – Are *you* going to run?
Holly:	Us? Er, no, we aren't. But our friends
20	Luke and Gwen are! Do you have any tips for them?
Ayla:	Yes: Always wear *real* running shoes – but never *new* shoes.
Holly:	Is there anything else?
25 Ayla:	Oh, and don't run too fast too early; you don't want a cramp!
Dave:	Have you ever won any awards?

Ayla:	Yes, I have. I won the 'Best Maths Student' award two years ago. But no sports awards – sorry! 30
Holly:	Have you ever had an accident?
Ayla:	Oh, I've had *lots* of accidents! Two years ago I had one at the mini marathon: I fell and broke my arm!
Dave:	Can you describe how you felt? 35
Ayla:	Well, it was strange: While I was running I felt fine, but *after* the race it really, really hurt.
Dave:	Oh, I've never broken anything.
Holly:	I have! I fell off a chair and broke my 40 arm when I was a little girl.
Ayla:	So you know what it's like. Ouch!

READING **10** **Match the parts**

1. Ayla has never run
2. She finished
3. Ayla broke her arm
4. Holly broke her arm
5. Ayla ran
6. Dave has been

a) lucky; he hasn't broken anything yet!
b) when she was just a little girl.
c) in a real marathon before.
d) with the fastest time last year.
e) when she fell two years ago.
f) in a half marathon two months ago.

LANGUAGE **11** **Signal words** → WB 50/13, 51/14 → G12

Find these signal words in the text. Which tenses do they go with?

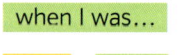 when I was…   last …   never

ever   after   yet   ago

→ △ 145/6

LANGUAGE   **12**   **Questions and answers**

Make questions and answers like the examples. Use the present perfect and simple past.

Examples: **Have** you ever **been** to England? – Yes, I have. I **was** in London last …
Have you ever **seen** a ghost? – No, but I **saw** a famous actor when I …

LANGUAGE   **13**   **Simple past or present perfect?**   → WB 51/15

→ △ 146/7
→ ▲ 146/8

Luke wrote his cousin Jan in Cracow an e-mail about a funny basketball game.
Put the verbs in the simple past or the present perfect. First look for signal words.

… I **1** (never see) a basketball game like the one I **2** (see) yesterday. It **3** (be) so embarrassing! First, one reporter almost **4** (become) sick in front of the camera and **5** (go) to find the toilet! "Er, er, we're so sorry: This **6** (never happen) before!" the other reporter **7** (say). After that it **8** (get) worse. Before the game the star player **9** (tell) a reporter: "I **10** (give) the crowd a great show in every game so far, and I can do that in this game too!" He **11** (be) right: Ten minutes later, he **12** (lose) his shorts when a player from the other team **13** (pull) too hard! And then, just when I thought, "I **14** (see) too many embarrassing things today," a strange man **15** (run) onto the court with no clothes on!

SPEAKING   **14**   **How to: Ask interview questions**   → WB 51/16–17

→ S16

a) *For her health project, Olivia is going to interview Nick Ashton, a member of the Greenwich Rugby Football Club (RFC). Read the internet profile about Nick she found.*

NICK ASHTON: Nick is 21 and joined RFC in 2014. Read about him!

Goals: – to play for England one day, of course!
– to get through the next season[1] with no broken arms, legs or anything else!

Nick likes … ☺
– getting the ball and sprinting[2] as far as he can (→ see Photo!).
– fast action sports like rugby!

Nick doesn't like… ☹
– all the attention[3] football gets.
– going to the weight room[4] every day. ("But I go anyway; rugby players need their muscles[5]!")

b) *Write questions that Olivia could ask Nick. The phrases can help you.*

c) *Act dialogues in small groups. One is Nick, the others ask interview questions.*

> **Useful phrases**
>
> Have you ever…? | Did you…? | Are you going to…? | What do you do every day / before big games / … | How often do you …? | Describe what you / how you … | Can you please tell me about … | What happened after you …? | Do you have any tips for …?

1 season ['siːzn] Saison | **2 to sprint** [sprɪnt] sprinten |
3 attention [ə'tenʃn] Aufmerksamkeit | **4 weight room**
['weɪt rʊm] Kraftraum | **5 muscle** ['mʌsl] Muskel

A picnic in the park → S21–22

VIEWING

1 Understanding the story so far

8 🎬 *Watch (00:00–03:55). Then match the sentences / the sentence parts below.*

1. Marley's ankle hurts.
2. Laura is going to stay with her grandad in Kent
3. Marley wants to watch the football match
4. Marley thinks it's unfair
5. Jinsoo's mum has made 'kimbap'¹.
6. At first, Jinsoo doesn't like the idea

a) but his dad needs his help in the attic.
b) that everyone is going to watch football and he can't.
c) that Alicia is going to come to Kent too.
d) It's typical Korean snack food.
e) and invites her friends to visit her.
f) He thinks he has twisted it.

SPEAKING

2 How's your ankle?

a) *Watch the rest of the film. What does Marley do? The phrases can help you.*

b) *What does Marley's father say at the end? Do you think he's right? Say why / why not. Think about it from Marley's point of view and from Mr Thompson's too. Look at the box again.*

> **Useful phrases**
>
> to fake an injury / a headache / …
> to teach somebody a lesson
> It's fair / unfair because …
> I think / don't think his father is right …
> Marley deserves it / doesn't deserve it …

c) *Your turn: Have you ever faked anything? Did you get away with it? Tell the class.*

VOCABULARY

3 The picnic → WB 52/18

a) *The friends are having different food for their picnic. Look at the photo and the food words and say what looks good.*

b) *Your turn: In class, talk about **your** 'perfect picnic'. What food from your country / your area / other countries could you have?*

kimbap   sandwiches (egg & cress² / cheese & tomato)

Scotch eggs³   quiche⁴   pasta salad⁵ with tuna⁶

---

1 kimbap [ˈkɪmbæp] *koreanischer Snack aus Seegras, Reis, Rindfleisch, Käse und Ei* | **2 cress** [krɛs] *Kresse* | **3 Scotch egg** [skɒtʃ ˈeg] *hart gekochtes Ei in Wurstbrät* | **4 quiche** [kiːʃ] *Quiche* | **5 pasta salad** [ˌpæstə ˈsæləd] *Nudelsalat* | **6 tuna** [ˈtjuːnə] *Thunfisch*

How to understand news reports and take notes → S18–20

For the task on pages 78–79, you need to know what the parts of a radio report are and what language is typical for a radio report. This page can help you.

1 A mountain rescue → WB 53/20

L 2/30 ◉

a) *Listen to a radio report about an accident in the mountains. Take notes in a grid.*

Time	Place	People	Event

b) *Use your notes and answer the questions.*

1. What was the accident?
2. Why did it happen?
3. What did the mountain rescue team do?
4. Why was the rescue difficult?

5. How serious was the accident?
6. How is the way the news presenter and the reporter speak different to the way the witnesses speak?

2 The language of a radio report → WB 53/21

Read the boxes. Then listen to the report again. Note down which phrases from the bigger box you can hear in the report.

*Also, note down **other** interesting or typical phrases for the news presenter, the reporter, the witness. Why do you think they are typical?*

Vocabulary skills

The situations are different, but the **language** of radio reports is often the same:

– **News presenters** and **reporters** stay more formal and use a language of facts.
– An **eyewitness** has just seen something dramatic, strange or maybe scary; the language he / she uses often shows more feelings.

Useful phrases

News presenter at radio station:
Hello / Good morning to all our listeners out there. | We've just received news of … | Now we're going to hear from our reporter at the scene: Can you describe the … / Can you tell us about the … | Stay with us for more …

Reporter at the scene:
What were you doing when …? | Where were you when …? | What have you seen? | Has anyone else …? | What else can you tell us?

Eyewitness at the scene:
I couldn't believe my eyes! | This is strange / dramatic / exciting / …: I've never seen anything like it! | I didn't know what was happening. | I was watching TV when suddenly I heard / saw …

The aliens have landed!

Imagine that aliens have landed on Earth – in Greenwich Park! In this Unit task, you and your group write your own radio report about this strange event. For the report, there are five roles: **three witnesses**; a **reporter** who interviews the witnesses; the **radio news presenter**. Your job is to write – and record – a fun report. Your report should be 3–4 minutes long. Be as creative as possible!

News presenter at radio station

Assistant at sweet shop

Greenwich man in garden

Doctor at hospital

Reporter in Greenwich Park

Step 1

The situation   → WB 54/22

In groups of five, look at the scenes above. Talk about what you think is happening / has happened in each scene. Look closely at the words in the box. You need them to talk about the pictures.

Martian | Mars | space | spaceship | UFO | light | sky | star | customer | stomachache | human | to land | to invade | to come in peace | to make friends | to get sick on (too much) chocolate | strange-looking | bright | friendly

Examples:
A: In this scene, you can see that the aliens have landed.
B: What's happening at the hospital? Have the aliens eaten too much chocolate?
C: Look at the park scene: It looks like the aliens want to make friends!

Martian [ˈmɑːʃn] Marsmensch | **space** [speɪs] Weltraum | **spaceship** [ˈspeɪsʃɪp] Raumschiff | **light** [laɪt] Licht | **sky** [skaɪ] Himmel | **customer** [ˈkʌstəmə] Kunde / Kundin | **human** [ˈhjuːmən] Mensch | **to invade** [ɪnˈveɪd] eindringen | **in peace** [ɪn ˈpiːs] in Frieden | **to make friends** [meɪk ˈfrendz] Freundschaft schließen | **to get sick on sth** [get ˈsɪk ɒn] sich an etw. den Magen verderben | **strange-looking** [ˈstreɪndʒ ˌlʊkɪŋ] seltsam aussehend | **bright** [braɪt] hell

D　Not far from the finish line …

> **Gwen:**
> I think that stupid cramp is gone. YES! And
> Luke is still doing fine too. … We're still
> 55　running fast: I think our time is going to
> be *really* good. … I want to see our photos
> on the TTS website! "Gwen Parker, the new
> running star". Sounds great! – OH NO!!!!!!!!!
> What's happening?!?! Oh no, I don't
> 60　want to fall!

E　Just after the race …

Luke:　Gwen, we did it, WE DID IT!

Gwen:　Yes, we did! And it feels GREAT!

Luke:　Well, *now* it feels great. But during
65　the race I had a bad cramp. You
started too fast for me!

Gwen:　*You* had a cramp? Oh, now I feel
better.

Luke:　I had a cramp and now *you* feel
70　better? I don't understand.

Gwen:　Well, I had a cramp too – but I
didn't want to tell you; I didn't
want to stop the race.

Luke:　And I didn't want to tell *you* and
75　hear, "You didn't train enough!"

Gwen:　Well, we *both* finished, yippee! And
'See with your Heart' gets some
money too!

Luke:　Well, they almost *didn't*: That
80　stupid dog and that stupid cat
almost ruined everything for us! I
couldn't believe my eyes when they
pulled out a smartphone and took
a selfie. That one boy fell because
85　of them, and we almost fell too!

Gwen:　They took a *selfie*? In the middle
of the race? Oh, I knew those two
were trouble!

Olivia:　*(suddenly)* Yes, that's what the race
90　officials thought too so they finally
took the dog and the cat out of the
race. – Look who I've found!

Luke:　Dave and Jay?!?!

Gwen:　YOU were the dog and the cat?!?!
Aaaargh!!!　95

Dave:　Don't be angry, please! We're really
sorry. We only wanted to surprise
you.

Jay:　Yes, we trained in secret, and ran
for the pets' charity!　100

Gwen:　But somebody *fell* because of you
two. Luke and I almost fell! I'm
sure that boy trained hard. Have
you ever thought of that?

Jay:　Well, er …　105

Dave:　We said sorry, Gwen.

Gwen:　Well, don't tell *me*. Have you told
the boy yet?

Dave:　Er, no.

Gwen:　Well, *tell* him. *(smiling now)* So we　110
can finally forgive you.

Luke:　But I'm not sure 'sorry' is enough.
How about a present for him?

Olivia:　That sounds good. I'm sure we all
have nice present ideas.　115

Gwen:　Yes boys, you must do something
nice for him. But you can do
something nice for me and Luke
too. – Luke, where's your phone?
Picture time!　120

Luke:　Oh yes – those silly costumes,
those faces in the next TTS
yearbook! Say CHEESE!

READING

1 Working with the text → WB 56/26

a) *Look at the text and talk about these questions.*

1. What different kinds of text are there in parts A–E?
2. Why do people run in a marathon? Find reasons in the text and say who gives them.
3. What can cause problems in a marathon race?
4. What do we learn about Gwen and Luke's hopes and fears?
5. What can you say about their relationship?

→ △ 147/9 b) *Use the text and the pictures to retell what happened.*

READING

2 What do you think?

 a) *Find adjectives to describe Gwen, Luke, Jay and Dave and their actions.*

→ △ 147/10 b) *Find positive and negative things in the story that they did. Use words from a) to discuss what you think about their actions. Here are some ideas:*

Positive	Negative
On the one hand it was **good** that … I think Gwen was **brave** … …	On the other hand it was really **stupid** … But it was also **dangerous** … …

VOCABULARY

3 Looking at spoken language

→ △ 147/11 *Read the dialogues and Gwen's thoughts out loud. How do Gwen and Luke talk to each other?*
→ ▲ 147/12 *What language do they use to express their feelings? Collect words and phrases you would like to use again in a mind map.*

WRITING

4 Another story → WB 56/27

→ S10–13 *Write about what **isn't** in the story. Choose one of these two topics. You can write a story, a dialogue or a comic. Use your vocabulary from Ex. 2.*

– Just for fun: The race from Jay and Dave's point of view.
– Can you forgive us: Jay and Dave talk to the boy who fell because of them.

Can you . . .

1. talk about experiences in your life / in somebody else's life?   Have you ever played rugby?
2. talk about things which have (just) happened?   I've hurt my foot!
3. use *just*, *already* and *yet*?   I haven't had my dinner yet.

LANGUAGE

1 Match the sentence halves.

1. I think you've broken
2. We've been to
3. I've never eaten
4. Jay has just written
5. Holly hasn't finished
6. I've already asked

a) a new chant.
b) in an Indian restaurant.
c) your ankle.
d) Olivia to help me with my project.
e) Buckingham Palace three times.
f) her homework yet.

LANGUAGE

2 Make dialogues about Luke and Dave

Example: Dave: write | your health report?   → Have you already written your report?
Luke: no | have | no time yet   → No, I haven't. I haven't had time yet.

1. Luke: find | interesting information on the internet yet?
   Dave: yes | find | yesterday after school.
2. Luke: Jay | draw | new mangas for his report yet?
   Dave: yes | draw | cool new characters at lunch.
3. Dave: see | two new manga comics yet?
   Luke: yes | already finish | one of them.
4. Luke: see | Olivia today?
   Dave: no | but send | text an hour ago.
5. Dave: Holly | write | about guinea pigs?
   Luke: hope not! | write | about guinea pigs last year.

LANGUAGE

3 BMX: Popular but a bit dirty!

Dave wrote a text for the health project about the history of BMX. Complete his text with the correct verb forms: simple past or present perfect.

The full name of BMX is 'bicycle motocross'. It is a sport that
1 (become) very popular with young people. It **2** (start)
with children in the USA in about 1970. At first, the children
3 (use) normal bikes on mud roads; there **4** (be) no special
BMX bikes. But then a few bicycle companies **5** (discover)
the sport, and the world **6** (have) its first BMX bikes. It's
a fast, dangerous sport, and there **7** (be) many serious
accidents. That's why many parents are *not* big fans. In one
survey with parents last year, BMX **8** (not be) at the top of
the list of 'favourite sports'. One mother said: "I **9** (see) dirty
football and rugby uniforms, but my children's BMX clothes
after a race? They're the worst!"

S 2/11–14
L 3/1–4 ◉

The summer¹ table

August was born² with a genetic defect and has 'facial issues³'. To other people, the highly intelligent boy looks like a monster. Everyone stares at him so he doesn't go to school; his mum teaches him at home. When he is about 10, his parents finally decide to send him to school. On his first day, Auggie has a
5 really hard time. The other children stare at him or ignore him completely. At lunchtime, Auggie feels really bad – his friend Jack Will isn't there, and because of⁴ his face, August has problems eating, too. When a girl, Summer, sits down at his table, he is very surprised.

"Hey, is somebody sitting here?"
10   I looked up, and a girl I never saw before was standing across from my table with a lunch tray⁵ full of food. She had long wavy brown hair, and wore a brown T-shirt with a purple peace sign⁶ on it.
15   "Uh, no," I said.
     She put her lunch tray on the table, dropped her rucksack on the floor, and sat down across from me. She started to eat the pasta with cheese sauce on her plate.
20   "Ugh," she said when she took the first bite. "Why didn't I bring a sandwich like you did?"
     "Yeah," I said.

"My name is Summer, by the way. What's yours?" 25
     "August."
     "Cool," she said.
     "Summer!"
     Another girl who was carrying⁷ a tray came over to the table. "Why are you 30 sitting here? Come back to the table."
     "There were too many people," Summer answered her. "Come sit here. There's more room."
     The other girl looked confused⁸ for a 35 second. I recognized⁹ her. She was sitting at another table with some friends a few minutes ago: They were looking at me and she had her hand over her mouth and was whispering. I guess Summer was one of the 40 girls at that table too.
     "Don't worry," the girl said and went away.
     Summer looked at me, smiled, and took another bite of her pasta. 45
     "Hey, our names match," she said, as she ate.
     I guess she noticed that¹⁰ I didn't know what she meant.
     "Summer? August?" she said and 50 smiled, her eyes open wide, as she waited for me to understand.
     "Oh, yeah," I said after a second.
     "We can make this the 'summer only'

1 **summer** ['sʌmə] Sommer | 2 **to be born** [bi 'bɔːn] geboren werden | 3 **facial issues** [ˌfeɪʃl 'ɪʃuːz] Gesichtsprobleme | 4 **because of** [bɪ'kɒz‿əv] wegen | 5 **tray** [treɪ] Tablett | 6 **peace sign** ['piːs saɪn] Friedenszeichen | 7 **to carry** ['kæri] tragen | 8 **confused** [kən'fjuːzd] verwirrt | 9 **to recognize** ['rekəgnaɪz] wiedererkennen | 10 **that** [ðæt] dass

4

55 lunch table," she said. "Only kids with summer names can sit here. Let's see, is there anyone here named June or July?"

"There's a Maya," I said.

"Technically, May is spring[11]," Summer
60 answered, "but if she wants to sit here, we can make an exception[12]." She said it as if[13] she already had a plan. "There's Julian. That's like the name Julia, which comes from July."

65 I didn't say anything.

"There's a kid named Reid in my English class," I said.

"Yeah, I know Reid, but how is Reid a summer name?" she asked.

70 "I don't know," I said. "I just imagine … it's like a reed of grass[14] in summer."

"Yeah, OK," she answered and pulled out her notebook[15]. "And Ms.[16] Petosa could[17] sit here, too. That sounds like the
75 word 'petal[18]', which is a summer thing too, I think."

"She's my tutor," I said.

"I have her for Maths," she answered and made a face[19].

She started to write the list of names 80 on a page of her notebook.

"So, who else?" she said.

When we finished lunch, we had a whole list of names of kids and teachers who could sit at our table if they wanted. 85 Most of the names weren't really summer names, but they were names that had some kind of connection to summer. I even found a way to put Jack Will's name on the list – I suggested that we could put 90 his name into a sentence about summer, like "Jack will go to the beach[20]," and Summer agreed that that was fine.

"But if someone doesn't have a summer name and wants to sit with us," she said 95 very seriously, "they can still sit here if they're nice, OK?"

"OK," I agreed. "Even if it's a winter name."

"Cool," she answered and gave me a 100 thumbs-up.

Summer looked like her name. She had a tan[21], and her eyes were green like the leaves of a tree.

'The Summer Table' from *WONDER* by R. J. Palacio

→ WB 58/1–4

11 **spring** [sprɪŋ] Frühling | 12 **exception** [ɪkˈsepʃn] Ausnahme | 13 **as if** [əz ˈɪf] als ob | 14 **reed of grass** [ˌriːd əv ˈɡrɑːs] Schilf | 15 **notebook** [ˈnəʊtbʊk] Notizbuch | 16 **Ms.** [mɪz] Frau *(Anrede)* | 17 **could** [kʊd] könnte | 18 **petal** [ˈpetl] Blütenblatt | 19 **to make a face** [meɪk ə ˈfeɪs] das Gesicht verziehen | 20 **beach** [biːtʃ] Strand | 21 **tan** [tæn] sonnengebräunte Haut

LANGUAGE

1 On tour on a London pedicab[1]

a) *Complete the text. Use adjectives or adverbs.*

The London pedicabs

Do you want to go on a ` 1 ` (different) kind of sightseeing tour?
Then hop on[2] ` 2 ` (quick) and enjoy London's sights and attractions
from the backseat[3] of a pedicab. Pedicabs are an ` 3 ` (exciting) and
environmentally friendly[4] way to travel around the city ` 4 ` (easy). Enjoy
the view, see all the ` 5 ` (famous) sights and get off anywhere you like.
Our ` 6 ` (friendly) drivers speak three languages and know all the ` 7 `
(important) facts and ` 8 ` (interesting) stories about London. And, of
course, they always drive ` 9 ` (slow) and ` 10 ` (careful)!

You can start your tour at different places, for example at Covent
Garden, with its shops, cafés and restaurants with ` 11 ` (fresh) food
from all over the world. You want to take a photo or buy something to
drink? – No problem. Our drivers work ` 12 ` (hard) to make your tour an
` 13 ` (amazing) experience. Have a look at Buckingham Palace and the
Changing of the Guard. Stop in front of the Houses of Parliament and
listen to the sound of Big Ben. You want to know where you can eat
` 14 ` (good) and ` 15 ` (cheap)? Or where you can buy ` 16 ` (cool) clothes?
Just ask our drivers!

Tours:
* ✿ Mini tour: 1 hour |
  £50 | 1–2 persons
* ✿ Shopping tour:
  1 hour | £30 |
  1–2 persons

b) *Would you like to see London in a pedicab? Say why/why not.*

c) *Where else could the pedicab tour go? Continue the text. Use adjectives and adverbs.*

LISTENING

2 A radio report: Shopping for souvenirs → WB 59/1–2

L 3/5

a) *Listen to the radio report and say where the reporter is and what the report is about.*

b) *Listen again. Copy the grid and fill in the missing information.*

	Mr Smith	Amir	American tourist
souvenir			
for			
price			
problem			

c) *What do you think is the best souvenir? What souvenir would you bring? Say why.*

1 pedicab [ˈpedɪkæb] Fahrradtaxi, Fahrradrikscha | **2 to hop on** [hɒp ˈɒn] (schnell) einsteigen | **3 backseat** [ˈbæksiːt]
Rücksitz | **4 environmentally friendly** [ɪnˌvaɪrənˌmentli ˈfrendli] umweltfreundlich

CABULARY

3 **A sports quiz** → WB 60/3–4

a) *You and your partner each make notes about one sport that you both like: where people play, what equipment they need, how many players there are in a team, etc. (For new words, use a dictionary.) Don't show each other your notes!*

b) *Write 5–6 quiz questions with the information in your notes.*

Example: Which of these football teams has never won the World Cup?
A. England   B. Poland   C. Italy

c) *Test your partner with your quiz! Who knows the most about the same sport?*

READING

4 **Are they crazy?** → WB 60/5

a) *Skim the text for the gist. Say what it is about in 2–3 sentences.*

BEN NEVIS

You've probably heard of Ben Nevis in Scotland[5]. With its 1344 metres it is the highest mountain in Great Britain. Each year 125,000 people climb this mountain and enjoy the great view from the top. It usually takes a few hours to get to the peak[6]. But if you go up on the first Saturday in September, you can see people who run up or down the mountain. You think they're crazy? Well, they probably are … They take part in the Ben Nevis race which takes place every year in early September. The race starts and finishes in Fort William. The runners do not only run up the mountain but also back down again – that's a distance of 9.9 miles with a height[7] difference of 1,340 metres. And some runners are really fast. In 1984 Kenny Stuart ran up and down the mountain in 1 hour, 25 minutes and 34 seconds – that's still the record[8] today.
To run up and down the mountain you must be really fit. Only runners with a lot of experience are allowed to take part in the race. For safety reasons[9] the number of runners is limited to[10] 600. The weather can change quickly in the mountains, so the runners must wear waterproofs[11], a hat, gloves and a whistle[12].
But who had this crazy idea anyway? The first person known to run up and down the mountain was William Swan. On September 27, 1895 he ran from Fort William to the top of the mountain in 2 hours and 41 minutes. He probably didn't know what he started …

b) *Scan the text. What numbers are there in the text and what do they mean? What does it tell you about 1. safety rules 2. the history of the race? Take notes.*

5 Scotland [ˈskɒtlənd] Schottland | **6 peak** [piːk] Gipfel, Bergspitze | **7 height** [haɪt] Höhe | **8 record** [ˈrekɔːd] Rekord | **9 safety reasons** [ˈseɪfti ˌriːzns] Sicherheitsgründe | **10 limited to** [ˈlɪmɪtɪd tə] begrenzt auf | **11 waterproofs** [ˈwɔːtəpruːfs] Regenkleidung | **12 whistle** [ˈwɪsl] Trillerpfeife

Find more online:
m2g8ws

English around the world

Many people in different countries around the world speak English. Learn about where and why, and listen to some different kinds of English.

SPEAKING

1 Which countries speak English?

a) *Which countries do you know where the people speak English?*

b) *On a map or in an atlas, show where these countries are.*

c) *Can you think of a time when you spoke English? Where were you and who did you speak to? The phrases can help.*

VIEWING

2 Speaking English

9 a) *Watch the film. What is it about?*

b) *Does Marley mention any countries you talked about in Ex. 1? Which ones?*

c) *Look at the stills and describe what happens in the two scenes.*

d) *Watch the film again. Say which statements are right. Correct the wrong ones.*

1. The American man works in England.
2. American English is not exactly the same as British English.
3. You can see English signs in China, India and in some other countries.
4. The South Korean man can't help the Romanian woman.

 e) *Act out one of these scenes:*

1. You're on holiday and make a new friend from another country.
2. You help an English-speaking person in your town.

READING

3 How English became a world language → WB 61/1

a) *Before you read: Why do you think so many people in the world speak English?*

b) *Read the text. Make a list of the reasons why so many people speak English today. Only take notes! Then use your notes to explain to your partner why English is so important today.*

More than 400 million people in the world today speak English as their first language, and more than 600 million speak it as a second or official language. The first important reason for this is that from about 1600, British sailors and merchants crossed the sea and started colonies. This went on for many years and the British Empire became huge. For example, Australia was a British colony; India and South Africa too. Today, the British king or queen is still head of state in many countries, e. g. Australia.

There's a second important reason why so many people speak English. After World War II, the USA became a superpower and started to influence the world in many new ways. American rock 'n' roll music and Hollywood films became popular almost everywhere. And later, new technology from America (the PC, the internet, the e-mail) made it possible to communicate in every last corner of the world. In English, of course!

LISTENING

4 Where are we from? → WB 61/2

L 3/7

a) *Listen to four people from different English-speaking regions or countries. Which place is each person from? Which ones did you find easy or difficult to understand? Why?*

b) *Listen again. In which place can you hear these words and expressions? Can you remember what they mean?*

cookie	sunnies	wee	loch
lads and lasses	I'm grand	G'day
candy	movie	What's the craic?

VOCABULARY

5 Your turn: English in your language

Collect words in German that are similar to or the same as words in English. Put the words into these categories. (Maybe you can think of more categories too.)

Clothes | Technology | Food | Sport | ...

Find more online: dd832q

Unit 5

Stay in touch

Special interest forums are a great way to meet friends online. I found 'Pet Paradise', and now Olivia and I have both got profiles.

A

I see you've got a new friend on Mousebook. Who's Jon?

He's just a friend, Tony. Don't be jealous!

SPEAKING

1 Media and TTS students: A survey

Read what TTS students say about different media in A–E. Which of the activities have you done this week?

VOCABULARY

2 Media collocations

→ △ 148/1   *Match these verbs and nouns to make phrases to talk about media.*

→ S3   **Example:** I like to change my profile and post new photos. What about you?

change	post	receive	send	read		profile	photo	text message	forum
talk to	reply to	play	join	check		social network	video game	video chat
chat	take part in	write	text	have		magazine	discussion	each other	friend

In Unit 5 you learn

… how to talk and write about communication in your life. You learn:

- media vocabulary and phrases
- the language of giving and getting advice
- modals and their substitute forms
- writing skills for letters and replies

I can't live without my smartphone – I check my messages all the time!

I usually read magazines online. I love the advice pages! But I buy print magazines too – for the posters.

C

This is my favourite video game. My cousin and I always compare our scores on video chat!

E

Social networks are cool. But nasty comments and cyber bullies *aren't* so cool …

LISTENING **3** **More about the survey** → WB 62/1–3

L 3/8–12 ⊚

a) *Listen and make a list of the media the TTS students use.*

b) *Listen again and take notes. What do the students say about the media?*

Useful phrases

Smartphones / Social networks / … are great because they're fun / practical / easy to use / …

… are great for meeting … / for staying in touch with … / for sharing information about …

Which media?	What's positive?	What's not so positive?
smartphone / mobile	texts / easy to stay in touch	texts from parents!
special interest forums	…	…

c) *Your turn: Talk about how you use the different media.*

L 3/13 ⊙ # Dear Ruby

Holly and Olivia have found an interesting problem in the 'agony aunt' pages of their favourite magazine.

JUST ASK RUBY!

Dear Ruby,

I'm writing to you because I don't know what to do. Last week I had a big fight with one of my best friends. Before the fight, we spent all our free time together. But now she has made friends with another girl and they're having a lot of fun. I know this because she posts photos of the two of them on the social network site we use. She acts like she's having a much better time without me! Whenever I see these photos, it really hurts my feelings. I'm not jealous, am I? Can you please help? I would really like to hear your advice.

Lauren

Dear Lauren,

You're having a hard time, aren't you? I'm sorry you're feeling so upset. I understand how hard it is to share a friend; it was the same with me when I was young. It doesn't mean you're a jealous person. As a first step, my advice is to be self-critical: Are you overreacting? Maybe the situation isn't as serious as you think. The next step is to talk to your friend in a friendly way and tell her how you feel. Why don't you invite her to your house after school? Or have you tried texting her? Things usually get better as soon as you talk. Another tip: Please stop looking at your social network site until you've talked to her. The photos only make you feel worse! I hope you two can be friends again very soon.

Ruby

READING **1** **Understanding the problem** → WB 63/4

→ ▲ 148/2 *Answer these questions about Lauren's letter and Ruby's reply.*

1. Why is Lauren writing to Ruby?
2. How does Lauren know about her friend's new friend?
3. When does Lauren feel really bad?
4. Compare how her friend acted before the fight and after (in Lauren's opinion).

LANGUAGE **2 Using linking words** → WB 63/5–6 → G13

→ △ 148/3

→ S13

Read what different teens say about how they use different social media websites.
Put these words in the gaps. There's sometimes more than one correct answer.

after   before   as soon as   until   whenever   like   because

1. I'm careful. I never give my phone number ▯ I've met a new friend face-to-face.
2. ▯ somebody starts asking too many personal questions, I just block them.
3. ▯ you post photos of yourself online, remember: ▯ you post them, they're probably on the internet forever!
4. I'm angry with my cousin ▯ she posted that awful photo of me at the lake.
5. My friend doesn't even know some of the people on her friends list! It's ▯ she doesn't care about real friends, she just wants a long list of 'friends'.
6. I don't get much attention online ▯ I don't post pictures of myself very often!

WRITING **3 Your turn: Media in your life**

Write 5–6 sentences about yourself like the ones you see in Ex. 2. Think about these ideas:

– How much information about yourself do you share online? Why? How often?
– Do you and your friends use media differently? How?

VOCABULARY **4 The right vocabulary for advice** → WB 64/7

a) *In the letters on page 92, you see some phrases with 'advice vocabulary' in* green .
In a grid like this one, match the phrases to the three categories.

Asking for advice	Giving advice	Showing understanding

b) *Here are some important advice phrases. Think of them as 'building blocks' for your own*
sentences about advice. Write a sentence with each phrase. You can write about the same
→ S3 *problem as on page 92, or about something different.*

Useful phrases

My advice is to be self-critical / to see it from the other side / to find a compromise.

Why don't you talk to your friend / invite your friend over / text your friend / …

The next step is to talk to / write to / …
It's always a good idea to talk / try / …

You're having a hard time / trouble with …
I'm sorry you're feeling sad / **you're** having trouble with …

Have you tried talking to him / texting her?
Stop looking at … / thinking about / worrying about / …

LANGUAGE **5** **Find the rule: Question tags** → WB 64/8 → G14

→ △ 149/4

a) *Look at the examples. What can you say about positive and negative forms?*

You**'re** having a hard time, **aren't** you?
The weather **is** nice today, **isn't** it?
You and Pia **haven't** told our secret,
    have you?
Ben **doesn't** like video games, **does** he?

b) *Make the correct question tags.*

1. That's a cool phone, …?
2. You can pay, …?
3. You aren't online often, …?
4. We need more time for our project, …?
5. She didn't write that awful post, …?
6. Ed hasn't got a new girlfriend, …?

L 3/16 ⊙ **c)** *Listen to the sentences from b). Are the people sure about the answer or not?*
→ ▲ 149/5   *Listen again and repeat the sentences.*

> **Across cultures**
>
> – In English, question tags are a good way to **start a conversation** and to **get feedback**. Example at a football match: "Hey, this is a great game, isn't it?" – "Yeah, it is. Is Manchester City your favourite team too?"
> – Also, it's important **to know this difference** with question tags: When it's a *real* question, your voice goes up. When it *isn't*, your voices go down. Just listen to the examples in **Ex. 5 c)**.

LISTENING **6** ⟨ **A song: Friends** ⟩ Aura Dione

L 3/17 ⊙
→ S9

Free, free to be myself
Free to need some time
Free to need some help
So I'm reaching baby, out
When I'm lonely in the crowd
When the silence[1] gets too loud
I'll be crashing[2] on some couch

And even if I never forget you baby
Tonight I'm gonna let your memory[3] baby
go, oh it's sad I know

But at least[4] I got my friends
Share a raincoat in the wind
They got my back[5] until the end
If I never fall in love again
Well at least I got my friends
Like a lifeboat in the dark
Saving me from the sharks[6]
Even though I got a broken heart
At least I got my friends, got my friends

Text: Aura Dione, Antonina Armato, Tim James, David Jost
© Koolmusic

a) *Which words/lines tell you what kind of a situation the main character is in?*

→ △ 149/6 **b)** *Your turn: What things are symbols of friendship in the song, and for* **you**? *Why?*

1 **silence** ['saɪləns] Stille | 2 **to crash** [kræʃ] schlafen *(ugs.)* | 3 **memory** ['mɛmri] Erinnerung | 4 **at least** [ət 'liːst] wenigstens | 5 **They got my back** [ðeɪ ˌgɒt maɪ 'bæk] Sie halten mir den Rücken frei; sie passen auf mich auf *(ugs.)* | 6 **shark** [ʃɑːk] Hai

L 3/18 ⊙

Forum? What forum?

Luke: Dad, I wasn't allowed to go over to Jay's house yesterday. But can I … er, what on earth are you doing? There's water everywhere!

5 **Dad:** Really? Where?

Luke: Very funny. What's happened?

Dad: There's a problem with one of the pipes. I must fix it before your mum comes home and goes crazy!

10 **Luke:** Dad, do you know what you're doing?

Dad: Of course! It's just taking longer than I thought. I had to have a good look at everything first.

Luke: You could look at a forum for help.

15 **Dad:** Forum? What forum? You mean on the internet? So I can't fix my own washing machine – is that what you think? I don't need the internet.

Luke: But you're wasting so much time!

20   I *cannot* believe you don't just look online – there's step-by-step advice for everything!

Dad: Well, when I was young, I wasn't able to look everything up on the internet.

25   But I still learned to do things my way, step-by-step.

Luke: Your way? Hm …

Dad: I've done this a million times before. You should watch me and learn! – Er,

30   what are you doing with *my* tablet?

Luke: Well, I can use it, can't I? Anyway, let's see … hm … Oh yes, look: I've found a great website. Hey, over 1,000 people have given it five stars!

Dad: You shouldn't believe everything you 35 read online, Luke!

Luke: OK, just listen. You see that knob on the right?

Dad: Yes, I think I can reach it.

Luke: You must turn it off, then you … 40

15 minutes later …

Luke: Yes! It's working! These forums are great! No, please, you needn't say "thanks". Advice is free!

Dad: Fantastic! I fixed it. I told you, didn't I? 45

Luke: Only because I'm a genius!

Dad: With a *very* big head. Now, may I have my tablet back, please?

READING   **7** **Luke knows best?**

a) *Luke and his dad have different ideas about how to solve the problem. What are they?*

b) *Have you ever had conversations like this one with family or friends? Tell the class.*

SPEAKING   **8** **The day I fixed my …**

👥 *Tell your partner about a time when you fixed something. How did you do it?*

→ △ 149/7

LANGUAGE **9** **Find the rule: *Can* and its substitute forms** → G15

a) *In which sentences from the text does **can** mean the same as the words in sentences A or B on the right?*

b) *Make more sentences for the two meanings of **can**.*

A: I'm good at Maths so **I'm able to** help my little brother with his homework.
B: My little brother **isn't allowed to** come into my room.

LANGUAGE **10** **Substitute forms: *Be able to, be allowed to* and *have to*** → WB 65/9–10

a) *Copy the grid into your folder. Find examples of the three substitute forms in the text and fill in your grid.*

→ △ 150/8–9

b) *What were you not able or not allowed to do in the past? What are you not able or not allowed to do now? Tell your partner.*

	Present	Past
können		
dürfen		
müssen		

Examples: When I was four, I **wasn't able to** swim. Now I can.
When I was ten, I **wasn't allowed to** have my own phone. Now I have one.
When I was five, I **didn't have to** do homework. Now I must.

LANGUAGE **11** **Should, shouldn't and could for advice** → WB 66/11–12 → G16

→ ▲ 150/10
→ △ 151/11

*Tony is having a very bad day. Look at his problems, then write sentences with advice for him. Use **should, shouldn't** or **could**. The ideas on the right can help.*

Example: Oh no, that was my dinner for Lou!
– Maybe you **could** take her to a restaurant.

1. I forgot Lou's birthday yesterday!
2. I've got a new neighbour.
3. I've left my money at home.
4. I want to do something nice for Dad.
5. I want to buy a new phone but haven't got enough money.
6. Someone has stolen my bike!

ask a friend   buy flowers
go to the police
take her to a restaurant ✔   say hello
take him to a football game
help your parents at home for pocket money

MEDIATION **12** **A German survey about young people and media**

 L3/20

Listen to part of a radio report about a German media survey. You want to share the most interesting information with your chat friend in Italy. What can you tell him/her in English?

13 Are you media mad?

→ ▲ 151/12 *Take the test and find out how media mad you are!*
Do you agree with your results? Why / why not?

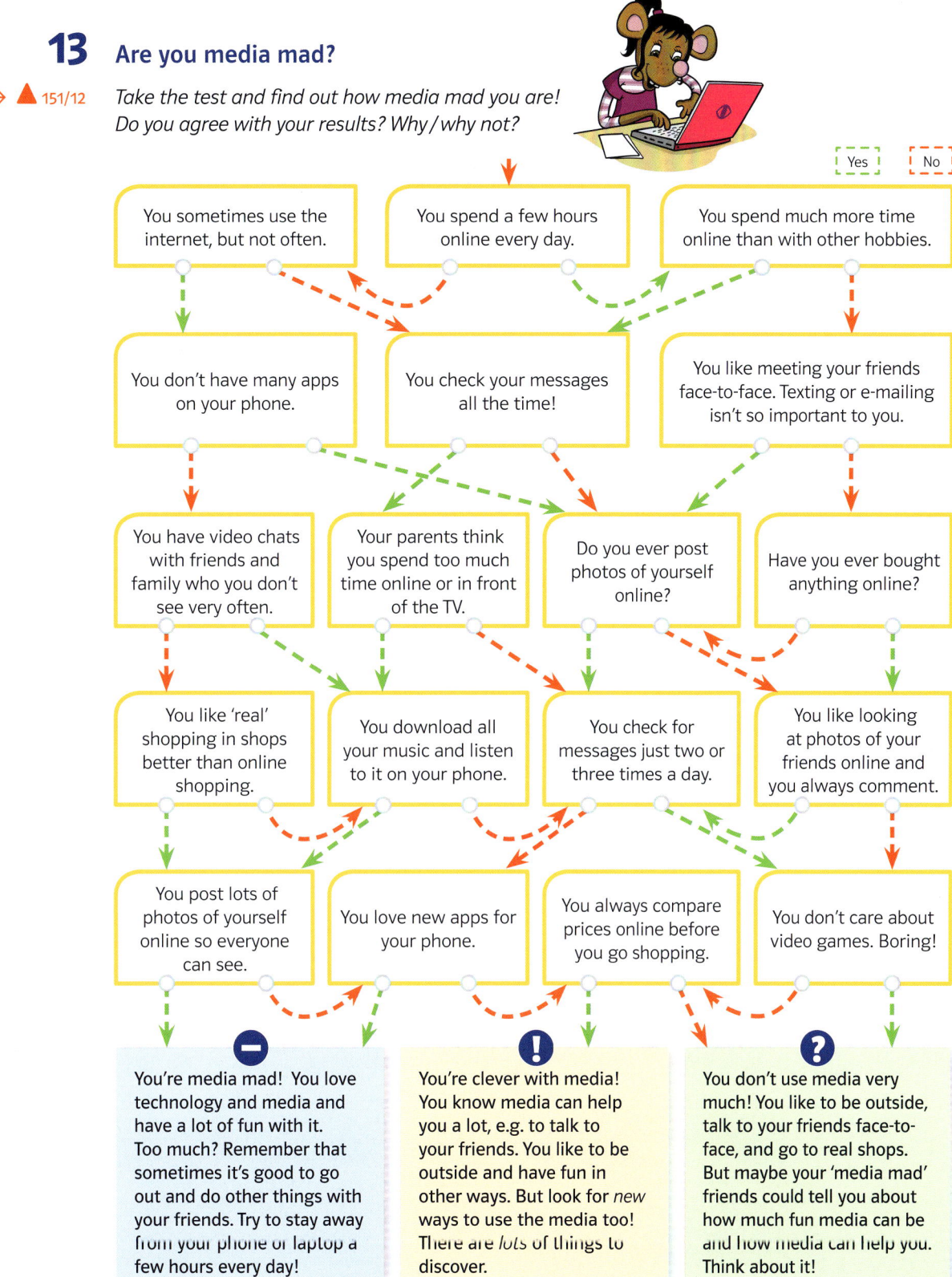

Yes   No

You sometimes use the internet, but not often.

You spend a few hours online every day.

You spend much more time online than with other hobbies.

You don't have many apps on your phone.

You check your messages all the time!

You like meeting your friends face-to-face. Texting or e-mailing isn't so important to you.

You have video chats with friends and family who you don't see very often.

Your parents think you spend too much time online or in front of the TV.

Do you ever post photos of yourself online?

Have you ever bought anything online?

You like 'real' shopping in shops better than online shopping.

You download all your music and listen to it on your phone.

You check for messages just two or three times a day.

You like looking at photos of your friends online and you always comment.

You post lots of photos of yourself online so everyone can see.

You love new apps for your phone.

You always compare prices online before you go shopping.

You don't care about video games. Boring!

⊖ You're media mad! You love technology and media and have a lot of fun with it. Too much? Remember that sometimes it's good to go out and do other things with your friends. Try to stay away from your phone or laptop a few hours every day!

! You're clever with media! You know media can help you a lot, e.g. to talk to your friends. You like to be outside and have fun in other ways. But look for *new* ways to use the media too! There are *lots* of things to discover.

? You don't use media very much! You like to be outside, talk to your friends face-to-face, and go to real shops. But maybe your 'media mad' friends could tell you about how much fun media can be and how media can help you. Think about it!

Where's Maisie? → S21–22

VIEWING

1 Little dog, big trouble → WB 67/13

a) *Have you ever lost a pet? How did you feel? Tell the class about it.*

10 ▣ b) *Watch the film and then talk about the roles of Laura, Nathan and Polly in the story.*

Examples: A: I think Nathan is awful. He's too busy with girls and then …
B: Laura has great friends! They all help …

c) *Now imagine you are Laura. She wants to tell Alicia about what happened with Maisie.*

Start like this: Alicia, I can't believe what Nathan did! He lost Maisie! He was …

SPEAKING

2 Media in the film scenes → WB 67/14–15

Watch the film again. How many different kinds of media can you see in the film? Say how they helped the friends to find Maisie.

SPEAKING

3 Close-ups

a) *First, read the skills box.*

> **Film skills**
>
> In Unit 1 you learned how music can help to show / describe feelings or atmosphere. Another way to do this in films is with **close-ups**: very close shots of a character's face. In this example, the girl isn't sure: Should she give Nathan her phone number, or not?
>
> With the camera so close, you can 'read' the question in her face!

A

B

b) *Look at scenes A and B from the film. What do the two close-ups tell us? The ideas on the right can help you.*

can't believe it | is happy again | loves her dog | wants to look cute / cool for Polly | thinks he's so cool | likes himself a lot | …

How to write a letter and a reply → S10–13

When you write a letter – to an agony aunt, for example – your letter should have different parts. This page shows you how to put a letter and a reply together.

1 The parts of a letter

a) *Read this letter to an agony aunt, and then read the reply. The box on the right shows you which parts of the letters there are. You need to know this for Ex. 2.*

Dear Ruby,

I'm writing to you because I just don't know what to do.
I'm 13, and a new friend has invited me to go on holiday with his family this summer, to Spain. They always go to really cool places, and we just go camping. We never have much money. Before I met my friend, camping was fun. But it doesn't sound fun now. My parents say: "No, you can't go." That isn't fair, is it? I feel like I'm missing a lot of fun. I'm angry with my parents. What do you think, Ruby?
Thanks for your help!

Yours, Ben

Begin with a greeting.

The main idea(s): In an advice letter, the main idea is the problem.

Ask for advice.

Say 'Thank you'.

Your name (often with 'Yours')

Dear Ben,

Yes, I understand that a cool holiday in Spain sounds like fun. But my advice is to ask yourself this: Is your friend really a good friend? Do you care about each other? Why don't you ask him to come with your family on a camping trip. If he's a good friend, you can have fun together anywhere, can't you? It needn't be on a beach in Spain.
I hope this advice helps!

Ruby

Begin with a greeting.

The main idea(s):
A reply should show understanding / feelings.

Give advice.

Finish your letter.

Name

> Look back at the phrases box on p. 93 for the language of advice.

b) *Say what you think about Ben's problem and Ruby's advice.*

2 Write your own letter and reply → WB 68/16–18

a) *Your partner writes a short letter to an agony aunt, and you write another short letter about a **different** problem. Choose one of the ideas below, or an idea of your own:*

- "My friends say I'm weird because I don't like their music."
- "My two best friends are good at everything and I'm not."

b) *When you're both finished, exchange letters and write a reply to each other with advice.*

Advice letters and replies: Our collection

In this task, you get the chance to talk more about advice for young people's problems. Later, after the different groups have collected and discussed advice for different problems, you're going to write letters and replies for a class advice collection.

Step 1

Choose a topic → WB 69/19

In groups of 4 or 6, choose one of the problems in the list below. Make sure there is at least one group for each question:

A. I want a pet, but my parents say "no".
B. My friends say, "You share too much information about yourself on the internet".
C. My parents never buy cool clothes for me. I look stupid!
D. I never have enough pocket money.
E. I'm only allowed to watch TV or play video games for an hour on weekday evenings. It isn't enough!

Step 2

Pair work: What do you think? → WB 69/20

*Before you talk to your group about advice for your problem, work **with a partner** in your group for a few minutes. Make notes while you talk about these questions:*

– What places / people could the person go to for help?
– What advice could you give?

> Look back at the **Stations** and the **Skills page** for help with advice.

Example:

A: As soon as I have a problem, I ask somebody in my family, or maybe a friend at the club I go to / on my football team / …
B: I've never written to an agony aunt, but a friend sometimes writes posts in advice forums.
A: And about the problem: Well, the person should … because it's always a good idea to …

> Hey Mick, you always have good advice. What do you think I should do about Lou?

Step 3

Write an 'agony aunt' letter → WB 70/21

a) *Back in your group, discuss the different pairs' ideas about your group's problem. Use your notes from Step 2.*

b) *Now write one letter to an agony aunt about your group's problem. Then put your letter into a class box.*

You know how to write letters. Just look at the **Skills page** again.

Step 4

Exchange questions → WB 70/22

Pick one of the letters from the box. As a group, discuss the problem and write a reply. Everyone in the group should help to check the letter:

– Is the form of the letter correct?
– Is the language for the advice correct?
– Is the advice helpful? How / Why?

That was a great reply. You talked about where you should go for help. That's an important first step!

I thought it was good because your advice was to find a compromise. But I didn't think it was so helpful to say …

Step 5

Present the problem and advice
→ WB 70/23

Tell the class about the problem you chose from the class box and the advice you wrote for that problem. (Speak freely; don't just read from the page!)

The rest of the class should think about these things during the discussion:
– What do you think of the advice?
– Why is it helpful / not so helpful?

Step 6

Organise your letters and replies

As a class, talk about which topics the different problems fit into. Then organise your letters and replies by those topics. Think of how you can make nice pages with pictures, comics, etc.

S 2/19–24
L 3/21–26

It's a disaster!

A Dave's dad, Frank, stopped his car in front
of his house. It was raining very hard – he
wasn't able to see the house from his car
but he was able to see that all the lights
5 were on. The storm was getting worse
every minute, with lots of thunder and
lightning. He waited for a while and then
quickly got out of the car, ran for the house
and opened the front door. As he went
10 inside, he nearly fell over all the bags and
shoes. "I see Dave's friends are here again!"
he thought. He shouted "Hello everyone!"
But there wasn't a sound. "Hello-o-o?!" he
called again. Nothing. "That's strange," he
15 thought.

> **Stop and think:**
> Why do you think the
> house is so quiet?

He looked in the kitchen – nobody was
there. Next, he looked in the living room
and saw Gwen, Holly and Olivia. "Hi girls!"
he said, but they didn't notice him because
20 they were watching a *loud* music video
on Olivia's laptop. Then he saw Jay in the
corner.

"How are you, Jay?" he asked, but Jay
was busy with text messages and music on
his tablet PC. Frank went upstairs. As soon 25
as he opened the door to Dave's bedroom,
he saw Dave and Luke. They were sitting
on the bed wearing headphones and
playing a video game – they didn't notice
Frank. "Well, they all look *very* happy to see 30
me, I must say!" he said to himself, as he
went back downstairs.

B Jay took off his headphones and tapped
the girls' shoulders. "I was thinking," he
said. "We should talk about that party we 35
want to have soon."

"Yeah, I was thinking about that too,"
Olivia answered. "We can have it at my
house. My dad and Claire say it's OK. Look,
I've already written the invitation." 40

"Great! Let's post a message with the
invitation and tell everyone to go to Olivia's
house on –"

"No!" Olivia shouted. "We can't just post
the invitation like *that*! A lot of people we 45
don't know could see it and come to my
house. No, we can only invite people face-
to-face. People we *know*."

"Olivia, it's much quicker by internet,"
Jay said. "Come on, let's just do it! It's fun! 50
He then grabbed Olivia's laptop.

"Jay, what are you doing?!" Olivia cried.

"I'm going to post it, what do you
think?" They all started fighting for the
laptop. At first they were laughing and 55
joking, but then the girls saw that Jay was
serious! They were horrified and tried to
push him away from the laptop, but Jay
was quicker. "Party on Friday 22nd at my
house, 52 Begbie Road. Come and have 60
fun!" it said in the invitation text. But just
as Jay was pressing 'post', there was a very
loud "BANG!" and everything went black.

C Suddenly, the house became very loud
65 and all the friends started shouting at the
same time: "What's happened?" – "I can't
see!" – "My computer has crashed!" – "Oh
no, we're offline too!" – "I can't find my
phone!" – "Help! I don't like the dark!"
70   Frank shouted, "Calm down, it's only
a power cut! Wait a moment while I find
some candles."
     "Did you really send that message?"
whispered Holly. "I don't know, I think so!"
75 Jay said.
     "To Olivia's friends?" Holly asked.
     "No. To *everyone*! But I'm not sure …"
He was really starting to worry now, but he
didn't want to tell the girls. Five minutes
80 later, they were all sitting round the
kitchen table in candlelight.
     "Dad, what do we need candles for?"
asked Dave. "Look, our phones have all got
torches!"
85   "Sometimes, the old ways are better!"
smiled Frank. "The only problem we have
right now," Frank went on, "is that we can't
cook – and I'm *really* hungry!"
     "How is that a problem?" asked Luke.
90 "Who needs to cook when there are pizza
apps?" Dave and Luke started to show
Mr Preston fantastic apps for his phone.
Mr Preston was impressed! But nobody
noticed that Jay wasn't speaking. "What
95 have I done?" he thought to himself.
"I was just showing off and I went a bit
crazy for a moment. Please tell me the
power cut stopped the message." Then he
said, "Luke, Dave: Can I borrow a phone?
100 I need to check something and I left mine
in the other room." But they were busy
with Mr Preston and his new pizza app.

D Frank was still talking about the old days.
"When I was young, we *talked* to each
105 other, we didn't text all the time."
     "Oh no, he *loves* this topic!" Dave
said and, as he spoke, there was a loud
CLICK, and all the lights were back on.

The girls ran to the living room and waited
nervously to get back online.   110
     "Come on, come on!" Holly said. And
suddenly they were online again. They
went on to their social network site and …
"Fantastic!" shouted Olivia. "The power cut
stopped the message! But let's teach Jay   115
a lesson." Gwen and Holly smiled at each
other.

E Jay walked slowly back into the living
room.
     "You're in *big* trouble now!" Olivia said. 120
     "How many messages are there?" he
whispered. His face was white. He felt sick.
"More than 50!" Holly said. "Listen to
these: 'You don't know us but we *love*
parties – see you there!', or 'Party? Cool! I 125
love meeting new people!'"
     Now Jay felt *really* sick. "It's a disaster!"
he said. Holly and Olivia were trying very
hard not to laugh.
     "What's so funny?" Jay asked.   130
     "Don't worry. The power cut stopped
your message. Nobody got it," Olivia said.
     "But you're lucky, Jay Azad!" Holly
added. "And you *really* should leave the
party invitations to us next time!"   135
     "That," said Jay, "is no problem at all!"

READING

1 Understanding the story → WB 71/24–25

a) *Do you think 'It's a disaster!' is a good title for the story? Say why or why not. What ideas for a different story title do you have?*

b) *There are two main characters in this story: One is Frank, and the other is Jay. Find sentences in the text that show how they both feel left out at some point in the story.*

   Example: He shouted "Hello everyone!" But there wasn't a sound. (Frank, lines 12–13)

→ △ 151/13
→ S16

c) *Do one of these role plays:*
   – *One of you is Frank, the other is Dave's mum. She asks him what happened.*
   Or:
   – *One of you is Jay, the other is Olivia. They talk about what happened and what they were feeling. Use ideas from the text.*

WRITING

2 Writing about pros and cons

→ S8

a) *Make a grid with examples of things people can do today with modern technology and examples of things people did or used when Frank was very young. There are a lot of examples in the text, but you can find more and add them to your grid.*

New world	Old world
– watch a video	– use candles
– send text messages	…
…	

→ S13

b) *What are the pros and cons of modern technology? First read the skills box. Then write about the two worlds. The phrases box can help you too.*

Writing skills

Use these words / phrases to link ideas and give information:

When things happen (time):
When my parents were young…, then …, now …, today …, before …, after …, as …, when …

Where things happen (place):
in the house, on my phone/PC, everywhere

Why things happen (reasons):
… because …

What else happens:
and …, or …, but …

How things happen:
easily, carefully, dangerously, more quickly, in a friendly way, without thinking, by internet, face-to-face

Useful phrases

Today we've got … | We can … | It's great that … because … | We weren't able to… before we had … | (Not) everything was …, I think … is better than … | But … can be dangerous. We should …

Unsocial Networking

→ Solutions p. 287

Can you . . .

1. talk about media in your life?	I use … to send / receive / post / chat / play / read / look up / take part in …
2. link ideas?	I do it when / after / before / because …
3. give advice to somebody?	Why don't you …? | You should … | You could … | Have you tried …ing …?
4. make question tags?	You like texting, don't you? You aren't sad, are you?
5. use substitute forms for modals?	He wasn't allowed / able to come with us. He had to do his History homework.

VOCABULARY

1 How do people use media?

Match the sentence parts and make sentences.

Example: When my grandma wants to chat with her sister, she calls her on the telephone.

1. my dad / want / relax
2. I / want / know / words of a song I've heard
3. my mum / work away from home
4. I / want / tell all my friends how great my holiday is
5. my sister / want / know about the coolest new clothes

a) post / it on my social network profile
b) send / me text messages
c) read / girls' magazines
d) look / it up on the internet
e) watch / football on TV

SPEAKING

2 What can you say to give these people advice?

1. Your brother hurts his foot and doesn't know if it's broken.
2. Your friend missed his favourite TV show.
3. Your sister doesn't know how to fix her bike.
4. Your friend tells you that someone posted really embarrassing photos of her on the internet.
5. Your friend's parents are angry with her: She isn't allowed to use her smartphone for a week.

LANGUAGE

3 Fill in the right forms: *can, be able to, be allowed to, must, have to*

When I was young, we 〔1〕 make phone calls from everywhere because there were no mobile phones. Now you 〔2〕 use your smartphones nearly everywhere. But you 〔3〕 use them at school, are you? There 〔4〕 be rules for using them, right? 30 years ago you 〔5〕 look for information in books. Today you 〔6〕 look things up on the internet. When we were young, we 〔7〕 watch TV only sometimes, but today you 〔8〕 watch videos online all day.

S 2/25–29
L 3/27–31 ◉

Ten-tonne truck

Zoe finds a rat in her room. She wants to train it like she trained her pet hamster (who could break-dance), but she knows she isn't allowed to keep any pets. Raj, a shopkeeper[1] who is the 'agony aunt' of the town, tells her to set Armitage the rat free[2] in the park.

5 "What am I going to do with him, Raj? I'm not allowed to keep him at home; he's the reason why I was suspended[3] from school. My stepmother hated my hamster, she is *never* going to let me keep a rat."

10 Raj thought for a moment. "Maybe you should set him free," he finally said.
"Free?" Zoe said, with a tear[4] in her eye.
"Yes. Rats shouldn't be pets …"
"But this little one is so cute …"

15 "Maybe, but he's going to grow[5]. He can't spend his whole life in your pocket."
"But I love him, Raj, I really do."
"I'm sure you do, Miss Zoe," Raj said. "And if you love him, you should set him
20 free."

So this was goodbye. Zoe knew deep down she would[6] never be able to keep Armitage for long. There were a hundred reasons, but the most important one was: HE WAS A RAT.   25

Children don't have rats as pets. They have cats and dogs and hamsters and mice and rabbits and tortoises. Some kids even have ponies, but never rats. Rats live underground, not in little girls' bedrooms.   30

Zoe walked sadly out of Raj's shop. It was true that sometimes he tried to sell his customers[7] a half-eaten chocolate bar, but all the kids in town knew that when they needed advice, he was the best.   35

And so she had to say goodbye to Armitage. Zoe took the long way back to her flat, through the park. She thought this was the perfect place to set little Armitage free. There were always bits of bread for   40
the ducks – Armitage could[8] eat these. He could drink from the pond and take a bath in it. And maybe there was a squirrel or two he could make friends with.

The little girl carried[9] the little rat in her   45
hand. It was the middle of the afternoon and there were just a few old ladies and their dogs in the park. Armitage wrapped his tail around her thumb – maybe he knew that something was wrong …   50

Zoe walked as slowly as possible. Finally, she reached the middle of the park. She was looking for a nice quiet place. Then she bent down[10] to the ground slowly and opened her hand. But Armitage didn't   55
move. He just stayed in her hand. It was breaking Zoe's heart …

---

1 **shopkeeper** [ʃɒpˈkiːpə] Ladenbesitzer | 2 **to set sb/sth free** [set ˈfriː] jmdn./etw. freilassen | 3 **to be suspended** [bi səˈspendɪd] (vorübergehend) der Schule verwiesen werden | 4 **tear** [tɪə] Träne | 5 **to grow** [grəʊ] wachsen | 6 **would** [wʊd] würde | 7 **customer** [ˈkʌstəmə] Kunde | 8 **could** [kʊd] könnte | 9 **to carry** [ˈkæri] tragen | 10 **to bend down** [bend ˈdaʊn] sich bücken

Zoe shook[11] her hand a little, but Armitage only held on tighter[12] to her fingers. She was fighting back tears when she picked the rat up gently[13] and put him carefully on the grass. Once again Armitage didn't move. He just looked up at her sadly. Zoe kissed him gently on his little pink nose.

"Goodbye, little friend," she whispered. "I'm going to miss[14] you."

A tear dropped from her eye.

The little rat turned his little head to one side, like a friend who was trying to understand her. This just made it harder for Zoe.

Finally, Zoe took a big breath and stood up. "Don't look back!" she told herself. But after a few steps she had to look one last time at the place she left him. To Zoe's surprise, Armitage wasn't there.

"He has already run away to the safety of the bushes," she thought. She looked at the grass, but it was long and he was short, and the grass didn't move. Zoe turned round and sadly started to walk home.

She left the park and crossed[15] the road. For a moment, there was no noise of cars, and in the silence, Zoe heard a small 'eek'. She turned round quickly, and in the middle of the road was Armitage.

He was following her!

"Armitage!" she shouted excitedly. He didn't want to be free; he wanted to be with her! She was so happy. Now she didn't have to imagine all kinds of terrible scenes any more: A hungry swan[16] couldn't eat him for dinner, and a ten-tonne truck couldn't run him over[17].

At that moment, she heard a loud thundering noise. Something came along the road towards Armitage, who was still moving slowly to get to Zoe. It was a ten-tonne truck!

Zoe wasn't able to move, she just watched the truck which was speeding[18] closer and closer towards Armitage. How could the driver see a baby rat in the road?

From: *Ratburger* by David Walliams → WB 73/1–4

11 **to shake** [ʃeɪk] schütteln | 12 **tight** [taɪt] fest | 13 **gently** [ˈdʒentli] sanft | 14 **to miss sb/sth** [mɪs] jmdn./etw. vermissen | 15 **to cross** [krɒs] überqueren | 16 **swan** [swɒn] Schwan | 17 **to run sth over** [rʌnˈəʊvə] etw. überfahren | 18 **to speed** [spiːd] rasen

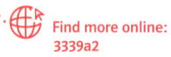

Find more online:
3339a2

Unit 6

Goodbye Greenwich

A A beach in Cornwall, in the south-west of England

B A medieval 'living history' show at Caerphilly Castle in Wales

SPEAKING

1 Parts of the British Isles

→ △ 152/1

Look at the pictures and find the places on the map at the back of your book. Which part of the British Isles do they belong to? Which part of them looks most interesting to you and why?

The United Kingdom includes Great Britain and Northern Ireland.

Yes, and most of Ireland is a separate country: the Republic of Ireland.

LISTENING

2 Come on Dave, don't be so negative!

L 4/1

a) *Dave is talking about his parents' plans and his mum's vet surgery. What is the problem from Dave's point of view? Listen and take notes.*

b) *Now talk about the different places that Dave and his friends discuss. Make a grid for your answers with these headings:*

→ S18–20

Place | Landscape | Things to do | Other information

In Unit 6 you learn
… how to talk about places in the British Isles.
You learn:
- to describe places
- to talk about plans for a journey
- to talk about the future with *will*
- to make conditional sentences

Pony trekking in Ireland

D The Edinburgh Festival in the Scottish capital

CABULARY **3** **Places** → WB 74/1–2

a) *Collect vocabulary in different categories like landscapes, sights, things to do.*

 b) *Each of you does the following: Take four cards and write **one** of your words / phrases from a) on each card. Shuffle all the cards and pick four. Choose a place in the British Isles and take turns to talk about it, with the words on your cards.*

c) *Your turn: Find information about a German region (e.g. the North Sea). Write a short text and present it.*

Useful phrases

high mountain | field | forest | sandy / rocky beach | wide river | deep lake | island | city | village | harbour | visit a castle | go hiking / climbing / mountain biking / (wind) surfing / pony trekking

Across cultures

Did you know that palm trees grow in the south-west of England? Some call it the **English Riviera**. Are there any surprising facts about the region where you live?

L 4/2 ◎ **Moving to the middle of nowhere**

Dave's parents have found a beautiful house near St Agnes, in the Cornish countryside.
Dave is very sad to leave.

Dave: Oh no, why do we have to move to the middle of nowhere? London is just fine. And I'll miss you so much!

5

Olivia: But the house looks fantastic! And your mum never wanted to live in the city. She'll be happy there with her new surgery and all the farm animals and pets to work with, won't she?

10

Dave: Yes, but will I be happy? Has anyone ever asked *me*? If I want to see farm animals, I can go to Mudchute Farm.

15 Luke: What about your dad? Will he find work there?

Dave: Well, he travels a lot anyway. He'll stay in London with Aunt Frances when he has to work there. I think it'll be OK for *him*. But me?

20

Holly: Oh Dave, I'll miss you too! I'm so sorry you won't be able to go to the park with us any longer.

Jay: And we won't be able to play video games together.

25

Gwen: Come on now, it's not the end of the world. There are games you can play online. Oh, and we'll text you and have lots of video chats together.

30 Olivia: And we'll come to visit you! Cornwall is a great place. Most British people go there for a holiday. I've been there with my mum.

Dave: That's nice for people on holiday – but *I'll* be in a new school, and   35
there'll be nobody I know. It'll be horrible. And I'm sure Sid will hate it too.

Jay: Don't worry, you'll make lots of new friends. But what about Olivia's idea? 40
We could go to Cornwall to visit you.

Holly: All of us together, in Cornwall? Wow! I'll ask my mum.

Luke: Well, maybe. I'll think about it. But we'll have to find the money first,   45
won't we?

Gwen: I'm sure we'll find a way to get there.

Olivia: Will it be OK for us to stay with Dave?

Luke: I'm sure it will. His parents are cool.   50

Dave: That's a wonderful idea. It'll be great to see you all there.

READING   **1**   **Questions about the future**   → WB 75/3

1.   What does Dave say about the Prestons' future in Cornwall?

2.   What do his friends say to make him feel better?

3.   What will the friends need to do before they go to Cornwall? Think about these things: parents, dates, transport, money.

Examples:

1.   He'll miss his friends. His mum will be happy …

2.   They'll miss him too. They'll text him …

3.   They'll have to ask their parents …

LANGUAGE

2 Rules for the *will* future → WB 75/4 → G17

*Find 4–5 sentences with **will** or **won't** in the text. Say if they're predictions about the future or spontaneous reactions / decisions. You see some examples on the right.*

Prediction	Spontaneous reaction / decision
I'll miss you. She'll be happy there.	I'll ask my mum. We'll text you.

LANGUAGE

3 How will we get there?

👥

→ △ 152/2
→ ▲ 152/3

Luke goes to a travel agent's to ask about the journey to St Agnes.

a) *Complete dialogue A with forms of the* **will future** *and read it with a partner.*

b) *Now do the same with dialogue B.*

> Train + bus: London Paddington to St Agnes
> Time: 6 – 7 hours
> Prices: £50 – £70
> Children under 12 must travel with an adult.
>
> Coach + bus: London Victoria to St Agnes
> Time: 8 hours
> Prices: £65 – £75
> Children under 14 must travel with an adult.

A

Luke: My friends and I want to go to Cornwall, but we're worried that tickets (be) expensive.

Assistant: Don't worry. It (not be) too expensive. But it depends on the date. Give me your dates and I (check) for you.
(a few minutes later)
Yes, on those dates, train tickets per person are £5 cheaper than by coach. – Oh, but now I see better prices for the next day. Between £10 and £15 cheaper by train.

Luke: £15 cheaper per person? Cool! My friends (like) that.

Assistant: Well, I can't promise £15, but it (be) a better price than a day earlier. – Oh, and children under 12 need to travel with a person who is 16 or older.

Luke: Oh, that (not be) a problem. – Anyway, I (talk) to my friends and come back.

B

Olivia: (we go) by train or by coach?

Luke: I think we (go) by train. It (be) cheaper and (not take) so long.

Gwen: And we (not have) to find an adult to go with us.

Holly: There's just one problem: Where (I get) the money?

LISTENING

4 Preparing for the trip → WB 75/5

L 4/5

Listen to the dialogue and answer the questions.

a) *What's Holly's problem? What can she do and who can help her?*

b) *What will these people do? Say one sentence about each person: Dave, Granny Rose, Luke, the girls, the boys, Luke's grandparents, Holly, Amber.*

VOCABULARY

5 How to: Book train tickets on the internet → WB 76/6

Luke wants to book tickets for the five friends and Granny Rose online. They want to leave next Sunday morning and return a week later.

→ △ 153/4
→ S9

a) *Help him to fill in the form (1). He clicks on "Buy train tickets". Then he chooses a connection and clicks on it. A new window shows details for this connection (2).*

Useful phrases

one-way / single ticket | return ticket | fee | to depart | to arrive | to change at … | outward journey | inward journey | price / fare | platform

2

Journey Summary				Outward Journey (9 Aug 2015)	
Depart		**Arrive**		**Travel by**	**Duration**
09:32	Greenwich	09:43	London Bridge	Train	00h 11 Calling Points
09:53	London Bridge	10:23	London Paddington	Tube	00h 30
10:43	London Paddington	16:46	Redruth	Train	06h 03 Calling Points
17:12	Redruth	17:46	St Agnes	Bus	00h 34

Text me these details   Add to calendar

b) *Match words and phrases from the phrases box with these definitions.*

1. to leave
2. to leave one train and get on another
3. a ticket to go to a place and back
4. going away to a place
5. this tells you what a ticket costs
6. to get to a place
7. a ticket to go to a place
8. going back to your starting place
9. extra money you have to pay

You often hear *will* future in weather forecasts.

MEDIATION

6 The weather forecast → WB 76/7

→ △ 153/5
→ S17

A British tourist who wants to do a 5-hour mountain climbing tour shows you this weather forecast for tomorrow. He asks you to tell him if he can go on his tour. What is your advice?

Wettervorhersage Oberallgäu: Während es heute bei Höchsttemperaturen über 30 Grad noch sehr heiß mit viel Sonne ist, zieht morgen eine Schlechtwetterfront von Südwesten herein. Es ist mit starken Unwettern und Hagel zu rechnen, vor allem Samstagnachmittag und -abend. Im Bergland besteht Gefahr durch orkanartige Windböen mit Geschwindigkeiten bis zu 105 km/h. Durch starke Niederschläge kann es zu Überflutungen kommen.

How to get information → S10–13

For the Unit task you'll need information about different parts of the British Isles:
England (e.g. Cornwall, or maybe London), Scotland, Wales and Ireland (Northern Ireland
or the Republic of Ireland).

1 Where to get information

*If you want to collect pictures and facts about
interesting places, you can write to a tourist
board and ask for free material. What else can
you do?*

2 Asking for information → WB 77/8–10

*Make four groups, one for each of the regions
you learned about on pages 108–109.
Find out e-mail addresses of organisations
that have interesting material. Then write a
polite e-mail to ask for the material. Some of
them don't give you their e-mail addresses
but ask you to fill in an internet contact
form. Make sure you don't write to the same
organisation about the same material more
than once!*

> **Writing skills**
>
> Before you send off your e-mail or contact
> form, **remember**:
> - Don't forget your greetings.
> - Who are you?
> - What do you want to do?
> - What do you need?
> - How do you ask for it politely?
> - What information about yourselves do
>   you need to give?

Dear Sir or Madam,

We are students of a German grammar school. We would like to do a project
about the British Isles and need information about Scotland for it.
Could you please send us some free material about interesting places in Scotland,
Scottish history and things to do in Scotland?
Here is our address:
...-Gymnasium
Class ...
...straße (XX)
D-(XXXXX) ...

Thank you very much for your help.

Best wishes,
The students of Class (...)

3 Working with the material

*When you have enough material, go through it together in your group.
Make notes of interesting ideas for a presentation, and look for the best photos.*

L4/6 ⊙   # Visit Cornwall – You'll love it!

Where is Cornwall?

If you look at a map of Great Britain, you'll find Cornwall in the far west. Look north, west or south of Cornwall and you'll find the same 'neighbour': the Atlantic Ocean. Cornwall's coastline is almost 300 miles long and gets more sun than any other part of the UK.

Why do more than 3 million tourists visit Cornwall every year?

If you like dramatic landscapes, beautiful fishing harbours and wonderful beaches and if you're into water sports, you'll find that Cornwall is just the right place for your holiday.
But Cornwall has more to offer than its coastline and water sports. There are lots of other outdoor activities, like adventure sports, pony trekking or golf. And if you aren't into sports at all, you can visit a lot of very interesting sights.
If you go to Bodmin Moor, you'll get to know a wild landscape with prehistoric monuments that you can explore on great walking trails. And if you visit the Eden Project near St Austell, you can look at beautiful and useful plants from around the world and learn about the environment. It's the most popular tourist attraction in Cornwall.
If you visit one of the museums, you'll learn a lot about Cornwall's Celtic past or its mining history. You can still see Celtic culture in Bronze Age monuments, Celtic crosses and Cornish place names. Like Irish, Scottish Gaelic or Welsh, Cornish is a Celtic language and a few people in Cornwall still speak it besides English – but you'll be very lucky if you hear it.
If you want to eat real Cornish food, you should try pasties[1]. (And if you're still hungry, try cream tea[2] with scones[3], clotted cream[4] and jam[5]!)
When you're here, don't forget to come in and say 'hello' at one of our many visitor centres!

11
Mehr zum
Thema Cornwall

READING   **7**   **Tourist information about Cornwall**   → WB 78/11

Olivia has found this text about Cornwall on the internet. Say what information there is about the geography, tourism, things to do, sights, history and food.

LANGUAGE   **8**   **What will happen if …?**   → WB 78/12   → G18

*Collect all the sentences with **if** from the text. They have two parts: an **if-clause** and a **main clause**. There are three basic patterns, but in one example the order is different:*

If …, … will …	If …, … can …	If …, … should … If …, try …

1 **pasty** ['pæsti] Pastete | 2 **cream tea** [ˌkriːm 'tiː] Nachmittagstee | 3 **scone** [skɒn] brötchenartiges Buttergebäck |
4 **clotted cream** [ˌklɒtɪd 'kriːm] Sahne *(aus erhitzter Milch)* | 5 **jam** [dʒæm] Marmelade

LANGUAGE **9** **Find the rule** → WB 78/13 → G18

a) *Match the three patterns with the meanings. Then write the rule and put it in your folder.*

1. If you go to Cornwall, you'll see a lot of beautiful beaches.
2. If you go to Cornwall, you can do water sports.
3. If you go to Cornwall, you should try cream tea.

A Advice
B Prediction
C Possibility

→ △ 153/6
→ ▲ 154/7

b) *In German, there's only one word for **if** and **when**. Can you explain the difference between sentences 1 and 2 with the information in brackets?*

A If I go to Cornwall, I'll go surfing. (I don't know if we'll go to Cornwall or to Italy.)
B When Dave goes to Cornwall, he'll miss his friends. (We know he'll go there, but we don't know when.)

LANGUAGE **10** **Go on with the story**

Play a game in class: One student starts with an if-sentence. The next student uses the main clause as an if-clause and makes a new sentence, and so on.

Example: If I go on holiday, I'll take my dog. → If I take my dog, he'll be happy. → If my dog is happy, he'll … → …

SPEAKING **11** **Languages in Britain**

Look at the photo. Which of the Cornish words can you understand?

> **Across cultures**
>
> Everybody in the British Isles speaks English. But Cornwall, Ireland, Scotland, Wales and the Isle of Man still have their own **Celtic languages**. What languages do people in your class speak besides German? Do people speak in a local dialect or with an accent?

LISTENING **12** **Announcements**

L 4/8–11 ◉

a) *Mr Preston travels a lot. Listen to four little dialogues and find out this information for each scene. Take notes:*

→ S20

1. where he is
2. where he wants to go
3. what sight they talk about
4. what the announcement is about.

b) *Say in what way the fourth dialogue is different from the other three.*

SPEAKING

13   Role play: At the travel agent's → WB 79/14–16

→ S16

One of you is an assistant at a travel agent's. The other chooses one of these roles:
A: A father who wants to travel with his wife and young children; B: A teenager who wants to travel with her mum; or C: a young couple who is interested in sports. They all want to go to Cornwall. Use the useful phrases to make dialogues. (You can also look back at Ex. 3 on p. 111.)

> **Useful phrases**
>
> | **Assistant:** | **Customer:** |
> |---|---|
> | Hello, what can I do for you? | I'd like to travel to … with … |
> | How long would you like to stay? | Over the weekend / two weeks / … |
> | If you're into …, you'll … | We love … / We're into … |
> | Do you want to go by car, by train or by coach? Do you need a ticket? | How long does it take? |
> | | We need … tickets. |
> | Would you like to book a room / a flat / a house? | How much is it? |
> | | Oh, I think that's too expensive. |
> | If you want to …, you can … | Yes, that's fine. Thank you. |

READING

14   British history: A poem about the Romans

→ ▲ 154/8

a) *Explain what the poem says about the Romans and what they did in Britain.*

The Romans in Britain
(A history in 40 words)

by Judith Nicholls

The Romans gave us aqueducts
fine buildings and straight[1] roads,
where all those Roman legionaries
marched with heavy loads[2].

They gave us central heating[3],
good laws[4], a peaceful[5] home …
Then after just four centuries
they shuffled back to Rome.

> **Useful phrases**
>
> to build (a bridge, a road, a town) |
> to supply somebody (with water, food) |
> to rule (a country)

 **b)** *Think of how you could complete this little poem about Britain.*

Great Britain is an island.
It is in the North …
It's got green fields and mountains.
It's where I'd like to …

The biggest city is …
It's got a lot to show.
There's always something happening.
It's where I'd like to…

1 straight [streɪt] gerade | **2 heavy load** [ˌhevi ˈləʊd] schwere Last | **3 central heating** [ˌsentrl ˈhiːtɪŋ]
Zentralheizung | **4 law** [lɔː] *hier:* Gesetz | **5 peaceful** [ˈpiːsfl] friedlich

L 4/12 ◎

If I had my way[1]

Dave: It's so unfair. My parents can do what they want, but I can't. If I were an adult, I could choose where I wanted to live.

5 Luke: Yeah, and if I had my way, you'd stay here in Greenwich with us.

Jay *(rapping and clapping hands)*:
         I would if I could, but I can't, so I won't …

10 Luke: Jay, can you stop being silly? This isn't funny!

Jay: OK, OK, you know I'm sad about Dave too. But let's try to make the most of the time that's left. You have to live
15   with things you can't change.

Luke: You're always so smart[2]!

Dave: Guys[3], stop fighting! Jay is right. We should try to have some fun while we're together. Let's call the girls and
20   organise a big farewell party[4].

Jay: A party? Wow! Remember last year? It would be great if we had another party like my surprise party!

Luke: If I had more money, I'd buy a cool
25   new costume, but I've already spent

my pocket money. – Anyway, it would be a good idea if you asked your parents first.

Dave: That's no problem. I've already asked them. They would do anything if it   30 cheered me up[5] a bit.

Luke: That's typical! But they wouldn't stay here, would they?

Dave: Luke, please stop being so negative. If all the people were like you, nobody   35 would have any more fun.

Jay: Yes, listen to Dave! It would really help if you tried to be a bit more positive.

Luke: Hm. Maybe you're right. So let's have   40 the coolest party ever!

READING

1 Who says what?

a) *What advice does Jay have for Dave and Luke? Is it good advice? Say why or why not.*

🖊 b) *Complete the sentences with the right information from the text.*

→ △ 154/9

Example: If **Dave** were an adult, **he** could choose where **he** wanted to live.

1. If ▮ were an adult, ▮ could choose where ▮ wanted to live. ✔
2. If ▮ had ▮ way, ▮ would stay here in Greenwich with ▮.
3. ▮ says ▮ would be great if ▮ had another party like ▮ surprise party.
4. ▮ says ▮ would be a good idea if ▮ asked ▮ parents first.
5. If ▮ had more money, ▮ would buy a cool new costume.
6. ▮'s parents would do anything if ▮ cheered ▮ up a bit.
7. ▮ says that if ▮ were like ▮, ▮ would have any more fun.
8. ▮ says ▮ would really help if ▮ tried to be a bit more positive.

---

1 **If I had my way** [ɪfˌaɪ hæd ˈmaɪˌweɪ] Wenn es nach mir ginge | 2 **smart** [smɑːt] clever | 3 **Guys…!** [gaɪz] Jungs…!
(Anrede; ugs.) | 4 **farewell party** [feəˈwel ˌpɑːti] Abschiedsfeier | 5 **to cheer sb up** [tʃɪərˌʌp] jmdn. aufmuntern

LANGUAGE

2 Find the rule → WB 80/17 → G19

Look at these if-sentences and say what verb forms you can use in the if-clause and the main clause. When can you use these if-sentences?

If-clause	Main clause	
If we **had** more time, If we **went** by coach, If the weather **was / were** better,	we **could visit** you. the journey **would take** longer. we'**d / would go** for a walk.	(But we haven't.) (But we'll go by train.) (But it's raining.)

I wouldn't do that if I were you!

If I **was / were** …
If he / she / it **was / were** …
If we / you / they **were** …

LANGUAGE

3 Find the right verb forms → WB 80/18–19

→ △ 155/10
→ ▲ 155/11

1. If I ▢ (live) in Cornwall, I ▢ (go) surfing every day.
2. If you ▢ (go) to school in England, you ▢ (have to) wear school uniform.
3. If we ▢ (be) adults, we ▢ (travel) by train alone.
4. If I ▢ (train) harder, I ▢ (be) a better runner.

5. If I ▢ (have) a better job, I ▢ (get) more money.
6. If they ▢ (have) more money, they ▢ (buy) new phones.
7. If there ▢ (be) a cinema in the village, we ▢ (go) there and watch a film.
8. If I ▢ (be) you, I ▢ (be) more careful on these trails.

LANGUAGE

4 If I had my way, …

*Write down five sentences as in the example. Compare them in class.
Find somebody who has written at least one of your sentences too.*

Example: If I had my way, school would start at 10 o'clock.

SPEAKING

5 What would you do if …?

Ask and answer questions like these.

Example: If somebody stole my bike, I'd be really angry. I'd call the police …

1. … somebody stole your bike?
2. … somebody broke your smartphone?

3. … your dog ran away?
4. … you had an accident in a forest?

The caves → S21–22

SPEAKING

1 Things to do in the country

→ △ 155/12 *Talk about which of these activities are interesting for you.*

1. feeding animals
2. milking cows
3. exploring a cave
4. swimming in a lake
5. playing in an adventure playground
6. reading ghost stories
7. walking
8. geocaching

VIEWING

2 Themes → WB 81/20

12 ▣ *Watch the film. Then say which themes below play a role in the film. Explain why/why not. Which of them are more important/the most important?*

1. food
2. city and country life
3. school
4. children and adults
5. stories
6. sports
7. love
8. ghosts

VIEWING

3 Suspense: What's going to happen?

✏ *Watch the film again, find examples of the ideas below and take notes. They can help you to talk about elements that create suspense in a story.*

Story: What about …
- *Laura's grandpa?*
- *ghosts?*
- *getting lost?*
- *phones, maps and torches?*

Acting: What about …
- *people's faces?*

Audiovisual effects: What about …
- *darkness?*
- *strange sounds, a voice in the caves?*
- *dramatic music?*

Film skills

Elements that create suspense:
- clues in the story about what could happen
- acting
- music
- light
- sounds

WRITING

4 Laura and her grandpa

🙎 *Write a scene that comes after the last scene in the film:*
→ S15 *Laura and her grandpa talk about what has really happened and why. Act it and film it.*

Our big British Isles quiz

You're going to work in four groups. You're going to make question cards for a quiz about the British Isles (Wales, England, etc.). You can use information in this book and from other sources. When you're finished, you'll be able to play a quiz game.

Step 1

Get organised   → WB 82/22–23

Make four groups of 4–6, one for a different part of the British Isles. In your group, agree on 16 interesting sights or places in your region. Each of you makes 2–4 question cards so you have one for each sight in the end.

For ideas, look at **this unit** and **the other units** in the book. Use the information material you got from **books**, the **internet** and **tourist boards**.

Step 2

Prepare your cards

Make cards that look like this on the front and back. But don't finish them until you've done Step 3.

Tower of London

(A question about the sight / place / thing)
Which of these animals never lived at the Tower?

(Three answers, two of which are wrong)
a) a polar bear that loved to fish
b) a raven that was able to talk
c) a zebra that liked beer

(The right answer)

Step 3

Test your cards → WB 83/24

a) *Show a picture of the sight / place / thing you want to use for the front of your card. Read the question and the three answers. The others guess which answer is right. Correct them if they're wrong. You can give tips to help them.*

b) *Are the questions, answers and tips OK? If a quiz question is too difficult, make changes or give more tips.*

c) *Now make your cards.*

Useful phrases

Ideas for tips:
In this place you can …
It's famous for …
One of the attractions here is …
If you want to …, you will … here.
If you're interested in history, you
should …
It's in the north / east / south / west.
… built it.

Step 4

Play the quiz game in your groups → WB 83/25

– *Shuffle the 16 cards for your group and place them on a table face down.*
– *Each group draws four cards from each group.*
– *In each group, shuffle all the cards again.*
– *Every player draws the same number of cards. One player starts and uses a card for the person next to him / her. If the person gets the answer right, he / she can keep the card.*
– *When you've used all the cards once, the person with the most cards wins!*

Step 5

Your 'British Isles Top 5'

a) *Copy an outline of the map of Britain at the back of this book.*

b) *Mark your 'Top 5' sights / places on the map. Write information about them next to each one.*

c) *Gallery walk: Look at the other posters and try to guess the sights / places.*

I think that's the capital of Scotland. Do you know its name?

Edinburgh?

polar bear [ˈpəʊlə ˌbeə] Eisbär | **to fish** [fɪʃ] Fische fangen | **zebra** [ˈzebrə] | **beer** [bɪə] Bier

S 2/33–37
L 4/13–17 ⊙ **Things will get better**

A "Come in, come in!" Mrs Preston said from the hall of the big old house by the sea. "I'll make some tea."

"We can't have tea, Mum," Dave said.
5 "There's no electricity, remember?"

"Oh, yes," she answered. "Well, a glass of water then?"

"Er … OK, yes please, Mrs Preston," Olivia said.

10 "Hi," Dave said to his friends and his granny. "Thanks for coming. Good journey?"

"Yeah, the journey was fine, thanks," Luke answered. "But *you* don't look fine.
15 What's the matter? Is everything OK?"

"No, not really," Dave said. "We've been here a week, and there's no electricity yet. Dad is in London, the cat has run away, I haven't got any friends and I'm really
20 missing my old life in Greenwich. It's awful here. I hate it."

"Oh, Dave!" Granny Rose said. "Don't be sad. You've only been here a week. Things will get better. You know they will."

B "Here are your glasses of water," Mrs Preston said. Then she looked at one of the glasses. "Oh dear," she said "Why is this water brown? I think we've got a problem with the water now too."

"Let's go out," Dave said to his friends. 30 "We'll go up to the coastal path, to the old mine. Is that OK, Mum?"

"Yes, that's fine," Dave's mum answered. "See you later. I'll call a plumber."

"But it's Sunday," Granny Rose said. 35 "If you call a plumber on a Sunday, it'll be *really* expensive."

C The friends were standing on a hill by an old building. It had a tall chimney, but no roof. There was a strong wind from the sea, 40 and it brought lots of big black clouds.

"This old building looks a bit scary," Holly whispered.

"Don't be silly. It's just one of many old mine buildings in this area. Tin was really 45 important here," Olivia said. "Going right back to Celtic times. Tin from Cornwall went all over the world. But now there's almost no tin left."

"Looks like a great place for 50 geocaching!" Luke said excitedly as he grabbed his smartphone. "Let's see if there's a cache somewhere near here. – Yes, there must be a difficult puzzle cache."

"Really?" Dave asked, "Let's solve the 55 puzzle and get to that cache!"

Suddenly a deep voice behind them boomed, "Hey you, what are you doing here?! Keep away from MY treasure!"

The friends were scared. They turned 60 around and saw a big man with a serious face. He was wearing a kind of skirt and trousers. He had wild hair and looked dangerous, not only because of the long spear in his hand. 65

"I'm sorry, we – we didn't want to steal anything from you. We didn't know the cache was yours," Dave said. He was really scared.

Suddenly the sun came out again and 70 the man's face went from scary to much friendlier.

"Hello!" he said to Dave. "I was only joking. Have you just moved into number 7?"

75   "Er, yes," Dave said. "And you are a Celtic warrior?"

"I'm Bob," the man said. "Your new neighbour."

"Ah," Dave said. "So you're on your way
80 to a fancy dress party, aren't you?"

The others just looked at Bob's strange clothes and said nothing.

"Oh, don't worry!" Bob laughed. "I don't always wear these clothes. I'm in the local
85 history society. We do shows about the history of Cornwall. These are clothes from Celtic times."

"Right," Dave said. "Nice to meet you."

"I just came up to say hello," Bob said.
90 "Tea at my house anyone?"

D "This is my wife, Helen," Bob said.

The friends were standing in the kitchen of Bob's house. "And these are my children, Jago and Tamara." The boy and girl were
95 both about 13. "Good old Cornish names."

"Hello Dave. I'm Jago," the boy said.

"We're twins," the girl said. "Do you like computers, Dave?"

"Not now, Tamara," Bob said. "I'm sure
100 Dave doesn't want to hear about your new computer games."

Then Olivia saw a big bag of tools on the kitchen floor.

"What do you do, Mr … er …?
105   "Call me Bob. I'm a plumber. And Helen here's an electrician. We do the plumbing

and electrics for half the village. Well, the *whole* village, really."

Then Bob's bag of tools moved. A cat came out of it.   110

"That's the cat that moved in here last week," Bob said.

"Sid!" Dave shouted. "There you are!"

E An hour later, there were thirteen people and a cat in Dave's garden. The friends, Bob 115 and his family, Granny Rose and Dave's parents were all sitting around a big garden table. There was tea and a cake.

"We were on the train before you," Granny Rose said to Dave's dad. "I didn't 120 know you were coming today."

"Change of plan at work," Dave's dad said. "I can be here all this week."

"Thanks again for fixing the water," Dave's mum said to Bob. "Are you sure I 125 can't pay you for …"

"No, no," Bob said. "It was a five-minute job, and we're neighbours. But I'll have another piece of Rose's cake, if that's OK."

"And I'll have a look at your electrics   130 tomorrow morning," Helen added.

Dave turned to Luke. "I think it'll be OK here after all," he said.

READING

1 Understanding the text → WB 84/26

→ S5–7 a) *Find headings for parts A–E of the story.*

b) *Answer these questions.*

1. What problems do the Prestons have in their new home?
2. What do the friends think of Bob at first? What do we get to know about him?
3. Think of what Granny Rose said at the end of part A. At the end of the story, was she right? Explain.

SPEAKING

2 Help for Dave

Talk about what everyone can do to make Dave happier in his new home.

Example: Tamara and Jago can play computer games with him.

WRITING

3 Creative writing → WB 84/27

→ S10–13 a) *Write a diary entry for one of the characters about what happened on their first day in Cornwall and what he / she felt.*

b) *Write a postcard from one of Dave's friends to his / her parents at home.*

Writing skills

A **diary entry** is a very personal text. Usually nobody else reads it. It's like writing to a close friend. Put the date at the top and start writing about what happened, what was important and how you feel about it. You can also write about your hopes and plans for the future.

Greetings from St Agnes

Dear Mum and Dad,

How are you? We arrived in St Agnes yesterday. There is a beautiful harbour with nice sailboats, and we're camping really close to the sea. The weather is great, and we've spent a lot of time at the beach.

See you soon,

Megan

→ Solutions p. 287

Can you ...

1. say what will happen in the future?   Tomorrow there will be ...
2. talk about the future with 'if'?   If you ..., you can / will / should ...
3. talk about places and regions?   ‹ If you went ..., you could / would ... ›
   It's in ... | It has got ... | There are ... | You can ... there.
4. talk about travelling?   We can go by ... | It takes ... | We'll have to ...

LANGUAGE

1 Tomorrow's weather forecast

Complete the weather forecast with the correct forms of the verbs in the box.

Tomorrow ▮1▮ a nice day. There ▮2▮ a lot of sun. There ▮3▮ too many clouds. In the morning, it ▮4▮ cool, but it ▮5▮ nicer in the afternoon. It ▮6▮ a fine day for outdoor activities. You can be sure it ▮7▮ . But in the evening there ▮8▮ more wind, and at night the weather ▮9▮ . Clouds ▮10▮ and at about 12 o'clock it ▮11▮ to rain.

be (5x)

not be

change

get

move in

not rain

start

LANGUAGE

2 Make if-sentences

a) *Use the ideas to say what will happen.*

1. you like surfing / you love Cornwall
2. we run / we not be late
3. you not do homework / you not be allowed to play with your computer
4. it not rain / we go swimming
5. we not book the train tickets now / they be more expensive
6. Mum work late / we cook dinner for her

b) ‹ *Use the ideas to say what could / would happen.* ›

1. my dad find a good job / I get more pocket money
2. my granny have time / we go to London
3. I be you / I not eat so much chocolate
4. we get lost / we use my smartphone to find the way home
5. the shops be open on Sundays / we go shopping now
6. I be you / I not post those photos!

LANGUAGE

3 *If* or *when*?

1. ... I get up, I'll make breakfast. – ... I get up before you, I'll make breakfast.
2. I won't do my homework today ... my teacher doesn't want it tomorrow. – I'll do my homework ... I'm at home after school.

S 2/38–41
L 4/18–21 ◉

A harp¹ on the water – a Welsh legend

Most countries have their legends – stories handed down from generation to generation. These stories talk of kings and queens, of fights between good and bad, rich and poor. Maybe you know the legend of Robin Hood, or of King Arthur? This one from Wales is about what happened to a very cruel² king.

5   Long long ago, at the beginning of time on this island, there was a very cruel king who lived in a stone palace where the lake of Bala is now. People said about him: "He kills³ who he can," and it was true – he
10 killed many.

One day, not long after he became king, and while he was still a young man, he was walking in his garden and thinking about cruelty when he suddenly heard a
15 voice. It sounded like something between a silver bell and a bird's cry⁴ and it said: "Vengeance⁵ will come. Vengeance will come." Then he heard a second voice, farther away than the first. It asked: "When
20 will it come? When will it come?" Then the first voice replied: "In the third generation.

The third generation." At this he laughed loudly and shouted through the garden: "If it doesn't come before that, why should I care?"
25

And he planned to be crueller than ever.

Years later, the king's three sons⁶ were born⁷ and they were even crueller than he was. One day he was again walking
30 in the garden when he heard the same voices. They were crying the same words: "Vengeance will come. When will it come? In the third generation, the third generation." Again he laughed loudly.
35 "I laugh in the face of vengeance," he shouted. And he hurried back into the palace to teach his sons more cruelty.

Years passed⁸, until the day when the whole palace was celebrating the birth of
40 a son to the king's son and heir⁹. The king sent his guards out into the country. They had to tell everyone who loved the king (and their own lives too) to hurry to the palace to celebrate. One guard had to find
45 a harp player with white hair who lived high up in the hills; he should play music for all the people who came to eat and dance in the palace that night.

The harp player didn't want to come,
50 but he had to. When he saw the silver candlesticks, the golden cups and the beautiful dresses of the ladies, it felt like a strange dream and he couldn't say a word. He wasn't in the mood to play as he
55 watched the faces of the king and his sons

1 **harp** [hɑːp] Harfe | 2 **cruel** [ˈkruːəl] grausam | 3 **to kill** [kɪl] töten | 4 **cry** [kraɪ] Ruf, Schrei | 5 **vengeance** [ˈvendʒns] Rache | 6 **son** [sʌn] Sohn | 7 **to be born** [bi ˈbɔːn] geboren werden | 8 **to pass** [pɑːs] vorübergehen | 9 **heir** [eə] Thronfolger

silent[16]. The moon moved behind a black cloud. In the dark the harp player couldn't see his hand in front of him and the noise of water below told him that it was dangerous to move. 85

He suddenly thought that he was crazy to follow the voice of a bird, and he remembered sadly that his harp was back at the palace. "I must go back before the 90 dancing starts!" he shouted. But when he thought of those cruel faces he was so horrified that he couldn't move. He was so tired and it was so dark … He fell asleep quickly. 95

In the morning, he got up and rubbed[17] the sleep from his eyes. Then he rubbed them again and again because when he looked towards the palace, there was no palace there! He saw only a huge, calm lake 100 where before there were walls and towers[18]. And his harp was swimming on the water towards him.

with their hard smiles and ice-cold eyes. But the king said: "Play!", and so he had to play.

60　At midnight[10] there was a break between the eating and dancing. The harp player was left alone, with nothing to eat and drink, in a quiet corner. Suddenly he heard a clear voice which said: "Vengeance
65 will come. Vengeance will come." He turned to the window, and in the light of the moon[11] he could see a small brown bird which was flying[12] around in the garden. It seemed[13] to invite him to follow!

70　He was very tired, but he stood up and left the palace. The bird flew in front of him and showed him the path[14] he should take. At the palace wall he stopped for a moment, but "Vengeance, vengeance!" the
75 brown bird cried. Now it seemed as easy to go on as to go back. So they went on and on, until the harp player could see the hill in front of them.

　When they reached[15] the top of the
80 hill at last, he was so tired that he had to sit down. For the first time the bird was

'A Harp on the Water' from *Welsh Legends and Folktales* by Gwyn Jones

→ WB 86/1–3

10 **midnight** [ˈmɪdnaɪt] Mitternacht | **11** **moon** [muːn] Mond | **12** **to fly** [flaɪ] fliegen | **13** **to seem** [siːm] scheinen | **14** **path** [pɑːθ] Pfad | **15** **to reach** [riːtʃ] erreichen | **16** **silent** [ˈsaɪlənt] still | **17** **to rub** [rʌb] reiben | **18** **tower** [taʊə] Turm

VOCABULARY

1 Offline for a month

a) *Sally is a 14-year old blogger from London. Last month she was offline for four weeks. Read about her experience. Fill in the gaps. Put the verbs in the right tense.*

to spend | to send | face-to-face | to post | to download | to stay in touch | to watch | offline | social networks | to see | challenge | phone | media mad | to get

SALLY'S BLOG

MY MONTH OFFLINE – A REAL CHALLENGE!

I'm [1]! I use the computer and the internet *very* often. I've got a smartphone, a tablet and a laptop – yes, I [2] a lot of time online. "When I was young we didn't have all those things," my Aunt Elizabeth told me one day. "I bet you can't live for a week [3]." "Ha," I said. "Of course I can. I can even do it for a month! You'll see!"

Well, that's how it started. I wasn't able to [4] with my friends on my phone or on [5] for four weeks. When my friends met in town they [6] me texts but I wasn't able to read them because I didn't have my [7] anymore. They [8] photos I wasn't able to [9], and when they [10] videos or [11] new music and then talked about how great it all was, I didn't know what they were talking about. And once, my friend Anne forgot that I was offline. At school, she asked me angrily, "Why didn't you come to my party?!" "*What* party?" I replied. "My birthday party!" Anne answered. Oops, I never [12] her invitation! So that wasn't so great.

But I also discovered that I had more time for other things when I was offline. I read more books, I did more sports and I talked to people [13] more often. But now I'm happy to be online again and tell you about this experience. Try it. It's a real [14]!

b) *Would you be able to stay offline for a month? Say why / why not.*

MEDIATION

2 A new computer game

Your little brother has a new computer game, but the instructions are in English and he doesn't understand everything. Explain the game to him. (Remember: In mediation, you don't need to know every word when you explain something; just the main ideas!)

Welcome to **Jungle World**, where Jolly Joe and his monkey friends swing from tree to tree and try to grab as much fruit as they can! But they have to be careful – the jungle is a dangerous place full of wild animals who want the fruit *and* you! Choose which monkey you want to be and give him / her a name. Then start your adventure through the jungle. With S-P-A-C-E your monkey jumps. Press ← → if you want to move left or right and press ↑ ↓ to go up or down. Try to grab as much fruit as you can – the more you get, the more points you get! You find different kinds of small fruit in the trees – but watch out: There are snakes in the trees too! The fruit on the ground is bigger, but be careful there too: Before you can grab some fruit, a tiger or lion could grab *you*! Enjoy **Jungle World**.

WRITING

3 A postcard from ...

Have a look at the material you collected for the Task in Unit 6. Imagine you've been to one of the places. Write a postcard to your friend / your grandma / … . Tell them …

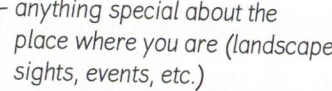

Greetings from Scotland –
The Highland Games

- *what you did*
- *what the weather was like*
- *anything special about the place where you are (landscape, sights, events, etc.)*
- *anything strange / interesting / exciting that happened to you*
- *any special food you ate*

LISTENING

4 Travelling around the world: Announcements

L 4/22

a) *Listen to five announcements and say where the people are. Which words helped you to find out about where they are?*

b) *Listen again. Who is the announcement important for? What is the most important information for these people?*

c) *Your turn: Write your own announcement and read it to your partner. Your partner has to guess where you are.*

WRITING

5 The world 50 years from now

*In a short text, make predictions about the future. What will life be like 50 (or 100, 200) years from now? Use the **will** future in your text, and think of these ideas:*

how people will live / travel | what people will eat / drink | what school / nature / technology will be like | how people will communicate with each other

forest skyscrapers to live in

robots for cleaning the house

Find more online:
h9j6vx

British stories and legends

Every country has special places where famous historical people lived or important events happened. When we don't know all the facts, we like to hear strange and wonderful stories about them. But how much is really true?

SPEAKING

1 Warm-up

Talk about famous historical people you know about in your country or in Britain.

READING

2 Typical ingredients of legends

a) *Read the text. Which ingredients do you like in a story or legend? Why?*

Legends are stories about people in history – but usually they aren't completely true. Often, writers have taken historical events and changed them a bit to make the stories more exciting, or maybe to show the difference between right and wrong more clearly. Legends have colourful characters like brave kings and cruel queens, or magical characters like wizards. There are heroes ('good guys') and villains ('bad guys') who have dangerous fights – of course, the good guy usually wins! Popular heroes are often brave knights, but sometimes they're just normal men who do brave things to help other people. Villains can be dangerous criminals or very powerful people who use their power in a bad way. And finally, there are more modern legends from popular books, like Sherlock Holmes, a private detective who solved mysterious crimes. He never lived at all, but people all over the world love to think he did!

b) *Look at the stills of Jinsoo and Marley. They're playing the roles of three famous British legends. What do you think the stories are about? What do you know about them?*

> ### Useful phrases
>
> **Nouns:** king | queen | wizard | hero / heroine | villain | knight | robber | outlaw
>
> **Adjectives:** colourful | magical | brave | cruel | dangerous | powerful | mysterious
>
> **Phrases:** to have a fight | to hide in the forest | to use your power | to solve a crime

VIEWING **3** **Stories and legends (1)**

13 🎬 a) *Watch the film and take notes about the three legends.*

b) *Match the sentence parts. Find the correct statements for each character.*

1. Sherlock Holmes was a private detective.
2. Robin Hood was a famous outlaw.
3. King Arthur was a powerful king.

a) Dr Watson was his assistant.
b) Many people think Tintagel was his castle.
c) He lived in Sherwood Forest, near Nottingham.
d) He lived in Baker Street in London.
e) His knights sat at the Round Table.
f) He loved Maid Marian.
g) He solved many mysterious crimes.
h) He stole from the rich and gave to the poor.

VIEWING **4** **Stories and legends (2)** → WB 87/1–2

a) *Watch the film again. Which characters have which props?*

b) *Your turn: Read the skills box. Then find out about another character from a legend or story, maybe a woman (like Boudicca, a Celtic queen who fought against the Romans; Vivien, the Lady[6] of the Lake who gave King Arthur his sword[7] Excalibur; or Miss Marple, a detective in Agatha Christie's crime stories.) Which costume, props or set could you give that character in a film? Why?*

c) *Role play: In groups of three, each of you chooses to be one of the characters. Your characters meet. Talk to each other about*

1. where you live
2. what you do
3. what you wear and carry
4. what's good and bad about your life.

Example:
A: Hi there. I'm Robin, I help the poor.
B: And I'm Miss Marple. I love to solve mysterious crimes.
C: …

bell | castle | bow and arrow[1] |
gloves | cape[2] | crown[3] |
lucky charm | magnifying glass[4] | cap[5]

Film skills

A film uses more than pictures, sounds and words to tell a story. It also uses **costumes**, **props** and a **set**. The characters wear **costumes** and they carry or use **props**. We can also see where they live – this is called the **set**.

Example:
If you want to show that a woman is a queen, she can wear a crown and beautiful clothes and live in a castle.

Robin, you don't think you're the *only* hero in this forest, do you?

Of course not, Marian.

1 **bow and arrow** [ˌbəʊ ən ˈærəʊ] Pfeil und Bogen | 2 **cape** [keɪp] Umhang |
3 **crown** [kraʊn] Krone | 4 **magnifying glass** [ˈmæɡnɪfaɪŋ ˌɡlɑːs] Lupe |
5 **cap** [kæp] Kappe; Mütze | 6 **lady** [ˈleɪdi] Herrin; Dame | 7 **sword** [sɔːd] Schwert

Legende

Diese Symbole und Erklärungen zeigen dir, wie du mit den Hilfen, Aufgaben und Aktivitäten auf den *Diff pool*-Seiten arbeiten kannst.

△ Hilfe zur Unit-Aufgabe | oder eine leichtere Variante der Unit-Aufgabe | oder eine zusätzliche Aufgabe

▲ eine zusätzliche Herausforderung

Unit 1

△ **1 Feelings** → Help with Check-in, p. 9/3

How can you feel in these situations? Match the feelings with the sentences. There's often more than one answer.

1. There's a test in English tomorrow.
2. Your team won a football match.
3. You forgot your homework – again.
4. You know all the answers in class today.
5. You're the new student.
6. You're alone, and you don't know what to do.
7. You're at the park and are playing with your friends.
8. You meet your favourite star.
9. You can't find your lucky charm.
10. You have chocolate on your white jeans and everyone can see it.

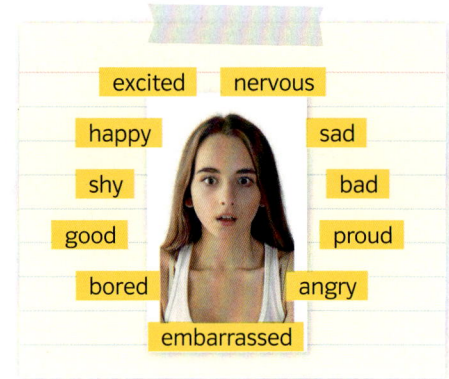

▲ **2 Charity work** → After Station 1, p. 10/1

*Do you know any children in charity projects? What can **you** do to raise money? Write down some ideas and prepare a short talk for the class.*

△ **3 Irregular simple past forms** → Instead of Station 1, p. 10/2 b)

Put in the correct past forms. Use the verbs below.

Two years ago the students 1 (do) fun activities and 2 (get) money for Comic Relief. They 3 (bring) the money to school. Then the school 4 (put) all the money together and 5 (give) it to the charity. Red Nose Day 6 (be) a non-uniform day, so everyone 7 (come) to school in different clothes. But they all 8 (wear) something red. Of course they all 9 (have) red noses too. Some students 10 (take) funny photos for the school website.

got   brought   gave   was   took   wore   had   put   did   came

⚠ **4** Sounds → After Station 1, p. 11/3

How do you say these simple past forms? Put them in the right box, then read them to your partner. Can you hear the difference?

played   stopped   acted   danced   collected   chased

laughed   watched   wanted   started   looked   turned   jumped

[d]	[t]	[ɪd]
played	stopped	acted

⚠ **5** The star of the show → Instead of Station 1, p. 11/5

What does Sherlock tell his dog friends the next day? Write the text again in his words, and use the verbs in the simple past below.

Start: I **did** lots of great tricks in the comedy show yesterday.

1. Sherlock does lots of great tricks in the comedy show.   2. First he jumps over a big box.
3. Then he runs around and chases his tail.   4. After that he dances on a skateboard, and when Olivia starts to play the sax he also sings.   5. The people love it.   6. They laugh and clap and give lots of money to Comic Relief.   7. Luke and his friends try to do their best too, but everyone's eyes are on Sherlock.   8. He feels so happy and proud – he is the real star of the show!

was   did ✔   ran   danced   sang   chased   loved   started

tried   laughed   gave   were   clapped   jumped   felt

⚠ **6** A report about a special activity → Help with Station 1, p. 12/7

What did these people do to raise money for charity? The words below can help you.

sell old things | flea market

make cakes and biscuits | cake sale

run for charity | find sponsors | pay money per metre

organise talent show | sell tickets | sell drinks

△ **7** **What they didn't do and what they did** → After Station 2, p. 14/12

👥 *Tony was tired last week, but Lou wasn't – so they didn't do things together. What didn't they do? What did they do? Take turns!*

Example: You: Tony didn't go skating with Lou, he read a book.
        Your partner: Lou didn't read a book, she went skating in the park.

go skating in the park   read a book

swim in the boating lake   watch TV

play tennis with a friend   sleep on the sofa

buy cheese at Greenwich Market   listen to music

prepare dinner for her friends   play a computer game

▲ **8** **A perfect day** → After Station 2, p. 14/12

👥 *Think of something you did on a perfect day. (It needn't be true). Now your partner must find out what it was. He / She can ask questions like these:*

Did you do something funny / exciting? Did you do it at home / in the park? Did you do it with friends / parents / alone? Were you nervous / excited / happy?

Think of more questions. Take notes, and then tell your classmates what your partner did on his / her perfect day!

△ **9** **The new forms** → After Station 3, p. 17/20 b)

Tony and Lou are fighting! What do they say?

Tony: I'm **1** (big) than you, Lou!
Lou: OK, I'm not as **2** (big) as you, but I am **3** (nice).
Tony: Maybe. But I'm **4** (popular) than you!
Lou: Oh no, you aren't. That's because I'm **5** (funny) than you.
Tony: You aren't as **6** (funny) as I am. Your jokes are **7** (bad) than my jokes! And I'm **8** (fast) than you.
Lou: That's because you're **9** (tall). But I'm **10** (intelligent). I can use my skates – and then I'm **11** (fast) than you!

△ **10 Say what's different** → Instead of Station 3, p. 17/21

Make sentences with comparisons.

Example: 1. Wales is smaller than England.

1. Wales is ▮ ▮ (small) England.
2. The weather today is ▮ ▮ (bad) yesterday.
3. Route B is ▮ ▮ (easy) route A.
4. The courses aren't ▮ ▮ ▮ (expensive) most people think.
5. I'm not ▮ ▮ ▮ (nervous) I was about new challenges.

△ **11 Who's the tallest?** → After Station 3, p. 17/22

Find out about your classmates! Choose one of the ideas in the box, find two partners and stand next to each other! Who is taller than you? Who has got the most interesting hobby? When you have got a group, shout "Stop!" and present your group to the class. Find the next group.

tall / short	young / old	boring / interesting hobby	big / small family

long / short way to school	young / old parents	silly / nice brother / sister

▲ **12 The best thing ever** → After Station 3, p. 17/22

*Choose two of these things and write a short text about them. Use **than** and **as … as** too. You can start like this: The tastiest meal I ever had was … It was tastier than…*

tasty meal[1]	good film	nice teacher	funny book	exciting holiday	bad joke

△ **13 The secret** → Help with Story, p. 20/3 b)

You can use these ideas and phrases to write your scene.

1. Look! I think that window … / … help me up?
2. Hey, here's another … / Do you think it's …? / Shshsh, quiet! / Don't … noise!
3. There's a light[2] …! / I think it's … window! / Let's throw …
4. Who's there? / Oh, it's you! / I heard …
5. We can use this to … / I can climb up, and then I can open …

1 tasty meal ['teɪsti 'mi:l] leckeres Essen; leckere Mahlzeit | **2 light** [laɪt] Licht

Unit 2

△ **1** **This is a fantastic school!** → After Check-in, p. 29/2

✏ **a)** *What do you think is important for a good school? Make a list of ten things.*

👥 **b)** *In groups of three or four, take turns to say an idea on your list. Give yourself one point[1] for each idea on your list when no other student has that same idea. If others in the group have the same idea, nobody gets a point. Who's got the most points?*

△ **2** **A school trip which was really cool** → After Station 1, p. 31/3

✏ *Do you need **who** / **that**, **which** / **that** or **whose**? Put in the right relative pronoun.*

The teacher **1** lessons we like the most is Mrs Jordan. Last year, she took us on a class trip and the coolest place **2** we visited was the Tower of London. Two men **3** costumes were black and red and very funny asked us about our visit. They were 'Beefeaters'[2]. They're the men **4** show the Tower to all the visitors. They told us about the ghosts **5** voices you can hear if you're quiet enough. They're the ghosts of all the people **6** lost their heads in the Tower many, many years ago!

△ **3** **Contact clauses** → After Station 1, p. 31/4 b)

*Read the sentence pairs. Which sentence in each pair **doesn't** need a relative pronoun?*

1. a) Lots of children that are interested in history go to the museum.
   b) Lots of children that I know go to the museum.
2. a) The art which you can see all around our school gives us lots of ideas!
   b) The art which is all around our school gives us lots of ideas!
3. a) I'm friends with lots of the students who go to Dance class.
   b) I'm friends with lots of the students who I see at Dance class.
4. a) This is a website which I use a lot for my homework.
   b) This is a website which helps me a lot with my homework.
5. a) I think the school trips that we go on are fun.
   b) I think the school trips that help us to understand history are fun.
6. a) Students who walk to school often get there earlier than me!
   b) Students who I see from the car window often get there earlier than me!

1 point [pɔɪnt] Punkt | **2 Beefeater** [ˈbiːfˈiːtə] königlicher Leibgardist

4 Make one sentence from two → After Station 1, p. 31/5

Replace[3] the words in blue with a relative pronoun and make a new sentence.

Examples: Last lesson we talked about a famous person. We all know him.
→ Last lesson we talked about a famous person **who / that** we all know.
The Cooking Club organises competitions. They're really exciting.
→ The Cooking Club organises competitions **which / that** are really exciting.

1. At TTS, there are lots of clubs and activities. You can do them outside.
2. I'm playing tennis with a new friend. He can run really fast!
3. Last lesson we watched a film. It was really interesting.
4. In Drama Club we learn about different film stars. I like them very much.
5. I can show you a cool wall painting. We made it yesterday.
6. Do you know the new girl? She's talking to Luke.

5 Puzzles → After Station 1, p. 31/5

a) *Complete the sentences with **who / that**, **which / that** or **whose**.*

1. It's something ▨ has four legs[4] but can't walk.
2. It's something ▨ you must break before you can eat it!
3. I'm someone ▨ is always cold but I must never feel warm!
4. It's something ▨ is yours but your friends use it more than you do!
5. I'm a person ▨ chair is a throne[5].
6. It's something ▨ is tall when it's new and not so tall when it's old!

b) *Can you guess the answers?*

Answers: a table | an egg | a snowman[6] | your name | a king / a queen | a candle

6 How to: Write prompt cards → Instead of Station 1, p. 32/6

Copy this prompt card about Queen Mary and Christopher Wren and fill in the right information for each heading.

Who:
What:

When:
Where:

Greenwich | cut the hospital in half | hospital between her house and the river | liked the sea | queen was upset | Christopher Wren | wanted a hospital | famous architect | 1692 | Wren had a very good idea | Mary

3 Replace … [rɪˈpleɪs] Ersetze … | **4 leg** [leg] Bein | **5 throne** [θrəʊn] Thron | **6 snowman** [ˈsnəʊmæn] Schneemann

△ **7** **Gwen's timetable** → Help with Station 1, p. 32/7

These pictures can help you to understand what Gwen, Holly and Olivia are talking about.

△ **8** **School subjects** → Help with Station 1, p. 32/8 a)

These words and phrases can help you to compare your timetable with Gwen's.

Useful phrases	
Our school day starts at 7:30 / …	Gwen and I have the same subjects, but I also have lessons in …
We have … lessons in the afternoon / every day / only on Mondays / Tuesdays / …	In Maths / History / RE / … we learn / talk about … / we often work on projects.
There's a break at … Lunch is from … till …	We have lots of after-school clubs / activities / …

▲ **9** **School subjects** → After Station 1, p. 32/8 b)

👥 *Take turns to describe a lesson that you had last week. Don't say which lesson you're talking about! Your partner must guess the lesson.*

Example: Last week I had a lesson in which we built a …

△ **10** **The mice's Cooking Club** → After Station 2, p. 33/9

What are / were the mice doing in Cooking Club? Put in the correct verb forms.

It's Friday, 10:00	Last Friday, 10:00
1. I **am** mak**ing** a cheesecake.	1. I **was** mak**ing** a cheesecake.
2. Tony **is learning** how to make pizza.	2. Tony ▮ how to make pizza.
3. Hey Lou, you ▮ Tony's cheese!	3. Hey Lou, you **were** eat**ing** Tony's cheese!
4. Sophie and Alex **are** prepar**ing** a pie.	4. Sophie and Alex ▮ a pie.
5. We ▮ for tips on the internet.	5. We **were** look**ing** for tips on the internet.

▲ 11 Act it out and guess! → After Station 2, p. 33/9

*One student leaves the classroom. 3–4 other students act an activity **without** words. When the teacher shouts "Stop!", everyone stops. Now the student comes back in and sees the 'frozen'[1] students. With yes/no questions, he/she must guess what the others were doing.*

> Were you eating something?

> No, we weren't.

△ 12 When or while? → After Station 2, p. 34/10

*Fill the gaps with **when** or **while**.*

1. We were watching a film ▨ Mum came home.
2. ▨ I saw my brother, he was buying lots of sweets.
3. I read a whole magazine ▨ I was waiting for the bus.
4. ▨ my dog was sleeping, my cat stole his dinner!
5. Amber was preparing a presentation ▨ her phone rang.
6. ▨ the friends were walking home from school, they discovered a new shop.

▲ 13 A crazy day at home → After Station 2, p. 34/10

Use these photos and write a short story about a crazy day at home. Think of your own crazy ideas too. Use the simple past and the past progressive.

Start like this:
First, breakfast was crazy. While Mum was…, our dog … her breakfast! Then, while Mum and Dad were …, we … in the kitchen. But when …

▲ 14 Write a dialogue → Instead of Story, p. 42/3 c)

After his fight with Jay, Luke talks to his mum. Write their conversation and use words which show that Luke had very strong feelings about what happened.

Start like this: Mum: You look **really** angry, Luke. Is anything wrong?
Luke: I had an **absolutely awful** fight with Jay today …

1 **frozen** ['frəʊzn] *hier:* erstarrt

Unit 3

△ **1 Choose your London** → Help with Check-in, p. 51/3

Here are some useful phrases that can help you to discuss where you want to go.

Useful phrases

I'd like to visit … It's free. | I think … is the best place. Let's go there!

We must see …, it's fantastic. | Can we go to …? I hear it's really great.

I'm sure it's fun to …, so I really want to …

△ **2 What are they going to do next week?** → After Station 1, p. 52/3

Monday	Tuesday	Wednesday	Thursday	Friday
Amir and Jay – go to the cinema	*Amir – go shopping with Aunt Yasmin, buy a London T-shirt*	*Amir – meet Jay's friends in the afternoon*	*Amir and Shahid – visit Cutty Sark*	*Amir and Jay – have a sleepover at Luke's house*

Amir tells his mum about these plans in an e-mail – what does he write?

Start like this: Dear Mum, I can't call you very often next week because I have so many plans! On Monday, Jay and I are going to go … On Tuesday, Aunt Yasmin is going to …

△ **3 What's going to happen?** → Help with Station 1, p. 53/4

These words can help you to write about the people in the picture on p. 53:

open the door | clean the street | take the bus | buy an ice cream

give some money | go to the cinema | play the saxophone

Start: 1. The old man and woman are going to sit down. **2.** The man is going to …

△ **4 Guess my plans for tomorrow** → Help with Station 1, p. 53/5

What can you do where? These ideas can help you to guess your partner's plans. Match the activities with the right places first.

1. London Dungeon
2. London Eye
3. Royal Observatory
4. Shakespeare's Globe
5. Brick Lane

a) learn about the theatre, watch a Shakespeare play
b) stand on the time line, watch the time ball fall down
c) buy great clothes, see street art
d) get a great view of London
e) hear horror stories, see ghosts

△ **5 The photo story** → Help with Station 2, p. 55/7

Olivia, Holly, Amir and Jay all have different feelings about the food challenge.
These ideas help you to think of something that they might say about it.

Jay	Olivia	Holly	Amir
really like music ǀ fantastic street shows ǀ not so hungry	like a challenge ǀ try something exciting ǀ find cafés boring	doesn't know where the cafés are ǀ try to find something special ǀ everything so expensive	nervous ǀ not know where to look ǀ happy to go with Olivia

▲ **6 A game: Why didn't you buy any food?** → After Station 2, p. 55/7

👥 🖊 *One of you is Jay, one of you is Olivia. Olivia starts with the question below. Jay must quickly give three different answers. Olivia chooses one and writes it down. Then it's her turn to answer with three different sentences. Jay chooses one, writes it down and goes on with three different sentences. Go on like this till you have the perfect dialogue.*

Start: Olivia: Why didn't you buy any food?

I didn't feel hungry any more.
I was watching the street shows
   and they were great.
I didn't have any money.

What about your pocket
   money?
Why not?
Maybe someone stole it!

I forgot it at home.
…

△ **7 Compound words with *some* and *any*** → After Station 2, p. 55/9

🖊 **a)** *Fill the gaps with **some** or **any**.*

Jay: Let's buy 〔1〕 drinks. I have 〔2〕 money left.
Olivia: Oh, no! I don't want 〔3〕 drinks, and I'm still
          hungry. Have you got 〔4〕 crisps left, Holly?
Holly: No, sorry. I haven't got 〔5〕 crisps, but I've got
          〔6〕 biscuits.

b) *Complete the words with **some** or **any**.*

Amir hasn't bought 〔1〕 **thing** for his mum yet, so the
friends are looking for souvenir shops. "How much do you want to spend?" Jay wants to
know.
"Well, I can't buy 〔2〕 **thing** expensive, I've only got a few pounds. But I need 〔3〕 **thing** for
my mum – maybe there's 〔4〕 **thing** in this little shop?" Amir answers.
"I don't think so. Look at the prices! Let's go 〔5〕 **where** else," Holly says. "What about
Greenwich Market? Or does 〔6〕 **one** have a better idea?"

▲ 8 Sherlock, you crazy dog! → After Station 2, p. 55/9

Luke's mum is away at the weekend. She wrote a note for the family – but Sherlock found it and now it's in pieces! Match the parts and write a new note in the right order.

1. You needn't buy
2. Remember: someone must
3. I had to get to the station, so
4. There's something
5. Lots of love for
6. Can someone please
7. I don't want to find
8. Everybody should
9. Hi everyone, I hope

a) clean the windows?
b) in the fridge for you, please check.
c) anything for dinner.
d) clean up a bit.
e) any food on the sofa when I come back.
f) you can manage without me!
g) I didn't do everything before I left.
h) take Sherlock for a walk tomorrow morning.
i) everybody, Mum.

△ 9 Complete the text → Instead of Station 2, p. 55/10

Fill the gaps with these words. Use each word only once.

Holly: What can we do till we meet Shahid later? Has **1** got a good suggestion?

Jay: It must be **2** that costs **3** – we haven't got any money left.

Olivia: Let's just walk around. I'm sure that's fun for **4** new in London like Amir. There are lots of interesting things to see **5** you look. What do you think, Amir?

Amir: Well, if **6** wants to make a different suggestion – yes, I'd like that.

Holly: Is there **7** special you'd like to go or **8** special you'd like to see?

Amir: Well, **9** is special for me – it's all amazing. But I'd love to walk near the river.

Jay: Is that OK with **10** ? – Great, come on, let's go and find the Thames!

nothing
everywhere
anybody
someone
something

everybody
everything
nobody
anywhere
anything

△ 10 Adverbs → After Station 3, p. 57/15

Here are some tips for people who visit London. Find the right adverb for each sentence.

Always cross[1] the street **1** (careful). Remember: In England cars drive[2] on the left! Sometimes people in England speak very **2** (fast). You can always ask people to talk **3** (slow) and **4** (clear). They're usually friendly when you ask them **5** (polite). You should try **6** (hard) to understand, but if you have problems, don't react[3] **7** (nervous). When you get back home, you can talk **8** (happy) about the great things you did in London!

1 to cross [krɒs] überqueren | **2 to drive** [draɪv] fahren | **3 to react** [riˈækt] reagieren

△ **11 Act it out!** → After Station 3, p. 57/15

Write these activities on cards. One of you choooses an activity and acts it without words. The others guess what you're doing, and how.

sing loudly   jump quickly

dance slowly   look around nervously

talk excitedly   walk carefully

write fast   smile happily

△ **12 Adjective or adverb?** → After Station 3, p. 57/16

Decide if you need the adjective or the adverb in these sentences.

1. When Amir came to London, he was ▮▮ because he travelled alone. At Victoria Station he looked around ▮▮ to find Jay and his aunt and uncle. (nervous)
2. But he was also ▮▮: Jay always talked so ▮▮ about all the things you can do in London! (excited)
3. Amir, Jay and his aunt and uncle went home by bus. The old London buses are very ▮▮. They travel around the city very ▮▮ so tourists can have a ▮▮ look at all the sights. You can see them very ▮▮ from the top of a real London bus. (slow, good)
4. On the bus, Amir smiled ▮▮. A whole week in London! And he was ▮▮ to see his cousin and his family. (happy)

▲ **13 Adjective or adverb?** → After Station 3, p. 57/16

From the two boxes, choose an activity and an adjective. Then write sentences about yourself – and use the adverb form too!

Example: I'm good at sports, but I don't play football very well. I'm nervous before a test, but I don't …

| walk to school |
| do my homework |
| talk to teachers |
| dance │ sing |
| pop songs │ go |
| cycling │ … |

| good │ nervous │ |
| excited │ happy │ |
| angry │ crazy │ |
| loud │ slow │ |
| fast │ … |

▲ **14 A treasure in the Thames** → Instead of Story, p. 64/4

Think of something the friends find in the Thames: a gold coin, an old ring, a statue, an oil lamp … Tell the story of how they find it, what they do with it, etc.

Unit 4

△ **1** **Talk about sports** → Help with Check-In, p. 68/2 b)

*Two students made these word clouds. What are their favourite sports? You can use the words to talk about the sports **you** are interested in.*

racket fun match player tennis ball judo exciting skating outside partner

karate costume team practice show gymnastics music dancing hip hop ballet interesting

▲ **2** **Have you really done that?** → After Station 1, p. 71/3

*Work with a partner. Each of you writes down six very strange or exciting activities. **One** of them must be an activity that you have really done. Exchange your activities and find out which one your partner has done.*

eat worms – take a llama to the park – go water-skiing with my granny – play with a tarantula[1] – sleep in a haunted house[2]

△ **3** **Great runners** → After Station 1, p. 73/7

Lisa and Mark help to organise the London Marathon; they need great runners. Put the verbs into the present perfect.

Lisa: We need some great runners this year. Mark, **1** (you write an e-mail to) last year's winners?

Mark: Yes, I have. But I **2** (get) answers from everyone yet. What about the German twins[3], Klara and Lena – I **3** (find) some info about them on the internet.

Lisa: **4** (they win) anything yet? I **5** (never hear) of them.

Mark: They **6** (run) in a few important races. Klara won one big marathon last year, the Frankfurt City Marathon. Lena **7** (win) yet, but she was 'Best European' in the Hamburg Marathon. They always run together.

Lisa: **8** (you check) if they have a website?

Mark: Of course I have. Here, I **9** (copy) the contact details for you. Let's write them an e-mail. We **10** (not have) famous twins in the Marathon yet, have we?

Lisa: No, it's a good idea to ask them. But wait till I **11** (look) at their website first!

1 **tarantula** [təˈræntjələ] Vogelspinne | 2 **haunted house** [ˌhɔːntɪd ˈhaʊs] Geisterhaus | 3 **twins** [twɪnz] Zwillinge

▲ **4 Write a profile about Brandon** → After Station 2, p. 73/7

*For a magazine, write a short profile about a rich[4] and famous young actor, Brandon Fairchild. What has he **already** / **just** / **never done**, or **not yet done**? What is he **going to do** in the future? Use the ideas below for the profile, but also add some of your own ideas. Be creative! (Use a dictionary for help with new words.)*

already ✔	buy a cool house in Hollywood / travel around the world in private jet
never ✘	have a famous girlfriend
just ✔	get award[5] for 'Coolest Actor'
not yet ✘	find a new house in London
future plans ✔	buy his own ship / win an Oscar

△ **5 Children and accidents** → Help with Station 2, p. 73/9

These words can help you to tell your partner in English about the German survey.

young people	often	get hurt[6]
have accidents	per cent[7]	every year
injury[8]	see a doctor	small children

> Remember, your partner only needs to understand **the main ideas**. You needn't try to translate everything word for word!

△ **6 Questions and answers** → Help with Station 2, p. 75/12

Here are some ideas for your questions and answers.

Activities:
watch a … / join a …
win an important match / race
play tennis / rugby / handball
run for charity / run for fun
have an accident / a serious injury
finish first / last in a race
enjoy a Sports lesson

When (simple past):
last year / week / month
when I was smaller / a baby / younger
yesterday
in May / January / October / …

When (present perfect):
never / before / yet / ever

---

4 rich [rɪtʃ] reich | **5 award** [əˈwɔːd] Auszeichnung; Preis | **6 to get hurt** [getˈhɜːt] sich verletzen |
7 per cent [pəˈsent] Prozent | **8 injury** [ˈɪndʒəri] Verletzung

△ 7 Boys' day! → After Station 3, p. 75/13

Dave and Jay are on the phone. They want to have a picnic in the park with Luke, and then go to the match between Greenwich RFC and Sidcup RFC.

Complete their phone call with the right verb form in the simple past or present perfect. Sometimes you just need a short answer.

Dave: So what's the plan for Saturday, Jay? You **1** (not tell) us yet!

Jay: Oh yes, I **2** ! We **3** (talk) about it yesterday in the Maths lesson.

Dave: Really? I can't remember. Sorry! – Anyway, what **4** (you say) yesterday?

Jay: I have tickets for the rugby match between Greenwich and Sidcup! My dad **5** (buy) them as a present for me and two friends!

Dave: Hey, you've got a cool dad. – So when are we going to meet?

Jay: Well, I **6** (think) it would be a good idea to have a picnic in the park first.

Dave: Cool. And what **7** (Luke say) when you **8** (tell) him?

Jay: He thinks it sounds great too. He **9** (already ask) his dad for help with the food. Can you buy some drinks, Dave?

Dave: No problem. My mum **10** (just give) me some extra pocket money because I **11** (do) well in the Maths test last week. So what drinks do we want?

Jay: Just lemonade and water?

Dave: OK. **12** (you ask) the girls if they want to come, Jay?

Jay: The girls?! No, I **13** . It's a *boys'* day, remember? And they **14** (not ask) *us* to come to their sleepover party last weekend, did they?

Dave: No, but who would *want* to be at their sleepover?!

▲ 8 A game: Who is it? → After Station 3, p. 75/13

1. *Choose a famous star, a person in the class or somebody else **everybody** knows.*
2. *On a card, write five activities this person has already / never done, or did at some time. But don't write his / her name!*
3. *Then collect and shuffle¹ all the cards.*
4. *Take turns to read out the information. The others must guess who it is.*

Example:
- started to play football when he was five
- has played for Schalke and Bayern
- has been a member of the German national football team since² 2009
- became the world's best goalkeeper³ in January 2014
- won the World Cup in 2014

Answer: Manuel Neuer

1 **to shuffle** ['ʃʌfl] mischen | 2 **since** [sɪns] seit |
3 **goalkeeper** ['gəʊlˌkiːpə] Torwart

9 The London Mini Marathon → Help with Story, p. 82/1b)

These words and phrases for the three pictures can help you to retell the story.

When the race started, Gwen was … | Olivia wasn't there, so … | Gwen was a bit worried about … | She told Luke, "Don't …" | Luke saw two people in …

Ten minutes later, she felt … | She told herself … | The two runners in the funny costumes were … | They were getting … | But Luke and Gwen were still …

Suddenly, … pulled out a phone and … chaos … | Another runner … | But Gwen and Luke finished … | Olivia found out that the dog and cat were …

10 What's the person like? → Help with Story, p. 82/2

*Which of these words can you use if you want to say something **positive** about someone? Which ones are **negative**? Make two lists. Some of the words can help you to describe the children and their actions.*

brave unfriendly stupid fast polite crazy clever
careful helpful funny silly interesting great
good boring confident friendly popular awful nice

11 Useful phrases from the story → Help with Story, p. 82/3

Complete the phrases; you know them from the story. This can help with your mind map.

1. "My charity does a lot of really important work, so it really ▢ to me."
2. "Olivia can't join us. That's ▢, isn't it?"
3. "You're silly, not me! So ▢ me silly."
4. "This ▢ great! After all that training, this is the moment, *my* moment!"
5. "There are so many people here, and it's my first marathon! I'm ▢! You too?"

12 A game: Frozen image⁴! → After Story, p. 82/3

Get together in groups of four or five. Choose a scene from the story and practise a frozen image of that scene. (Practise in another room so your classmates can't see you.) Back in the classroom, the others then shout "One… two… freeze⁵!" and your group does its frozen image. Your classmates must guess the scene and explain how they guessed.

4 **frozen image** [ˌfrəʊznˈɪmɪdʒ] erstarrtes Bild | 5 **to freeze** [friːz] erstarren

Unit 5

△ **1** **Media collocations** → Instead of Check-in, p. 90/2

✎ **a)** *Write down all the media collocations in the text.*

> Tony loves the world of media! He checks his text messages all the time. He loves texting his friends. He sends and receives text messages during lessons too. (Bad boy!) And Tony has joined a popular social network: He's on Mousebook, of course. He regularly posts photos and changes his profile. It's important for Tony to stay in touch with his friends, so he often talks to them on video chat. At weekends, he often plays video games or takes part in discussions. It's easy to forget the time when you're online! Lou isn't so happy about this: Tony doesn't always reply to her text messages quickly enough, and she has to check his profile on Mousebook to see what he's doing!

b) *You can use some of the verbs with more than one noun, e.g., you can **change** your **profile** and you can **check** your **profile** too. How many different media collocations of nouns and verbs can you find?*

▲ **2** **Ruby's answer** → After Station 1, p. 92/1

👥
✎ *Work with a partner. On little pieces of paper, write down the different bits of advice that Ruby has for Lauren. Then put the pieces of paper face down on the table. Take turns to pick one up and talk about it. Do you think it's good advice? Why / Why not? What other bits of advice do **you** have for Lauren? Talk about them.*

△ **3** **Using linking words: Tony and his phone** → After Station 1, p. 93/2

✎ *Read what Tony's friend Robby says about Tony. Use these words to make one sentence out of the two. There's sometimes more than one way!*

Example: Tony plays video games too often.
He doesn't call me. → **Whenever** Tony plays video games, he doesn't call me.

> after   before   as soon as
> whenever   because   when

1. He got a new smartphone for his birthday. We often saw each other before that.
2. Tony can't leave his phone alone for one minute. He's really into texting.
3. I wanted to go to the cinema with him yesterday. He said "yes".
4. At the cinema, someone said, "You must turn off your phone. The film is starting."
5. Tony heard that. He was shocked.
6. Sometimes a phone rings at the cinema. It always makes the other people angry.

△ 4 A game: Who's the fastest? → After Station 1, p. 94/5

1. *Write short positive and negative statements on little pieces of paper.*
   Example: This is a cool T-shirt.
2. *Your teacher then collects the papers.*
3. *Now stand up in two lines. Your teacher reads out a sentence from your list to the first two students in the lines.*
4. *You must complete the sentence with the right question tag.*
   Example: This is a cool T-shirt, **isn't it**?

The student who gives the right answer first joins the queue again; the other student must sit down.

▲ 5 You can hear the difference, can't you? → After Station 1, p. 94/5 c)

*You and your partner write six sentences with question tags – three of them must be **real** questions. Take turns to read your sentences to each other. Your partner must listen closely and then answer. Remember: A real question needs a real answer, not just a short answer!*

△ 6 Symbols of friendship → Help with Station 1, 94/6 b)

Here are some phrases and ideas for talking about symbols of friendship.

Useful phrases

A symbol can be **something you do**, like … when you wear the same clothes / colours | when you have a secret together | when you talk about / help each other with problems | …

A symbol can be **a thing**, like … a photo together | a mascot keyring[1] / a mascot toy | special words for things | favourite stickers | …

△ 7 The day I fixed my . . . → Help with Station 2, p. 95/8

Ask yourself these questions before you talk to your partner:

What did you fix? | Did it belong to you or to someone else? | Why did you fix it and not buy a new one? | Where did you look for help / advice? | Did you ask anybody for help? | Was it easy to fix? | How long did it take you? | Does it still work?

1 **mascot keyring** [ˌmæskət ˈkiːrɪŋ] Maskottchen-Schlüsselanhänger

△ **8** **The older you are, the more you can do . . .** → Instead of Station 2, p. 96/10 b)

*Look at the list of things Olivia can do now. Say what you think she **wasn't allowed to do** when she was four years old, what she **wasn't able to do**, and what she **didn't have to do** then.*

Examples:
- When Olivia was four, she wasn't able to read a book. Now she can. / Now she loves to read.
- When Olivia was four, she didn't have to …

- go cyling	- help her mum in the kitchen
- read a book	- watch TV in the evening
- go shopping	- make models
- go to school	- join a social network
- do homework	- have a sleepover

△ **9** **'Fun' in Scotland . . .** → After Station 2, p. 96/10 b)

🖉 *Complete Holly and Dave's dialogue with the right forms.*

Dave: Hi Holly! Back from Scotland? Did you enjoy your holiday?

Holly: Well, not really. You know I wanted to visit the castle in Edinburgh, but I [1] . My mum said it was too expensive.

Dave: Oh, that's too bad. But you [2] to take some photos of the castle, weren't you?

Holly: Yes, of course. That doesn't cost anything. Amber and I [3] to go shopping on the Royal Mile, so that was good. We went all the way down to Hollyrood House, but we [4] to go inside: "Too expensive", mum said. *Again.*

Dave: When I was in Edinburgh last summer, I didn't want to visit any old castles, but I [5] to visit *lots* of them! My parents *always* take me to museums and castles.

Holly: Well Scotland has lots of beautiful lakes. I'm sure you went swimming, right?

Dave: Wrong! My mum always says, "Forget it, the water is too cold. No swimming!" So no, we [6] to go swimming. We [7] to visit all the different sights.

Holly: Hm, it sounds like you and I [8] to have the best time there. Maybe next time!

▲ **10** **Giving and taking advice** → After Station 2, p. 96/11

👥 *On cards, write down situations where **you** might
🖉 need advice. (The ideas on the right can help you.)
Put them face down on the table, between you
and your partner. Take turns to choose a card,
read the situation to your partner, and say what
advice you have for him/her.*

not good at school

trouble with teacher

fight with friend

not enough pocket money

small room   …

△ 11 You could do that, but I think you should... → After Station 2, p. 96/11

*Read these situations and decide what advice you want to give. Do you need **could** or **should**?*
(Remember, there's a difference! Check G16 for help.)

1. Oh no. I left my smartphone at home!
   (use mine)
2. This phone doesn't work at all.
   (buy a new one)
3. Do you like this photo? I want to post it.
   (not post private photos)
4. My computer has been so slow!
   (let me check it)
5. Hmm, 'World of Heroes' or 'Super Talents' –
   which game is better? (try both)
6. Susan is still angry because I sent her
   that text. (tell her you're sorry)
7. I think my profile is boring.
   (write something interesting / exciting)

Oh, I've got the worst headache!

I could make some tea, Tony. That always helps you.

▲ 12 Media mad → After Station 2, p. 97/13

When you read a flow chart, always start at the top and work down, step by step. First read the text in the middle box in the first line, and then decide if you must follow the red (= no) or green (= yes) flash. Are you surprised about your results?

Work with a partner. Choose a box for your partner (e.g. 'five / four' is the box with "You don't care about video games"). Your partner must find the box and comment on it. Then it's his / her turn.

Example: A: Two / two. "You check your messages all the time!"
            B: I don't know. When I'm bored I often check them. But when I'm with my friends, I don't do that. What about you?

△ 13 Writing a dialogue → Help with Story, p. 104/1c)

Here are some ideas to help you write your dialogue.

Mrs Preston:	When did you get …	Was anybody … ?	Didn't you ask them what…	What happened when …	That sounds like a lot of fun, but …
Mr Preston:	When I got home, I wasn't able …	I was angry because…	I found some candles and thought …	The kids used their smartphones to …
Jay:	I was thinking about the party we wanted to have and …	It takes so long to write …	I'm sorry, I wasn't thinking when I …	I was so worried when…
Olivia:	Don't you know how dangerous it is to … ?	Why didn't you wait for … ?	We were really lucky that …	I think next time you should …	But it's OK, don't worry …

Unit 6

△ 1 Talking about places → Help with Check-In, p. 108/1

Where should these people go on holiday?

Start like this: Lou should go to Wales. She can visit …

1. Lou likes stories about the past and she likes to visit old castles.
2. Sandy loves horses and she likes to be outside every day.
3. Andrew is interested in music and traditions.
   He loves watching shows and listening to traditional songs.
4. Ellen is a good swimmer and loves the sea. She thinks it's great to walk along the beach and look for treasures.

△ 2 Frequently asked questions → After Station 1, p. 111/3

Work with a partner and fill in the gaps. Take turns to ask and answer the questions.

1. ▭ rain today?
2. What ▭ do ten years from now?
3. ▭ meet friends after school?
4. Where ▭ spend your holidays?
5. When ▭ do your homework?
6. ▭ watch a scary film with me?
7. ▭ buy me some ice cream?
8. Where ▭ live when you're 30?

▲ 3 Mediation: At a German station → After Station 1, p. 111/3

*An English boy is trying to buy a ticket at a German station. He's talking to a man who doesn't speak English. Can you help the boy? Try to use the **will** future where you can.*

Boy: Excuse me, I need to take the next train to Cologne. Will it wait a few more minutes?

Man: *Entschuldigung, ich spreche kein Englisch.*

You: *Dieser Junge muss …*

Man: *Ach so. Nein, der Zug wartet nicht. Aber ich bin sicher, der nächste Zug wird ihm besser gefallen. Es ist ein Express-Zug.*

You: Sorry, the train … But the man is sure …

Boy: Express train? Won't … expensive?

You: …

Man: *Warte kurz, ich schaue nach.*

You: …

Man: *Nein, es wird sogar günstiger! Und er wird früher in Köln ankommen als der frühere Zug!*

You: No, he says it'll … And, he says …

Boy: Cool! I … earlier and I … more money for my visit in Cologne! – Yes, I think I … buy that ticket.

You: Great, but I must go now or my train … leave without me!

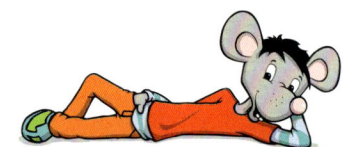

4 Buying train tickets on the internet → After Station 1, p. 112/5

Fill in the new travel words.

price   inward   arrive   one-way   return   change   fee   depart   outward

First, Luke forgets to click on **1** , but he doesn't only need the **2** for a **3** ticket. So he has to fill in the dates for the **4** journey and then the **5** journey. He clicks on **6** , but then he remembers that he doesn't know how long the journey takes. So he chooses the time he wants to **7** . He learns that for St Agnes you have to **8** at London Bridge and Paddington. Then he wants to know how much the booking[1] **9** is.

5 What will the weather be like? → Help with Station 1, p. 112/6

Here are weather pictures and words to help you with exercise 6 on page 112.

Start like this: Today the weather is still … | But tomorrow it'll be… |
Temperatures[2] will … | There will be …

lots of sun

temperatures up to 30 degrees[3]

no wind

partly cloudy

not too much wind

warm   24 degrees

storm   thunder

lots of wind

temperatures fall to 17 degrees

6 Do we really need to leave Greenwich? → After Station 2, p. 115/9

*Read Dave and Mr Preston's dialogue and decide if you need **if** or **when**.*

Dad: Dave, your mum just doesn't feel at home in Greenwich any more. You'll understand **1** you're older.

Dave: But I'm *not* older, Dad. It's *now*, I'm young, and I know that **2** we leave Greenwich, I'll be really sad.

Dad: Yes, you're right. But **3** you don't try to change your point of view, things will never get better. Can you please try, for me and for your mum?

Dave: Well,… **4** I try to be happier, will you do something special for me?

Dad: **5** I say yes, will it cost a lot, Dave?

Dave: No, it won't. Don't worry about money. Anyway, three weeks from now, **6** we're in our new house, I know I'll be sad. But, **7** I have a party for my friends, I'll feel *much* better, I know it! May I? PLEASE …?

1 **booking** [ˈbʊkɪŋ] Reservierung | 2 **temperature** [ˈtɛmprətʃə] Temperatur | 3 **degree** [dɪˈgriː] Grad

one hundred and fifty-three **153**

▲ **7** **German tourist attractions** → After Station 2, p. 115/9

🖊 *Match the tourist attractions with the places or regions in Germany. Write tips for tourists, using **if + will / can / should** or the **imperative**. Add more information if you like. Remember: When you write your sentences, you can start with the **if-clause** or with the **main clause**!*

| lots of Roman buildings
fish market in the harbour
a famous cake
Germany's capital
a very big cathedral (church)
Germany's biggest island
a boat trip to a famous rock
a beautiful palace | go
see
visit
like
enjoy | Berlin
the Black Forest
Cologne
Hamburg
Loreley
Neuschwanstein Castle
Rügen
Trier |

▲ **8** **A poem about your home town** → After Station 2, 116/14

🖊 *Write a poem about your town or area. The word groups below rhyme[1]; they can help you with your poem. Maybe you can think of more words in English that rhyme?*

| city | be | sea | me | free | | like | bike | hike |

| village | language | manage | image | | site | bright | night | right | light |

| live | give | active | | run | fun | sun | one |

△ **9** ⟨**Who says what?**⟩ → Instead of Station 3, p. 117/1

Match the sentence parts. Sometimes you have to add a pronoun (I, you …) too!

1. If Dave were an adult,
2. If he had his way,
3. Jay says it would be great
4. Luke says it would be a good idea
5. If Luke had more money,
6. Dave's parents would do anything
7. Dave says that if all people were like Luke,
8. Jay says it would really help

a) nobody would have any more fun.
b) … would stay here in Greenwich with … friends.
c) if … had another party like … surprise party.
d) … could choose where … wants to live.
e) if … tried to be a bit more positive.
f) … would buy a cool new costume.
g) if … cheered … up[2] a bit.
h) if … asked his parents first.

> If I were king, cheese would be free for EVERY mouse!

1 **to rhyme** [raɪm] sich reimen | **2** **to cheer up** [tʃɪərˈʌp] fröhlicher werden

6

△ **10** ⟨ If the weather were … ⟩ → After Station 3, p. 118/3

*Look at the photos and words. With **if**, write what the children could do.*

Start like this: If the weather were nice today, I / we / my family could …

| weather nice today \| go to the beach | not break arm \| go surfing | finish home-work \| play football | tidy room \| find favourite T-shirt | fix bike \| not be late for cinema |

▲ **11** ⟨ Time for some fun ⟩ → After Station 3, p. 118/3

*Think of fun sentences; they needn't be true at all. Write five of them down. Now work with a partner. Read out your sentence; your partner must find an **if-clause** for it. You can use the ideas in the box below, or ideas of your own.*

Example: A: I know an alien with superpowers[3]!
B: If I knew an alien with superpowers, he could do my homework for me!

know an alien with superpowers   win the lottery[4]   get tickets for any show that you want

money grows on trees   see a UFO   be a Hollywood film star

△ **12** **Things to do in the country** → Help with Action UK!, p. 119/1

Match these activities with phrases and words from the box.

1. feeding animals
2. milking cows
3. exploring a cave
4. swimming in a lake
5. playing in an adventure playground
6. reading ghost stories
7. walking
8. geocaching

Useful phrases

I think … is dangerous / scary / exciting / boring / fantastic / a lot of fun / …

I like farms, so … is the activity for me!

… is fantastic / great / … for small children, but I like more interesting / more exciting / … activities like …

I don't like sports, so I'm not into …

3 **superpowers** [ˈsuːpəˌpaʊəz] Superkräfte | 4 **lottery** [ˈlɒtri] Lotterie

Vocabulary

S1 Vokabelheft

Führe ein dreispaltiges Vokabelheft, in dem du auch neue Vokabeln notieren kannst, die nicht in der Wortliste stehen. Die erste Spalte ist für die englische Vokabel bestimmt, die zweite für die Übersetzung und die dritte für Beispielsätze oder alles, was dir hilft, dir die Bedeutung zu merken, z. B. Bilder, *mind maps*, Beziehungen zu anderen Wörtern, auch in anderen Sprachen.

S2 Vokabelkartei

Es lohnt sich, eine Vokabelkartei anzulegen, um Vokabeln zu lernen. Sie besteht aus Karteikarten für die Vokabeln und einem Karton mit fünf Fächern für die Karten.
Schreibe das englische Wort auf die Vorderseite der Karteikarte und die deutsche Bedeutung auf die Rückseite. Zusätzlich kannst du weitere Merkhilfen notieren. Stelle zunächst alle Karten ins erste Fach.
Übe jeden Tag fünf bis zehn Minuten, und zwar so: Nimm eine Karte nach der anderen heraus und überprüfe, ob du die Übersetzung weißt (deutsch – englisch, englisch – deutsch). Wenn ja, stellst du die Karte ins zweite Fach. Mache weiter, bis das erste Fach leer ist. Das zweite Fach bearbeitest du dann genauso, allerdings nicht jeden Tag, sondern nur einmal in der Woche, das dritte Fach alle zwei Wochen usw.

S3 Wörter im Zusammenhang

Wörter sind die Bausteine der Sprache. Du musst sie natürlich lernen und jedes für sich verstehen. Zur Beherrschung einer Sprache gehört aber auch zu wissen, welche Kombinationen dieser Bausteine möglich sind. Deshalb ist es wichtig, mit den Wörtern schon die richtigen Kombinationen mitzulernen. Schreibe Wörter möglichst immer in typischen Zusammenhängen auf.

Mit Verben kannst du passende Ergänzungen mitlernen, z. B.:

*to **read** a book, a magazine, a comic, a manga*
*to **write** a letter, an e-mail, an invitation, a blog*
*to **go** swimming, shopping, home, away, to the cinema*

Du solltest auch wissen, wann bestimmte grammatische Formen auf bestimmte Wörter folgen. Schreibe dir passende Beispiele zusammen mit der Vokabel auf, z. B.:

*I would like **to** swim, **to** read, **to** go shopping*
*I like swim**ing**, read**ing**, go**ing** shopping*

Welche die richtigen Präpositionen sind, muss man in jeder Sprache auswendig lernen. Notiere auch dafür Beispiele und lerne sie, z.B.:

*The party is **on** Friday, **at** seven, **at** the weekend.*
*My house is **in** Dover Street. We're **on** the road to London.*
*London is **on** the Thames.*

S4 Methoden

Du hast schon mehrere Methoden gelernt, wie du dir Vokabeln besser einprägen kannst:

- Klebezettel mit englischen Wörtern an die entsprechenden Gegenstände in deinem Zimmer kleben

- Wörter als Bildwörter oder mit passenden Bildern aufmalen

- Wörter zusammen mit anderen, die zu einem Thema gehören, in *mind maps* anordnen

- Wörter pantomimisch darstellen und gegenseitig erraten lassen

- Wörter aussprechen, zusammen mit ihrer Übersetzung und vielleicht einem Beispielsatz aufnehmen und immer wieder anhören

- Wörter mit ähnlichen Wörtern in anderen Sprachen notieren

- Wörter, die miteinander in Beziehung stehen, zusammen notieren, z. B. verwandte Wörter, Gegensatzpaare, zusammengehörige Paare

Reading

S5 Schnelllesetechniken

Normalerweise denkst du während des Lesens nicht darüber nach, wie du dabei vorgehst. Wenn du aber eine Aufgabe zu einem Text bekommst oder eine bestimmte Information suchst, liest du bewusster und gezielter. Diese Techniken helfen dir, wenn die Zeit begrenzt ist.

Skimming („den Rahm abschöpfen")	Scanning („maschinell durchsuchen")
Wenn du danach gefragt wirst, worum es in einem Text geht, sollst du ihn nicht einfach nacherzählen, sondern nur das Wichtigste *(gist)* zusammenfassen. Dazu kannst du den ganzen Text überfliegen und darauf achten, ob bestimmte Wörter *(key words)* oder Personen häufiger vorkommen. Auch die Überschrift oder Bilder können dir helfen einzuschätzen, was wichtig ist und was nicht. Diese Art des Schnelllesens nennt man *skimming*.	Wenn du nach bestimmten Einzelheiten *(details)* in einem Text gefragt wirst, musst du ihn überfliegen und die Stellen mit der wichtigen Information finden. Dazu suchst du gezielt nach passenden Stichwörtern *(key words)*. Sie zeigen an, welche Teile du genauer lesen solltest, um die gesuchte Information zu bekommen. Diese Art des Überfliegens nennt man auch *scanning*.

S6 Wichtige Inhalte von Texten herausfinden

Wenn du einen Text liest, solltest du danach immer folgende Fragen beantworten können:

Who ...?
Wer ist beteiligt?

What ...?
Was geschieht?

When ...?
Wann?

Where ...?
Wo?

Dazu kannst du Schnelllesetechniken anwenden, Markierungen im Text machen und dir Fragen und Anmerkungen notieren (S8). Wenn du den Text noch genauer liest, kannst du weitere Fragen beantworten, z. B. Warum geschieht etwas? Wenn es eine Geschichte ist, wer erzählt sie? Für wen wurde der Text geschrieben (Adressat)?

S7 Gliederung als Hilfe

Um einen Text besser zu verstehen, kann es dir helfen, ihn in mehrere Abschnitte zu gliedern. Orientiere dich dabei z. B. an Absätzen und inhaltlichen Punkten, die du dir markiert hast. Überlege anschließend, was in den einzelnen Teilen jeweils das Wichtigste ist und formuliere passende Überschriften. Dies erleichtert es dir, Zusammenfassungen von Texten zu geben oder *Mediation*-Aufgaben zu lösen.

A *Henry hopes to play the lead*

B *Henry is disappointed*

C *Henry sees the positive side of things*

S8 Textbearbeitung mit Markierungen und Notizen

Im geliehenen Buch darfst du das zwar nicht, aber auf
Kopien oder in Arbeitsheften solltest du dir angewöhnen,
wichtige Stellen in Texten zu markieren und Randnotizen
zu machen (z. B. Fragen oder
Anmerkungen). Verwende
am besten verschiedene
Farben: Markiere z. B. wichtige
inhaltliche Punkte grün
und Informationen zu den
Personen blau. Wörter, die du
nachschlagen musst, solltest du
auch hervorheben. Unterstreiche
sie beispielsweise und notiere
die richtige Übersetzung am
Rand. So fällt dir das erneute
Lesen leichter.

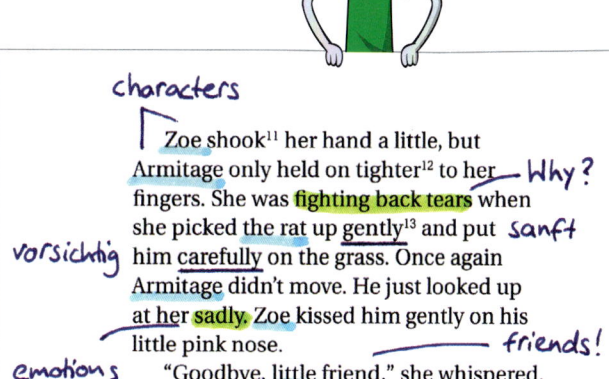

S9 Umgang mit neuen Wörtern

Viele Wörter kannst du schon verstehen, obwohl du sie noch nicht gelernt hast.

1. Ähnlichkeit mit Wörtern, die du schon kennst
Oft haben verwandte Wörter den gleichen Stamm, aber andere Vorsilben oder Endungen.
Wenn du z. B. *happy* schon kennst, wirst du *unhappy* sicher auch verstehen. Englische
Wörter haben oft keine Endungen, aber es gibt sie in verschiedenen Wortarten. Wenn du
also das Wort *guide* als Nomen kennst, kannst du dir bestimmt denken, was das Verb *to
guide* oder die Zusammensetzung *travel guide* bedeutet.

2. Ähnlichkeit mit Wörtern, die du aus einer anderen Sprache kennst
Viele englische Wörter gibt es genauso oder ähnlich auch im Deutschen, z. B. *computer*,
hobby oder *pony*. Manchmal hilft dir auch ein Wort, das du aus einer anderen Sprache
kennst (Französisch, Latein, …) ein englisches Wort zu verstehen, z. B. weil es ähnlich
geschrieben wird oder ähnlich klingt.

3. Verstehen der Wörter im Zusammenhang
Manchmal kannst du dir anhand eines Bildes oder einer Überschrift denken, was ein
Wort in einem Text bedeutet. Und wenn du alle Wörter in einem Satz verstehst außer
einem, kann dieses oft nur eine bestimmte Bedeutung haben. Was bedeutet z. B. *return*
in diesem Satz?
*My dog ran away, and I was really happy when he **returned** after three days.*

Und wenn du doch im Wörterbuch nachschlagen musst, helfen dir die Tipps auf S. 21.

Writing

S10 Planung deines Textes

Überlege, für wen dein Text bestimmt ist (Adressat) und welchen Zweck er erfüllen soll. Vor dem Schreiben machst du dir am besten einen Plan: Notiere in Stichwörtern, was in der Einleitung, dem Hauptteil und dem Schluss deines Textes stehen soll. So vergisst du nichts Wichtiges und findest auch leichter eine schöne Einleitung und einen guten Schluss.

S11 Textsorten und ihre Besonderheiten

Du kennst schon einige wichtige Textsorten und ihre Haupteigenschaften:

E-mail, letter, postcard, invitation	Achte auf die richtige Anrede für den Adressaten, z.B. *Dear …*, Grußformeln am Schluss, z.B. *Yours/Love/Best wishes*, und beachte die Höflichkeitsregeln. Denke bei einem Brief an die Angabe der Empfänger- und Absenderadresse und an das Datum.
Story	Wenn du eine Geschichte vervollständigen sollst, muss dein Teil zum vorgegebenen Text passen. Vermeide also inhaltliche Widersprüche. Außerdem sollten die Erzählperspektive und die Erzählzeit nicht wechseln. Meistens sind Geschichten im *past tense* geschrieben. Gestalte deine Geschichten sprachlich abwechslungsreich und schmücke sie aus.
Dialogue	Wenn du einen Dialog, z.B. für eine Filmszene, schreibst, denke daran, dass du echte mündliche Sprache verwendest, also z.B. *short forms*, *question tags*, verstärkende Ausdrücke usw.
Report	Bei einem Bericht ist die Vollständigkeit und Verständlichkeit der sachlichen Informationen das Wichtigste. Er wird im *past tense* geschrieben.
Prompt cards	Wenn du dich auf eine Präsentation vorbereitest, notiere auf Karteikarten nur Stichwörter, die dich an die einzelnen Punkte des Vortrags erinnern. Schreibe z.B. wichtige Namen, Ereignisse, Orte und Daten unter die Überschriften *Who, What, Where, When*.
Flyer	Ein Flyer sollte gut lesbar sein (Schriftart- und größe) und alle wichtigen Informationen enthalten: *Who?, What?, When?, Where?, Why?* Formuliere außerdem einen ansprechenden Slogan.
Diary entry	Ein Tagebucheintrag erzählt und kommentiert vergangene und erwartete Ereignisse aus der ganz persönlichen Sicht einer Person und ist normalerweise nicht für andere Leser bestimmt.

S12 Überarbeitung deines Textes

Wenn du einen Entwurf erstellt hast, liest du ihn am besten noch einmal gründlich durch. Meistens entdeckst du so noch einige Fehler und kannst holprige Formulierungen verbessern. Nimm dabei eine Checkliste zur Hilfe (siehe rechts), damit du nichts Wichtiges vergisst. Es ist auch eine gute Übung, die Texte mit einem Partner zu tauschen.

Checkliste

Rechtschreibung:
- Wörter richtig geschrieben?
- Am Satzanfang groß?
- Getrennt oder zusammen?

Grammatik:
- Richtige Zeitformen?
- Richtige Formenbildung?

Inhalt:
- Alle wesentlichen Punkte enthalten?
- Keine inhaltlichen Fehler?
- Zusammenhänge erkennbar und logisch?

S13 Sprachliche Verbesserungen

Je größer dein Wortschatz wird, desto mehr Möglichkeiten eröffnen sich dir beim Schreiben von Texten.

Einzelne Sätze kannst du genauer und interessanter gestalten, indem du z. B. Nomen durch Adjektive oder durch weitere Nomen näher beschreibst. Verben kannst du durch adverbiale Bestimmungen ergänzen. Vergleiche die unterschiedliche Information in den beiden folgenden Sätzen:

A *I went to the shop.*

B *I went to the* `big` `pet` *shop* *in Greenwich* *with my sister* *last Saturday*.

Deinen gesamten Text kannst du flüssiger gestalten, indem du die Sätze miteinander verknüpfst. So werden logische Zusammenhänge klarer und der Text liest sich leichter. Vergleiche die beiden folgenden Textausschnitte. Der erste wirkt durch die unverbundenen Hauptsätze abgehackt. Der zweite enthält auch Satzgefüge aus Haupt- und Nebensätzen, die mit Hilfe von Bindewörtern *(linking words)* logische Zusammenhänge herstellen. Außerdem geben die vielen Adjektive und Adverbien genauere Informationen und machen den Text interessanter.

A *I went to the shop. I wanted a guinea pig. We looked at all the guinea pigs. I didn't like them. We wanted to leave.*
A girl came in with a box. She brought back a guinea pig. It was cute! I bought it. I'm happy.

B *I went to the big pet shop in Greenwich with my sister last Saturday* **because** *I wanted to buy a nice guinea pig. We looked at all the guinea pigs,* **but** *I didn't like them.* **Just when** *I wanted to leave, a girl came in with a box. She brought back a guinea pig* **which** *was really cute.* **So** *I bought it* **and** *I'm very happy now.*

Speaking

S14 Sprechen üben

Sprechen lernt man nur durch Sprechen. Du solltest dir angewöhnen, im Englischunterricht immer englisch zu sprechen, ob mit deiner Lehrerin/deinem Lehrer oder in der Partner- und Gruppenarbeit. Um Sprechen zu üben, solltest du allerdings viel mehr sprechen als nur im Unterricht. Vielleicht üben deine Freunde, Eltern oder Geschwister mit dir?

Eine Voraussetzung für das richtige Sprechen ist natürlich, dass du übst, die englischen Wörter richtig auszusprechen. Beim Lernen mit dem Buch kann dir die Lautschrift dabei helfen. Sage sie dir immer wieder laut vor. Einfacher und einprägsamer ist es natürlich, die Vokabeln richtig ausge-sprochen anzuhören und nachzusprechen. Hilfsmittel dafür sind Audio-CDs mit den Schülerbuchtexten, Lernsoftware oder Online-Wörterbücher, in denen du jedes Wort anklicken und anhören kannst.

Übe schwierig auszusprechende Laute, die anders sind als im Deutschen, z. B. das stimmhafte oder stimmlose *th* oder das *w* im Kontrast zum *v* oder ein stimmhaftes *d* oder *g* am Wortende. Dazu kannst du (lustige) Sätze erfinden, sie dir immer wieder vorsprechen und dabei das Tempo steigern, bis die Aussprache zuverlässig klappt.

Wenn du ganze Texte hörst, bekommst du ein Gefühl dafür, wie die Wörter im Textzusammenhang ausgesprochen werden. Die Aussprache unterscheidet sich manchmal stark von der Aussprache der Einzelwörter. Aufeinander treffende Laute werden z. B. häufig miteinander verbunden.

Du hast auch schon gehört, wie die Betonung die Aussprache beeinflussen kann, wenn jemand besonders starke Gefühle ausdrücken will. Das kannst du auch üben.

They **th**ought of **the th**ree **th**ousand **th**ankful **th**ieves.

Why **w**ork **w**ith **v**ocabulary **w**hen you can **v**isit a **w**onderful **v**illage **w**orld?

She wante**d** her ba**g** back and sai**d** what a nice hat she ha**d**.

This is th**e end of t**he story. They know ove**r a** hundred different stories.

It's **so** unfair! Why doesn't anyone **ever** ask **me** what I'm feeling?

S15 Gesprochene Sprache

Auch beim Sprechen kommt es auf die Situation und deinen Gesprächspartner an, wie du dich ausdrückst. Denke z. B. auch an Höflichkeitsregeln.
In der gesprochenen Sprache ist es normal, dass Pausen, unvollständige Sätze, Wiederholungen oder Füllwörter vorkommen:

- Während bei Gleichaltrigen ein *Hi!* als Begrüßung ausreicht, ist Lehrpersonen oder fremden Erwachsenen gegenüber ein *Good morning! / Good morning …* eher angemessen.
- Statt *I want …* sagst du höflicher *I would like …* oder *Could I please have …?*
- Entscheidungsfragen beantwortest du mit Kurzantworten, nicht einfach mit *Yes* oder *No: Yes, I do. No, I'm not.*

*Well, I – I really don't know. It's – **er**, maybe you want to …?*

Es ist wichtig, einem Dialogpartner immer das Gefühl zu geben, dass er einbezogen wird. Dazu dienen *feedback phrases,* Nachfragen und *question tags.*

*Then we went to the city farm, Mudchute, **you know**. And there was this cute little pig – **you saw it too, didn't you? Guess what Linda did when she saw it!***

S16 Mündliche Aufgaben und ihre Besonderheiten

Es ist viel wichtiger, dass du regelmäßig länger zusammenhängend sprichst, als dass jedes Wort perfekt ausgesprochen und die Grammatik absolut korrekt ist. Wie wäre es, wenn jeder in deiner Klasse in einer Englischstunde eine Minute lang Englisch über ein selbst gewähltes Thema spricht? Hier findest du ein paar Tipps für bestimmte mündliche Aufgaben:

Interview	Sei höflich, aber scheue dich nicht nachzufragen, wenn du etwas nicht sofort verstehst. Achte bei der Fragestellung auf die richtige Zeitform und das richtige Hilfsverb. Antworte auch in der passenden Zeitform.
Asking/ Showing the way	Auch hier ist Höflichkeit wichtig und ganz bestimmte Vokabeln wie *go down X Street, go straight on, go past/turn left/right into Y Lane, it's on the left / right / opposite Z.*
Role play	Versetze dich in deine Rolle und versuche nachzufühlen, was die Person weiß und was sie denkt und fühlt. Verwende typische Merkmale der gesprochenen Sprache und unterstütze deine Worte mit Mimik und Gestik.
Presentation	Bereite deine Präsentation gut vor. Recherchiere die Fakten gründlich. Überlege, was dir wichtig ist und was du sagen möchtest. Besorge Material, das du zeigen willst, und bereite es so auf, dass es gut aussieht und verständlich ist. Mache dir einen Ablaufplan. Schreibe dir Notizen auf *prompt cards.* Versuche frei zu sprechen und nicht abzulesen. Übe deine Präsentation vorher und stoppe die Zeit, die du brauchst.

Mediation

S17 Bearbeitung von Mediationsaufgaben

Mediation ist die Übertragung wichtiger Informationen aus einem gesprochenen oder geschriebenen Text in eine andere Sprache, z.B. aus dem Englischen ins Deutsche oder umgekehrt. Das machst du, wenn du einen Text für jemanden zusammenfassen sollst, der die Sprache des Ausgangstexts nicht versteht. Gelegentlich kann es auch sein, dass du dolmetschen musst, also zwischen Gesprächspartnern vermittelst, die nicht dieselbe Sprache sprechen. Ganz wichtig: Es geht bei der *Mediation* niemals um eine wörtliche Übersetzung *(translation)*!

Lies dir die *Mediation*-Aufgabe gut durch und beachte besonders folgende Dinge:

Adressat:
Für wen ist die Information bestimmt?

--→ Je nachdem, wer die Person ist und wie viel sie schon weiß, sprichst du sie unterschiedlich an.

Ausgangstext

Zweck:
Wozu benötigt die Person die Information?

--→ Du musst nur die Informationen wiedergeben, die für den Adressaten in der jeweiligen Situation wichtig sind. Alles andere kannst du weglassen. Es kann aber auch vorkommen, dass du Dinge zusätzlich erklären musst.

wichtige Info

Beispiel: Dein Ausgangstext ist die Infobroschüre eines Museums, die alle Öffnungszeiten und Eintrittspreise enthält. Wenn dein Gegenüber dich fragt, ob das Museum heute geöffnet ist, musst du nicht unbedingt sagen, wann es sonst noch geöffnet oder geschlossen ist. Will die Person den Eintrittspreis wissen, kommt es auf ihr Alter an und darauf, ob sie allein oder mit einer Gruppe unterwegs ist.

Einen schriftlichen Ausgangstext kannst du in Ruhe durchlesen und die wichtigen Informationen auswählen. Dabei helfen dir alle Techniken, die auf S.158 / 159 unter *Reading* beschrieben sind. Formuliere die entsprechenden Inhalte so, dass der Adressat sie gut verstehen kann.
Bei einer Dolmetscheraufgabe wird eine echte mündliche Gesprächssituation simuliert. Deshalb musst du schneller reagieren, um möglichst viel von dem sinngemäß wiederzugeben, was die Gesprächspartner zueinander sagen.

Wenn dir ein Wort in der Zielsprache nicht einfällt, umschreibe es mit anderen Worten *(paraphrasing)*. Beachte bei der schriftlichen und mündlichen Bearbeitung von *Mediation*-Aufgaben außerdem die Tipps unter *Writing* und *Speaking* (siehe S.160–163)

Listening

S18 Hörverstehen üben

Grundsätzlich ist es zur Übung immer sinnvoll, viele echte englische
Texte anzuhören, z. B. Nachrichten oder Kindersendungen in Radio
und Fernsehen oder Hörbücher. Dabei ist es nicht schlimm,
wenn du nicht jedes Wort verstehst. Dir wird außerdem auffallen,
wie unterschiedlich die Aussprache des Englischen je nach
Herkunft des Sprechers sein kann.

S19 Techniken des Hörverstehens

Analog zum Lesen gibt es auch beim Hörverstehen unterschiedliche Techniken. Beim *Listening
for gist* geht es darum, das Wichtigste in einem Hörtext zu erkennen und zusammenzufassen.
Beim *Listening for detail* hingegen sollst du einem Hörtext bestimmte Einzelheiten
entnehmen.

Listening for gist	Listening for detail
Welche Wörter und Themen kommen mehrmals vor und spielen deshalb vermutlich eine wichtige Rolle? Höre besonders auf diese und fasse die wichtigsten Inhalte des Textes zusammen.	Nach welchen bestimmten Einzelheiten im Text wirst du gefragt? Höre besonders auf Wörter, die du in der Antwort erwartest, und die Informationen dazu.

Auch beim Hörverstehen hilft eine Tabelle wie beim Leseverstehen. Du kannst darin während
des Hörens deine Notizen machen.

Who ...?   *What ...?*   *When ...?*   *Where ...?*

S20 Typische Hörverstehenssituationen

Manchmal hilft dir beim Hörverstehen auch die Kenntnis von typischen Textsorten
und Situationen. Wenn du die Textsorte des Hörtextes kennst, überlege dir, worauf es
beim Telefonieren, beim Dolmetschen, bei Präsentationen, Durchsagen, Radio- oder
Fernsehsendungen ankommt und welche Themen jeweils zu erwarten sind. Gelegentlich
geben dir auch Bilder Hinweise zur entsprechenden Situation: Wenn z. B. bestimmte Personen
oder Orte dargestellt sind, kannst du leichter einschätzen, worum es in dem Hörtext geht.
Achte beim Hören auf Geräusche sowie Stimme und Tonfall des Sprechers. In echten
Gesprächssituationen oder Filmen können dir auch Gestik und Mimik das Verständnis
erleichtern.

Film skills/Viewing

S21 Inhalt und Gliederung

Ein Film ist auch eine Art Text. Deshalb lassen sich viele ähnliche Fragen dazu stellen:

– Worum geht es?
– Wird eine Geschichte erzählt?
– Welche Personen spielen mit?
– Welches sind die Hauptpersonen?
– Was passiert in welcher Reihenfolge?
– Wann und wo passiert es?

– Welche Gliederung und welche Themen sind zu erkennen?
– Aus wessen Sicht wird die Geschichte erzählt?
– Wer hat den Film gemacht, für welches Publikum und wozu?

Das Anschauen und Verstehen eines Films verlangt dir jedoch nicht nur das Verständnis der Sprache ab, sondern du musst auch auf viele weitere Dinge achten.

S22 Wichtige filmische Aspekte

Wie stellen die Schauspieler den Charakter der Personen dar, die sie verkörpern? Wie drücken sie Gefühle aus?

--➤ Achte vor allem auf Sprache, Mimik und Gestik. Aber auch Kleidung oder Frisuren können eine Rolle spielen.

Wie werden Handlungsort und -zeit dargestellt *(setting)*?
--➤ Achte auf Landschaften, Gebäude und Innenräume, Kleidung und Gegenstände.

Wie wird eine bestimmte Atmosphäre geschaffen *(atmosphere)*?
--➤ Achte auf Licht, Farben, Musik, Geräusche.

Wie unterstützt die Musik den Inhalt des Films?
--➤ Beachte, wann welche Musik ertönt und wann sie wechselt.

Wie helfen bestimmte Kameraeinstellungen den Inhalt deutlicher darzustellen *(shot)*?
--➤ Achte z. B. auf Nahaufnahmen *(close-ups)*.

Wie wird Spannung erzeugt *(suspense)*?
--➤ Achte auf Vorandeutungen, Musik, Licht, Geräusche und natürlich die Gestik und Mimik der Schauspieler.

Mit der Zeit wirst du weitere filmische Mittel kennen lernen, die bestimmte Wirkungen auf den Zuschauer erzeugen.

Kooperative Lernformen

Hier findest du die Erklärung für einige ausgewählte Methoden der kooperativen Arbeit.

S23 Think – Pair – Share

1. *Think:* Du sammelst still mögliche Lösungen zu der Aufgabe. Du kannst deine Ideen in Stichpunkten notieren.
2. *Pair:* Zusammen mit deinem Partner besprichst du leise deine gesammelten Ideen.
3. *Share:* Im Klassengespräch meldet ihr euch und teilt euren Mitschülern die Ergebnisse eurer Partnergespräche mit.

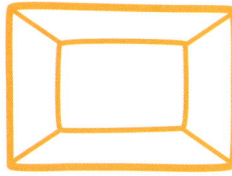

Variante: *Placemat* in Vierergruppen

S24 Milling around (Marktplatz)

Du gehst durch das Klassenzimmer, erfragst von deinen Mitschülern bestimmte Informationen und gibst auch selbst Auskunft. Versuche mit möglichst vielen Mitschülern zu sprechen und verschiedene Informationen zu sammeln. Ihr könnt auch ein Signal vereinbaren, zu dem ihr eure Gesprächspartner wechselt.

S25 Inside outside circle (Kugellager)

1. Bildet zwei Stuhlkreise, einen inneren und einen äußeren.
2. Setzt euch in den Stuhlkreisen so hin, dass immer ein Schüler des äußeren und des inneren Stuhlkreises sich gegenüber sitzen.
3. Stellt euch gegenseitig eure Fragen und beantwortet diese.
4. Rutscht im inneren oder äußeren Kreis nach dem Ende der Gesprächsrunde einen Platz weiter und beginnt ein Gespräch mit einem neuen Mitschüler.

S26 Bus stop (Lerntempoduett)

Sobald du deine Aufgabe fertig bearbeitet hast, gehst du zu einem vereinbarten Treffpunkt, dem *bus stop*. Dort wartest du auf den nächsten Mitschüler, der fertig ist, und zusammen besprecht und vergleicht ihr eure Lösungen. Anschließend verlasst ihr den *bus stop* und bearbeitet die nächste Aufgabe.

S27 Gallery walk (Museumsgang)

1. *Group work:* In der Gruppe erarbeitet ihr ein Thema und haltet euer Ergebnis, z. B. auf einem Poster, fest.
2. *Gallery walk.* Es werden neue Gruppen gebildet. In jeder Gruppe ist ein Schüler jeder Ausgangsgruppe. Jede Gruppe betrachtet die verschiedenen Ergebnisse der Gruppenarbeiten. Jeder präsentiert nun in der neuen Gruppe das Ergebnis seiner Ausgangsgruppe.

Grammar

Liebe Schülerin, lieber Schüler,
jede Sprache besteht aus bestimmten Bausteinen und funktioniert nach bestimmten Regeln.
Die Bausteine sind z.B. einzelne Wörter (Vokabeln). Die Regeln für ihre Zusammensetzung
nennt man Grammatik. Diese musst du außer den Vokabeln lernen, damit du dich verständigen
kannst und damit es nicht zu Missverständnissen kommt.

Jedes Grammatikkapitel (**G**) behandelt Themen, die auf bestimmten Seiten vorne in den *Units*
vorkommen (z.B. Seiten 10–11). Erklärungen, Bilder und Tabellen helfen dir, …
– die Grammatik zu verstehen,
– beim Nachholen, wenn du ein paar Stunden gefehlt hast,
– bei den Hausaufgaben,
– beim Wiederholen,
– bei der Vorbereitung auf Tests und Klassenarbeiten

Regeln sind mit einem blauen Punkt (**o**) gekennzeichnet.
Ein Ausrufezeichen (**!**) bedeutet, dass du hier besonders
aufpassen musst. Mit kleinen Aufgaben (**Test yourself**)
kannst du überprüfen, ob du alles verstanden hast.
Die Lösungen findest du ab Seite 288.

> Hier ist eine Liste aller grammatischen Begriffe aus diesem Buch in alphabetischer Reihenfolge zum Nachschlagen. Links findest du den englischen Begriff, in der Mitte ein Beispiel und rechts den deutschen Ausdruck.

Grammatical terms

English term		Example	Deutsche Bezeichnung
adjective	G4, G5	exciting, easy, young	*Adjektiv*
comparison of adjectives	G4	After the adventure course I was **more confident**.	*Steigerung der Adjektive*
comparisons with adjectives	G5	Wales is**n't as big as** England or Scotland, but it's **bigger than** Northern Ireland.	*Vergleiche mit Adjektiven*
adverb of manner	G10	The Raven Master's job is to look after the ravens **carefully**.	*Adverb der Art und Weise*
comparison of adverbs	G11	Our guides know London's history **better** than anyone.	*Steigerung der Adverbien*
compounds of some, any, every and no	G9	Listen, **everybody**. What can we do for lunch? Are there any cafés **anywhere** near here?	*Zusammensetzungen mit some, any, every und no*
conditional clause type 1	G18	**If** you **like** beaches, you**'ll find** that Cornwall is just the right place for you.	*Bedingungssatz Typ 1*

English term		Example	Deutsche Bezeichnung
conditional clause type 2	G19	**If** I **were** an adult, I **could choose** where I wanted to live.	*Bedingungssatz Typ 2*
defining relative clause	G6	My presentation is about two queens **that lived in Greenwich**.	*notwendiger Relativsatz*
contact clause	G6b	Christopher Wren is **an architect we** talked about in our Art lesson.	*notwendiger Relativsatz ohne Relativpronomen*
going-to future	G8	Jay and Amir **are going to visit** the British Museum.	*Futur mit* going to
modal auxiliary	G15, G16	can, can't, must, needn't, mustn't, should(n't), could	*Modalverb, modales Hilfsverb*
substitute form	G15	When I was ten, I **wasn't allowed to** have my own smartphone.	*Ersatzform*
past participle	G12	Gwen and Luke have already **prepared** for the trials. Olivia has **hurt** her foot.	*Partizip Perfekt*
past progressive	G7	Jack **was making** a bee hotel when he hit his thumb.	*Verlaufsform der Vergangenheit*
present perfect simple	G12	**Have** you ever **seen** the London Marathon?	*einfache Form des Perfekts*
question tag	G14	You're having a hard time, **aren't you**?	*Bestätigungsfrage, Frageanhängsel*
simple past	G1–G3	Lenny Henry **started** Comic Relief in 1985.	*einfache Form der Vergangenheit*
irregular verb	G1	came, had, met, wore	*unregelmäßiges Verb*
regular verb	G1	answered, played, watched	*regelmäßiges Verb*
questions	G2	Did the police arrest the man? What did he take from the shop?	*Fragen*
negating statements	G3	The man **didn't break** any shop windows.	*Aussagesätze verneinen*
subordinate clauses of comparison, time, reason	G13	The girl wrote to an agony aunt **because** she had a problem. **Before** we had an argument, we spent all our free time together.	*Nebensätze des Vergleichs (Komparativsätze), der Zeit (Temporalsätze), des Grundes (Kausalsätze)*
will future	G17	I'**ll miss** you so much!	*Futur mit* will

Unit 1

G1 **Two years ago we raised lots of money.**
Seiten 10–12
Die einfache Form der Vergangenheit
The simple past

> Lenny Henry **started** Comic Relief in 1985 to help people in Africa. On the first Red Nose Day in 1988 people **wore** red noses, **did** fun activities to raise money and **watched** a big comedy show on TV. That **was** many years ago, but today people still do the same things.

> *Das* simple past *verwendest du, um über eine Handlung oder ein Ereignis zu sprechen, das in der Vergangenheit liegt und abgeschlossen ist.*
> *Du findest es oft in Berichten und Geschichten.*

○ *Bei der Bildung des* simple past *unterscheidest du zwischen regelmäßigen und unregelmäßigen Verben. Anders als bei den Gegenwartsformen sind sie in allen Personen gleich.*

○ *Das* simple past *von* **regelmäßigen Verben** *bildest du aus der* **Grundform des Verbs + -ed**. *Doch bevor du* -ed *anhängst, musst du folgende Besonderheiten bei der Schreibweise beachten:*

normal	stummes -e	einfacher Konsonant	y nach Konsonant
play – play**ed**	like – lik**ed**	plan – plan**ned**	try – tr**ied**

○ *Beachte, dass* -ed *auf drei verschiedene Weisen ausgesprochen wird. Sprich …*

[d] *nach Vokalen gefolgt von stimmhaften Konsonanten:*	love – lov**ed**, organise – organis**ed**
[t] *nach stimmlosen Konsonanten:*	help – help**ed**, like – lik**ed**
[ɪd] *nach* [t] *oder* [d]:	need – need**ed**, paint – paint**ed**

○ *Bei unregelmäßigen Verben musst du die Formen des* simple past *auswendig lernen.*

come – came [keɪm]	have – had [hæd]
do – did [dɪd]	make – made [meɪd]
go – went [went]	put – put [pʊt]
get – got [gɒt]	see – saw [sɔ:]
give – gave [geɪv]	take – took [tʊk]

> *Das Verb* be *hat im* simple past *zwei Formen:*
> I / He / She / It **was** … [wɒz]
> We / You / They **were** … [wɜ:]
> *Die verneinten Formen lauten* **wasn't** *und* **weren't**.

Auf Seite 284 findest du weitere unregelmäßige Verben. Im Dictionary erkennst du sie am ˟.

○ Im Englischen verwendest du das simple past, *um eine abgeschlossene Handlung der Vergangenheit wiederzugeben. Im Deutschen kannst du dafür das Präteritum (z.B. er spielte, er ging) oder aber das Perfekt (z.B. er hat gespielt, er ist gegangen) verwenden. Vergleiche:*

Zeitangaben wie yesterday, last week / month / year, in 1985 oder two years ago können dir den Gebrauch des simple past signalisieren.

Letztes Jahr **haben** wir viel Geld **gesammelt**. – Last year we **raised** lots of money.

Test yourself Complete the e-mail. Use the verbs in the simple past.

> Dear Olivia,
> Thank you for your e-mail and the photos. I like them a lot.
> You (want) to know about our charity event. Well, last month we (organise) an event in the park and we (plan) lots of activities. First there (be) games for students, parents and teachers. After that we (sell) cakes. In the afternoon the students in Year 7 (do) some really cool tricks. And then it (be) the turn of the students in Year 8. They (create) a comedy show. The girls (want) to look funny so they (paint) their faces and (wear) some funny costumes too. In the evening the school band (sing) in the park – lots of people (come) to listen. Michael (be) the real star of their show. He (do) some cool moves!
> We (raise) 400 euros in just one day!
> Write soon.
> Pia

G2 How did they know?

Fragen in der einfachen Form der Vergangenheit
Questions in the simple past

Seiten 13–15

Policeman:	**Where were** you last Saturday evening?
Man:	Last Saturday evening? Let me think … Oh yes. On Saturday evening I was at the cinema.
Policeman:	**What** time **did** the film **finish**?
Man:	At about 10 p.m.
Policeman:	**Did** you **go** home right away?
Man:	Well, … **no, I didn't**. I walked along Trafalgar Road before I went home.
Policeman:	Um, … Trafalgar Road?

Bei Fragen unterscheidest du zwischen Entscheidungsfragen und Ergänzungsfragen.
Entscheidungsfragen *beantwortest du im Deutschen mit „ja" oder „nein". **Ergänzungsfragen** enthalten ein Fragewort* (what, who, where, when, why, how).

○ *Du kennst schon die Fragebildung im* simple present:

(Fragewort)	do / does	Subjekt	Vollverb	restlicher Satz	Antwort
	Do	**you**	**go**	shopping at the market?	– Yes, I **do**.
When	**do**	**you**	**go**	shopping at the market?	– I usually go there in the mornings.
	Does	**Olivia**	**go**	shopping on Sundays?	– No, she **doesn't**.
Why	**does**	**Olivia**	**go**	shopping on Saturdays?	– Because she's got time then.

○ *Im* **simple past** *hat das Hilfsverb* do *nur eine Form, nämlich* **did**. *Nach dem Subjekt folgt die* **Grundform des Vollverbs**, *weil das Hilfsverb bereits die Vergangenheit ausdrückt.*

(Fragewort)	did	Subjekt	Vollverb	restlicher Satz	Antwort
	Did	the police	**arrest**	the man?	– Yes, they **did**.
	Did	the man	**take**	any money?	– No, he **didn't**.
What	**did**	he	**take**	from the shop?	– He took some T-shirts, sports shoes and a bike.

○ *Enthält die Frage eine Form von* be, *verwendest du im* simple past *bei* I / he / she / it **was** *und bei* we / you / they **were**.

(Fragewort)	was / were	Subjekt	restlicher Satz	Antwort
	Was	the man	in Trafalgar Road last Saturday?	– Yes, he **was**.
	Were	there	any photos of him in Trafalgar Road?	– No, there **weren't**.
Where	**were**	you	yesterday evening?	– I was at the cinema.
Who	**was**		with you?	– My friend was with me.

❗ *Wenn* who *oder* what *Subjekt des Fragesatzes sind, darfst du das Hilfsverb* did *nicht verwenden. Die Fragebildung funktioniert dann genauso wie im Deutschen:*

Who phoned the police?   – *Wer rief die Polizei an?*
What happened on 4th September?   – *Was geschah am 4. September?*

> *Du brauchst ein „not' in deiner Frage? Kein Problem! Es schließt sich direkt an das Hilfsverb bzw. die Form von* be *an:* Why did**n't** you go home after the film?, Why were**n't** you at home?

Test yourself *Work in pairs. After somebody broke into a sports shop in Trafalgar Road, the police got a tip from an anonymous caller. Write down four questions that the police asked the caller. Then give them to your partner to answer.* **Example:**

Policeman: What did the man look like?
Caller: He had brown hair and big ears.

G3 The police didn't know what the man looked like.
Seiten 13–15

Aussagesätze in der einfachen Form der Vergangenheit verneinen
Negating statements in the simple past

Yesterday evening a man broke into a sports shop in Trafalgar Road. He came in through the door, so he **didn't break** any shop windows. He took ten pairs of expensive sports shoes, some T-shirts and a bike. He **didn't take** any money or computers. Luckily, there **weren't** any people in the shop.

Mit didn't, wasn't / weren't *kannst du sagen, dass jemand etwas nicht gemacht hat oder etwas nicht geschehen ist.*

○ *Aussagesätze im* simple present *kennst du schon. Du verneinst sie, indem du ein Hilfsverb einsetzt und es verneinst:*
I / You / We / They   **don't** like dogs.
He / She / It   **doesn't** like dogs.

○ *Im* **simple past** *hat das verneinte Hilfsverb do nur eine Form, nämlich* **didn't**. *Danach folgt die* **Grundform des Vollverbs**, *weil das Hilfsverb bereits die Vergangenheit ausdrückt.*

➕	➖
The man **took** a bike.	The man **didn't take** any money.
The shoes **looked** nice.	The shoes **didn't look** cheap.
He **did** judo on Friday.	He **didn't do** any other sport.

○ *Ist im Satz eine Form von* be *vorhanden, verwendest du bei* I / he / she / it **wasn't** *und bei* we / you / they **weren't**.

➕	➖
The man **was** young.	The man **wasn't** old.
There **were** people in the street.	There **weren't** any people in the shop.

○ *Sätze mit modalen Hilfsverben (*can, can't, must, mustn't, needn't*) kannst du noch nicht in der Vergangenheit verwenden. Das lernst du erst in* **Unit 5 / G15**.

Test yourself *Complete the article. Use the verbs in the simple past.*

8th September

Man arrested
Greenwich. On 4th September a young man (break into) a sports shop in Trafalgar Road. Yesterday the police (arrest) him. They (not know) what he (look) like at first. But then they (get) an anonymous phone call. The caller (not give) them much information, but she (give) them an address in Greenwich. When the police (get to) the house, two women (be) there but the man (not be). So they (wait) till he (come) home and then they (arrest) him – he (not try) to run away. The police (find) the sports shoes and the T-shirts in the loft, but they (not find) the bike.

G4 An adventure course helps students to be more confident.   Seiten 16–17
Steigerung der Adjektive
Comparison of adjectives

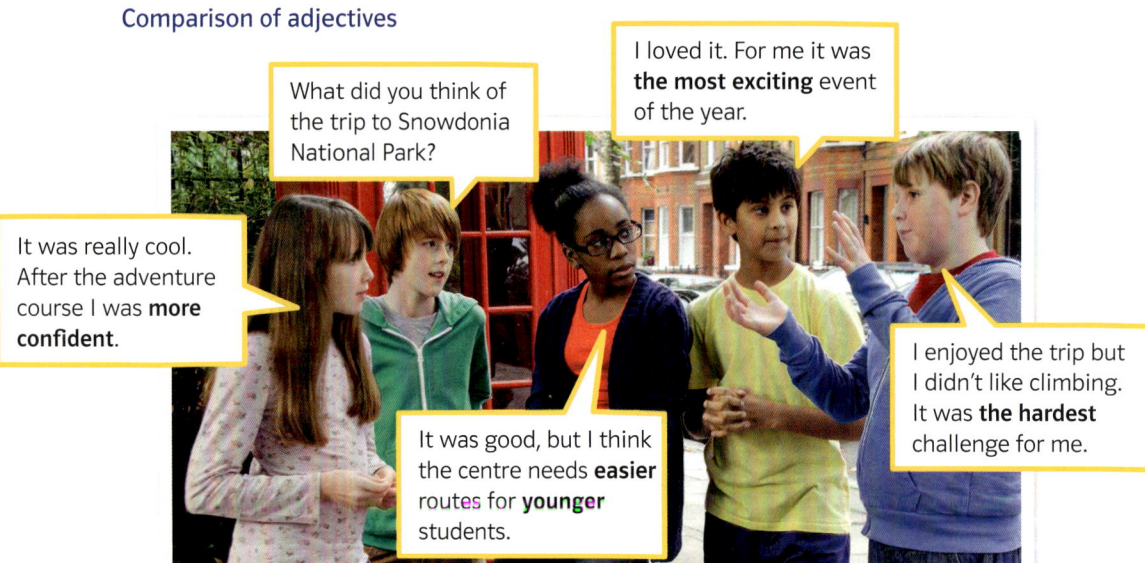

What did you think of the trip to Snowdonia National Park?

I loved it. For me it was **the most exciting** event of the year.

It was really cool. After the adventure course I was **more confident**.

It was good, but I think the centre needs **easier** routes for **younger** students.

I enjoyed the trip but I didn't like climbing. It was **the hardest** challenge for me.

> *Du verwendest Adjektive und ihre Steigerungsformen, um Lebewesen und Sachen näher zu beschreiben und um sie miteinander zu vergleichen.*

○ *Es gibt zwei Möglichkeiten Adjektive zu steigern. Welche du benötigst, hängt von der Anzahl der Silben ab, die die Grundform des Adjektivs (Positiv) hat.*

○ *Einsilbige Adjektive und zweisilbige Adjektive, die auf -y enden, steigerst du, indem du -er (1. Steigerung / Komparativ) bzw. -est (2. Steigerung / Superlativ) an die Grundform des Adjektivs anhängst.*

○ Fast alle anderen **zweisilbigen Adjektive** sowie **alle Adjektive mit mehr als zwei Silben** steigerst du, indem du **more** (*1. Steigerung / Komparativ*) bzw. **most** (*2. Steigerung / Superlativ*) **vor** die **Grundform** des Adjektivs setzt.

Grundform	1. Steigerung	2. Steigerung	Besonderheiten
einsilbige Adjektive			
hard	hard**er**	the hard**est**	–
big	bi**gg**er	the bi**gg**est	*Endkonsonant wird nach kurzem Vokal verdoppelt*
nic**e**	nic**er**	the nic**est**	*stummes -e am Ende des Adjektivs fällt weg*
zweisilbige Adjektive auf -y			
eas**y**	eas**ier**	the eas**iest**	*y wird zu i, wenn das Adjektiv auf Konsonant + -y endet (außer:* shy*)*
funn**y**	funn**ier**	the funn**iest**	
andere zweisilbige Adjektive sowie mehrsilbige Adjektive			
awful	**more** awful	the **most** awful	–
interesting	**more** interesting	the **most** interesting	–

(linke Randspalte oben: *Endungen -er, -est*; linke Randspalte unten: *more, most*)

❗ Beachte, dass **zweisilbige Adjektive**, die **auf -le, -ow oder -er** enden, mit -er / -est gesteigert werden:
simp**le** *(einfach)* – simp**er** – the simp**est**   (*e am Ende des Adjektivs fällt weg*)
narr**ow** *(eng, schmal)* – narro**er** – the narro**est**
clev**er** *(klug, schlau)* – cleve**er** – the cleve**est**

❗ Einige wenige Adjektive werden unregelmäßig gesteigert. Diese musst du auswendig lernen:
bad – worse – the worst
good – better – the best

Test yourself **a)** *Copy the grid into your exercise book and fill it in.*

Grundform	1. Steigerung	2. Steigerung
big		
		the worst
	happier	
important		

b) *Write sentences and describe the pictures.*

tall

expensive

Luke is tall.
Holly is … .
But Olivia is the … of the three.

The red car is … .
The blue … .
But … .

busy road

good idea

Hook Lane is … .
King's Street is … .
But London Road … .

Luke has got a … .
Holly's idea is … .
But Dave has got … .

G5 Outdoor activities are as important as lessons in the classroom. Seiten 16–17

Gleich oder verschieden: Vergleiche mit Adjektiven
The same or different: Making comparisons with adjectives

DID YOU KNOW …?

1. Wales is part of the UK. It is**n't as big as** England or Scotland, but it's **bigger than** Northern Ireland.
2. Mount Snowdon (1,085 m) is the highest mountain in Wales. But it is**n't higher than** Ben Nevis (1,343 m) in Scotland.
3. The River Severn (362 km) is the longest river in the UK. It is **as long as** the River Neckar in Germany.

Vergleiche mit Adjektiven benutzt du, um Lebewesen oder Sachen miteinander zu vergleichen.

○ *Wenn die Lebewesen oder Sachen in Bezug auf eine Eigenschaft* gleich *sind, benutzt du* **as +** *Grundform* **+ as***:*
The River Severn is **as long as** the River Neckar.   *… genauso/so lang wie …*

○ *Wenn die Lebewesen oder Sachen in Bezug auf eine Eigenschaft* **verschieden** *sind, benutzt du entweder* **not as** + *Grundform* + **as** *oder* **1.** *Steigerung* + **than**:

Wales is**n't as big as** England.   *… nicht so groß wie …*
Wales is **bigger than** Northern Ireland.   *… größer als …*
Is climbing **more dangerous than** gorge scrambling? *… gefährlicher als …*

❗ *Verwechsle nicht* **than** *(als) und* **then** *(dann)!*

Test yourself *Write sentences and compare the rivers, cities, mountains and regions.*

big   small   short   high   long

Rhine: 1,233 km
Spree: 400 km
Oder: 854 km

Düsseldorf: 590,000
Stuttgart: 590,000
Cologne: 1 million

Brocken: 1,141 m
Feldberg: 1,493 m
Großer Arber: 1,455 m

the Saarland: 2,570 km²
Hesse: 21,100 km²
Saxony: 18,415 km²

Unit 2

G6 **The queen who loved parties**   Seiten 30–31
Notwendige Relativsätze
Defining relative clauses

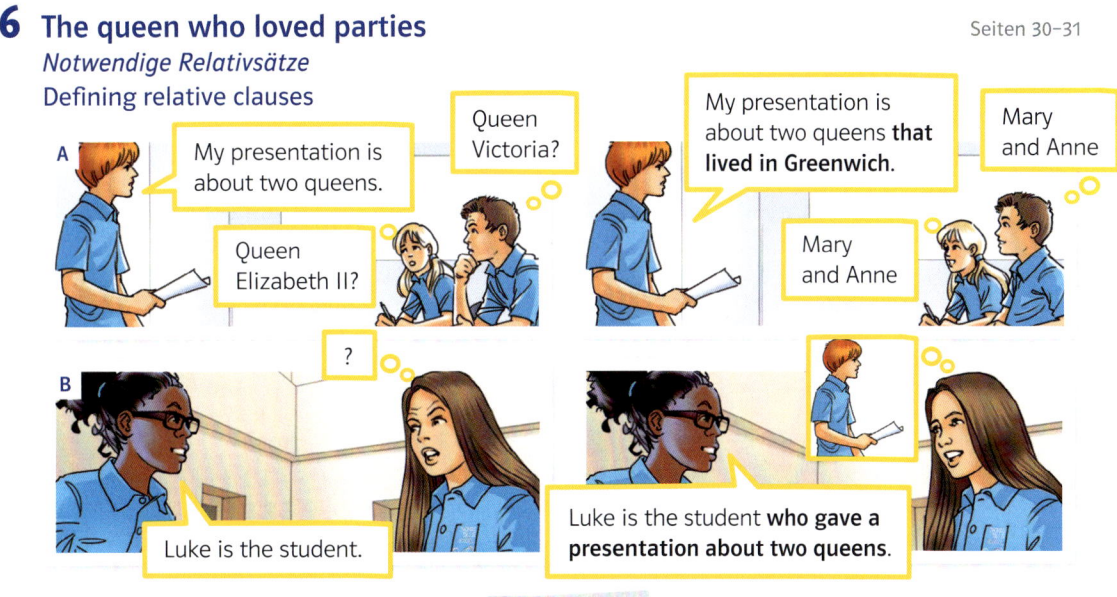

Relativsätze sind Nebensätze, die ein Nomen (Bezugswort) näher beschreiben oder definieren. Notwendige Relativsätze werden deshalb so genannt, well der Hauptsatz ohne die im Relativsatz enthaltene Information nicht eindeutig (A) oder nicht verständlich wäre (B):

○ *Relativsätze leitest du durch ein* **Relativpronomen** *ein. Du verwendest …*

who *für Personen*

which *für Sachen*

that *für Personen oder Sachen*

○ *Das Relativpronomen* **whose** *(dt. deren, dessen) benutzt du, um Besitz oder Zugehörigkeit auszudrücken.*

○ *Das* **Relativpronomen** *steht meist direkt nach dem* **Bezugswort** *und leitet den Relativsatz ein. Danach folgt die* **notwendige Information** *.*

My presentation is about **two queens** . They **lived in Greenwich** .
My presentation is about **two queens** who / that **lived in Greenwich** .
In meinem Vortrag geht es um zwei Königinnen, die in Greenwich lebten.

❗ *Im Gegensatz zum Deutschen trennst du solche notwendigen Relativsätze nicht durch Kommas vom Hauptsatz ab.*

○ *Relativpronomen können Subjekt oder Objekt des notwendigen Relativsatzes sein:*

a) **Relativpronomen als Subjekt**

○ *Die Relativpronomen* **who**, **which** *und* **that** *darfst du* **nie weglassen**, *wenn sie Subjekt im Relativsatz sind.*

Hauptsätze	Hauptsatz + Relativsatz
Anne was **a queen** . She loved parties.	Anne was **a queen** who / that loved parties.
Do you know **the big building** ? It's across the river.	Do you know **the big building** which / that is across the river?
That's the **woman** . Her husband gave her a house for parties.	That's the **woman** whose husband gave her a house for parties.

b) **Relativpronomen als Objekt**

○ *Die Relativpronomen* **who**, **which** *und* **that** *kannst du* **weglassen**, **wenn** *sie* **Objekt** *im Relativsatz sind. Das erkennst du am* **neuen Subjekt** *nach dem Relativpronomen. Solche Relativsätze nennt man* contact clauses, *weil sie ohne Relativpronomen in direktem Kontakt zum Hauptsatz stehen.*

Hauptsätze	Hauptsatz + Relativsatz
Christopher Wren was **an architect** . We talked about him in Art.	Christopher Wren was **an architect** (who / that) **we** talked about in Art.
The hospital was near the river. Wren built it.	**The hospital** (which / that) **Wren** built was near the river.
The architect was Christopher Wren. Mary chose his design.	**The architect** whose design **Mary** chose was Christopher Wren.

Test yourself a) *Complete the dialogues. Use the correct relative pronoun.*

1. Dave: Have you got any music … people listened to at Anne's parties? You can use it in your presentation.
   Luke: Yes, I have. But I'm not sure. I don't like the songs … they played in the 17th century.
   Dave: Well, don't worry about that. Luke, what's that under the table?
   Luke: Oh, thanks, Dave. This is the photo of the Queen's House … I'm looking for.

2. Jay: Who was Christopher Wren?
   Olivia: He was the famous architect … designs you can see in London.
   Jay: Really?
   Olivia: Yes, he was the man … designed the Royal Naval College, the Royal Observatory, St Paul's Cathedral and many other buildings.
   Jay: Cool! Those are all buildings … I know.

b) *Which of the sentences in a) can you use without the relative pronoun?*

G7 What were they doing when Sally fell into the pond?

Seiten 33–34

Die Verlaufsform der Vergangenheit
The past progressive

Look! That's Jack. He **was making** a bee hotel when he hit his thumb.

And do you remember Kate and Filip? They hit a water pipe while they **were digging** a hole.

Das **past progressive** ist eine Zeitform der Vergangenheit. Damit beschreibst du nicht das Ergebnis einer Handlung (→ G1), sondern den **Verlauf einer Handlung zu einem bestimmten Zeitpunkt in der Vergangenheit**. Du kennst auch schon das present progressive, mit dem du ausdrückst, dass eine Handlung jetzt gerade im Verlauf ist.

○ *Mit dem* past progressive *kannst du drei verschiedene Situationen beschreiben:*

a) *Die Handlung befand sich zu einem bestimmten Zeitpunkt in der Vergangenheit noch im Verlauf, sie war also noch nicht abgeschlossen:*

9:30 → 10:30	At 10 o'clock yesterday Kate and Filip **were digging** a hole.
	Gestern um 10 Uhr hoben Kate und Filip gerade ein Loch aus.

b) *Eine Handlung befand sich noch im Verlauf, als eine neue Handlung oder ein neues Ereignis einsetzte. Diese(s) steht im* **simple past**:

simple past ↓	Jack **was making** a bee hotel when he **hit** his thumb.
past progressive →	*Jack baute gerade ein Bienenhaus, als er sich auf den Daumen schlug.*

c) *Zwei Handlungen befanden sich gleichzeitig im Verlauf:*

～～～→	While the girls **were taking** photos, Filip and Kate **were digging** a hole.
～～～→	*Während die Mädchen gerade Fotos machten, hoben Filip und Kate ein Loch aus.*

○ *Du bildest das* past progressive *aus der Vergangenheitsform von* **be (was/were)** *und dem* **present participle** *(= Verb + -ing).*

Aussage:	Henry **was putting up** a sign when he fell off his ladder.
Verneinung:	Kate and Filip **weren't taking** photos.
Ergänzungsfrage:	What **was** Jack **doing** when he hit his thumb?
Entscheidungsfrage mit Kurzantwort:	**Was** Jack **making** a bee hotel when he hit his thumb? – Yes, he **was**. / No, he **wasn't**.

❗ *Das* past progressive *gibt es im Deutschen nicht. Du kannst es mit „gerade dabei sein, etwas zu tun" wiedergeben. Sieh dir dazu die Übersetzungen in a) – c) noch einmal an.*

Test yourself *What were the students doing at 4 p.m. yesterday? Work in pairs and make dialogues. Use the past progressive.*

Jay – Dance class

Luke – Football Club

Holly – Sign Language Club

Olivia – Netball Club

A: Was Luke playing basketball at 4 o'clock yesterday?
B: No, he wasn't. He was playing football with his friends.

Unit 3

G8 **It's going to be fun.**

Seiten 52–53

Das Futur mit going to
The going-to future

What **are** you **going to do** tomorrow? **Are** you **going to see** more sights in Greenwich?

No, we aren't. We**'re going to visit** the British Museum with Olivia and Holly.

Mit dem going-to future *drückst du feststehende Pläne und Absichten für die nahe Zukunft aus. Du verwendest es auch, wenn es bereits jetzt deutliche Anzeichen dafür gibt, wie die Zukunft werden wird:* A visit to London **is going to be** fun.

○ *Das* going-to future *bildest du aus einer* **Form von be (am/is/are) + going to + Grundform des Verbs**:

Aussage:	The boys **are going to visit** the British Museum with Olivia and Holly.
Verneinung:	Jay **isn't going to go** alone.
Ergänzungsfrage:	What **are** you **going to do** tomorrow, Amir?
Entscheidungsfrage mit Kurzantwort:	**Are** you **going to see** more sights in Greenwich? – Yes, I **am**. / No, I**'m not**.

❗ *Um etwas Zukünftiges auszudrücken, kannst du im Deutschen neben dem Futur oft auch das Präsens verwenden. Im Englischen geht das nicht. Vergleiche:*
We**'re going to visit** London next week.
Wir **werden** *nächste Woche London* **besuchen**.
Wir **besuchen** *nächste Woche London.*

Wörter wie tomorrow *und* next week *können dir den Gebrauch des* going-to future *anzeigen.*

Test yourself *What are/aren't the people going to do tomorrow? Look at the pictures and write sentences.*

Jay

Amir

Olivia and Holly

Shahid

Mrs Azad

Mr Azad

G9 It's something important.
Zusammensetzungen mit some, any, every *und* no
The compounds of *some, any, every* and *no*

Seiten 54–55

> Listen, **everybody**. What can we do for lunch? Are there any cafés **anywhere** near here?

> Follow me, there's a great place **somewhere** around the corner here.

Mit den Zusammensetzungen von some, any, every *und* no *kannst du allgemein über Dinge, Menschen und Orte sprechen.*

○ *Das kennst du schon:*
Some *benutzt du in positiven Aussagen:* Jay has got **some** money.
oder in höflichen Bitten, Angeboten oder Vorschlägen, wenn du eine positive Antwort erwartest: Can you give me **some** money, please? – Yes, sure.

Any *benutzt du in Fragen und zur Verneinung:*
Are there **any** cheap cafés near here? – No, there are**n't any** cheap cafés near here.

○ *Für* some *und* any *gibt es Zusammen-setzungen mit* -body/-one *("jemand"),* -thing *("etwas") und* -where *("irgendwo").* *Du verwendest sie auf die gleiche Weise wie* some *und* any.

> Somebody *und* someone *bzw.* anybody *und* anyone *sind bedeutungsgleich.*

Zusammensetzungen mit **some**	
somebody / someone:	I can't see the show – **someone** tall is standing in front of me.
something:	I'm hungry. I need **something** to eat.
somewhere:	I know a good café. It's **somewhere** near Covent Garden.
Zusammensetzungen mit **any**	
anybody / anyone:	Did you ask **anyone**?
anything:	He hasn't got **anything**!
anywhere:	Are there any cheap cafés **anywhere**?

○ *Auch von* no *und* every *gibt es Zusammensetzungen mit* -body/-one, -thing *und* -where. *Sie drücken jeweils das Gegenteil aus:*

Zusammensetzungen mit **every**	⟷	Zusammensetzungen mit **no**
Everybody likes London.		Olivia bets **nobody** can beat her.
jeder, alle		*niemand, keiner*
Everything is OK.		The British Museum costs **nothing**.
alles		*nichts*
There are people **everywhere**.		There's **nowhere** to sit.
überall		*nirgends, nirgendwo*

❗ *Beachte den Unterschied zwischen* everybody/-one *und* anybody/-one:
Everybody in my class likes London. (ausnahmslos) Jeder …
Anybody can visit Tate Britain. It's free. Jeder (x-beliebige) …
Mit anybody/-one *ist keine bestimmte Person gemeint, sondern jeder x-beliebige. In dieser Bedeutung kann es auch in positiven Aussagesätzen und* if-*Sätzen verwendet werden.*

> Nobody *und* no one *sind bedeutungsgleich. Beachte aber, dass* no one *nicht zusammengeschrieben wird.*

❗ Everybody/-one *und* anybody/-one *sind Singularformen. Die dazugehörigen Pronomen und Possessivbegleiter stehen aber meist im Plural:*
Everybody pays for **their** own Oyster card.
Anybody at the Tube station can tell you where you can buy an Oyster card if you ask **them**.

Test yourself   *Complete the dialogue.*

> Amir: Listen, (*alle*). I want to buy a little present for my aunt to say 'thank you'. Is there a good shop (*irgendwo*)?
>
> Olivia: What are you thinking of?
>
> Amir: Well, it must be (*etwas*) special, but it mustn't be (*nichts*) expensive.
>
> Jay: (*Alles*) is expensive in London!
>
> Holly: That's not true! I know a good shop where (*nichts*) costs more than £10.
>
> Amir: OK. Let's go there and see if we can find (*etwas*) for her.

G10   Now we're going slowly past the Tower of London.

Seiten 56–57

Adverbien der Art und Weise
Adverbs of manner

> Welcome to the Tower of London!
> Many people come here **specially** to see the Crown Jewels. You too, I guess. But let me tell you about the ravens first. Look, there's the Raven Master! His job is to look after the ravens **carefully**.

> *Mit Adverbien bestimmst du ein Verb näher.*
> *Du beschreibst also, wie etwas getan wird.*
> *Zur Erinnerung: Mit Adjektiven beschreibst du ein Nomen näher.*

- *Die meisten Adverbien bildest du aus dem **Adjektiv** und der Endung **-ly** oder **-ally**.*
Adverbien stehen in der Regel am Satzende, jedoch vor einer Orts- und Zeitangabe.

Adjektiv + -ly:	The bus is going **slowly** past the Tower of London. You can see the Tower of London **clearly** on the left.
Adjektiv auf -ic + -ally:	The Beefeaters explain the history of the Tower **fantastically**. "Help!" shouted the little boy **dramatically** when the ravens came near.

❗ *Beachte folgende Rechtschreibregeln:*

a) *Endet das Adjektiv auf -y, wird y zu i:* angry → angrily, happy → happily;
    außer: shy → shyly.

b) *Endet das Adjektiv auf -le, fällt e weg:* comfortable → comfortably, terrible → terribly

❗ *Merke dir folgende Ausnahmen:*

good → well	The guide gave us some tips about where to eat **well**.
fast → fast	The Tube takes you very **fast** through London.
hard → hard	Ravens can bite very **hard**.

❗ *Wenn **feel** oder eine **Form von be** das einzige Verb im Satz ist, benutzt du kein Adverb, sondern ein **Adjektiv**, z.B.:* The guide is **nice**.

Test yourself *Read the tips and complete the sentences. Do you need an adjective or an adverb?*

Tips for London visitors

1. Buy an Oyster card and travel by public transport (cheap) and (comfortable).
2. Stand on Westminster Bridge and take (fantastic) photos of Big Ben.
3. On a (nice) day, take a picnic with you and have lunch in one of London's (great) parks.
4. Go to the British Museum and learn about money, animals and ships. It's (free)!
5. Visit Madame Tussauds. The museum shows famous people very (realistic).
6. If you're in London for a day or two only, take a sightseeing bus. Most guides know London and its history (good).

G11 You can see London faster and more easily with a guide.

Seiten 56–57

Steigerung der Adverbien

The comparison of adverbs

EXPLORE LONDON BY BUS

Only £16

Buy a ticket for one of our sightseeing buses and you can see London **faster** and **more easily** than if you explore alone. Our guides know London's history **better** than anyone.

Mit den Steigerungsformen der Adverbien kannst du Vorgänge vergleichen.

- ***Einsilbige Adverbien** steigerst du auf **-er** (1. Steigerung / Komparativ) bzw. **-est** (2. Steigerung / Superlativ).*
- *Alle **Adverbien**, die **auf -ly** enden **oder mehrsilbig** sind, steigerst du mit **more** (1. Steigerung / Komparativ) bzw. **most** (2. Steigerung / Superlativ).*

	Grundform	1. Steigerung	2. Steigerung
	einsilbige Adverbien		
Endungen -er, -est	(run) fast	fast**er**	fast**est**
	(try) hard	hard**er**	hard**est**
	(jump) high	high**er**	high**est**
	(go) near	near**er**	near**est**
	Adverbien auf -ly sowie mehrsilbige Adverbien		
more, most	(finish) easily	**more** easily	**most** easily
	(do) quickly	**more** quickly	**most** quickly
	(talk) interestingly	**more** interestingly	**most** interestingly
	(sit) comfortably	**more** comfortably	**most** comfortably

❗ *Beachte, dass die Formen von* **early earlier** *und* **earliest** *lauten, obwohl* early *auf* -ly *endet.*

❗ *Merke dir folgende Ausnahmen:*

badly – worse – worst   well – better – best
much – more – most   little – less – least

Test yourself *Look at the table and make comparisons.*

Example: A lion runs **faster** than a bear. A horse runs **fastest**.

animal	run fast	eat little	sleep long	weigh much
horse	70 km/h	6 kg	4 h	400 kg
bear	50 km/h	40 kg	6 h (in summer)	380 kg
lion	60 km/h	10 kg	13 h	180 kg
pig	45 km/h	1,5 kg	13 h	100 kg
cat	45 km/h	250 g	15 h	4 kg

Unit 4

G12 **Have you ever run in a marathon?**   Seiten 70–75
Die einfache Form des Perfekts
The present perfect simple

Have you ever **seen** the London Marathon?

Of course, I **have**. It starts right here in Greenwich Park.

Mit dem present perfect simple verbindest du die Vergangenheit mit der Gegenwart.

○ *Mit dem* present perfect simple *kannst du verschiedene Situationen beschreiben:*

a) *Mit* Have you ever … *fragst du, ob jemand etwas schon ein- oder mehrmals gemacht hat.*

Have you ever …?	**Has** Jay **ever run** in a marathon? – No, he **hasn't**. He **has never run** one mile.
In den Antworten auf die Frage findest du oft eines dieser Signalwörter: never, before, only ever, … times.	**Have** Dave and Holly **ever run** in big races? – No, Dave **hasn't run** in big races **before**. And Holly **has only ever run** in short races.
	Have the Elliots **ever watched** the London Marathon? – Yes, they **have**. They**'ve watched** it **three times**.

b) *Mit dem* present perfect simple *kannst du sagen, dass eine Handlung bereits, gerade erst oder noch nicht abgeschlossen wurde:*

already *(schon, bereits)*	Olivia **has already prepared** for the trials.
just *(gerade erst, eben)*	Gwen **has just had** an idea.
not yet *(noch nicht)*	The girls **haven't left** for school **yet**.

Die Signalwörter never, only, ever, already und just stehen direkt nach dem Hilfsverb.

c) *Außerdem kannst du ausdrücken, dass eine Handlung irgendwann in der Vergangenheit stattfand und das Ergebnis dieser Handlung bis in die Gegenwart spürbar bzw. sichtbar ist:*

I**'ve hurt** my foot. It hurts when I walk.
Olivia **has bought** new running shoes. They're still clean.

○ *Du bildest das* present perfect simple *aus einer Form von* have (have/has) *und dem* past participle.

Das past participle *von regelmäßigen Verben entspricht ihrer Form im* simple past *(→G1). Die Formen von unregelmäßigen Verben musst du lernen. Du findest sie in der 3. Spalte auf den Seiten 284–285.*

Aussage:	I**'ve run** in races before, but not in a big race like a marathon.
Verneinung:	Jay **hasn't run** one mile.
Ergänzungsfrage:	Who **has heard** of the mini marathon?
Entscheidungsfrage mit Kurzantwort:	**Has** Dave ever **run** in race? – Yes, he **has**. / No, he **hasn't**.

🔴 *Beachte die Unterschiede zum Deutschen:*
a) *Das* present perfect simple *bildest du immer mit* have / has + past participle. *Vergleiche:*
I**'ve hurt** my foot. = Ich **habe** mir den Fuß **verletzt.**
I **haven't left** yet. = Ich **bin** noch nicht **losgegangen**.

b) *Auch in Sätzen, die das* present perfect simple *beinhalten, gilt im Englischen die Regel*
S – V – O. *Das* **Objekt** *steht also nach der Verbform.*
Olivia **has hurt** **her foot** .
Olivia **hat** sich **den Fuß** **verletzt**.

🔴 *Anders als im Deutschen sind das* simple past (→G1) *und das* present perfect simple *nicht beliebig austauschbar, um Handlungen oder Ereignisse in der Vergangenheit zu beschreiben. Das* **present perfect simple** *verwendest du, um zu sagen, dass etwas stattgefunden hat. Wenn du genau berichtest, wann und unter welchen Umständen etwas stattgefunden hat, verwendest du das* **simple past**.

I**'ve** already **run** in a marathon.

past	present	future

My dad **ran** in a marathon when he was 20.

Test yourself **a)** *You and your classmates are talking about Sports Day. Make questions and write them in your exercise book.*

Have you …	(prepare) (buy) already (start) ever (hurt) (find)	eating healthy food? a name for your team yet? your foot while you were playing sports? for Sports Day yet? new sports shoes yet?

b) *Work in small groups. Ask and answer the questions from a).*

Example:
Sabrina: Have you prepared for Sports Day yet?
Martin: Yes, I have. I've already run around the park three times.
Ella: Yes, I have. I went jogging yesterday.

Unit 5

G13 I'm writing to you because I need your advice.

Seiten 92–93

Nebensätze der Zeit, des Grundes und des Vergleichs
Subordinate clauses of time, reason and comparison

Do you often buy *TeenLife*?

Well, Claire buys it for me **when** she goes shopping. I like it **because** there are interesting texts and great posters in it.

Du kannst Nebensätze verwenden, wenn du deiner Hauptaussage zusätzliche Informationen hinzufügen möchtest. Mit den aus Haupt- und Nebensatz entstehenden Satzgefügen stellst du logische Verbindungen her. Sie sind stilistisch eleganter als hintereinander gereihte Hauptsätze.

a) *Nebensätze der Zeit (= Temporalsätze):*

after *(nachdem)*	**After** I spoke to my friend, I felt much better.
as soon as *(sobald)*	Things often get better **as soon as** you talk to somebody about it.
before *(bevor, ehe, vor)*	**Before** they had an argument, Lauren spent a lot of her free time with her friend.
until *(bis)*	Never give your address **until** you've really met your new friend face-to-face.
when *(wenn)*	Ask your parents, older sister or brother **when** you need advice.
whenever *(jedes Mal, wenn)*	**Whenever** you want to put photos of other people online, ask them first.

b) *Nebensätze des Grundes (= Kausalsätze):*

because *(weil)*	Lauren wrote to an agony aunt **because** she had a problem.

c) *Nebensätze des Vergleichs (= Komparativsätze):*

like *(als ob)*	My friend acts **like** she's having a much better time without me.

❗ *Beachte, dass die Satzstellung im Deutschen anders ist als im Englischen. Im Englischen bleibt die Reihenfolge* **Subjekt** – **Verbform** – **Objekt** *sowohl im Haupt- als auch Nebensatz immer erhalten. Vergleiche:*
After **I** **spoke** to my friend, **I** **felt** much better.
Nachdem **ich** mit meinem Freund **gesprochen hatte** , **fühlte** **ich** mich besser.

❗ *Wenn du dir die Beispiele in a) – c) einmal genauer anschaust, wirst du feststellen, dass Nebensätze sowohl nach dem Hauptsatz als auch vor dem Hauptsatz stehen können. Steht der* **Hauptsatz vor** *dem* **Nebensatz** *, setzt du* **kein Komma** *, weil die Konjunktion die Sätze trennt. Steht der* **Nebensatz vor** *dem* **Hauptsatz** *, trennst du beide durch* **ein Komma** *.*

Test yourself   *Read the posts of some* TeenLife *readers. Complete the sentences with the correct linking word. Add commas where you need them.*

Joe: I like your magazine … it's always got interesting news on my favourite stars in it.
Ginny: I buy *TeenLife* … I get my pocket money from my parents. I love it!
Michael: The concert photos are fantastic. When I look at them it's … I'm there.
Lisa: … I read Ruby's advice I think she really understands our problems.
Sheila: … I tried the make-up which came with the magazine last week I'm not going to buy *TeenLife* again! It looked awful on my face.

G14   You watched the match last night, didn't you?   Seite 92, 94
Bestätigungsfragen
Question tags

You're having a hard time, **aren't you**?

Yes, I'm feeling very upset. Arsenal lost their match at the weekend.

Bestätigungsfragen sind kurze Fragen am Ende eines Aussagesatzes. Sie entsprechen dem deutschen „nicht wahr?", „oder?" bzw. „stimmt's?" und kommen häufig im mündlichen Sprachgebrauch vor.

○ *Du bildest Bestätigungsfragen, indem du das* **Hilfsverb** *des Hauptsatzes* **mit anderer Polung** *wiederholst – bejahte Hauptsätze verneinst du; verneinte Hauptsätze bejahst du.*

present progressive	You're having a hard time, aren't you?
past progressive	Many players were playing badly, weren't they?
present perfect simple	You've never seen a match live in the stadium before, have you?
going-to future	Jay isn't going to watch a match live, is he?

o *Wenn ein **Name das Subjekt im Hauptsatz** ist, benutzt du **in der Bestätigungsfrage** immer das passende **Personalpronomen**, z.B.: **Jay** isn't going to watch a match live, is **he**?*

o *Enthält der Hauptsatz eine **Form von** be **oder** can, so steht diese ebenso in der Bestätigungsfrage.*

| *Form von* be | Luke is an Arsenal fan, isn't he? |
| *Modalverb* can | Jay is good at dancing, but he can't play football well, can he? |

❗ *Beachte den folgenden Unterschied beim Verb* be *in der 1. Person Singular:*
Luke: I'm late for football practice, aren't I?

o *Steht im Hauptsatz kein Hilfsverb, sondern nur ein **Vollverb** (knows, talked, …), verwendest du eine **Form von** do. Die Zeitform richtet sich nach dem Hauptsatz.*

| simple present | Luke knows a lot about football, doesn't he? |
| simple past | We talked about this in PE, didn't we? |

❗ *Denke daran, die Bestätigungsfrage durch Komma vom Hauptsatz abzutrennen! Steigt die Intonation in der Bestätigungsfrage, handelt es sich um eine echte Frage. Fällt die Intonation, kennt der Sprecher bereits die Antwort.*

❗ *Ist* have *die einzige Verbform im Hauptsatz, handelt es sich um ein Vollverb und muss in der Bestätigungsfrage durch* do *ersetzt werden. Ist es Teil einer zusammengesetzten Form, ist es ein Hilfsverb und wird in die Bestätigungsfrage übernommen:*

simple present	We often have a little party after the match, don't we?
simple past	The team had a lot of bad luck, didn't they?
present perfect simple	They've just had a bad day, haven't they?

❗ *Apostroph + s kann für* is *oder* has *stehen. Vergleiche:*
Luke's a good football player, isn't he?
Luke's never been more than ten minutes late, has he?

Test yourself *Complete the dialogues. Add the correct question tags. Remember to look at the subject and verb form carefully.*

1. Olivia: Miss Brown played an interesting song in class today, …?
   Holly: Its title was *Life before media technology*, …?
   Jay: Yes, and it's a really cool song, …?
   Holly: Well, yeah. I liked it.

2. Luke: We're going to work on our media project this afternoon, …?
   Dave: Of course. Let's meet in front of the school after lessons and go to my house.
   Luke: Good idea. With Jamie and Irina it's always very noisy at our house, …?
   Dave: That's true! If we concentrate, perhaps we can finish the project today.
   Luke: I'm not sure. We haven't worked on this kind of project before, …? So we don't really know how long it's going to take us, …?
   Dave: That's right. But you've already collected some ideas, …?
   Luke: Well, erm …

G15 I wasn't allowed to go over to Jay's house yesterday.

Seite 95-96

Modalverben und ihre Ersatzformen
Modals and their substitute forms

Luke: Let's look for help on the internet.
Dad: Well when I was young, I **wasn't able to** look everything up on the internet. But I still learned to do things my way.

> *Die Modalverben* can, may, can't, mustn't, must *und* needn't *kannst du nur im* simple present *verwenden. Ihre Ersatzform verwendest du vor allem für alle anderen Zeitformen.*

	Modalverb	Ersatzform im simple present	Ersatzform im simple past
Erlaubnis / Verbot — **be allowed to**	can	Olivia **is allowed to** use her parents' computer when she likes.	She **was allowed to** play a game on it last weekend.
	can't / mustn't	You **aren't allowed to** chat with your friends all day.	In my last school we **weren't allowed to** use computers just for fun.
	may	**Am** I **allowed to** use your tablet, Dad?	**Were** you **allowed to** use your dad's tablet when you were younger?
(Un)Fähigkeit — **be able to**	can	Luke **is able to** help his dad with the washing machine.	He **was able to** find help on the internet.
	can't	Luke and Jamie **aren't able to** swim very fast.	When the boys were four, they **weren't able to** swim.

	Modalverb	Ersatzform im simple present	Ersatzform im simple past
(Keine) Notwendigkeit have to	must	I **have to** show Dad this advice. Mrs Elliot **has to** do the washing.	He **had to** ask somebody for help. She **had to** do the shopping yesterday.
	needn't	You **don't have to** look for the phone number. I've got it. Mr Elliot **doesn't have to** work in the evenings.	We **didn't have to** wait long until the man came to fix the pipe. He **didn't have to** pay for Luke's advice.

Test yourself *Complete Luke's message. Use the substitute forms in the simple past.*

Hi,
Guess what. When I came home from school, there was water everywhere on the kitchen floor.
Something was wrong with the washing machine and Dad (musste) fix it before Mum came home.
Dad had no idea what he was doing … But I (durfte) use his tablet and check for advice in a forum.
I (konnte) find a great website quickly. It was very helpful. All we (mussten) do was turn the knob off.
So we (konnten) solve the problem in 20 minutes and Mum (konnte) use the washing machine when
she came home.
See you at school on Monday.
Luke

G16 You could look at a forum for help.
Die Modalverben should, shouldn't *und* could
The modals *should*, *shouldn't* and *could*

Seite 95-96

Have you got a problem? Well, you **could** look at a forum for help. But you **shouldn't** believe everything you read online.

Mit den Modalverben should, shouldn't *und* could *kannst du jemandem etwas vorschlagen oder raten.*

○ *Die Modalverben* should, shouldn't *und* could *funktionieren wie die Modalverben, die du schon kennst: Du verwendest sie im* simple present, *sie sind in allen Personen gleich und nach ihnen folgt immer ein Vollverb in der Grundform. Vergleiche:*

Mr Elliot **could look** for help on the internet.	*Herr Elliot* **könnte** *im Internet nach Hilfe* **suchen**.
They **should ask** their parents for advice.	*Sie* **sollten** *ihre Eltern um Rat* **fragen**.
You **shouldn't try** to fix everything yourself.	*Du* **solltest nicht versuchen**, *alles selbst zu reparieren.*

Test yourself *What should, could or shouldn't they do? Give advice.*

1. Olivia: In netball I pushed a girl while we were playing. She fell and hurt her hand.
2. Jay: I've ruined Dave's book.
3. Holly: Mr Fluff often explores under my bed. It's difficult to get him out when he needs to go to bed.
4. Dave: Last weekend I pulled out some flowers in Granny's garden. I thought they were weeds[1].

Unit 6

G17 I'll miss you so much!
Das Futur mit will
Will future

Seiten 110–112

> But the house looks fantastic! I'm sure your mum **will be** happy there with all the farm animals to work with.

> I'**ll miss** you so much!

> *Du verwendest das Futur mit* will *für spontane Entscheidungen, Versprechen, Hoffnungen und Vorhersagen, die die Zukunft betreffen.*

Mit dem will future …
a) *drückst du spontane Entscheidungen oder Versprechen aus.*

I'**ll text** you.
Holly and I **will visit** you in Cornwall.

b) *machst du Vorhersagen über zukünftige Ereignisse.*
(Der Sprecher kann diese nicht beeinflussen.)

Gwen:	We'**ll miss** you, Dave.
Assistant:	The trip to St Agnes **will take** about seven hours.

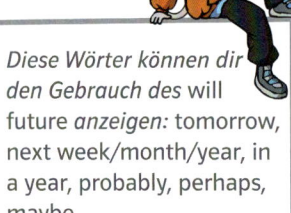

> *Diese Wörter können dir den Gebrauch des* will future *anzeigen:* tomorrow, next week/month/year, in a year, probably, perhaps, maybe.

1 **weeds** [wiːdz] Unkraut

c) *sagst du, was jemand über ein zukünftiges Ereignis denkt, hofft oder vermutet. Diese Sätze beginnen häufig mit* I hope, I think *oder* I'm sure.

Jay:	I think you**'ll make** lots of new friends quickly.
Dave:	I'm sure Sid **will hate** his new home.

○ *Das* will future *bildest du für alle Personen aus dem Hilfsverb* **will (not) + Grundform des Verbs.** *Die Kurzform lautet* 'll *bzw. bei verneinten Sätzen* won't.

Aussage:	Dave hopes that his friends **will visit** him in St Agnes.
Verneinung:	Aunt Frances **won't come** to Cornwall with them.
Ergänzungsfrage:	What do you think Dave's new school **will be** like?
Entscheidungsfrage mit Kurzantwort:	**Will** your dad **find** work there? – Yes, he **will**. / No, he **won't**.

❗ *Um die Zukunftsform der Modalverben zu bilden, brauchst du ihre Ersatzformen (→G15):*

can, can't → (not) be able to:	Dave hopes his friends **will be able to** find enough money to visit him in St Agnes. … *werden in der Lage sein* …
can, can't, may, mustn't → (not) be allowed to:	The friends **won't be allowed to** go to Cornwall without an adult. … *werden nicht* … *dürfen*
must, needn't → (not) have to:	Holly **will have to** ask her mum for money. … *wird* … *müssen*

❗ *Mit dem* going-to *und dem* will future *kennst du zwei Zeitformen der Zukunft. Möchtest du über Zukünftiges sprechen, musst du abwägen:*
Für feststehende **Pläne** *oder* **Absichten** → going-to future (→G8):
The Prestons **are going to move** to Cornwall in summer.
Für **spontane Entscheidungen** → will future:
"I need to put all my things into boxes." – "Don't worry. I**'ll help** you."
Für **Vermutungen, Hoffnungen** *oder* **Vorhersagen** → will future:
I think Dave **will be** OK in Cornwall.

❗ *Verwechsle nicht „Ich will …"* (= I want to …) *und "I will …"* (= Ich werde …).

Test yourself *What do the friends say when Dave isn't with them? Complete the sentences.*

1. Olivia: I hope Dave … his new school. (love)
2. Holly: I'm sure the Prestons … Granny Rose and Aunt Frances in London soon. (visit)
3. Luke: I don't think the new home … a problem for Sid. There are lots of fields and he … . He … new cat friends quickly. He … ! (be / be able to run around / make / not get bored)
4. Gwen: I hope Dave … us. (not forget)

G18 If you look at a map of Great Britain, you'll find Cornwall in the far west.

Seiten 114-115

Bedingungssätze Typ 1
Conditional clauses type 1

> **If** you **like** beaches and fishing harbours, you**'ll find** that Cornwall is just the right place for you.

> Well, you **can** go fishing **if** we **go** to Cornwall. What do you think?

Mit dem Bedingungssatz Typ 1 drückst du aus, was unter einer bestimmten Bedingung passieren wird. Der Sprecher hält die Bedingung für erfüllbar.

○ *Um Vorhersagen zu machen, verwendest du im* if-Satz *das* simple present *und im* **Hauptsatz** *das* **will future**.

if-*Satz* (simple present)	*Hauptsatz* (will future)
If you **look** at a map,	you**'ll see** that Cornwall is on the Atlantic Ocean.
If the friends **visit** Dave in Cornwall,	they **won't get** bored.

○ **Im Hauptsatz** *kann statt des* will future *auch ein* **Modalverb + Grundform des Verbs** *oder der* **Imperativ** *stehen.*

if-*Satz* (simple present)	*Hauptsatz* (*Modalverb + Grundform des Verbs; Imperativ*)
If you **aren't** into sports,	you **can** go to a museum. (Möglichkeit)
If you **want** to learn about the environment,	you **should** visit the Eden Project. (Ratschlag)
If you **go** to Cornwall,	**try** real Cornish food. (Ratschlag / Aufforderung)

❗ *Das deutsche Wort „wenn" hat im Englischen zwei Bedeutungen:*
a) *Mit* if *betonst du eine Bedingung:*
   If we go on a beach holiday, I'll try surfing.
b) *Mit* when *betonst du den zeitlichen Zusammenhang:*
   We'll see Dave **when** he visits his granny in London.

Du kannst die Reihenfolge von if-Satz und Hauptsatz auch tauschen. Dann entfällt allerdings das Komma.

Test yourself   *There's a teacher from Scotland at your school. In the next holidays he wants to travel around Germany. Tell him what he can and should do.*

Example: If you go to Berlin, you can visit the Brandenburg Gate.
If you go to Leipzig, you should try "Leipziger Lerche".
If you visit Frankfurt, you'll see lots of tall buildings.

G19 ⟨If I were an adult, I could choose where I wanted to live.⟩

Seiten 117–118

Bedingungssätze Typ 2
Conditional clauses type 2

It **would be** great
if we **had** a party.

OK, but it **would be** a good idea
if you **asked** your parents first, Dave.

*Mit dem Bedingungssatz Typ 2 drückst
du eine Bedingung aus, die nicht oder
nicht so einfach zu erfüllen ist.*

○ *Im* **if**-*Satz verwendest du das* **simple past** *und im* **Hauptsatz** *would(n't) / could(n't) +*
Grundform des Verbs (= conditional).

if-*Satz* (simple past)	Hauptsatz (conditional)
If Dave **had** the choice,	he **wouldn't move** to Cornwall.
Wenn Dave die Wahl hätte, würde er nicht nach Cornwall ziehen.	
If Cornwall **wasn't** so far from Greenwich,	the friends **could see** each other more often.
Wenn Cornwall nicht so weit von Greenwich weg wäre, könnten sich die Freunde öfter sehen.	

*Nach I / he / she / it
kannst du was oder
were verwenden,
wobei was eher
umgangssprachlich ist.*

*Du kannst die Reihenfolge
von if-Satz und Hauptsatz
wie bei Typ 1 (→G18)
tauschen. Dann entfällt
das Komma.*

❗ *Das* simple past *im* if-Satz *drückt eine Bedingung aus und keine Handlung in der
Vergangenheit.*

❗ *Schau dir noch einmal die Übersetzungen oben an! Im Deutschen verwendest du sowohl für die
Übersetzung des* if-Satzes *als auch für den Hauptsatz den Konjunktiv.*

❗ *Im* if-Satz *darf normalerweise kein* would *oder* could *stehen.*

Test yourself *Complete the sentences with your own ideas.*

1. If I (be) an adult, …
2. My mum/dad (do) anything if …
3. If I (get) more pocket money, …
4. If I (not live) in a town/village, …

Vocabulary

Im **Vocabulary** findest du alle wichtigen englischen Wörter und Redewendungen aus *Green Line* 2. Sie stehen in der Reihenfolge, in der sie im Buch vorkommen. Diese Wörter solltest du lernen und anwenden können. Andere nützliche Wörter und Begriffe (z. B. Arbeitsanweisungen), die du **nicht** auswendig lernen musst, findest du ab S. 281. Das *Vocabulary* ist in drei Spalten aufgeteilt:

- Links stehen die englischen Wörter und Sätze. In Klammern ist die Lautschrift aufgeführt. Sie zeigt dir, wie du das Wort oder den Satz aussprichst. Die Erklärung der Lautschrift findest du am Ende dieser Seite.
- In der Mitte steht die deutsche Übersetzung.
- Rechts findest du Beispielsätze, Erklärungen, Bilder oder Hinweise auf Besonderheiten.

In *Green Line* findest du manchmal neue Wörter in Fußnoten unten auf einer Seite. Auch diese helfen dir, die Texte zu verstehen. Du musst sie aber nicht lernen.

Auf das *Vocabulary* folgt das **Dictionary (English – German, German – English)**. Falls du ein Wort vergessen hast, kannst du in diesen alphabetischen Wortlisten nachsehen.

Englische Begriffe wie *e-mail*, *cool* oder *cornflakes*, die du auch im Deutschen verwendest, stehen nicht im *Vocabulary*. Du kannst ihre Aussprache und Übersetzung aber im *Dictionary* nachschlagen. Das gleiche gilt für Wörter, die auf Englisch und Deutsch fast gleich geschrieben und ausgesprochen werden, wie z. B. *park* oder *partner*.

Abkürzungen und Zeichen

pl	Mehrzahl (Plural)	↔	ist das Gegenteil von
sg	Einzahl (Singular)	→	ist verwandt mit
ugs	umgangssprachlich	=	entspricht
5	In dieser Übung kommen die Wörter vor.	*Fr./Lat.*	verwandte Wörter in anderen Fremdsprachen
!	Achtung!		

Englische Laute

Mitlaute (Konsonanten)

[b]	**b**ed	[p]	**p**icture
[d]	**d**ay	[r]	**r**ed
[ð]	**th**e	[s]	**s**ix
[f]	**f**amily	[ʃ]	**sh**e
[g]	**g**o	[t]	**t**en
[ŋ]	morni**ng**	[tʃ]	**ch**air
[h]	**h**ouse	[v]	**v**ideo
[j]	**y**ou	[w]	**w**e, **o**ne
[k]	**c**an, mil**k**	[z]	ea**s**y
[l]	**l**etter	[ʒ]	revi**s**ion
[m]	**m**an	[dʒ]	**p**age
[n]	**n**o	[θ]	**th**ank you

Selbstlaute (Vokale)

[ɑː]	c**a**r	[i]	happ**y**
[æ]	**a**pple	[iː]	t**ea**cher
[e]	p**e**n	[ɒ]	d**o**g
[ə]	**a**gain	[ɔː]	b**a**ll
[ɜː]	g**i**rl	[ʊ]	b**oo**k
[ʌ]	b**u**t	[u]	Jan**u**ary
[ɪ]	**i**t	[uː]	t**oo**, tw**o**

Doppellaute

[aɪ]	**I**, m**y**
[aʊ]	n**ow**, m**ou**se
[eɪ]	n**a**me, th**ey**
[eə]	th**ere**, p**air**
[ɪə]	h**ere**, id**ea**
[əʊ]	hell**o**
[ɔɪ]	b**oy**
[ʊə]	s**ure**

[ː]	der vorangehende Laut ist lang, z. B. *you* [juː]	[']	die folgende Silbe trägt den Hauptakzent
[‿]	der Bindebogen zeigt, dass zwei Wörter in der Aussprache verbunden werden	[ˌ]	die folgende Silbe trägt den Nebenakzent

Unit 1 My friends and I

Check-in

past [pɑːst]	Vergangenheit	'Today' is now, 'yesterday' is the *past*.
feeling [ˈfiːlɪŋ]	Gefühl	*feeling* → to feel
that [ðæt]	der; dem; den; die; das *(Relativpronomen)*	
caught on camera [ˌkɔːt ˌɒn ˈkæmrə]	ertappt; mit der Kamera festgehalten	
embarrassing [ɪmˈbærəsɪŋ]	peinlich	In the photo Jay is wearing an *embarrassing* outfit.
to **end up** [ˌend ˈʌp]	enden; landen	
yearbook [ˈjɪəbʊk]	Jahrbuch	A book with information about events and students at the school.
round of boxing [ˌraʊnd əv ˈbɒksɪŋ]	Boxrunde	
nose [nəʊz]	Nase	They look funny with their red *noses*.
eye [aɪ]	Auge	
lovebirds *(pl)* [ˈlʌvˌbɜːdz]	Turteltauben	
to **lie** [laɪ]	lügen	The camera never *lies*!
trip [trɪp]	Trip; Reise; Ausflug; Fahrt	Let's go on a fun *trip* at the weekend!
guy [gaɪ]	Typ; Kerl; *(Pl.)* Leute	Our new classmate is a really cool *guy*.
2 **himself** [hɪmˈself]	(er) selbst; sich (selbst)	You mustn't help him. He wants to do everything *himself*.
3 **shy** [ʃaɪ]	schüchtern	Are you *shy*? – Yes, I am. That's why I don't like parties.
embarrassed [ɪmˈbærəst]	verlegen	*embarrassed* → embarrassing *Fr.* embarrassé/-e
proud (of) [ˈpraʊd əv]	stolz (auf)	Jay is *proud of* himself because he is good at singing.
American [əˈmerɪkən]	Amerikanisch; amerikanisch; aus Amerika; Amerikaner/-in	Yearbooks are an *American* tradition.
report [rɪˈpɔːt]	Bericht; Meldung	Who can write the *report* about the class trip?
during *(+ noun)* [ˈdjʊərɪŋ]	während *(+ Nomen)*	Don't eat *during* lessons.
highlight [ˈhaɪlaɪt]	Highlight; Höhepunkt	

Describing a person's character

He**'s** a very **shy** person. It isn't easy for him to give presentations.	schüchtern
She's good at lots of things so she**'s** always **confident** that she can do almost anything.	zuversichtlich; selbstbewusst
He**'s** so **brave**. He's never scared.	tapfer; mutig
She**'s** a **nice / friendly / unfriendly / funny** person.	nett / freundlich / unfreundlich / lustig
He**'s lucky** because he**'s happy**.	Glück haben / glücklich sein

Describe a person to your partner. Who is it?

Station 1: I love Red Nose Day

(the) best [best]	(der/die/das) Beste	I always try to do *my best* when there's a class test.
ago [əˈgəʊ]	vor *(zeitlich)*	**!** *Ago* steht meistens am Satzende: I did my homework two days *ago*.
to **raise money** [ˌreɪz ˈmʌni]	Geld sammeln	Charities *raise money*.
in need [ɪn ˈniːd]	bedürftig; in Not	*in need* → to need
also [ˈɔːlsəʊ]	auch	I like football and I *also* like basketball. = I like football and I like basketball too.
that's how [ðæts ˈhaʊ]	so	Look at Luke. *That's how* you play football – he's good!
noticeboard [ˈnəʊtɪsbɔːd]	schwarzes Brett	Olivia saw a Red Nose Day poster on the school *noticeboard*.
month [mʌnθ]	Monat	day – week – *month* – year
in the end [ˌɪn ði ˌend]	schließlich; zum Schluss	
real [rɪəl]	echt; richtig; wirklich	Not everything you see on TV is *real*. *real* → really
collection [kəˈlekʃn]	Kollektion; Sammlung	*collection* → to collect *Fr.* collection *(f)*
I can't wait till next time. [aɪ kɑːnt ˌweɪt tɪl nekst ˈtaɪm]	Ich kann es bis zum nächsten Mal kaum erwarten.	
2 **non-** [nɒn]	nicht-	Red Nose Day is a *non*-uniform day.
5 **the next day** [ðə ˌnekst ˈdeɪ]	am nächsten Tag	What did Luke tell his friends *the next day*?
yesterday [ˈjestədeɪ]	gestern	*yesterday* – today – tomorrow
6 **pyjamas** *(pl)* [pɪˈdʒɑːməz]	Schlafanzug; Pyjama	Do you wear *pyjamas* in bed?
to **enjoy** [ɪnˈdʒɔɪ]	genießen; sich freuen an	The party was great. I really *enjoyed* it.
comment [ˈkɒment]	Kommentar	This is a serious problem, so I don't need your funny *comments*!

to **turn off** [ˌtɜːnˈɒf]	abschalten; ausschalten	Please *turn off* the TV. It's time to go to bed.
hard [hɑːd]	hart; schwer; schwierig	I find German *hard*.
for ... [fɔː; fə]	... lang	Sherlock can swim *for* 30 minutes.
to **think of** [ˈθɪŋkˌəv]	(sich) ausdenken; sich etwas einfallen lassen	Can you *think of* other things to do at the weekend?
7	**nervous** [ˈnɜːvəs]	nervös; aufgeregt	I felt *nervous* before the class test. *Fr.* nerveux/nerveuse
8	**sale** [seɪl]	Verkauf	*sale* → to sell
to **keep going** [ˌkiːp ˈɡəʊɪŋ]	aufrechterhalten	A quick answer *keeps* the conversation *going*.

Station 2: How did they know?

coach [kəʊtʃ]	Reisebus	A big bus (for holidays or long trips).
someone [ˈsʌmwʌn]	jemand	*someone* = somebody
missing [ˈmɪsɪŋ]	fehlend; verschwunden	What's the *missing* word? "I really ... you."
solution [səˈluːʃn]	Lösung	Let's find a *solution* for your problem. *Fr.* solution (f)
anonymous [ənˈɒnɪməs]	anonym	
police [pəˈliːs]	Polizei	! The *police* <u>are</u> looking for a dangerous man. *Fr.* police (f)
to **arrest** [əˈrest]	festnehmen; verhaften	The police *arrested* two men. *Fr.* arrêter
what the man looked like [ˌwɒt ðə mæn ˈlʊkt laɪk]	wie der Mann aussah	I didn't see the man. I don't know *what he looks like*.
taxi [ˈtæksi]	Taxi	
driver [ˈdraɪvə]	Fahrer/-in	! My uncle is <u>a</u> taxi *driver*. = Mein Onkel ist Taxifahrer.
mechanic [məˈkænɪk]	Mechaniker/-in; Kfz-Mechaniker/-in	
farmer [ˈfɑːmə]	Farmer/-in; Landwirt/-in	*farmer* → farm
postman [ˈpəʊstmən]	Briefträger	
clue [kluː]	Hinweis; Spur	The man's name is the *clue*.
13	**friendly** [ˈfrendli]	freundlich; nett	I always try to be *friendly* to everyone. *friendly* → friend
14	**all day** [ɔːl ˈdeɪ]	den ganzen Tag	What did you do *all day* on Saturday?
15	**singer** [ˈsɪŋə]	Sänger/-in	Jay thinks he's a *singer*. *singer* → to sing
16	**dream** [driːm]	Traum	In my *dream* I was James Bond.

Station 3: Everyone can enjoy a challenge

challenge [ˈtʃælɪndʒ]	Herausforderung	
course [kɔːs]	Kurs	They organise sports *courses* for school groups. *Lat.* cursus *(m)*
mountain [ˈmaʊntɪn]	Berg	
forest [ˈfɒrɪst]	Wald	There are lots of trees in a *forest*. *Fr.* forêt *(f)*
adventure [ədˈventʃə]	Abenteuer	*Adventure* stories tell about exciting events.
confident [ˈkɒnfɪdnt]	selbstsicher; selbstbewusst	*Lat.* confidens
walking [ˈwɔːkɪŋ]	Wandern	**!** Wenn man *-ing* an ein Verb anhängt, wird es zum Hauptwort (Nomen): walk – *walking*, climb – climbing
climbing [ˈklaɪmɪŋ]	Klettern	**!** Achtung Aussprache.
gorge scrambling [ˈgɔːdʒ ˌskræmblɪŋ]	Schluchtenklettern	
route [ruːt]	Strecke; Route	*Fr.* route *(f)*
than [ðæn]	als *(bei Vergleichen)*	Her English is better *than* her French.
the worst [ðə ˈwɜːst]	der/die/das schlimmste; der/die/das schlechteste	*the worst* ↔ the best

Outdoor activities

to **play** football / tennis	Fußball / Tennis spielen
to **go** skating / swimming / climbing / gorge scrambling	inlineskaten / schwimmen / schluchtenklettern gehen
to **ride** your bike / a horse	Fahrrad fahren / reiten
to **run**	laufen; rennen
to **go for a walk** in a park / in a forest / in the mountains	im Park / im Wald / in den Bergen spazieren gehen
to **climb** a mountain	einen Berg besteigen
to **do** gorge scrambling / mountain climbing	schluchtenklettern / bergsteigen

Tell your partner what you'd like to do in your holidays.

18 **separate** [ˈseprət]	separat; getrennt; verschieden	Wales is a *separate* country. *Lat.* separatus/-a/-um
Celtic [ˈkeltɪk; ˈseltɪk]	keltisch	*Fr.* celtique
Welsh [welʃ]	walisisch; Walisisch; Waliser/-in	*Welsh* people are from Wales. Some of them still speak *Welsh*.
22 **low** [ləʊ]	niedrig	

tall [tɔ:l]	groß; hoch	Olivia is *taller* than Lucy.
high [haɪ]	hoch; groß	*high* ↔ low

Comparing things

Tony: My house is **big**.
Lou: My sister's house is **bigger**.
Tony: I think my house is **the biggest**.

Lou: Your joke is **good**. But my joke is **better**.
Tony: No, my joke is **the best**.

Lou: Football is **exciting**, but tennis is **more exciting**, and inline skating is **the most exciting** sport.

Compare the things in your schoolbag with a partner's things.

Story: It was amazing

amazing [əˈmeɪzɪŋ]	unglaublich; toll; erstaunlich	That's an *amazing* story!
planet [ˈplænɪt]	Planet	
sheep, sheep *(pl)* [ʃi:p]	Schaf	
sign [saɪn]	Zeichen; Schild	In Wales the *signs* are in Welsh. *Lat.* signum *(nt)*
road [rəʊd]	Straße	I live in King's *Road*.
soon [su:n]	bald	in a short time from now; a short time later
field [fi:ld]	Feld; Spielfeld; Wiese; Weide; Acker	On farms there are *fields*.
Welcome! [ˈwelkəm]	Willkommen!	
instructor [ɪnˈstrʌktə]	Lehrer/-in; Betreuer/-in	An *instructor* shows you how to do things. *Lat.* instructor *(m)*
few [fju:]	wenige	! He's got a *few* friends. = ... ein paar Freunde. He's got *few* friends. = ... wenige Freunde.
meal [mi:l]	Mahlzeit; Essen	Lunch is a *meal*.
a bit [ə ˈbɪt]	ein bisschen; ein wenig	

cold [kəʊld]	kalt	The nights in Wales were a bit *cold*.
torch [tɔːtʃ]	Fackel; Taschenlampe	
to **go for a walk** [ˌgəʊ fər ə ˈwɔːk]	spazieren gehen	It's nice today. Let's *go for a walk*.
the dark [ðə ˈdɑːk]	Dunkelheit	in *the dark* = im Dunkeln
noise [nɔɪz]	Lärm; Geräusch	What all the *noise*? I can't sleep!
dark [dɑːk]	dunkel	*dark* → the dark
night walk [ˈnaɪt wɔːk]	Nachtwanderung	
against [əˈgenst]	gegen	It was *against* the rules.
to **be asleep** [ˌbi əˈsliːp]	schlafen	*to be asleep* = to sleep
to **tiptoe** [ˈtɪptəʊ]	auf Zehenspitzen gehen	They *tiptoed* back to their rooms.
cloudy [ˈklaʊdi]	bedeckt; bewölkt	On a *cloudy* night you can't see the stars.
battery [ˈbætri]	Batterie; Akku	*Fr.* batterie *(f)*
no idea [ˌnəʊ aɪˈdɪə]	keine Ahnung	Which is the right way? – I have *no idea*!
locked [lɒkt]	abgeschlossen	*locked* ↔ open
trouble [ˈtrʌbl]	Ärger; Probleme; Schwierig-keiten	We didn't want *trouble* with our teacher.
secret [ˈsiːkrət]	Geheimnis	Don't tell the others, it's a *secret*. *Fr.* secret *(m)*
memory [ˈmemri]	Erinnerung; Gedächtnis	We all have great *memories* of our school trip. *Lat.* memoria *(f)*
4 **travel report** [ˌtrævl rɪˈpɔːt]	Reisebericht	Do you like Dave's *travel report* about the class trip?

Skills: How to use a dictionary

1 **electronic** [ˌelekˈtrɒnɪk]	elektronisch	Do you use an *electronic* dictionary?
search [sɜːtʃ]	Suche; Such-	Write the word in the *search* box.
meaning [ˈmiːnɪŋ]	Bedeutung; Sinn	What's the *meaning* of 'to describe'?

Unit task: Our travel report

spaceship [ˈspeɪsʃɪp]	Raumschiff	In science fiction stories there are often *spaceships*.
beginning [bɪˈgɪnɪŋ]	Anfang; Beginn	*beginning* ↔ end

Action UK! The new boy

1 to **sneak around** [ˌsniːk əˈraʊnd]	herumschleichen	
lemon [ˈlemən]	Zitrone	

	surprising [sə'praɪzɪŋ]	überraschend	*surprising* → surprise
2	**filmmaker** ['fɪlm,meɪkə]	Filmemacher/-in	A *filmmaker* makes films.
	mood [muːd]	Stimmung; Laune	Can you describe the *mood* in that scene?
	unfriendly [ʌn'frendli]	unfreundlich	*unfriendly* ↔ friendly
	hurt [hɜːt]	verletzt	He made some really unfriendly comments and now I feel *hurt*.
	aggressive [ə'gresɪv]	aggressiv	**!** Achtung Aussprache. *Fr.* agressif/agressive
	scary ['skeəri]	unheimlich; gruselig; beängstigend	*scary* → to be scared

Unit 2 Let's discover TTS!

Check-in

	to **discover** [dɪ'skʌvə]	entdecken	The students *discover* Thomas Tallis School.
	painting ['peɪntɪŋ]	Malerei; Gemälde	*painting* → to paint
	assembly [ə'sembli]	Versammlung; Morgenappell	
	hall [hɔːl]	Halle; Saal	In the *hall*, the students meet for Assembly.
	competition [,kɒmpə'tɪʃn]	Wettbewerb; Turnier	There's a painting *competition* at our school this year. *Fr.* compétition *(f)*
	to **belong (to)** [bɪ'lɒŋ (tə)]	gehören (zu)	
	with special needs [wɪð ,speʃl 'niːdz]	behindert	Students *with special needs* belong to TTS too.
	art [ɑːt]	Kunst	Not every painting is *art*! *Lat.* ars *(f)*
1	**subject** ['sʌbdʒɪkt]	Schulfach	What *subjects* do you like?
	exam [ɪg'zæm]	Examen; Prüfung	An *exam* is an important test *Fr.* examen *(m)*
	drama ['drɑːmə]	Theater; Drama	In *Drama* class, you can learn how to be an actor.
	studies *(pl)* ['stʌdiz]	Studium; Lernen; Arbeit für die Schule	My favourite subject is Film *Studies*. *Lat.* studēre
	fashion ['fæʃn]	Mode	In *Fashion* lessons you learn about clothes.

to **offer** [ˈɒfə]	anbieten	Can I *offer* you something to drink? *Fr.* offrir
additional [əˈdɪʃnl]	zusätzlich	
birdwatching [ˈbɜːdˌwɒtʃɪŋ]	Vogelbeobachtung	*Birdwatching* is an additional activity at TTS.
chess [tʃes]	Schach	
2 **fantastic** [fænˈtæstɪk]	fantastisch; großartig	*fantastic* = great *Fr.* fantastique
reaction [rɪˈækʃn]	Reaktion	
3 **positive** [ˈpɒzətɪv]	positiv	Give *positive* feedback and be friendly when your feedback isn't so *positive*.
introduction [ˌɪntrəˈdʌkʃn]	Einführung; Einleitung; Vorstellung	the *introduction* of a presentation = the first part of a presentation
lively [ˈlaɪvli]	lebendig	Holly's presentation was interesting and *lively*.

Station 1: The queen who loved parties

queen [kwiːn]	Königin	Elizabeth II is the *Queen* of England.
who [huː]	der; dem; den; die *(Relativpronomen)*	Pia is the girl *who* comes from Germany.
history [ˈhɪstri]	Geschichte	*Lat.* historia *(f)*
husband [ˈhʌzbənd]	Ehemann	My dad is my mum's *husband*.
beautiful [ˈbjuːtɪfl]	schön; hübsch; wunderbar	
view [vjuː]	Aussicht; Sicht; Ausblick; Blick	Anne's house had a beautiful *view* of the Thames.
which [wɪtʃ]	der; die; das; dem; den *(Relativpronomen)*	The subject *which* I like most is English.
ghost [ɡəʊst]	Geist	Sometimes there are stories of *ghosts* in old houses.
as [æz; əz]	als	
hospital [ˈhɒspɪtl]	Hospital; Krankenhaus	Later they used the house as a *hospital*. *Fr.* hôpital *(m)*
to **build, built** [bɪld; bɪlt]	bauen	
architect [ˈɑːkɪtekt]	Architekt/-in	Which *architect* built the museum? *Lat.* architectus *(m)*
whose [huːz]	dessen; deren *(Relativpronomen)*	
design [dɪˈzaɪn]	Design; Gestaltung; Entwurf	

	to **choose, chose** [tʃuːz; tʃəʊz]	auswählen; wählen	Christopher Wren was the architect whose design Anne *chose*.
	upset [ʌpˈset]	aufgebracht; bestürzt	Why are you so *upset*? – My brother lost my phone!
	to **cut, cut (off)** [kʌt; kʌt (ɒf)]	schneiden; abschneiden	Anne wanted to *cut off* Wren's head.
	that's why [ðæts ˈwaɪ]	deshalb	Luke hurt his hand. *That's why* he didn't do his homework.
	to **leave, left** [liːv; left]	verlassen; lassen; abfahren	
	space [speɪs]	Raum; Fläche; Platz; Ort	Please leave some *space* for my picture on the wall.
3	**wife, wives** *(pl)* [waɪf, waɪvz]	Ehefrau	Mr and Mrs Preston are husband and *wife*.
	by the river [baɪ ðə ˈrɪvə]	am Fluss	Christopher Wren built the hospital *by the river*.
4	to **be interested in** [bi ˈɪntrəstɪd ˌɪn]	interessiert sein an; sich interessieren für	Are you *interested in* history?
	to **try on** [traɪ ˈɒn]	anprobieren	That's a nice T-shirt. Why don't you *try* it *on*, Olivia?
5	**finally** [ˈfaɪnli]	schließlich; endlich; zum Schluss; letztlich	first – then – *finally* *Lat.* finis *(m)*
	to **design** [dɪˈzaɪn]	entwerfen; gestalten	*to design* → design
7	**partially sighted** [ˌpɑːʃəli ˈsaɪtɪd]	sehbehindert	Gwen is the new girl who is *partially sighted*.
8	**registration** [ˌredʒɪsˈtreɪʃn]	Anwesenheitskontrolle	*Registration* is before lessons.
	Technology [tekˈnɒlədʒi]	Technik; Computerunterricht	
	Science [saɪəns]	Naturwissenschaften	*Lat.* scientia *(f)*
	Maths [mæθs]	Mathematik; Mathe	*Fr.* maths *(f) (pl)*
	RE *(= Religious Education)* [ˌɑːrˈiː; rɪˌlɪdʒəs ˌedʒʊˈkeɪʃn]	Religion *(Schulfach)*	
	French [frenʃ]	französisch; Französisch	
	Humanities *(pl)* [hjuːˈmænətiz]	Sozialwissenschaften	*Lat.* humanitas *(f)*
	PE *(= Physical Education)* [ˌpiːˈiː; ˌfɪzɪkl ˌedʒʊˈkeɪʃn]	Sportunterricht	In *PE* you do lots of sport.

Subjects at school

English	Englisch	**Music**	Musik
German	Deutsch	**Humanities**	Sozialwissenschaften
French	Französisch	**Technology**	Technik
Maths	Mathe	**Science**	Naturwissenschaften
PE	Sport	**RE**	Religion
Art	Kunst		

Make you own fantasy timetable and compare it with your partner's.

Station 2: Everyone was doing a really great job!

to **join** [dʒɔɪn]	beitreten; sich anschließen; verbinden	Let's *join* the Computer Club!
Eco [ɪkəʊ]	Öko-	
article [ˈɑːtɪkl]	Artikel; Bericht *(in einer Zeitschrift, Zeitung)*	On the TTS website there are lots of *articles* about clubs. *Fr.* article *(m)*
wildlife [ˈwaɪldlaɪf]	Tierwelt *(in freier Wildbahn)*	The Eco Club did a *wildlife* project.
to **get started** [ˌget ˈstɑːtɪd]	anfangen	*to get started* = to start
sun [sʌn]	Sonne	
to **shine, shone** [ʃaɪn; ʃɒn]	scheinen; glänzen	The sun is *shining* – let's go swimming.
bee [biː]	Biene	
to **hum** [hʌm]	summen	
to **look forward to** [ˌlʊk ˈfɔːwəd tə]	sich freuen auf	I'm *looking forward to* my grandma's visit next week.
to **put up, put up** [ˌpʊt ˈʌp; ˌpʊt ˈʌp]	aufstellen; errichten; aufhängen	*to put up* → to put
hotel [həʊˈtel]	Hotel	
to **dig, dug** [dɪg; dʌg]	graben	
hole [həʊl]	Loch	They dug a *hole* in the garden.
pond [pɒnd]	Teich	
to **hang up, hung up** [ˌhæŋ ˈʌp; ˌhʌŋ ˈʌp]	aufhängen	You can *hang up* a bird house in your garden.
bird [bɜːd]	Vogel	
ever [ˈevə]	jemals	It was our funniest project *ever*!
9	**member** [ˈmembə]	Mitglied	Dave is a *member* of the Preston family. *Fr.* membre *(m)*
10	**pipe** [paɪp]	Rohr; Rohrleitung	He broke a *pipe* and now there's water everywhere!
to **fall off, fell off** [ˌfɔːl ˈɒf; ˌfel ˈɒf]	herunterfallen; hinunterfallen	

ladder ['lædə]	Leiter		Be careful! Don't fall off the *ladder*.
fox [fɒks]	Fuchs		
to **steal, stole** [stiːl; stəʊl]	stehlen		A fox *stole* the students' lunch.
thumb [θʌm]	Daumen		
hammer ['hæmə]	Hammer		She hit her thumb with the *hammer*.
corner ['kɔːnə]	Ecke		Most rooms have four *corners*.
13 to **welcome** ['welkəm]	willkommen heißen		Let's go and *welcome* our new classmates.

Action UK! The film star

1 **one day** [wʌn 'deɪ]	eines Tages	Jay wants to be a famous singer *one day*.
actor ['æktə]	Schauspieler	*actor* → to act *Lat.* actor (m)
dancer ['dɑːnsə]	Tänzer/-in	*dancer* → to dance
pilot ['paɪlət]	Pilot/-in	
police officer [pə'liːsˌɒfɪsə]	Polizeibeamter	

Jobs

Who?		What he / she does, and where
actor	Schauspieler/-in	to act, to sing, to dance, to speak, drama
architect	Architekt/-in	to plan, to design, to build
coach	Trainer/-in	sport, dancing
dancer	Tänzer/-in	to dance, drama, music
driver	Fahrer/-in	to drive a car / taxi
farmer	Bauer/Bäuerin	to work on a farm, to look after the animals
instructor	Betreuer/-in	to look after people in a course
police officer	Polizist/-in	to arrest somebody
postman/ postwoman	Postbote/Postbotin; Briefträger/-in	to bring mail
sailor	Matrose/Matrosin	to work on a ship
singer	Sänger/-in	to sing, song, music
teacher	Lehrer/-in	to work at school, to help students
vet	Tierarzt/Tierärztin	to work in a surgery, to help pets / farm animals

Which jobs do you like and why?

3	**advice** [əd'vaɪs]	Rat; Ratschlag	What *advice* can you give me?
	to **panic** ['pænɪk]	panisch werden	Don't *panic*! *Fr.* paniquer
	to **relax** [rɪ'læks]	sich entspannen; sich ausruhen; sich beruhigen	Just *relax*!
	Take a deep breath. [ˌteɪk ə ˌdiːp 'breθ]	Atme(t) tief ein.	
	to **thank** [θæŋk]	danken	*to thank* → Thank you.
4	**such** [sʌtʃ]	solch; solche/-r/-s	It was *such* a good film!
	impressed [ɪm'prest]	beeindruckt	The friends were *impressed* with Jay's dancing and singing.

Skills: How to give a good presentation

1	**fact** [fækt]	Fakt; Tatsache	I know a lot of *facts* about King James and his wife Anne. *Lat.* factum (nt)
	on time [ɒn 'taɪm]	pünktlich	Be *on time*. = Don't be late.
	take a look at [ˌteɪk ə 'lʊk ˌæt]	einen Blick werfen auf	Let's *take a look at* this design.
	to **be connected** [bi kə'nektɪd]	zusammenhängen; in Zusammenhang stehen	
	topic ['tɒpɪk]	Thema	This story is connected with the *topic* of my presentation.
	contact ['kɒntækt]	Kontakt	
	audience ['ɔːdiəns]	Publikum	Make eye contact with your *audience* during a presentation.

Unit task: Join our club!

juggling ['dʒʌglɪŋ]	Jonglieren	
foreign language [ˌfɒrɪn 'læŋgwɪdʒ]	Fromdcpracho	A lot of British students learn French as their first *foreign language*.
fanzine [fæn'ziːn]	Fanzeitschrift	
life, lives *(pl)* [laɪf, laɪvz]	Leben	*life* → to live

Story: What a wonderful world

wonderful ['wʌndəfl]	wunderbar	*wonderful* = great = fantastic
news *(sg)* [njuːz]	Nachricht(en); Neuigkeit(en)	! That's good *news*. = Das ist eine gute Nachricht.
earth [ɜːθ]	Erdboden; Erde; die Erde	
dinosaur ['daɪnəsɔː]	Dinosaurier	
to **have to** ['hæv tə]	müssen	They *have to* make a poster for the competition.

to **share** [ʃeə]	teilen	Jay doesn't want to *share* his ideas with Luke.
anyone else [ˌeniwʌn ˈels]	jemand anderes	Don't tell the story to *anyone else*.
to **enter** [ˈentə]	hineingehen; betreten; eintreten; *hier:* mitmachen	He *entered* the competition. The teacher *entered* the room.
on my own [ˌɒn maɪˈəʊn]	allein; für mich	If you're *on your own*, you're alone.
side [saɪd]	Seite	
dirty [ˈdɜːti]	dreckig; schmutzig	I can't wear this T-shirt because it's *dirty*.
to **notice** [ˈnəʊtɪs]	bemerken; wahrnehmen	Did you *notice* anything strange about the woman?
to **lie, lay** [laɪ; leɪ]	liegen	My phone is *lying* on the table.
could [kʊd]	könnte/-n	
moment [ˈməʊmənt]	Moment; Augenblick	! Achtung Betonung.
class [klɑːs]	*hier:* Unterricht	In *class*, sometimes you work on your own, sometimes with your classmates.
break [breɪk]	Pause	After the first two lessons we always have *break*.
quickly [ˈkwɪkli]	schnell	Jay looked at the exercise book *quickly*.
He couldn't believe his eyes. [hi ˌkʊdnt bɪˌliːv hɪz ˈaɪz]	Er traute seinen Augen nicht.	*I couldn't believe my eyes* when I got a dog for my birthday.
flower [flaʊə]	Blume	
clever [ˈklevə]	schlau; klug	What a *clever* idea!
yours [jɔːz]	dein/-er/-e/-es; eure/-r/-s; Ihr/-e	This is my drawing. Is that one *yours*?
nearly [ˈnɪəli]	fast; annähernd	My presentation is *nearly* finished.
to **calm down** [ˌkɑːm ˈdaʊn]	sich beruhigen	! Das „l" in *calm* wird nicht ausgesprochen.
mine [maɪn]	mein/-er/-e/-es	*mine* ↔ yours
to **push** [pʊʃ]	stoßen; schieben; schubsen	He *pushed* me – and I fell over. That wasn't nice!
to **turn (a)round** [ˌtɜːn (ə)ˈraʊnd]	(sich) umdrehen; wenden	When they heard a voice behind them, they *turned (a)round*.
arm [ɑːm]	Arm	
fight [faɪt]	Kampf; Streit	
idiot [ˈɪdiət]	Idiot/-in	! Achtung Betonung.
to **turn back** [tɜːn ˈbæk]	umkehren; zurückgehen	*to turn back* → to turn (a)round → to turn off
nobody [ˈnəʊbədi]	niemand	
ready [ˈredi]	fertig; bereit	Let's get *ready* for school now.
to **plant** [plɑːnt]	pflanzen; anpflanzen	Let's *plant* some flowers in the garden.
3 **strong** [strɒŋ]	stark	
absolutely [ˌæbsəˈluːtli]	absolut; völlig	*Lat.* absolutus/-a/-um
to **hate** [heɪt]	hassen; nicht mögen	*to hate* ↔ to love

Feelings and reactions

She **feels nervous / embarrassed / hurt** because …	nervös / verlegen / verletzt
I'**m impressed / surprised**.	beeindruckt / überrascht
He'**s in an aggressive mood**.	in aggressiver Stimmung

Draw a face. Can your partner guess what feeling it shows?

Check-out

1	**nature** [ˈneɪtʃə]	Natur	I only watch films about *nature*. *Lat.* natura *(f)*
	to **make friends** [ˌmeɪk ˈfrendz]	Freundschaft schließen	I *made* lots of *friends* at my new school.
2	**alarm clock** [əˈlɑːm ˌklɒk]	Wecker	

Across cultures 1 London: A special city

	huge [hjuːdʒ]	riesig; riesengroß; gewaltig	Berlin is a big city. London is a *huge* city.
	capital [ˈkæpɪtl]	Hauptstadt	London is the *capital* of England. *Lat.* capitalis
1	**multi-ethnic** [ˌmʌltiˈeθnɪk]	Vielvölker-; international	London is a *multi-ethnic* city.
	sight [saɪt]	Sehenswürdigkeit; Anblick	A *sight* is an interesting thing to see in a city.
	underground [ˈʌndəɡraʊnd]	U-Bahn	Let's go by *underground*.
	the **Tube** [ðə ˈtjuːb]	die Londoner U-Bahn	Another name for the London underground is *the Tube*.
	carnival [ˈkɑːnɪvl]	Karneval	What costume do you want to wear at the *carnival*?
	originally [əˈrɪdʒnli]	ursprünglich	
	Roman [ˈrəʊmən]	Römer/-in; römisch	London was originally a *Roman* town. *Lat.* Romanus/-a/-um
	airport [ˈeəpɔːt]	Flughafen	London has got five *airports*. *Fr.* aéroport *(m)*
	million [ˈmɪljən]	Million	1,000,000
	large [lɑːdʒ]	groß; riesig	London is the third *largest* city in Europe.
	bell [bel]	Glocke	
2	**guard** [ɡɑːd]	Wache; Wächter/-in	There are always *guards* in front of Buckingham Palace.
	identity [aɪˈdentəti]	Identität	*Fr.* identité *(f)*

Unit 3 London is amazing!

Check-in

flair [fleə]	Flair; Atmosphäre	Brick Lane has a multi-ethnic *flair*.
wax figure ['wæks ˌfɪɡə]	Wachsfigur	At Madame Tussauds you can see *wax figures* of famous people.

Station 1: It's going to be fun

	to **stay with** ['steɪ wɪð]	wohnen bei	Amir is *staying with* the Azads.
	this afternoon [ðɪs ˈɑːftənuːn]	heute Nachmittag	yesterday afternoon – *this afternoon* – tomorrow afternoon
	18-year-old [ˌeɪtiːn ˈjɪərˌəʊld]	18-jährig	My sister is 18. I've got an *18-year-old* sister.
	to **persuade** [pəˈsweɪd]	überreden	Jay wants to *persuade* his brother to come with them. *Lat.* persuadēre
	probably [ˈprɒbəbli]	möglicherweise; wahrscheinlich	
1	to **travel** [ˈtrævl]	fahren; reisen	This year I'd like to *travel* to England.
	public transport *(no pl)* [ˌpʌblɪk ˈtrænspɔːt]	öffentliche Verkehrsmittel	*public transport* = the Underground, buses, trains
	smartcard [ˈsmɑːtkɑːd]	Chipkarte	
	to **top up** [tɒp ˈʌp]	aufladen	Jay *topped up* his Oyster card yesterday. Now he must *top up* his phone too.
	credit [ˈkredɪt]	Guthaben	I must top up my phone. There's no *credit* on it.
4	**wheelchair** [ˈwiːltʃeə]	Rollstuhl	 *wheelchair* → chair
5	**zoo** [zuː]	Zoo; Tierpark	There are lots of animals in a *zoo*.
	musician [mjuːˈzɪʃn]	Musiker/-in	*musician* → music *Fr.* musicien *(m)*/musicienne *(f)*
6	to **get around** [ˌget əˈraʊnd]	*hier:* sich fortbewegen	What's the best way to *get around* London? – By Tube.
	to **change (onto)** [tʃeɪndʒ (ˈɒntʊ)]	umsteigen (in)	To get to Buckingham Palace from here, you *change onto* the Victoria line.
	north [nɔːθ]	Norden; Nord-	
	south [saʊθ]	Süden; Süd-	

stop [stɒp]	Haltestelle; Halt	The next *stop* is Elephant & Castle. *stop* → to stop
to get off, got off (a bus/ train) [ˌget ˈɒf; ˌgɒt ˈɒf]	aussteigen (aus einem Bus/ Zug)	Let's *get off* the Underground and take the bus.

Station 2: Good idea!

to deal, dealt (with) [diːl; delt (wɪð)]	sich befassen (mit); umgehen (mit)	We've got a problem so let's *deal with* it.
a while [ə ˈwaɪl]	eine Weile	*a while* = a little time
to mean, meant [miːn; ment]	meinen; bedeuten	You think the new boy is strange? What do you *mean*? I think he's nice.
girlfriend [ˈgɜːlfrend]	Freundin *(in einer Paarbezie- hung)*	Shahid has a *girlfriend*.
souvenir [ˌsuːvnˈɪə]	Souvenir; Andenken	I'd like to buy a *souvenir* of London.
anywhere [ˈeniweə]	irgendwo; überall (egal, wo)	Are there any souvenir shops *anywhere*?
everybody [ˈevribɒdi]	jeder; alle	all the people
… where to go. [ˌweə tə ˈgəʊ]	… wohin ich gehen kann.	I don't know *where to go*.
to follow [ˈfɒləʊ]	folgen; hinterhergehen; befolgen	The bird is *following* the man.
I bet [aɪ ˈbet]	ich wette	
to beat, beat [biːt; biːt]	schlagen; besiegen	I bet nobody can *beat* Arsenal this year!
one *(sg)*/**ones** *(pl)* [wʌn/wʌnz]	eine/-r/-s	Wenn du im Englischen ein Nomen nicht wiederholen möchtest, kannst du es durch *one/ones* ersetzen: This sandwich is big, that *one* is bigger.
11 **pro** [prəʊ]	Argument dafür	*Lat.* pro
con [kɒn]	Argument dagegen	*Lat.* contra
far [fɑː]	weit	Is Big Ben *far* from Buckingham Palace?

Station 3: They can bite very hard

to bite, bit [baɪt; bɪt]	beißen	Does your dog *bite*? It looks a bit scary!
hard [hɑːd]	*hier:* stark	In tennis you must hit the ball *hard*.
tour [tʊə]	Tour; Fahrt; Rundgang	
guide [gaɪd]	Führer/-in; Reiseführer	A person or a book that gives you information (e.g. about a city or a museum). *Fr.* guide *(m) (f)*
to become, became [bɪˈkʌm, bɪˈkeɪm]	werden	William the Conqueror *became* king of England in 1066.
castle [ˈkɑːsl]	Schloss; Burg	! Das „t" in *castle* wird nicht gesprochen.

prison ['prɪzn]	Gefängnis	*Fr.* prison *(f)*
lion [laɪən]	Löwe	

Fr. lion *(m)*

bear [beə]	Bär	
crown jewels [ˌkraʊn 'dʒuːəlz]	Kronjuwelen	The Tower is a museum where you can see the *Crown Jewels*.
Beefeater ['biːfˌiːtə]	königlicher Leibgardist	
raven ['reɪvn]	Rabe	

raven master ['reɪvn ˌmɑːstə]	Herr der Raben	The *raven master* looks after the ravens in the Tower.
careful ['keəfl]	vorsichtig; sorgfältig	
safe [seɪf]	sicher; ungefährlich	*safe* ↔ dangerous
close [kləʊs]	nahe	Do'nt go too *close* to the ravens.
13 **audio tour** ['ɔːdiəʊ ˌtʊə]	Audioführung	**!** Achtung Aussprache. *Fr.* audio-; *Lat.* audire
treasure ['treʒə]	Schatz	Just look and you can find real *treasures* in the Thames.
15 to **jump back** [ˌdʒʌmpˌ'bæk]	zurückspringen; *hier:* zurückschrecken	My mum *jumps back* when she sees a mouse.

Action UK! A day out in London

a day out in ... [ə ˌdeɪ ˌ'aʊt ɪn]	ein Tag in …	What would you like to do on *a day out in* London?
2 **out and about** [ˌaʊt ˌən ə'baʊt]	unterwegs	
3 **adult** ['ædʌlt]	Erwachsene/-r	*adult* ↔ child
sightseeing ['saɪtsiːɪŋ]	Sightseeing-; Besichtigungs-	
normal ['nɔːml]	normal	Is it better to take the sightseeing bus or the *normal* one?
4 **choice** [tʃɔɪs]	Wahl; Auswahl	*choice* → to choose *Fr.* choix *(f)*
location [ləʊ'keɪʃn]	Handlungsort; Lage; Standort	The *location* of the film is a famous street in London. *Lat.* locus *(m)*
crowd [kraʊd]	Menschenmenge	A lot of people all together in one place.

Out and about in the city

to **take** the bus / the Underground	den Bus / die U-Bahn nehmen
to **go for a walk** in the streets / in a park / along the river	in den Straßen / im Park / am Fluss entlang spazieren gehen
to **sit** in a café / restaurant	in einem Café / Restaurant sitzen
to **have** lunch / dinner	zu Mittag / zu Abend essen
to **go** shopping / to the cinema	einkaufen / ins Kino gehen
to **visit** a sight / a tourist attraction / a museum / a historical building / the zoo	eine Sehenswürdigkeit / eine Touristenattraktion / ein Museum / ein historisches Gebäude / den Zoo besichtigen; besuchen
to **see** famous people / the sights / lots of interesting things	berühmte Leute / die Sehenswürdigkeiten / viele interessante Dinge sehen
to **listen** to street musicians / an audio tour	Straßenmusikern / einer Audioguide-Führung zuhören
to **watch** a football game / a street show	ein Fußballspiel / eine Straßenshow ansehen

What would you like to do in London?

Skills: How to find information on the internet

1	**attraction** [əˈtrækʃn]	Attraktion; Sehenswürdigkeit	The London Eye is one of the city's most popular *attractions*.
	basic [ˈbeɪsɪk]	grundlegend; Grund-	In the first two years of English you learn a lot of *basic* words.
	display [dɪˈspleɪ]	Ausstellung	The Natural History Museum has a great *display* with strange animals at the moment.

Unit task: Our London tour

on foot [ɒn ˈfʊt]	zu Fuß	by car/train/bus, *but: on foot*
distance [ˈdɪstns]	Distanz; Entfernung	What's the *distance* from here to there? *Fr.* distance *(f)*
realistic [ˌrɪəˈlɪstɪk]	realistisch	Are your plans *realistic*?
material [məˈtɪəriəl]	Material	

Story: I'm a mudlark

mudlark ['mʌdlɑːk]	*jemand, der im Schlamm nach Sachen sucht, die er dann verkaufen kann*	
high tide ['haɪ ˌtaɪd]	Flut	
low tide ['ləʊ ˌtaɪd]	Ebbe	The River Thames has two faces – one at high tide, one at *low tide*.
to **flow out** [fləʊ ˈaʊt]	hinausfließen	Rivers *flow out* into the sea.
towards [təˈwɔːdz]	in Richtung; auf … zu; darauf zu	Look, that man is coming *towards* us.
central ['sentrl]	zentral; Zentral-	*central* → centre *Lat.* centrum *(nt)*
heart [hɑːt]	Herz; *hier:* Zentrum	the *heart* of London = the centre of London
metre ['miːtə]	Meter	
muddy ['mʌdi]	schlammig	
bank [bæŋk]	Ufer	A river has two *banks*.
wobbly ['wɒbli]	wackelig	
bridge [brɪdʒ]	Brücke	A *bridge* goes over a river.

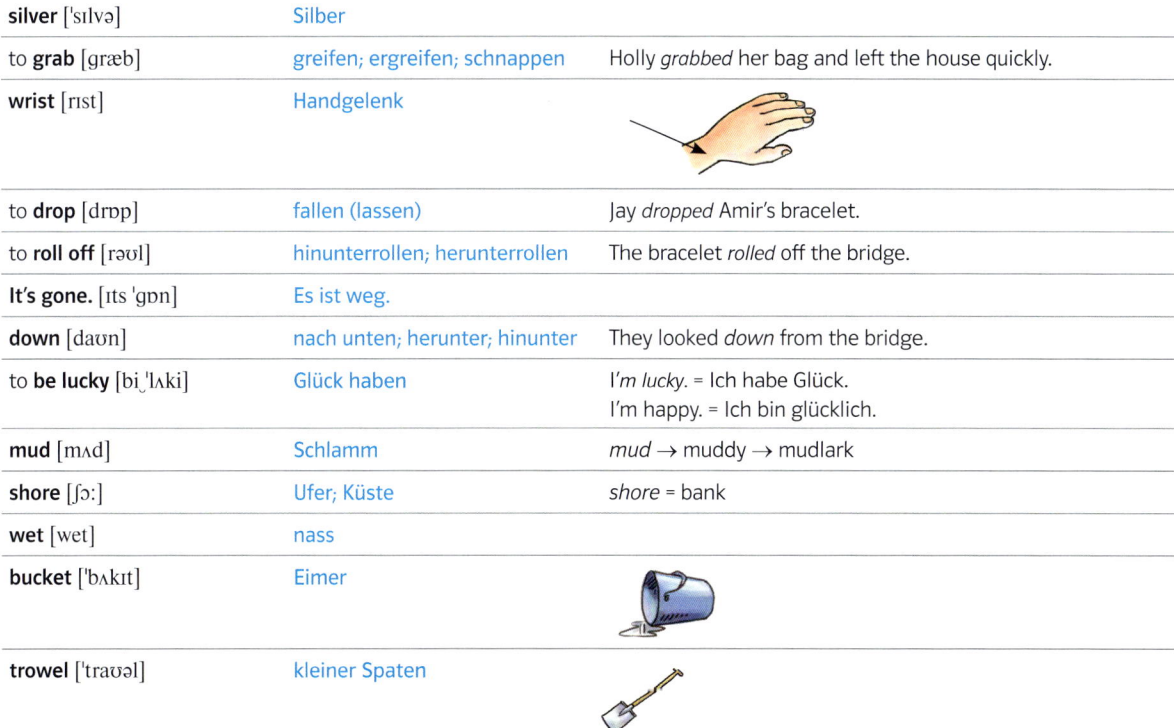

silver ['sɪlvə]	Silber	
to **grab** [græb]	greifen; ergreifen; schnappen	Holly *grabbed* her bag and left the house quickly.
wrist [rɪst]	Handgelenk	
to **drop** [drɒp]	fallen (lassen)	Jay *dropped* Amir's bracelet.
to **roll off** [rəʊl]	hinunterrollen; herunterrollen	The bracelet *rolled* off the bridge.
It's gone. [ɪts ˈgɒn]	Es ist weg.	
down [daʊn]	nach unten; herunter; hinunter	They looked *down* from the bridge.
to **be lucky** [bi ˈlʌki]	Glück haben	I'm *lucky*. = Ich habe Glück. I'm happy. = Ich bin glücklich.
mud [mʌd]	Schlamm	*mud* → muddy → mudlark
shore [ʃɔː]	Ufer; Küste	*shore* = bank
wet [wet]	nass	
bucket ['bʌkɪt]	Eimer	
trowel ['traʊəl]	kleiner Spaten	

century [ˈsenʃri]	Jahrhundert	We live in the 21st *century*.
anyway [ˈeniweɪ]	trotzdem; jedenfalls; sowieso	
pollution [pəˈluːʃn]	Verschmutzung	*Pollution* made the river dirty.
dead [ded]	tot	
to wash up [ˌwɒʃ ˈʌp]	angespült werden	Dead animals *washed up* on the river banks.
all the time [ˌɔːl ðə ˈtaɪm]	die ganze Zeit	I use my phone almost *all the time*.
human body [ˌhjuːmən ˈbɒdi]	menschlicher Körper	
clay pipe [ˈkleɪ paɪp]	Tonpfeife	
at first [ət ˈfɜːst]	zuerst; zunächst	*At first* Luke didn't like Jay very much, but then they became good friends.
key [kiː]	Schlüssel	
to scream [skriːm]	schreien; kreischen	Holly *screamed* because she found something awful.
coconut [ˈkəʊkənʌt]	Kokosnuss	
dramatic [drəˈmætɪk]	dramatisch	*dramatic* → drama *Fr.* dramatique
hour [aʊə]	Stunde	There are 24 *hours* in a day. *Lat.* hora *(f)*
to be surprised [bi səˈpraɪzd]	überrascht sein	They *were surprised* about all the 'treasure' in the mud!
2 **modern** [ˈmɒdn]	modern	Smartphones are *modern* technology. *Fr.* moderne

Water words

sea – river – lake – pond	Meer – Fluss – See – Teich
high tide – low tide – wave	Flut – Ebbe – Welle
to flow out – to flow towards … – to wash up	hinausfließen – in Richtung … fließen – anspülen
bank – shore	Ufer
bridge	Brücke
mud – muddy – wet	Schlamm – schlammig – nass
ship – boat	Schiff – Boot

Check-out

3 **comfortable** [ˈkʌmftəbl]	komfortabel; bequem	This sofa is really *comfortable*.
carpet [ˈkɑːpɪt]	Teppich	

Unit 4 Sport is good for you!

Check-in

experience [ɪkˈspɪərɪəns]	Erfahrung	What interesting *experiences* can you tell us about?
health [helθ]	Gesundheit	*health* → healthy
accident [ˈæksɪdnt]	Unfall	My sister had a bike *accident*. *Fr.* accident *(m)*
camel racing [ˈkæml ˌreɪsɪŋ]	Kamelrennen	Is *camel racing* really a sport?
marathon [ˈmærəθn]	Marathon	
1 **radio** [ˈreɪdɪəʊ]	Radio	! Achtung Aussprache. *Fr.* radio *(f)*
programme [ˈprəʊgræm]	Programm; Sendung	There's an interesting *programme* about camel racing on TV now. *Fr.* programme *(m)*
runner [ˈrʌnə]	Läufer/-in	*runner* → to run
race [reɪs]	Wettlauf; Rennen	Can we watch the bike *race* on TV, Mum?
net [net]	Netz	For tennis, you need a *net*.
to **lose, lost, lost** [luːz; lɒst; lɒst]	verlieren	Our team *lost* again!
match [mætʃ]	Spiel; Match	a game (of football/…)
racquet [ˈrækɪt]	Schläger	
court [kɔːt]	Spielfeld	! a tennis *court* – a football field
to **pass** [pɑːs]	zupassen; zuspielen	
to **kick** [kɪk]	schießen; treten	'Pass' means to throw or *kick* the ball to another player in the same team.
stadium [ˈsteɪdɪəm]	Stadion	
score [skɔː]	Punktestand; Spielstand	At the end of the match the *score* was 2-2.
point [pɔɪnt]	Punkt	That's right. One *point* for your team.
to **catch, caught, caught** [kætʃ; kɔːt; kɔːt]	fangen	*to catch* a ball ↔ to throw a ball
pitch [pɪtʃ]	Spielfeld; Platz	You play rugby on a *pitch*.
2 **the … the** [ðə … ðə]	je … desto	*The* quicker you are with your homework, *the* earlier you can meet your friends.
4 **equipment** [ɪˈkwɪpmənt]	Ausstattung; Ausrüstung	*equipment* = things you need for sports activities

individual [ˌɪndɪˈvɪdʒuəl]	individuell; einzeln	Do you do an *individual* sport or a team sport? *Lat.* individuus/-a/-um

Station 1: Have you ever run in a marathon?

right here [ˌraɪt ˈhɪə]	genau hier	The marathon starts *right here*.
until [ʌnˈtɪl]	bis; erst wenn	You can't run in a marathon *until* you're 18.
11-year-old [ɪˌlevnˈjɪərəʊld]	11-Jährige/-r	The mini marathon is for *11-* to *18-year-olds*.
running [ˈrʌnɪŋ]	Laufen; Rennen	Gwen loves *running*.
trial [traɪəl]	Qualifikation	There are *trials* in sports to find the best runners or players.
Who's in? [huːzˌˈɪn]	Wer macht mit?; Wer ist dabei?	
to **be in** [biˈɪn]	dabei sein; mitmachen	Are you going to run? Well, I'*m in*, and I hope you are too!
run [rʌn]	Rennen; Lauf	*a run* → to run → runner
to **look out** [ˌlʊkˈaʊt]	aufpassen	*Look out*, everyone! I'm going to win this race!
1 **area** [ˈeəriə]	Areal; Gebiet; Fläche	What sports events are there in your *area*?
2 **before** [bɪˈfɔː]	schon einmal; vorher; zuvor	Have you been here *before*? Or is this your first trip?
4 **leg** [leg]	Bein	

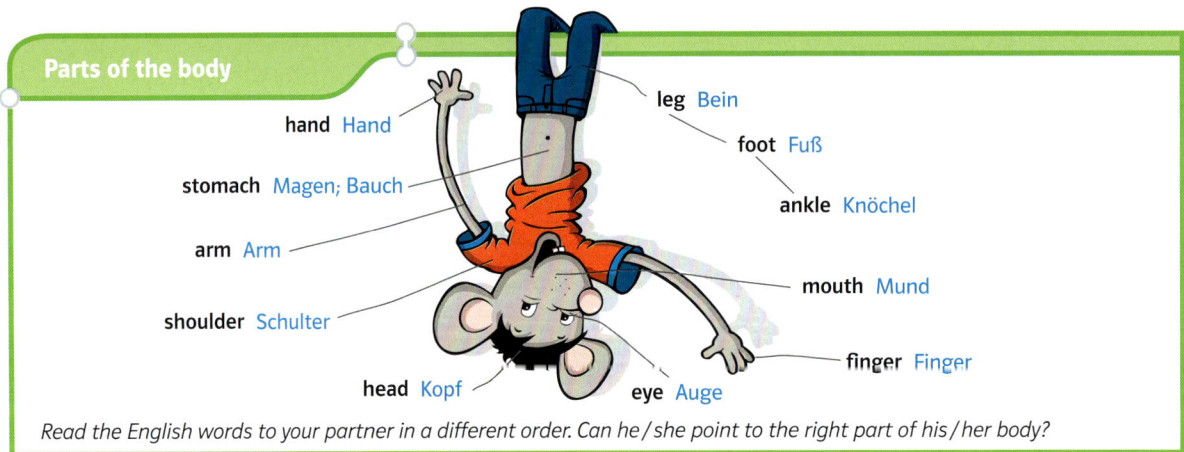

Parts of the body

hand   Hand

stomach   Magen; Bauch

arm   Arm

shoulder   Schulter

head   Kopf

eye   Auge

leg   Bein

foot   Fuß

ankle   Knöchel

mouth   Mund

finger   Finger

Read the English words to your partner in a different order. Can he / she point to the right part of his / her body?

Station 2: Have you been to the doctor's yet?

doctor [ˈdɒktə]	Arzt/Ärztin	**!** Beachte den Unterschied: Have you seen the *doctor* yet? Have you been to the *doctor's* yet? *doctor's* ist die Abkürzung für *doctor's surgery*. *Fr.* docteur *(m)*
yet [jet]	schon; noch	Have you asked your parents about the party *yet*?

to **leave, left, left** [liːv; left; left]	losgehen	
not … yet [nɒt ˈjet]	noch nicht	The friends have*n't* left for the marathon *yet*.
to **train** [treɪn]	trainieren	Luke plays football. He *trains* every day.
to **hurt, hurt, hurt** [hɜːt; hɜːt; hɜːt]	verletzen; weh tun	I *hurt* my leg last month, and it still *hurts* now.
to **twist your ankle** [ˌtwɪst jɔːr ˈæŋkl]	sich den Knöchel verrenken	
pain [peɪn]	Schmerz	I've got a really bad *pain* in my left foot.
unfair [ʌnˈfeə]	unfair	*unfair* ↔ fair
Bye! [baɪ]	Tschüss!	*bye* ↔ hello
6 **mile** [maɪl]	Meile *(brit. Längenmaß)*	1 *mile* = 1,609 metres
chant [tʃɑːnt]	Sprechgesang	*Lat.* cantare
to **cheer** [tʃɪə]	anfeuern; jubeln; zujubeln	Jay is writing a chant to *cheer* the runners in the marathon.
8 to **have a look (at)** [ˌhæv ə ˈlʊk]	anschauen	Let's *have a look* at it. = Let's look at it.
shouldn't [ˈʃʊdnt]	sollte(n) nicht	Olivia *shouldn't* run in the marathon with ankle problems.
prescription [prɪˈskrɪpʃn]	Rezept *(für Arzneimittel)*	*Lat.* praescribere
ointment [ˈɔɪntmənt]	Salbe	The doctor gave Olivia a prescription for an *ointment*.
shoulder [ˈʃəʊldə]	Schulter	
headache *(no pl)* [ˈhedeɪk]	Kopfschmerzen; Kopfweh	**!** *headache* steht immer im Singular: I've got a bad *headache*. *headache* → head
backache [ˈbækeɪk]	Rückenschmerzen; Rückenweh	
stomachache [ˈstʌməkeɪk]	Bauchschmerzen; Bauchweh	
to **feel sick** [ˌfiːl ˈsɪk]	Übelkeit verspüren; sich schlecht fühlen	I *feel sick*. = Mir ist schlecht/übel.
cold [kəʊld]	Erkältung	
cough [kɒf]	Husten	
fever [ˈfiːvə]	Fieber	People with a cold often have a cough and a *fever*. *Fr.* fièvre *(f)*
pill [pɪl]	Pille; Tablette	The doctor wrote a prescription for some *pills*.

I twisted my ankle in PE today. Ouch!

Health

to **have an accident**	einen Unfall haben
to **call the emergency service**	den Rettungsdienst rufen
to **hurt your foot / arm / leg/ …**	sich den Fuß / Arm / das Bein / … verletzen
to **twist your ankle**	sich den Knöchel verrenken
to **feel a pain in** …	Schmerzen haben in / an …
to **get a prescription**	ein Rezept bekommen
to **put ointment on** …	… einsalben
to **take pills**	Tabletten nehmen
to **have a headache / backache / stomachache**	Kopfweh / Rückenweh / Bauchweh haben
to **feel bad / sick**	sich schlecht / krank fühlen
to **catch a cold / cough / fever**	eine Erkältung / Husten / Fieber bekommen

I don't feel well today. Maybe I've caught a cold.

With a partner, make more doctor dialogues as on p. 73.

Station 3: An interview with Ayla

should [ʃʊd]	sollte; solltest; sollten; solltet	In a race you *should* wear real running shoes, an you *shouldn't* run too fast.
cramp [kræmp]	Krampf	
award [əˈwɔːd]	Auszeichnung; Preis	Ayla has won a Maths *award* but no sports *award*.
… what it's like [ˌwɒt ɪts ˈlaɪk]	… wie das ist	Do you know *what it's like* when you break something?
13 **almost** [ˈɔːlməʊst]	fast; beinahe	It's *almost* 8 o'clock! You're late for school.
player [ˈpleɪə]	Spieler/-in; Mitspieler/-in	*player* → to play
so far [ˌsəʊ ˈfɑː]	bis jetzt	The players have given the people a great show *so far*.

Action UK! A picnic in the park

1 **attic** [ˈætɪk]	Dachboden	
Korean [kəˈriːən]	koreanisch; Koreanisch; Koreaner/-in	There was *Korean* food at the picnic.
2 **to fake** [feɪk]	vortäuschen; fälschen	
injury [ˈɪndʒəri]	Verletzung	Who faked an *injury* in the film?
to **teach somebody a lesson** [ˌtiːtʃ ə ˈlesn]	jmdm. eine Lehre/Lektion erteilen	That wasn't a nice thing to do. Let's *teach him a lesson*.
to **teach, taught, taught** [tiːtʃ; tɔːt; tɔːt]	unterrichten; lehren; beibringen	*to teach* → teacher

to **deserve** [dɪˈzɜ:v]	verdienen	The others are angry with you, but you *deserved* it. You tricked them!
point of view [ˌpɔɪnt̬ˌəv ˈvju:]	Standpunkt; Ansicht; Perspektive	Who's right and who's wrong from your *point of view*?
to **get away with** [ˌgetˌəˈweɪ wɪð]	davonkommen mit	Marley didn't *get away with* it.

Skills: How to understand news reports and take notes

1	**rescue** [ˈreskju:]	Rettung	Here is a report about a *rescue* in the mountains.
	difficult [ˈdɪfɪklt]	schwierig	*difficult* ↔ easy *Fr.* difficil/-e; *Lat.* difficilis/-e
	witness [ˈwɪtnəs]	Zeuge/Zeugin	The police is looking for *witnesses* for the accident.
2	**eyewitness** [ˈaɪwɪtnəs]	Augenzeuge/Augenzeugin	The reporter is talking to an *eyewitness* in front of the camera.
	station [ˈsteɪʃn]	Sender	What's your favourite radio *station*?
	listener [ˈlɪsənə]	Zuhörer/-in	*listener* → to listen
	to **receive** [rɪˈsi:v]	empfangen; erhalten; bekommen	A formal word for 'to get'. *Fr.* recevoir; *Lat.* recipere
	scene [si:n]	Schauplatz	The reporter was trying to get to the *scene* of the accident.

Unit task: The aliens have landed!

to **land** [lænd]	landen	Do you believe that aliens have ever *landed* on Earth?
to **record** [rɪˈkɔ:d]	aufnehmen; aufzeichnen	Let's *record* the scene with a camera.
assistant [əˈsɪstnt]	Assistent/-in; Verkäufer/-in	❗ Achtung Schreibung und Aussprache.
to **end** [end]	enden; beenden	*to end* ↔ to start *to end* → end
over [ˈəʊvə]	vorüber; vorbei	School is *over* at 3:15.

Story: Hey, don't call me silly!

to **let go (of)** [ˌlet ˈgəʊ (əv)]	loslassen	Don't *let go of* my hand, Gwen!
silly [ˈsɪli]	Dummkopf	
fancy dress [ˈfænsi dres]	Verkleidung; Kostüm	
to **breathe** [bri:ð]	atmen	
to **keep up, kept, up, kept up (with)** [ˌki:pˈʌp; ˌkeptˈʌp; ˌkeptˈʌp (wɪð)]	mithalten (mit); Schritt halten (mit)	Can Luke *keep up with* Gwen? = Is Luke fast enough?

to **be worried** [bɪ ˈwʌrɪd]	beunruhigt sein; besorgt sein	Don't *be worried* = Don't worry
to **get in the way** [ˌɡet ɪn ðə ˈweɪ]	stören; im Weg stehen	The people in the costumes shouldn't *get in the way* of the runners.
stomach [ˈstʌmək]	Magen; Bauch	*Fr.* estomac *(m)* 
glasses *(pl)* [ˈɡlɑːsɪz]	Brille	**!** *glasses* steht immer im Plural: My *glasses* are broken. I need new ones.
finish line [ˈfɪnɪʃ ˌlaɪn]	Ziellinie	At the end of a run there's always a *finish line*.
stupid [ˈstjuːpɪd]	dumm; blöd	The *stupid* cat and dog almost ruined the race for Gwen and Luke.
to **be gone** [bɪ ˈɡɒn]	verschwunden sein; weg sein	Near the end of the race, Gwen's cramp *was gone*.
We did it! [ˌwiː ˈdɪd ɪt]	Wir haben es geschafft!	*Luke and Gwen did it!*
both [bəʊθ]	beide	Luke and Gwen *both* finished the race.
to **ruin** [ˈruːɪn]	ruinieren; zerstören	Jay and Dave almost *ruined* the race for Luke and Gwen.
official [əˈfɪʃl]	Schiedsrichter/-in	In a race there are always *officials*.
to **surprise** [səˈpraɪz]	überraschen	*to surprise → surprise*
in secret [ɪn ˈsiːkrət]	heimlich	Jay and Dave trained *in secret*. No one knew about it. *in secret → a secret*
because of [bɪˈkɒz ˌəv]	wegen	My feet really hurt *because of* my new shoes.
to **forgive, forgave, forgiven** [fəˈɡɪv; fəˈɡeɪv; fəˈɡɪvn]	vergeben; verzeihen	Can Gwen *forgive* them?
1 **reason** [ˈriːzn]	Grund	Why did you do it? What was the *reason*? *Fr.* raison *(f)*
to **cause** [kɔːz]	verursachen	What or who *caused* the accident?
hope [həʊp]	Hoffnung	*hope → to hope*
fear [fɪə]	Angst; Furcht; Befürchtung	The feeling you have when you are scared.
relationship [rɪˈleɪʃnʃɪp]	Beziehung	Is the *relationship* between you and your neighbours a good one?
2 **On the one hand …, (but) on the other hand …** [ɒn ðəˌwʌn ˌhænd … (bʌt) ɒn ðiˌʌðə ˌhænd …]	Einerseits …, (aber) andererseits …	*On the one hand* he'd like to be a better runner, *but on the other hand* he doesn't want to train very hard.

> I almost did it! I can already see the finish line.

Positive and negative words

What you think of something:	easy, good, great, interesting, useful; *stronger words:* amazing, fantastic, perfect	bad, boring, dangerous, difficult; *stronger words:* awful, scary
What you think of a person:	beautiful, creative, cute, fair, friendly, fun, funny, good, polite, popular	aggressive, boring, rude, silly, stupid, unfair, unfriendly
How a person feels:	confident, good, happy, lucky	bad, embarrassed, lonely, sad, shy, unhappy, unlucky

Which of the words are opposites? Write them down together.

Check-out

3	bicycle motocross [ˌbaɪsɪkl ˈməʊtəʊkrɒs]	Fahrradmotocross	The word 'bike' is short for 'bicycle'.

Across cultures 2 English around the world

1	summer camp [ˈsʌmə kæmp]	Sommerferienlager	I only spoke English when I was at *summer camp* last year.
2	to mention [ˈmenʃn]	erwähnen	Did I *mention* that I have a cool new phone? *Fr.* mentionner
	statement [ˈsteɪtmənt]	Aussage; Behauptung; Erklärung	to make a *statement* = to say something
	exactly [ɪɡˈzæktli]	genau	I don't understand. What *exactly* do you mean? *Lat.* exactus/-a/-um
	as [æz]	wie	My favourite music is not the same *as* yours.
	South Korean [ˌsaʊθ kəˈriːən]	Südkoreaner/-in; südkorea-nisch; Südkoreanisch	
	Romanian [rʊˈmeɪniən]	Rumäne/Rumänin; rumänisch; Rumänisch	
3	first language [ˌfɜːst ˈlæŋɡwɪdʒ]	Muttersprache	My *first language* is German.
	official language [əˌfɪʃl ˈlæŋɡwɪdʒ]	Amtssprache	In India, English is an *official language*.
	merchant [ˈmɜːtʃənt]	Kaufmann, Händler	A *merchant* sells and buys things.
	to cross [krɒs]	überqueren; kreuzen	You need to *cross* the street to get to the shoe shop.
	colony [ˈkɒləni]	Kolonie	Many years ago, Germany had *colonies* too. *Fr.* colonie *(f)*; *Lat.* colonia *(f)*

for example [fər‿ɪgˈzɑːmpl]	zum Beispiel	I speak four languages, *for example* English and French.
head of state [ˌhed‿əv ˈsteɪt]	Staatsoberhaupt	The British queen is *head of state* in Australia.
superpower [ˈsuːpəˌpaʊə]	Supermacht	Will China and India be the next *superpowers*?
to **influence** [ˈɪnfluəns]	beeinflussen	The USA has *influenced* the world in different ways. **!** Im Englischen verwendet man für „USA" immer die Einzahl (The USA has …), im Deutschen aber die Mehrzahl (Die USA haben …).
technology [tekˈnɒlədʒi]	Technologie	
to **communicate** [kəˈmjuːnɪkeɪt]	kommunizieren; sich verständigen	An easy way to *communicate* with people is to speak to them. *Lat.* communicare
4 **region** [ˈriːdʒn]	Region; Gegend	What *region* in Germany do you come from? *Lat.* regio *(f)*
expression [ɪkˈspreʃn]	Ausdruck; Wendung; Äußerung	We often use English *expressions* in German. *Lat.* expressio *(f)*

Unit 5 Stay in touch

Check-in

to **stay in touch (with)** [ˌsteɪ ɪn ˈtʌtʃ (wɪð)]	in Kontakt bleiben (mit)	E-mails are a good way to *stay in touch* with your friends.
media [ˈmiːdiə]	Medien	Radio, TV and the internet are all *media*. *Fr.* médias *(f) (pl)*; *Lat.* medium *(nt)*
letter [ˈletə]	Brief	 *Lat.* littera *(f)*
interest [ˈɪntrəst]	Interesse	*interest* → interesting → be interested
paradise [ˈpærədaɪs]	Paradies	*Fr.* paradis *(m)*
print [prɪnt]	gedruckt; Druck-	
for [fɔː; fə]	wegen	I buy print magazines *for* the posters.
social network [ˌsəʊʃl ˈnetwɜːk]	soziales Netzwerk	You can chat with all kinds of people in *social networks*.
nasty [ˈnɑːsti]	garstig; gemein	*nasty* ↔ nice
cyber bully [ˌsaɪbə ˈbʊli]	*jemand, der andere in sozialen Netzwerken belästigt oder mobbed*	*Cyber bullies* write nasty comments in social networks.
2 to **change** [tʃeɪndʒ]	wechseln; (sich) ändern	I *changed* my phone number. A stupid cyber bully was sending me nasty texts. *Fr.* changer
to **post** [pəʊst]	online stellen; posten	Have you *posted* the photos of the class trip?

to **take part (in)** [ˌteɪk ˈpɑːt (ɪn)]	teilnehmen (an)	Let's *take part in* the new Drama Club at school.
to **text** [tekst]	eine SMS schicken	*to text* → text message
discussion [dɪˈskʌʃn]	Diskussion	*discussion* → to discuss
3 **practical** [ˈpræktɪkl]	praktisch	Smartphones are *practical* to stay in touch with friends. *Fr.* pratique
mobile [ˈməʊbaɪl]	Handy; Mobiltelefon	*mobile* = phone

Media collocations

to check	checken, überprüfen	my e-mails / my profile / my friend's profile	meine E-Mails / mein Profil / das Profil meines Freundes
to change	ändern	my profile	mein Profil
to post to share	posten; hochladen teilen	photos / information about …	Fotos / Informationen über …
to read / to write / to reply to	lesen / schreiben / antworten auf	texts / text messages / e-mails	SMS-Nachrichten / E-Mails
to send / to receive	senden / empfangen	texts / text messages / e-mails / photos / information	SMS-Nachrichten / E-Mails / Fotos / Informationen
to chat with to text to stay in touch with	chatten mit eine SMS schreiben in Kontakt bleiben mit	a friend	einem Freund
to join to take part in	beitreten teilnehmen an	a discussion / a social network / a forum	einer Diskussion / einem sozialen Netzwerk / einem Forum
to have to take part in	führen teilnehmen an	a discussion / a video chat	eine Diskussion / einen Videochat einer Diskussion / einem Videochat
to play	spielen	video games	Computerspiele

Station 1: Dear Ruby

agony aunt [ˈæɡəniˌɑːnt]	Kummerkastentante	Lauren didn't want to talk about her problem with her friends or her family. So she wrote a letter to her favourite magazine's *agony aunt*.
teen [tiːn]	Jugend-	*teen* → teenager

… **what to do.** ['wɒt tə du:]	… was ich tun soll.	I don't know *what to do*.
to **spend, spent, spent** [spend; spent; spent]	verbringen *(Zeit)*	She *spends* all her free time with her dog.
the two of them [ðə 'tu:_əv ðəm]	beide	My brothers sent me a photo of *the two of them*.
site [saɪt]	Webseite	
to **act like** ['ækt laɪk]	tun als ob	My sister often *acts like* a baby.
whenever [wen'evə]	wann immer; jedes Mal, wenn; so oft	*Whenever* I ask my brother for something, he says "no".
self-critical ['self͵krɪtɪkl]	selbstkritisch	The agony aunt's advice is to be *self-critical*. I think she's right.
to **overreact** [͵əʊvəri'ækt]	überreagieren	I know you're angry with him, but don't *overreact* and say bad things about him, OK?
as soon as [əz 'su:n͵əz]	sobald	Things usually get better *as soon as* you talk to the person you're fighting with.
to **make somebody do something** [meɪk]	jmdn. dazu bringen, etw. zu tun	My friend's texts *make* me *feel bad*.
1 **opinion** [ə'pɪnjən]	Meinung	In my *opinion* … = I think … *Lat.* opinio (f)
2 **face-to-face** [͵feɪstə'feɪs]	*hier:* persönlich; von Angesicht zu Angesicht	It's fun to meet people *face-to-face* and not just in social networks.
to **block** [blɒk]	blockieren; abblocken	You can *block* messages from people you don't like.
forever [fə'revə]	für immer; ewig	Photos that you post on the internet never go away. They can stay there *forever*.
to **care (about)** ['keər͵əbaʊt]	wichtig nehmen; sich kümmern (um); sich interessieren (für)	If you *care about* something then it's important to you.
attention [ə'tenʃn]	Aufmerksamkeit; Beachtung	*Fr.* attention (f); *Lat.* attentio (f)
myself [maɪ'self]	ich/mir/mich (selbst); selber	*myself* → yourself → himself
4 **understanding** [͵ʌndə'stændɪŋ]	Verständnis	What can you say to show *understanding*?
compromise ['kɒmprəmaɪz]	Kompromiss	It isn't always easy to find a *compromise*. *Fr.* compromis (m)
to **worry** ['wʌri]	sich Sorgen machen	Don't *worry* about your friend. Everything is OK now.
5 **up** [ʌp]	hinauf; nach oben	She looked *up* and down the street.
6 **friendship** ['frendʃɪp]	Freundschaft	I've got lots of friends. I think *friendship* is very important.

Station 2: Forum? What forum?

to **be allowed to (do sth)** [bɪˌəˈlaʊd tə]	dürfen	Students *aren't allowed to* use mobiles at school.
to **go over to** [ˌgəʊ ˈəʊvə tə]	hinübergehen zu; zu jmdm. nach Hause gehen	Come on, let's *go over* to your house.
What on earth ...? [ˌwɒt: ɒn ˈɜːθ]	Was um alles in der Welt ...?	*What on earth* is this?
to **fix** [fɪks]	reparieren; befestigen	My bike is broken. Can you *fix* it?
to **go crazy** [ˌgəʊ ˈkreɪzi]	ausflippen; durchdrehen; verrückt werden	I think I'm *going crazy*: I don't understand the Maths homework at all!
to **take, took, taken** [teɪk; tʊk; ˈteɪkn]	dauern; (Zeit) brauchen	It *takes* two hours to get to London by train.
washing machine [ˈwɒʃɪŋ məˌʃiːn]	Waschmaschine	*washing machine* → to wash
to **waste** [weɪst]	verschwenden	You're *wasting* your time, Dad!
cannot [ˈkænɒt]	kann nicht; können nicht	*cannot* = can't
step-by-step [ˌstepbaɪˈstep]	Schritt-für-Schritt-	On the internet, there's *step-by-step* advice for everything.
to **be able to (do sth)** [bɪˌˈeɪbl tə]	fähig sein zu; können; dürfen	When my grandma lived in the next town, we *were able to* see her often. Now she lives in another town.
still [stɪl]	dennoch	I don't have any money, but I'm *still* going to go to London.
I've done this a million times before. [ˌaɪv dʌn ðɪs ə ˌmɪljən taɪmz bɪˈfɔː]	Ich habe das schon eine Million Mal gemacht.	
knob [nɒb]	Griff	Cupboard doors often have *knobs*.
to **reach** [riːtʃ]	erreichen; dran kommen	My mum put the chocolate on top of the cupboard so my little sister can't *reach* it.
to **work** [wɜːk]	*hier:* funktionieren	Is the washing machine *working* again?
genius [ˈdʒiːniəs]	Genie	*Fr.* génie *(m)*
With a very big head! [ˌwɪð ə ˌveri bɪg ˈhed]	Und ein Angeber!	
may [meɪ]	(vielleicht) können; dürfen	! Wenn du auf Englisch nach etwas fragst oder um etwas bittest, beginne deine Frage mit *may*: *May* I take another piece of cake, please?
13 **mad** [mæd]	verrückt	My parents think that I'm media *mad*.
result [rɪˈzʌlt]	Ergebnis; Resultat	Have we got the test *results* yet? Who got the most points? *Fr.* résultat *(m)*
to **(e-)mail** [ˈiːmeɪl]	mailen; per E-Mail schicken	Could you *e-mail* me your part of the class project? I can *mail* you my part too.
to **download** [ˌdaʊnˈləʊd]	herunterladen *(aus dem Internet)*	

to **comment (on)** [ˈkɒmentˌ(ɒn)]	kommentieren	Please don't *comment* on my test results; I didn't do very well at all! *to comment* → a comment
to **stay away from** [ˌsteɪ əˈweɪ frəm]	fernbleiben von; meiden	*Stay away from* too much chocolate. It isn't good for your health.
in other ways [ɪn ˈʌðə weɪz]	auf andere Weise	I don't need my phone all the time. I can have fun *in other ways* too.

Skills: How to write a letter and a reply

1	**camping** [ˈkæmpɪŋ]	Camping; Zelten	We go *camping* every year!
	to **miss** [mɪs]	verpassen; versäumen	Hey, you *missed* a great party! Where were you?
	Yours … [jɔːz]	Viele Grüße … *(am Ende von Briefen und Mails)*	! You can end a letter or e-mail like this.
	to **begin, began, begun** [bɪˈgɪn; bɪˈgæn; bɪˈgʌn]	beginnen; anfangen	How do you *begin* a letter or e-mail?
	beach [biːtʃ]	Strand	
2	**weird** [wɪəd]	merkwürdig; seltsam; sonderbar	*weird* = strange

Unit task: Advice letters and replies: Our collection

chance [tʃɑːns]	Chance; Gelegenheit; Möglichkeit	Give me another *chance*, please!
weekday [ˈwiːkdeɪ]	Wochentag	On *weekday* mornings I usually go to school.
to **do about** [ˈduː əˌbaʊt]	unternehmen wegen	What can I *do about* my teacher? I don't think she likes me.

Story: It's a disaster!

disaster [dɪˈzɑːstə]	Desaster; Katastrophe; Unglück	Frank's day was a *disaster*. *Fr.* désastre *(m)*
to **rain** [reɪn]	regnen	It's *raining*!
light [laɪt]	Licht; Lampe	At night you need *light*.
to **be on** [biˈɒn]	an sein; laufen	The race *is on*.
thunder *(no pl)* [ˈθʌndə]	Donner	In a storm there's usually *thunder* and lightning.

lightning *(no pl)* [ˈlaɪtnɪŋ]	Blitz	
to **get out of** [get ˌaʊt‿əv]	aussteigen	He *got out of* the car quickly and ran to the house.
front door [ˌfrʌnt ˈdɔː]	Haustür	Every house has a *front door*.
upstairs [ʌpˈsteəz]	nach oben; im Obergeschoss; oben	
headphones *(pl)* [ˈhedfəʊnz]	Kopfhörer	Take my *headphones* and listen to this!
downstairs [ˌdaʊnˈsteəz]	nach unten; im Untergeschoss; unten	*downstairs* ↔ upstairs
to **tap** [tæp]	antippen	Jay *tapped* Olivia's shoulder.
to **cry** [kraɪ]	schreien; rufen	*to cry* = to shout **Fr.** crier
to **fight, fought, fought** [faɪt; fɔːt; fɔːt]	kämpfen; (sich) streiten	My brother and I often *fight*.
to **joke** [dʒəʊk]	scherzen	Don't worry, I'm only *joking*! *to joke* → a joke **Lat.** iocus *(m)*
to **press** [pres]	drücken; pressen	**Fr.** presser
to **go black** [ˌgəʊ ˈblæk]	schwarz werden	After the bang everything *went black*.
to **crash** [kræʃ]	abstürzen	Has your computer ever *crashed*?
power cut [ˈpaʊə ˌkʌt]	Stromausfall	
round [raʊnd]	um … herum	Five minutes later they all sat *round* the table.
candlelight *(no pl)* [ˈkændlaɪt]	Kerzenlicht	
only [ˈəʊnli]	einzige/-r/-s	I'm the *only* girl in my tutor group without glasses.
right now [ˌraɪt ˈnaʊ]	jetzt gleich; sofort; gerade	*Right now* I don't have any problems.
to **cook** [kʊk]	kochen	Have you ever *cooked* an Indian curry?
to **show off** [ʃəʊ ˈɒf]	angeben	My brother always *shows off* with his expensive smartphone.
to **borrow** [ˈbɒrəʊ]	(sich) ausleihen	Can I *borrow* this t-shirt? – OK, but please remember to give it back.
1 to **feel left out** [ˌfiːl left ˈaʊt]	sich ausgeschlossen fühlen	Did Frank *feel left out*?
2 to **link** [lɪŋk]	verbinden	

Unit 6 Goodbye Greenwich

Check-in

journey [ˈdʒɜːni]	Reise; Fahrt	On our *journey* through England we met a lot of nice people.
future [ˈfjuːtʃə]	Zukunft	What will the *future* be like?
medieval [ˌmediˈiːvl]	mittelalterlich	Is every castle *medieval*? – No, of course not. *Fr.* médiéval/-e
living history show [ˌlɪvɪŋ ˈhɪstəri ˌʃəʊ]	Show, in der historischer Alltag nachgespielt wird	
pony trekking [ˈpəʊni ˌtrekɪŋ]	Ponyreiten im Gelände	You go *pony trekking* in the country.
Scottish [ˈskɒtɪʃ]	schottisch	Edinburgh is the *Scottish* capital.
1 to **include** [ɪnˈkluːd]	einschließen; beinhalten	The trip will be expensive, but the price *includes* all our meals. *Lat.* includere
2 **negative** [ˈnegətɪv]	negativ; verneint	*negative* ↔ positive *Fr.* négatif/négative
landscape [ˈlændskeɪp]	Landschaft	
3 **sandy** [ˈsændi]	sandig; Sand-	
rocky [ˈrɒki]	felsig; steinig	Not every beach is sandy. Many are *rocky*.
wide [waɪd]	breit; weit; ausgedehnt	This table is too *wide*, we can't get it through the door.
deep [diːp]	tief	You mustn't go into *deep* water if you can't swim.
island [ˈaɪlənd]	Insel	The British Isles are a group of *islands*.
harbour [ˈhɑːbə]	Hafen	The weather is bad, so the boats are staying in the *harbour*.
hiking [ˈhaɪkɪŋ]	Wandern	Wales is great for *hiking*.
mountain biking [ˈmaʊntɪn ˌbaɪkɪŋ]	Mountainbikefahren	
(wind)surfing [ˈ(wɪnd)sɜːfɪŋ]	(Wind-)Surfen	! Beachte: Surfen und Windsurfen sind verschiedene Sportarten.
palm tree [ˈpɑːm ˌtriː]	Palme	
to **grow, grew, grown** [grəʊ; gruː; grəʊn]	wachsen	All kinds of flowers *grow* in our garden.

Parts of the British Isles

The British Isles — Scotland, Northern Ireland, Wales, Republic of Ireland, England

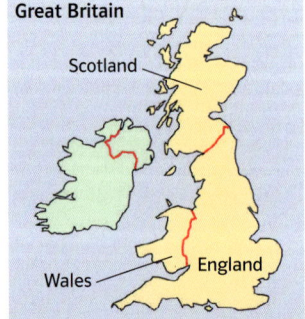

Great Britain — Scotland, Wales, England

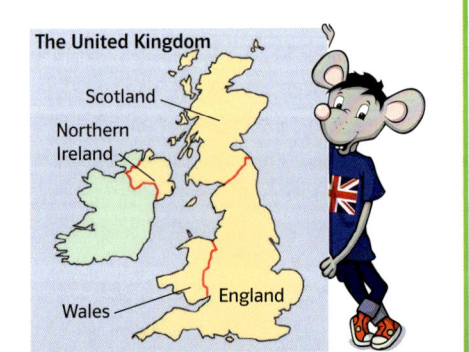

The United Kingdom — Scotland, Northern Ireland, Wales, England

Places and what you can do there

Places		Activities	
in a city / town	in einer Stadt	to visit a museum / castle to go to a festival to get to know the capital of …	ein Museum / Schloss besichtigen ein Festival besuchen die Hauptstadt von … kennen lernen
in the fields in the forest	auf den Wiesen und Feldern im Wald	to go hiking / mountain biking / pony trekking to go for a walk	wandern / Mountainbike fahren / wanderreiten gehen spazieren gehen
in the mountains	in den Bergen	to go climbing / hiking / mountain biking / pony trekking to go for a walk to climb a mountain	klettern / … einen Berg besteigen

on an island
at the seaside,
  by the sea,
  on the coast
on the beach,
  on the shore
on the river bank,
  on the shore
	auf einer Insel
	am Meer, an der Küste
	
	am Strand, am Meeresufer
	
	am Flussufer
		to go climbing / hiking / mountain biking / pony trekking
		to go for a walk
		to climb a mountain
		
		to go fishing
			klettern / …
			
			angeln gehen

in the sea in a river in a lake	im Meer in einem Fluss in einem See	to go swimming / surfing / windsurfing	schwimmen / surfen / windsurfen gehen

Station 1: Moving to the middle of nowhere

to **move (house)** [muːv (haʊs)]	umziehen	When you *move house*, you leave your old home and go to live in a new one. *Lat.* movēre
nowhere ['nəʊweə]	nirgendwo; nirgendwohin	*nowhere* → somewhere → everywhere

Cornish [ˈkɔːnɪʃ]	aus/in Cornwall	Dave and his parents are going to move to a *Cornish* town.
countryside [ˈkʌntrisaɪd]	Land	in the *countryside* = auf dem Land
to **miss** [mɪs]	vermissen	I *miss* you. = Du fehlst mir.
to **stay** [steɪ]	übernachten	We *stayed* at a really nice hotel.
(not) any longer [nɒt ˌeni ˈlɒŋgə]	(nicht) mehr; (nicht) länger	I don't like it here; I don't want to stay here *any longer*.
all of us [ˈɔːl əv ˌʌs]	wir alle	
1 **transport** [ˈtrænspɔːt]	Verkehrsmittel; Transport	*Transport* can be expensive. *Lat.* transportare
3 **travel agent's** [ˈtrævl ˌeɪdʒnts]	Reisebüro	You can buy holidays at the *travel agent's*.
ticket [ˈtɪkɪt]	Fahrschein	*Fr.* ticket *(m)*
to **depend (on)** [dɪˈpend ˌ(ɒn)]	abhängen von	The price of the ticket *depends on* the date. *Fr.* dépendre (de)
per [pɜː; pə]	pro	The price for the tickets is £5 *per* person.
to **promise** [ˈprɒmɪs]	versprechen	Can his parents *promise* that Dave will like Cornwall?
5 to **book** [bʊk]	buchen; reservieren	You can *book* a ticket for a journey, a holiday, a table at a restaurant.
to **return** [rɪˈtɜːn]	zurückkehren; zurückfahren	*to return* = to go or come back *Fr.* retourner
form [fɔːm]	Formular	You often have to fill in *forms* on the internet.
to **click on** [ˈklɪk ˌɒn]	anklicken	*Click on* 'SEND' to send your e-mail.
connection [kəˈnekʃn]	Verbindung	What *connections* are there from Greenwich to St Agnes today?
one-way ticket [ˈwʌnweɪ ˌtɪkɪt]	einfache Fahrkarte	
single ticket [ˌsɪŋgl ˌtɪkɪt]	einfache Fahrkarte	*single ticket = one-way ticket*
return ticket [rɪˈtɜːn ˌtɪkɪt]	Hin- und Rückfahrkarte	*return ticket* ↔ one-way ticket
fee [fiː]	Gebühr	Is there an extra *fee* on the ticket?
to **depart** [dɪˈpɑːt]	abfahren	When does the train *depart*?
to **arrive** [əˈraɪv]	ankommen	And when does the next train *arrive*? *Fr.* arriver
outward [ˈaʊtwəd]	abfahrend	*Outward* trains leave the station.
inward [ˈɪnwəd]	ankommend	*Inward* trains arrive at the station.
fare [feə]	Fahrpreis	Is there a special *fare* for groups?
platform [ˈplætfɔːm]	Plattform; Bahnsteig	
to **get on (the bus)** [ˌget ˈɒn]	einsteigen (in den Bus)	*to get on* ↔ to get off
starting place [ˈstɑːtɪŋ pleɪs]	Startpunkt	

Travel words

to travel	reisen
travel agent's	Reisebüro
to take a journey / trip	eine Reise machen
transport	Transport
by train / coach / car / Underground	mit dem Zug / Bus / Auto / mit der-U-Bahn
station	Bahnhof, Station
airport	Flughafen
on the road	auf der Straße; unterwegs
one way; single / return	einfach / hin und zurück
outward / inward journey	Hinfahrt / Rückfahrt
to depart / arrive	abfahren / ankommen
to change	umsteigen

Tell your partner about a trip you took last summer / last year / …

6	weather forecast ['weðə ,fɔːkɑːst]	Wettervorhersage	It tells you what the weather will be like.

Weather words

It's / The weather is	cold	kalt
	warm	warm
	cloudy	wolkig; bewölkt
	sunny	sonnig
There is / are	clouds	Wolken
	sun	Sonne
	rain	Regen
	wind	Wind
	storm	Sturm
	thunder	Donner
	lightning	Blitz
It's raining. The sun is shining.		Es regnet. Die Sonne scheint.

Say what the weather is like today and what it will be like tomorrow.

Skills: How to get information

1	**tourist board** [ˈtʊərɪst bɔːd]	Touristeninformation	At a *tourist board* you can get information about a country or region.
2	**Dear Sir or Madam** [dɪə ˌsɜːrˌɔː ˈmædəm]	Sehr geehrte Dame, sehr geehrter Herr	You begin a formal letter like this.
	grammar school [ˈgræmə ˌskuːl]	Gymnasium	A school (in Britain) that is similar to the German 'Gymnasium'.
	Best wishes [ˌbest ˈwɪʃɪz]	Viele Grüße; Herzliche Grüße	You can finish a formal letter like this.
	to send off [send ˈɒf]	abschicken	Before you *send off* your e-mail, read it again.
	yourselves [jɔːˈselvz]	selber; ihr/euch/Sie/sich (selbst)	Did you enjoy *yourselves*? – Oh yes, the party was really great.

Station 2: Visit Cornwall – You'll love it!

in the far west [ɪn ðə fɑː ˈwest]	im äußersten Westen	Cornwall is *in the far west* of Great Britain.
coastline [ˈkəʊstlaɪn]	Küste; Küstenverlauf	Cornwall's *coastline* is almost 300 miles long.
fishing [ˈfɪʃɪŋ]	Angeln; Fischen; Fischerei	*fishing* → a fish
to get to know [ˌget tə ˈnəʊ]	kennen lernen	I would like to *get to know* your friends.
wild [waɪld]	wild	pets – farm animals – *wild* animals
prehistoric [ˌpriːhɪˈstɒrɪk]	vorgeschichtlich	
monument [ˈmɒnjəmənt]	Monument; Denkmal	In Cornwall you can visit lots of prehistoric *monuments*. *Lat.* monumentum (nt)
walking trail [ˈwɔːkɪŋ treɪl]	Wanderweg	On *walking trails* you can only go on foot.
plant [plɑːnt]	Pflanze	A tree is a *plant*.
from around the world [frɒm əˌraʊnd ðə ˈwɜːld]	aus aller Welt	In our town there are people *from around the world*.
environment [ɪnˈvaɪrnmənt]	Umwelt; Umgebung	Our *environment* is the world (or area) we live in. *Fr.* environnement (m)
mining [ˈmaɪnɪŋ]	Bergbau	Cornwall has a long *mining* history.
Bronze Age [ˈbrɒnz eɪdʒ]	Bronzezeit (ca. 2200–800 v. Chr.)	
cross [krɒs]	Kreuz	*Fr.* croix (f); *Lat.* crux (f)
Irish [ˈaɪrɪʃ]	irisch; Irisch	There are lots of nice *Irish* songs.

Gaelic ['geɪlɪk]	gälisch; Gälisch	*Gaelic* is a Celtic language.
besides [bɪ'saɪdz]	neben	Do you speak any languages *besides* German?
7 **geography** [dʒi'ɒɡrəfi]	Geografie; Erdkunde	What do you know about the *geography* of Cornwall?
tourism ['tʊərɪzm]	Tourismus	*tourism* → tour → tourist
11 **local** ['ləʊkl]	örtlich; lokal	The schools in your area are your *local* schools.
dialect ['daɪəlekt]	Dialekt	Do people speak a *dialect* where you live?
accent ['æksnt]	Akzent	My granny has a strong German accent when she speaks English.
12 **announcement** [ə'naʊnsmənt]	Ankündigung; Durchsage	I never understand the *announcements* at the station. *Lat.* annuntiare
13 **couple** ['kʌpl]	Paar	*Fr.* couple *(m)*
customer ['kʌstəmə]	Kunde/Kundin	A *customer* buys things in a shop. *customer* ↔ assistant
14 to **supply** [sə'plaɪ]	versorgen	Shops *supply* people with the things they need.
to **rule** [ruːl]	herrschen; regieren	Elizabeth II *rules* the UK.

Action UK! The caves

cave [keɪv]	Höhle	*Fr.* caverne *(f)*
1 to **feed, fed, fed** [fiːd; fed; fed]	füttern; ernähren	Did you *feed* the dog this morning? People must work to *feed* their families.
to **milk** [mɪlk]	melken	
cow [kaʊ]	Kuh	
geocaching ['dʒiː.əʊkæʃɪŋ]	Geocaching	
2 **love** [lʌv]	Liebe	*love* → to love
3 to **get lost** [ˌɡet 'lɒst]	verloren gehen; sich verirren	In a big city, it's easy to *get lost*.
darkness ['dɑːknəs]	Dunkelheit	*darkness* → dark

Story: Things will get better

to **get, got, got** [ɡet; ɡɒt; ɡɒt]	werden	If you learn more words, your English will *get* better.
to **come in** [ˌkʌm 'ɪn]	hereinkommen	Mrs Preston invites the friends to *come in*.
hall [hɔːl]	Flur; Diele; Korridor	
electricity [ˌelɪk'trɪsəti]	Elektrizität; Strom	If there's no *electricity*, you can't make tea. *Fr.* électricité *(f)*

What's the matter? [ˌwɒts ðə ˈmætə]	Was ist los?; Was hast du?	
Oh dear! [ˌəʊ ˈdɪə]	Oje!	I've hurt my leg. – *Oh dear!*
to **go out** [ˌgəʊ ˈaʊt]	ausgehen; hinausgehen	Let's *go out!*
coastal path [ˌkəʊstl ˈpɑːθ]	Küstenweg	
mine [maɪn]	Mine	*mine* → mining
plumber [ˈplʌmə]	Installateur/-in; Klempner/-in	A *plumber* can fix your water pipes.
hill [hɪl]	Berg; Hügel	Our house is on a *hill* and we've got a fantastic view.
by [baɪ]	bei; neben; an	*by* = next to
chimney [ˈtʃɪmni]	Kamin; Schornstein	
roof [ruːf]	Dach	a *roof* with a chimney
cloud [klaʊd]	Wolke	
tin [tɪn]	Zinn	There's an old *tin* mine near Dave's house.
to **go right back to** [ˌgəʊ raɪt ˈbæk tə]	zurückgehen auf	Cornwall's mining history *goes right back to* Celtic times.
to **solve** [sɒlv]	lösen	Dave and his friends want to *solve* the puzzle. *Lat.* solvere
to **boom** [buːm]	dröhnen	A loud voice *booms*.
to **keep away from** [ˌkiːpˌəˈweɪ frəm]	(sich) fernhalten von	*Keep away from* my chocolate!
skirt [skɜːt]	Rock	
trousers (pl) [ˈtraʊzəz]	Hose	! *trousers* steht immer im Plural: You've got cool *trousers*.
spear [spɪə]	Speer	The *spear* is broken.
to **move in/into** [ˌmuːvˌɪn/ˈɪntə]	einziehen in	Dave and his parents *moved into* a new house in Cornwall.
warrior [ˈwɒriə]	Krieger	
society [səˈsaɪəti]	Verein; Gesellschaft	Bob is a member of a local history *society*. *Fr.* société (f)
twin [twɪn]	Zwilling; Zwillings-	
tool [tuːl]	Werkzeug; Gerät	A plumber needs special *tools*.
electrician [ˌelɪkˈtrɪʃn]	Elektriker/-in	*electrician* → electricity
plumbing [ˈplʌmɪŋ]	Sanitärarbeit	*plumbing* → plumber

electrics [ɪˈlektrɪks]	Elektrik	An electrician can fix the *electrics* in your house.
change [tʃeɪndʒ]	Änderung; Veränderung; Wechsel	*change* → to change
to **turn to** [ˈtɜːn tə]	sich wenden an; sich zuwenden	I *turned to* him to say something but he wasn't there any more.

More jobs

Who?		What and where?
mechanic	Mechaniker/-in	to fix, car, tools
pilot	Pilot/-in	to travel, journey, airport
plumber	Klempner/-in, Sanitärinstallateur/-in	to fix, plumbing, tools
electrician	Elektriker/-in	to fix, electrics, electricity

3	**diary entry** [ˈdaɪəri entri]	Tagebucheintrag	A *diary entry* is a personal text in which you write about what happened and what you felt.
	nobody else [ˈnəʊbədi els]	niemand anderes	Only you and *nobody else* should read your diary entries.
	postcard [ˈpəʊstkɑːd]	Postkarte	I love it when I get a real *postcard* and not just photos in an e-mail!
	sailboat [ˈseɪlbəʊt]	Segelboot	
	to **camp** [kæmp]	campen; zelten	*to camp* → camping

Across cultures 3 British stories and legends

	legend [ˈledʒənd]	Legende; Sage	An old story – maybe true in parts.
2	ingredient [ɪnˈɡriːdiənt]	Zutat	Something is missing in this cake; hm, what *ingredient* did I forget?
	completely [kəmˈpliːtli]	völlig	What you're saying isn't *completely* true! Some of it's wrong, sorry.
	cruel [ˈkruːəl]	grausam	People are sometimes *cruel* to each other. *Fr.* cruel/-le
	magical [ˈmædʒɪkəl]	magisch; Zauber-	The world of Harry Potter is a *magical* world.
	wizard [ˈwɪzəd]	Zauberer	

hero, heroes *(pl)* [ˈhɪərəʊ, ˈhɪərəʊz]	Held	The most important character in a book or film, usually good and brave.
villain [ˈvɪlən]	Bösewicht	*villain* ↔ hero
knight [naɪt]	Ritter	
criminal [ˈkrɪmɪnəl]	Kriminelle/-r; Verbrecher/-in	*criminal* = villain *Lat.* criminalis
powerful [ˈpaʊəfl]	stark; mächtig	Who's the most *powerful* person in the world?
power [paʊə]	Kraft; Macht; Stärke	*power* → powerful
private detective [ˌpraɪvət dɪˈtektɪv]	Privatdetektiv/-in	There are lots of books and films about Sherlock Holmes, the famous *private detective*.
mysterious [mɪˈstɪərɪəs]	mysteriös; geheimnisvoll	
crime [kraɪm]	Verbrechen; Kriminalität	*crime* → criminal *Lat.* crimen *(nt)*
heroine [ˈherəʊɪn]	Heldin	Who is your favourite *heroine*?
robber [ˈrɒbə]	Räuber/-in	A *robber* is a criminal.
outlaw [ˈaʊtlɔː]	Geächtete/-r; Gesetzlose/-r	Robin Hood was a famous *outlaw*.
to hide, hid, hidden [haɪd; hɪd; ˈhɪdn]	(sich) verstecken	My sister sometimes *hides* my things. She thinks it's funny.
3 **the Round Table** [ðə ˌraʊnd ˈteɪbl]	die Tafelrunde	King Arthur and his knights met at the *Round Table*.
the rich [ðə rɪtʃ]	die Reichen	Robin Hood was famous because he stole money from *the rich*.
the poor [ðə pʊə]	die Armen	*the poor* ↔ the rich
4 **prop** [prɒp]	Requisite	You need lots of *props* for a film.
set [set]	Umgebung; Rahmen	A film's *set* shows where the people live, work, etc.
to carry [ˈkæri]	tragen	Can you *carry* this box for me, please?

You're my heroine, Lou!

Dictionary

In dieser alphabetischen Wortliste findest du das gesamte Vokabular von *Green Line* 1 und 2.
Namen stehen in einer extra Liste am Ende des ***Dictionary***.
Einträge, die aus mehreren Wörtern bestehen, kannst du meist unter verschiedenen
Stichwörtern nachschlagen. So ist z.B. *after all* unter *after* und unter *all* eingetragen.
Die Fundstellen stehen immer hinter dem jeweiligen Wort und zeigen dir an, wo es zum ersten Mal vorkommt, z. B.:
actor ['æktə] Schauspieler **II U2**, 36 kommt zum ersten Mal vor in Band 2, Unit 2, Seite 36
airport ['eəpɔːt] Flughafen **II AC1**, 48 kommt zum ersten Mal vor in Band 2, Across cultures 1, Seite 48
U = Unit, AC = Across cultures
Die mit * gekennzeichneten Verben sind unregelmäßig.
Die mit ° gekennzeichneten Vokabeln sind rezeptiv.

A

a [ə] ein/-e **I**
  a bit [ə 'bɪt] ein bisschen; ein wenig
  II U1, 18
  a couple of [ə 'kʌpl̩ əv] ein paar **I**
  a few [ə 'fjuː] ein paar; wenige; einige **I**
  a girl from Germany [ə ˌgɜːl frəm
  'dʒɜːməni] ein Mädchen aus Deutschland **I**
  a group of three [ə ˌgruːp əv 'θriː] eine
  Dreiergruppe **I**
  a little [ə 'lɪtl̩] ein wenig; etwas **I**
  a lot [ə 'lɒt] viel **I**
  a lot of [ə 'lɒt əv] viel/-e; eine Menge **I**
  a lot to learn [ə ˌlɒt tə 'lɜːn] viel zu
  lernen **I**
a.m. [ˌeɪ'em] vormittags *(Uhrzeit)* **I**
*to be **able** to (do sth) [bi ˌ'eɪbl̩ tə] fähig sein
  zu; können; dürfen **II U5**, 95
aboard [ə'bɔːd] an Bord **I**
about [ə'baʊt] ungefähr; circa; etwa **I**
about [ə'baʊt] über; von **I**
  out and **about** [ˌaʊt ən ə'baʊt] unterwegs
  II U3, 58
  What **about** …? ['wɒt ˌə baʊt] Wie wär's
  mit …?; Was ist mit …? **I**
  What is … **about**? [wɒt ˌɪz … ə'baʊt]
  Worum geht es in/im …? **I**
above [ə'bʌv] oben °**II U3**, 53
absolutely [ˌæbsə'luːtli] absolut; völlig
  II U2, 42
accent ['æksnt] Akzent **II U6**, 115
accident ['æksɪdnt] Unfall **II U4**, 69
across [ə'krɒs] auf der anderen Seite von;
  über; hinüber; herüber; quer durch **I**
  Across cultures [əˌkrɒs 'kʌltʃəz] Interkulturelles **I**
to **act** [ækt] spielen *(Theater)* **I**
  to **act** like [ˌækt laɪk] tun als ob **II U5**, 92
  to **act** out [ækt 'aʊt] nachspielen
  °**II AC2**, 88
  acting a scene [ˌæktɪŋ ə 'siːn] eine Theaterszene spielen **I**
acting ['æktɪŋ] Schauspielen °**II U6**, 119
action ['ækʃn] Handlung; Action; Aktion **I**
activity [æk'tɪvəti] Aktivität **I**

actor ['æktə] Schauspieler **II U2**, 36
to **add** [æd] hinzufügen; ergänzen **I**
additional [ə'dɪʃnl] zusätzlich **II U2**, 28
address [ə'dres] Adresse **I**
adjective ['ædʒɪktɪv] Adjektiv; Eigenschafts-
  wort °**II U1**, 16
adult ['ædʌlt] Erwachsene/-r **II U3**, 58
adventure [əd'ventʃə] Abenteuer **II U1**, 16
adverb ['ædvɜːb] Adverb °**II U3**, 51
advice [əd'vaɪs] Rat; Ratschlag **II U2**, 36
after ['ɑːftə] nach *(zeitlich)* **I**
  after all [ˌɑːftər 'ɔːl] doch; schließlich;
  immerhin **I**
  after that [ˌɑːftə 'ðæt] danach **I**
afternoon [ˌɑːftə'nuːn] Nachmittag **I**
  this **afternoon** [ðɪs 'ɑːftənuːn] heute
  Nachmittag **II U3**, 52
again [ə'gen] wieder; noch einmal; noch
  mal **I**
against [ə'genst] gegen **II U1**, 19
Bronze Age ['brɒnz eɪdʒ] Bronzezeit
  (ca. 2200–800 v. Chr.) **II U6**, 114
travel **agent's** ['trævl̩ ˌeɪdʒnts] Reisebüro
  II U6, 111
aggressive [ə'gresɪv] aggressiv **II U1**, 24
ago [ə'gəʊ] vor *(zeitlich)* **II U1**, 10
agony aunt ['ægəni ˌɑːnt] Kummerkastentante **II U5**, 92
to **agree** (on) [ə'griː] sich einigen (auf)
  °**II U6**, 120
to **agree** (with) [ə'griː] einer Meinung sein
  (mit); zustimmen °**II U5**, 97
airport ['eəpɔːt] Flughafen **II AC1**, 48
alarm clock [ə'lɑːm ˌklɒk] Wecker **II U2**, 43
alien ['eɪliən] Außerirdische/-r; außerirdi-
  sches Wesen **I**
all [ɔːl] alle/-s; ganz **I**
  after **all** [ˌɑːftər 'ɔːl] doch; schließlich;
  immerhin **I**
  all day [ɔːl 'deɪ] den ganzen Tag **II U1**, 14
  all night [ɔːl 'naɪt] die ganze Nacht **I**
  all over [ˌɔːl 'əʊvə] überall (in) **I**
  all the time [ˌɔːl ðə 'taɪm] die ganze Zeit
  II U3, 62
  at **all** [ət 'ɔːl] überhaupt **I**

  all of them [ˌɔːl əv ˌðem] alle **I**
  all of us [ˌɔːl əv ˌʌs] wir alle **II U6**, 110
bowling alley ['bəʊlɪŋ ˌæli] Bowlingbahn **I**
*to be **allowed** to (do sth) [bi ˌə'laʊd tə]
  dürfen **II U5**, 95
almost ['ɔːlməʊst] fast; beinahe **II U4**, 75
alone [ə'ləʊn] allein; ohne fremde Hilfe **I**
along [ə'lɒŋ] entlang **I**
alphabet ['ælfəbet] Alphabet **I**
alphabetical [ˌælfə'betɪkl] alphabetisch
  °**II U1**, 21
already [ɔːl'redi] schon; bereits **I**
also ['ɔːlsəʊ] auch **II U1**, 10
always ['ɔːlweɪz] immer; ständig **I**
amazing [ə'meɪzɪŋ] unglaublich; toll;
  erstaunlich **II U1**, 18
American [ə'merɪkən] Amerikanisch;
  amerikanisch; aus Amerika; Amerikaner/-
  in **II U1**, 9
an [ən] ein/eine **I**
and [ænd; ənd] und **I**
angry ['æŋgri] wütend; zornig; verärgert;
  böse **I**
animal ['ænɪməl] Tier **I**
ankle ['æŋkl] Fußgelenk; Fußknöchel
  II U4, 72
  to twist your **ankle** [ˌtwɪst jɔːr 'æŋkl] sich
  den Knöchel verrenken **II U4**, 72
announcement [ə'naʊnsmənt] Ankündigung; Durchsage **II U6**, 115
anonymous [ən'ɒnɪməs] anonym **II U1**, 13
another [ə'nʌðə] ein/-e andere/-r/-s; noch
  ein/-e; ein/-e andere/-r/-s **I**
answer ['ɑːnsə] Antwort **I**
  short **answer** [ˌʃɔːt 'ɑːnsə] Kurzantwort **I**
to **answer** ['ɑːnsə] antworten; beantworten **I**
  to **answer** the phone [ˌɑːnsə ðə 'fəʊn]
  einen Anruf entgegennehmen **I**
  answering machine ['ɑːnsrɪŋ məˌʃiːn]
  Anrufbeantworter **I**
any ['eni] irgendein/-e/-er; irgendwelche **I**
  not **any** more [ˌnɒt eni 'mɔː] nicht mehr **I**
  not … **any** [nɒt … eni] kein/-e **I**
anyone else [ˌeniwʌn 'els] jemand anderes
  II U2, 40

Anything else? [ˌenɪθɪŋ ˈels] Sonst noch etwas? I

not … **anything** [ˌnɒt ˈenɪθɪŋ] nichts I

anyway [ˈeniweɪ] trotzdem; jedenfalls; sowieso II U3, 62

anywhere [ˈeniweə] irgendwo; überall (egal, wo) II U3, 54

app [æp] App II U5, 97

apple [ˈæpl] Apfel I

April [ˈeɪprəl] April I

architect [ˈɑːkɪtekt] Architekt/-in II U2, 30

How **are** you? [ˌhaʊ ˈɑː jə] Wie geht es dir?; Wie geht es euch?; Wie geht es Ihnen? I

area [ˈeəriə] Areal; Gebiet; Fläche II U4, 70

arm [ɑːm] Arm II U2, 41

around [əˈraʊnd] um … herum; umher I

to turn **around** [ˌtɜːn(ə)ˈraʊnd] (sich) umdrehen; wenden II U2, 41

to **arrest** [əˈrest] festnehmen; verhaften II U1, 13

to **arrive** [əˈraɪv] ankommen II U6, 112

Art [ɑːt] Kunstunterricht I

art [ɑːt] Kunst II U2, 29

article [ˈɑːtɪkl] Artikel; Bericht (in einer Zeitschrift, Zeitung) II U2, 33

as [æz; əz] als II U2, 30

as [æz] während; indem I; wie II AC2, 88

as … as [əz … əz] so … wie I

as soon **as** [əz ˈsuːn əz] sobald II U5, 92

to **ask** [ɑːsk] fragen; bitten I

Ask about … [ˈɑːsk əˌbaʊt] Frage/Fragt nach … I

to **ask** for [ˈɑːsk fə] fragen nach; bitten um I

*to be **asleep** [ˌbi əˈsliːp] schlafen II U1, 19

*to fall **asleep** [ˌfɔːl əˈsliːp] einschlafen I

assembly [əˈsembli] Versammlung; Morgenappell II U2, 29

assistant [əˈsɪstnt] Assistent/-in; Verkäufer/-in II U4, 78

at [æt; ət] in; auf; bei; an; um (bei Uhrzeitangaben) I

at 7:30 [ət ˌsevn̩ ˈθɜːti] um halb acht I

at all [ət ˈɔːl] überhaupt I

at first [ət ˈfɜːst] zuerst; zunächst II U3, 63

at home [ət ˈhəʊm] zu Hause I

at last [ət ˈlɑːst] endlich; schließlich I

at least [ət ˈliːst] mindestens; wenigstens °II U3, 63

at the back of [ət ðə ˈbæk əv] hinten; am Ende; im hinteren Teil °II U3, 50

at the moment [ət ðə ˈməʊmənt] im Moment; gerade I

at the same time [ət ðə ˌseɪm ˈtaɪm] zur selben Zeit; gleichzeitig I

at the weekend [ət ðə ˌwiːˈkend] am Wochenende I

atlas [ˈætləs] Atlas II AC2, 88

atmosphere [ˈætməsfɪə] Atmosphäre; Stimmung °II U3, 58

attention [əˈtenʃn] Aufmerksamkeit; Beachtung II U5, 93

attic [ˈætɪk] Dachboden II U4, 76

attraction [əˈtrækʃn] Attraktion; Sehenswürdigkeit II U3, 59

audience [ˈɔːdiəns] Publikum II U2, 37

audio [ˈɔːdiəʊ] Audio-; Hör- I

audio tour [ˈɔːdiəʊ ˌtʊə] Audioführung II U3, 56

audio-visual effect [ˌɔːdiəʊvɪʒuəl ɪˈfekt] audiovisueller Effekt °II U1, 24

August [ˈɔːgəst] August I

aunt [ɑːnt] Tante I

agony **aunt** [ˈægəniˌɑːnt] Kummerkastentante II U5, 92

award [əˈwɔːd] Auszeichnung; Preis II U4, 74

away [əˈweɪ] weg I

right **away** [ˌraɪt əˈweɪ] sofort; gleich I

*to run **away** [ˌrʌn əˈweɪ] wegrennen I

*to throw **away** [ˌθrəʊ əˈweɪ] wegwerfen I

awful [ˈɔːfl] schrecklich; furchtbar I

B

baby [ˈbeɪbi] Baby; Säugling I

back [bæk] Rückseite; Rücken °II U6, 120

at the **back** of [ət ðə ˈbæk əv] hinten; am Ende; im hinteren Teil °II U3, 50

back to **back** [ˌbæk tʊ ˈbæk] Rücken an Rücken I

back [bæk] zurück I

*to go right **back** to [ˌgəʊ raɪt ˈbæk tə] zurückgehen auf II U6, 122

to turn **back** [tɜːn ˈbæk] umkehren; zurückgehen II U2, 41

backache [ˈbækeɪk] Rückenschmerzen; Rückenweh II U4, 73

background [ˈbækgraʊnd] Hintergrund I

bacon [ˈbeɪkn] Schinkenspeck; Speck I

bad [bæd] schlecht; böse; schlimm (ugs.) I

Too **bad**! [ˌtuː ˈbæd] Zu dumm!; Schade! I

badminton [ˈbædmɪntən] Badminton I

bag [bæg] Tasche; Tüte I

baked beans (pl) [ˌbeɪkt ˈbiːnz] weiße Bohnen in Tomatensoße I

ball [bɔːl] Ball I

banana [bəˈnɑːnə] Banane I

Bang! [bæŋ] Peng! II U5, 102

bank [bæŋk] Ufer II U3, 62

snack **bar** [ˈsnæk ˌbɑː] Café; Imbissstube I

bargain [ˈbɑːgɪn] Schnäppchen I

to **bark** [bɑːk] bellen I

basic [ˈbeɪsɪk] grundlegend; Grund- II U3, 59

basketball [ˈbɑːskɪtbɔːl] Basketball I

bath [bɑːθ] Bad; Badewanne I

bathroom [ˈbɑːθrʊm] Bad; Badezimmer I

battery [ˈbætri] Batterie; Akku II U1, 19

*to **be** [biː] sein I

*to **be** able to (do sth) [biˌeɪbl tə] fähig sein zu; können; dürfen II U5, 95

*to **be** about [biːˌəˈbaʊt] sich handeln um I

*to **be** allowed to (do sth) [bi əˈlaʊd tə] dürfen II U5, 95

*to **be** asleep [ˌbi əˈsliːp] schlafen II U1, 19

*to **be** connected [bi kəˈnektɪd] zusammenhängen; in Zusammenhang stehen II U2, 37

*to **be** gone [bi: ˈgɒn] verschwunden sein; weg sein II U4, 81

*to **be** good at [bi: ˈgʊd ət] gut sein in I

*to **be** in [biˌɪn] dabei sein; mitmachen II U4, 70

*to **be** in the way [bi: ɪn ðə ˈweɪ] im Weg sein/stehen I

*to **be** interested in [biˈɪntrəstɪd ɪn] interessiert sein an; sich interessieren für II U2, 31

*to **be** into [bi: ˈɪntə] mögen; stehen auf I

*to **be** jealous (of) [bi: ˈdʒeləs] eifersüchtig sein (auf); neidisch sein (auf) I

*to **be** late [bi: ˈleɪt] zu spät dran sein; zu spät kommen I

*to **be** lucky [biˌˈlʌki] Glück haben II U3, 62

*to **be** on [biˌˈɒn] an sein; laufen II U5, 102

*to **be** right [bi raɪt] recht haben I

*to **be** scared (of) [bi: ˈskeəd əv] Angst haben (vor) I

*to **be** sorry [bi: ˈsɒri] leid tun I

*to **be** surprised [bi səˈpraɪzd] überrascht sein II U3, 63

*to **be** unlucky [bi: ʌnˈlʌki] Pech haben I

*to **be** up to [biˌˈʌp tə] vorhaben °II U1, 24

*to **be** worried [bi ˈwʌrid] beunruhigt sein; besorgt sein II U4, 80

*to **be** worth [bi: ˈwɜːθ] wert sein I

*to **be** wrong [bi: ˈrɒŋ] unrecht haben; sich irren I

Be careful! [bi: ˈkeəfl] Vorsicht!; Pass/Passt auf! I

Be polite. [bi: pəˈlaɪt] Sei/Seid höflich. I

Here you **are**. [ˌhɪə juˈɑː] Bitte schön. I

How **are** you? [ˌhaʊ ˈɑː jə] Wie geht es dir?; Wie geht es euch?; Wie geht es Ihnen? I

How much **is**/**are** …? [ˌhaʊ ˈmʌtʃ ɪz/ɑː] Wie viel (kostet/kosten) …? I

I'm from … [ˌaɪm frɒm] Ich bin aus … I

Is this how you (do) …? [ɪz ˈðɪs haʊ jʊ ˌduː] Machst du so …? I

beach [biːtʃ] Strand II U5, 99

baked beans (pl) [ˌbeɪkt ˈbiːnz] weiße Bohnen in Tomatensoße I

bear [beə] Bär II U3, 56

*to **beat** [biːt] schlagen; besiegen II U3, 54

beautiful [ˈbjuːtɪfl] schön; hübsch; wunderbar II U2, 30

because [bɪˈkɒz] weil; da I

because of [bɪˈkɒz əv] wegen II U4, 81

*to **become** [bɪˈkʌm] werden II U3, 56

bed [bed] Bett I

*to go to **bed** [ˌgəʊ tə ˈbed] ins Bett gehen I

bedroom [ˈbedrʊm] Schlafzimmer I

bee [biː] Biene II U2, 33

Beefeater ['biːfˌiːtə] königlicher Leibgardist II U3, 56

before [bɪ'fɔː] vor (zeitlich); bevor I; schon einmal; vorher; zuvor II U4, 71

*to begin [bɪ'gɪn] beginnen; anfangen II U5, 99

beginning [bɪ'gɪnɪŋ] Anfang; Beginn II U1, 22

behind [bɪ'haɪnd] hinter I

to believe [bɪ'liːv] glauben I
He couldn't believe his eyes. [hi ˌkʊdnt bɪˌliːv hɪz ˌaɪz] Er traute seinen Augen nicht. II U2, 40

bell [bel] Glocke II AC1, 48

to belong (to) [bɪ'lɒŋ (tə)] gehören (zu) II U2, 29

below [bɪ'ləʊ] unterhalb; unten I

besides [bɪ'saɪdz] neben II U6, 114

(the) best [best] (der/die/das) Beste II U1, 10

best [best] beste/-r/-s; am besten I
Best wishes [ˌbest 'wɪʃɪz] Viele Grüße; Herzliche Grüße II U6, 113

I bet [aɪ 'bet] ich wette II U3, 54

better ['betə] besser; lieber I

between [bɪ'twiːn] zwischen I

bicycle motocross [ˌbaɪsɪkl 'məʊtəʊkrɒs] Fahrradmotocross II U4, 83

big [bɪg] groß I

bike [baɪk] Fahrrad I

mountain biking ['maʊntɪn ˌbaɪkɪŋ] Mountainbikefahren II U6, 109

bilingual [baɪ'lɪŋgwl] zweisprachig °II U1, 21

bird [bɜːd] Vogel II U2, 33

birdwatching ['bɜːdˌwɒtʃɪŋ] Vogelbeobachtung II U2, 28

birthday ['bɜːθdeɪ] Geburtstag I
Happy Birthday! [ˌhæpi 'bɜːθdeɪ] Alles Gute zum Geburtstag!; Herzlichen Glückwunsch zum Geburtstag! I

biscuit ['bɪskɪt] Keks I

a bit [ə 'bɪt] ein bisschen; ein wenig II U1, 18

*to bite [baɪt] beißen II U3, 56

black [blæk] schwarz I
*to go black [ˌgəʊ 'blæk] schwarz werden II U5, 102

building block ['bɪldɪŋ blɒk] Baustein °II U5, 93

to block [blɒk] blockieren; abblocken II U5, 93

*to blow out [ˌbləʊ 'aʊt] ausblasen; auspusten I

blue [bluː] blau I

BMX [ˌbiːem'eks] BMX II U4, 68

tourist board ['tʊərɪst bɔːd] Touristeninformation II U6, 113

boat [bəʊt] Boot I

boating lake ['bəʊtɪŋ ˌleɪk] See zum Rudern I

human body [ˌhjuːmən 'bɒdi] menschlicher Körper II U3, 62

bonfire ['bɒnfaɪə] Lagerfeuer; Freudenfeuer I

book [bʊk] Buch I
exercise book ['eksəsaɪz ˌbʊk] Übungsheft I

to book [bʊk] buchen; reservieren II U6, 112

to boom [buːm] dröhnen II U6, 122

bored [bɔːd] gelangweilt I

boring ['bɔːrɪŋ] langweilig I

to borrow ['bɒrəʊ] (sich) ausleihen II U5, 103

both [bəʊθ] beide II U4, 81

bottle ['bɒtl] Flasche I

bowl [bəʊl] Schale; Schälchen; Schüssel I

bowling alley ['bəʊlɪŋ ˌæli] Bowlingbahn I

box [bɒks] Box; Kasten; Schachtel; Kiste I

boxing ['bɒksɪŋ] Boxen II U1, 8
round of boxing [ˌraʊnd əv 'bɒksɪŋ] Boxrunde II U1, 8

boy [bɔɪ] Junge I
cabin boy [ˌkæbɪn ˌbɔɪ] Schiffsjunge I

bracelet ['breɪslət] Armband I

bracket ['brækɪt] Klammer °II U6, 115

brave [breɪv] mutig; tapfer I

bread [bred] Brot I

break [breɪk] Pause II U2, 40
half-term break [ˌhɑːftɜːm 'breɪk] Halbjahresferien I
lunch break ['lʌnʃbreɪk] Mittagspause I

*to break [breɪk] brechen; zerbrechen I

broken ['brəʊkn] gebrochen; kaputt I

breakfast ['brekfəst] Frühstück I
*to have breakfast [ˌhæv 'brekfəst] frühstücken I

Take a deep breath. [teɪk ə ˌdiːp 'breθ] Atme(t) tief ein. II U2, 36

to breathe [briːð] atmen II U4, 80

bridge [brɪdʒ] Brücke II U3, 62

*to bring [brɪŋ] bringen; mitbringen I

British ['brɪtɪʃ] britisch; Brite/Britin I

brochure ['brəʊʃə] Broschüre; Prospekt I

broken ['brəʊkn] gebrochen; kaputt I

Bronze Age ['brɒnz eɪdʒ] Bronzezeit (ca. 2200–800 v. Chr.) II U6, 114

brother ['brʌðə] Bruder I

brown [braʊn] braun I

bucket ['bʌkɪt] Eimer II U3, 62

*to build [bɪld] bauen II U2, 30

building ['bɪldɪŋ] Gebäude I

building block ['bɪldɪŋ blɒk] Baustein °II U5, 93

cyber bully [ˌsaɪbə 'bʊli] jemand, der andere in sozialen Netzwerken belästigt oder mobbed II U5, 91

*to give the bumps [ˌgɪv ðə 'bʌmps] hochleben lassen I

burger ['bɜːgə] Hamburger I

bus [bʌs] Bus I
bus station ['bʌs ˌsteɪʃn] Busbahnhof I

busy ['bɪzi] belebt; beschäftigt I

but [bʌt] aber I

*to buy [baɪ] kaufen I

buyer ['baɪə] Käufer/-in I

by [baɪ] bei; neben; an II U6, 122
by the river [baɪ ðə 'rɪvə] am Fluss II U2, 31

by (bike) [baɪ] mit (dem Fahrrad) I

Bye! [baɪ] Tschüss! II U4, 72

C

cabin boy ['kæbɪn ˌbɔɪ] Schiffsjunge I

cache [kæʃ] Cache II U6, 122

café ['kæfeɪ] Café I

cafeteria [ˌkæfə'tɪəriə] Cafeteria I

cake [keɪk] Kuchen; Torte I

(phone) call ['fəʊn ˌkɔːl] Anruf; Telefonanruf I

to call [kɔːl] nennen; anrufen; rufen I

caller ['kɔːlə] Anrufer/-in I

to calm down [ˌkɑːm 'daʊn] sich beruhigen II U2, 41

camel racing ['kæml ˌreɪsɪŋ] Kamelrennen II U4, 68

camera ['kæmrə] Fotoapparat; Kamera II U1, 8
caught on camera [ˌkɔːt ɒn 'kæmrə] ertappt; mit der Kamera festgehalten II U1, 8

summer camp ['sʌmə kæmp] Sommerferienlager II AC2, 88

to camp [kæmp] campen; zelten II U6, 124

camping ['kæmpɪŋ] Camping; Zelten II U5, 99

can [kæn] Dose; Büchse I

can [kæn; kən] können; dürfen I
can't [kɑːnt] kann nicht; können nicht I
Can you name …? ['kæn jʊ ˌneɪm] Kannst du … nennen? I

candle ['kændl] Kerze I

candlelight (no pl) ['kændlaɪt] Kerzenlicht II U5, 103

cannot ['kænɒt] kann nicht; können nicht II U5, 95

capital ['kæpɪtl] Hauptstadt II AC1, 48

capital letter [ˌkæpɪtl 'letə] Großbuchstabe I

captain ['kæptɪn] Kapitän/-in; Mannschaftsführer/-in I

car [kɑː] Auto I

card [kɑːd] Karte; Spielkarte I
prompt card ['prɒmpt kɑːd] Stichwortkarte; Rollenkarte °II U2, 32

to care (about) [ˌkeər ə'baʊt] wichtig nehmen; sich kümmern (um); sich interessieren (für) II U5, 93

careful ['keəfl] vorsichtig; sorgfältig II U3, 56
Be careful! [bi: 'keəfl] Vorsicht!; Pass/Passt auf! I

carnival ['kɑːnɪvl] Karneval II AC1, 48

carpet ['kɑːpɪt] Teppich II U3, 65

carrot ['kærət] Karotte; Möhre I

to carry ['kæri] tragen II AC3, 131

castle ['kɑːsl] Schloss; Burg II U3, 56

cat [kæt] Katze I

*to catch [kætʃ] fangen II U4, 68

category ['kætəgri] Kategorie; Klasse °II AC2, 89

caught on camera [kɔːt ˌɒn ˈkæmrə] ertappt; mit der Kamera festgehalten II U1, 8

to **cause** [kɔːz] verursachen II U4, 82

cave [keɪv] Höhle II U6, 119

to **celebrate** [ˈseləbreɪt] feiern I

Celtic [ˈkeltɪk; ˈseltɪk] keltisch II U1, 16

cent [sent] Cent *(Währung)* I

central [ˈsentrl] zentral; Zentral- II U3, 62

centre [ˈsentə] Zentrum; Center I
    community **centre** [kəˈmjuːnəti ˌsentə] Gemeindezentrum I
    leisure **centre** [ˈleʒə ˌsentə] Freizeitzentrum I
    tourist information **centre** [ˌtʊərɪst ɪnfəˈmeɪʃn ˌsentə] Touristeninformation I

century [ˈsenʃri] Jahrhundert II U3, 62

cereal *(no pl)* [ˈsɪəriəl] Frühstückszerealie; Getreideprodukt *(z. B. Cornflakes oder Müsli)* I

chair [tʃeə] Stuhl; Sessel I

challenge [ˈtʃælɪndʒ] Herausforderung II U1, 16

chance [tʃɑːns] Chance; Gelegenheit; Möglichkeit II U5, 100

change [tʃeɪndʒ] Änderung; Veränderung; Wechsel II U6, 123

to **change** [tʃeɪndʒ] wechseln; (sich) ändern II U5, 90

to **change** (onto) [tʃeɪndʒ (ˈɒntʊ)] umsteigen (in) II U3, 53

chant [tʃɑːnt] Sprechgesang II U4, 72

character [ˈkærəktə] Charakter; Figur I

charity [ˈtʃærɪti] Wohltätigkeitsverein; wohltätige Zwecke; Wohlfahrt I
    charity shop [ˈtʃærɪti ʃɒp] Second-Hand-Laden I

lucky **charm** [ˌlʌki ˈtʃɑːm] Glücksbringer; Talisman I

to **chase** [tʃeɪs] jagen; nachjagen I

chat room [ˈtʃæt rʊm] Chatroom II AC2, 88
    video **chat** [ˈvɪdɪəʊ ˌtʃæt] Videochat II U3, 50

to **chat** [tʃæt] plaudern; chatten *(sich online unterhalten)* I

cheap [tʃiːp] billig; preiswert I

to **check** [tʃek] überprüfen; prüfen; kontrollieren I

Check-in [ˈtʃekɪn] Einchecken I

checklist [ˈtʃeklɪst] Checkliste °II U4, 72

Check-out [ˈtʃekaʊt] Auschecken I

to **cheer** [tʃɪə] anfeuern; zujubeln; jubeln II U4, 72

cheese [tʃiːz] Käse I

chess [tʃes] Schach II U2, 28

chicken [ˈtʃɪkɪn] Huhn; Hähnchen I
    chicken tikka masala [ˌtʃɪkɪn ˌtɪkə məˈsɑːlə] indisches Hühnchengericht I

child, **children** *(pl)* [tʃaɪld; ˈtʃɪldrən] Kind I
    only **child** [ˌəʊnli ˈtʃaɪld] Einzelkind I

chimney [ˈtʃɪmni] Kamin; Schornstein II U6, 122

chips *(pl)* *(BE)* [tʃɪps] Pommes frites I

chocolate [ˈtʃɒklət] Schokolade I

choice [tʃɔɪs] Wahl; Auswahl II U3, 58

*to **choose** [tʃuːz] auswählen; wählen II U2, 30
    Choose … [tʃuːz] Wähle/Wählt … aus. I

Christmas [ˈkrɪsməs] Weihnachten I

church [tʃɜːtʃ] Kirche I

cinema [ˈsɪnəmə] Kino I

circle [ˈsɜːkl] Kreis; Ring I

city [ˈsɪti] Stadt; Großstadt I

to **clap** [klæp] klatschen I
    Clap your hands. [ˌklæp jɔː ˈhændz] Klatsch/Klatscht in die Hände. I

class [klɑːs] Klasse; Schulklasse I; Unterricht II U2, 40
    class display [ˈklɑːs dɪˌspleɪ] Ausstellung in der Klasse I
    class poster [ˈklɑːs ˌpəʊstə] Klassenposter I

classmate [ˈklɑːsmeɪt] Klassenkamerad/-in; Mitschüler/-in I

classroom [ˈklɑːsrʊm] Klassenzimmer I

contact clause [ˈkɒntækt ˌklɔːz] *Relativsatz ohne Relativpronomen* °II U2, 31
    defining relative **clause** [dɪˌfaɪnɪŋ ˈrelətɪv ˌklɔːz] notwendiger Relativsatz °II U2, 30
    if-**clause** [ˈɪf ˌklɔːz] if-Satz °II U6, 114
    main **clause** [ˈmeɪn ˌklɔːz] Hauptsatz °II U6, 114

clay pipe [ˈkleɪ paɪp] Tonpfeife II U3, 63

to **clean** [kliːn] säubern; reinigen I

to **clear** out [klɪərˈaʊt] ausräumen; entrümpeln I

clear [klɪə] klar; deutlich I

clever [ˈklevə] schlau; klug II U2, 41

click [klɪk] Klicken; Klick II U5, 103

to **click** on [ˈklɪk ˌɒn] anklicken II U6, 112

to **climb** [klaɪm] klettern; besteigen; steigen I

climbing [ˈklaɪmɪŋ] Klettern II U1, 16

clock [klɒk] Uhr II I
    alarm **clock** [əˈlɑːm ˌklɒk] Wecker II U2, 43
    o'**clock** [əˈklɒk] Uhr *(Zeitangabe bei vollen Stunden)* I

to **close** [kləʊz] schließen; zumachen I

close [kləʊs] eng; knapp I; nahe II U3, 56
    Look **closely** … [ˌlʊk ˈkləʊsli] Schau(t) genau … °II U4, 78
    That was **close**! [ˌðæt wəz ˈkləʊs] Das war knapp! I

close-up [ˈkləʊsʌp] Nahaufnahme °II U5, 98

clothes *(pl)* [kləʊðz] Kleider; Kleidung I

cloud [klaʊd] Wolke II U6, 122
    word **cloud** [ˈwɜːd ˌklaʊd] Wörterwolke °II U4, 68

cloudy [ˈklaʊdi] bedeckt; bewölkt II U1, 19

clown [klaʊn] Clown II U4, 80

club [klʌb] Klub; Verein; AG I
    Cooking **Club** [ˈkʊkɪŋ ˌklʌb] Koch-AG I

clue [kluː] Hinweis; Spur II U1, 13

coach [kəʊtʃ] Trainer/-in I; Reisebus II U1, 13

coastal path [ˌkəʊstl ˈpɑːθ] Küstenweg II U6, 122

coastline [ˈkəʊstlaɪn] Küste; Küstenverlauf II U6, 114

coconut [ˈkəʊkənʌt] Kokosnuss II U3, 63

coffee [ˈkɒfi] Kaffee I

coin [kɔɪn] Münze I

coke [ˈkəʊk] Cola I

cold [kəʊld] Erkältung II U4, 73

cold [kəʊld] kalt II U1, 18

to **collect** [kəˈlekt] sammeln I

collection [kəˈlekʃn] Kollektion; Sammlung II U1, 10

collocation [ˌkɒləˈkeɪʃn] Wortverbindung °II U5, 90

colony [ˈkɒləni] Kolonie II AC2, 89

colour [ˈkʌlə] Farbe I
    What **colour** is …? [ˌwɒt ˈkʌləˌɪz] Welche Farbe hat …? I

colourful [ˈkʌləfl] farbenfroh; bunt I

*to **come** [kʌm] kommen I
    *to **come** down [kʌm ˈdaʊn] herunterkommen I
    *to **come** in [kʌmˈɪn] hereinkommen II U6, 122
    Come on! [kʌmˈɒn] Komm schon!; Komm jetzt! I

comedian [kəˈmiːdiən] Komiker/-in; Comedian II U1, 10

comedy show [ˈkɒmədi ˌʃəʊ] Comedy Show II U1, 10

comfortable [ˈkʌmftəbl] komfortabel; bequem II U3, 65

comic [ˈkɒmɪk] Comicheft II U4, 82

comment [ˈkɒment] Kommentar II U1, 12

to **comment** (on) [ˈkɒmentˌ(ɒn)] kommentieren II U5, 97

to **communicate** [kəˈmjuːnɪkeɪt] kommunizieren; sich verständigen II AC2, 89

communication [kəˌmjuːnɪˈkeɪʃn] Kommunikation °II U5, 90

community centre [kəˈmjuːnəti ˌsentə] Gemeindezentrum I

comparative [kəmˈpærətɪv] Komparativ °II U1, 16

to **compare** (with/to) [kəmˈpeə] vergleichen (mit) I

comparison [kəmˈpærɪsn] Vergleich °II U3, 55

competition [ˌkɒmpəˈtɪʃn] Wettbewerb; Turnier II U2, 29

Complete … [kəmˈpliːt] Vervollständige/ Vervollständigt … I

completely [kəmˈpliːtli] völlig II AC3, 130

compound word [ˈkɒmpaʊnd wɜːd] Kompositum *(zusammengesetztes Wort)* °II U3, 55

compromise [ˈkɒmprəmaɪz] Kompromiss II U5, 93

computer [kəmˈpjuːtə] Computer I

con [kɒn] Argument dagegen II U3, 55

condition [kənˈdɪʃn] Kondition; Bedingung °II U6, 117

conditional sentence [kənˌdɪʃnl ˈsentəns] Bedingungssatz °II U6, 109

confident [ˈkɒnfɪdnt] selbstsicher; selbstbewusst II U1, 16

*to be connected [bi kəˈnektɪd] zusammenhängen; in Zusammenhang stehen II U2, 37

connection [kəˈnekʃn] Verbindung II U6, 112

contact [ˈkɒntækt] Kontakt II U2, 37
    contact clause [ˈkɒntækt ˌklɔːz] Relativsatz ohne Relativpronomen °II U2, 31

contest [ˈkɒntest] Wettkampf; Wettbewerb I

conversation [ˌkɒnvəˈseɪʃn] Konversation; Gespräch; Unterhaltung I

to convince [kənˈvɪns] überzeugen °II U2, 38

to cook [kʊk] kochen II U5, 103

cooker [ˈkʊkə] Herd I

cooking [ˈkʊkɪŋ] Kochen I
    Cooking Club [ˈkʊkɪŋ ˌklʌb] Koch-AG I

*to leave it to cool [ˌliːv ɪt tə ˈkuːl] kalt stellen I

cool [kuːl] cool; super I

to copy [ˈkɒpi] abschreiben; kopieren I

corner [ˈkɔːnə] Ecke II U2, 34

Cornish [ˈkɔːnɪʃ] in Cornwall II U6, 110

Correct … [kəˈrekt] Korrigiere/Korrigiert … I

correct [kəˈrekt] richtig; korrekt I

*to cost [kɒst] kosten I

costume [ˈkɒstjuːm] Kostüm I

cough [kɒf] Husten II U4, 73

could [kʊd] könnte/-n II U2, 40; konnte/-n II U5, 95

to count (on) [ˈkaʊnt ɒn] zählen (auf) I

country, countries (pl) [ˈkʌntri; ˈkʌntriz] Land I

countryside [ˈkʌntrisaɪd] Land II U6, 110

couple [ˈkʌpl] Paar II U6, 116
    a couple of [ə ˈkʌpl əv] ein paar I

course [kɔːs] Kurs II U1, 16
    of course [əv ˈkɔːs] natürlich; selbstverständlich I

court [kɔːt] Spielfeld II U4, 68

cousin [ˈkʌzn] Cousin/Cousine I

cow [kaʊ] Kuh II U6, 119

cramp [kræmp] Krampf II U4, 74

to crash [kræʃ] abstürzen II U5, 103

crazy [ˈkreɪzi] verrückt I
    *to go crazy [ˌɡəʊ ˈkreɪzi] ausflippen; durchdrehen; verrückt werden II U5, 95

cream [kriːm] Creme; Sahne I
    ice cream [aɪs ˈkriːm] Eis; Eiscreme I

to create [kriˈeɪt] schaffen; erschaffen; erfinden I

creative [kriˈeɪtɪv] kreativ I

credit [ˈkredɪt] Guthaben II U3, 52

cricket [ˈkrɪkɪt] Cricket II U4, 69

crime [kraɪm] Verbrechen; Kriminalität II AC3, 130

criminal [ˈkrɪmɪnəl] Kriminelle/-r; Verbrecher/-in II AC3, 130

crisp (BE) [krɪsp] Kartoffelchip I

cross [krɒs] Kreuz II U6, 114

to cross [krɒs] überqueren; kreuzen II AC2, 89
    *to keep your fingers crossed [ˌkiːp jɔː ˌfɪŋɡəz ˈkrɒst] die Daumen drücken I

crowd [kraʊd] Menschenmenge II U3, 58

crown jewels [ˌkraʊn ˈdʒuːəlz] Kronjuwelen II U3, 56

cruel [ˈkruːəl] grausam II AC3, 130

to cry [kraɪ] schreien; rufen II U5, 102

CU (= See you) [ˈsiː juː] Bis dann!; Bis … I

culture [ˈkʌltʃə] Kultur I
    Across cultures [əˌkrɒs ˈkʌltʃəz] Interkulturelles I

cupboard [ˈkʌbəd] Küchenschrank; Schrank I

curry [ˈkʌri] Curry (Gewürz oder Gericht) I

custard [ˈkʌstəd] Vanillesoße; Vanillepudding I

customer [ˈkʌstəmə] Kunde/Kundin II U6, 116

*to cut (off) [kʌt (ɒf)] schneiden; abschneiden II U2, 30

cute [kjuːt] niedlich; süß I

cyber bully [ˌsaɪbə ˈbʊli] jemand, der andere in sozialen Netzwerken belästigt oder mobbed II U5, 91

cycling [ˈsaɪklɪŋ] Radfahren I

D

dad [dæd] Papa I

to dance [dɑːns] tanzen I
    I like singing and dancing. [aɪ laɪk ˌsɪŋɪŋ ənd ˈdɑːnsɪŋ] Ich singe und tanze gern. I

dancer [ˈdɑːnsə] Tänzer/-in II U2, 36

dangerous [ˈdeɪndʒərəs] gefährlich I

the dark [ðə ˈdɑːk] Dunkelheit II U1, 18

dark [dɑːk] dunkel II U1, 18

darkness [ˈdɑːknəs] Dunkelheit II U6, 119

date [deɪt] Datum I

day [deɪ] Tag I
    all day [ɔːl ˈdeɪ] den ganzen Tag II U1, 14
    one day [wʌn ˈdeɪ] eines Tages II U2, 36
    a day out in … [ə ˌdeɪ ˈaʊt ɪn] ein Tag in … II U3, 58
    the next day [ðə ˌnekst ˈdeɪ] am nächsten Tag II U1, 11

dead [ded] tot II U3, 62

*to deal (with) [diːl] sich befassen mit; umgehen mit II U3, 54

Oh dear! [əʊ ˈdɪə] Oje! II U6, 122

Dear … [dɪə] Lieber …; Liebe … (Anrede in Briefen) I
    Dear Sir or Madam [dɪə ˌsɜːr ɔː ˈmædəm] Sehr geehrte Dame, sehr geehrter Herr II U6, 113

December [dɪˈsembə] Dezember I

to decide [dɪˈsaɪd] (sich) entscheiden I

decision [dɪˈsɪʒn] Entscheidung °II U6, 111
    *to make a decision [ˌmeɪk ə dɪˈsɪʒn] eine Entscheidung treffen °II U3, 61

deck [dek] Deck I

to decorate [ˈdekəreɪt] dekorieren; verzieren; schmücken I

decorations (pl) [ˌdekəˈreɪʃnz] Dekoration; Schmuck I

deep [diːp] tief II U6, 109

defining relative clause [dɪˌfaɪnɪŋ ˈrelətɪv ˌklɔːz] notwendiger Relativsatz °II U2, 30

definition [ˌdefɪˈnɪʃn] Definition °II U6, 112

to depart [dɪˈpɑːt] abfahren II U6, 112

to depend (on) [dɪˈpend ˌɒn] abhängen von II U6, 111

to describe [dɪˈskraɪb] beschreiben I

description [dɪˈskrɪpʃn] Beschreibung °II U3, 58

to deserve [dɪˈzɜːv] verdienen II U4, 76

design [dɪˈzaɪn] Design; Gestaltung; Entwurf II U2, 30

to design [dɪˈzaɪn] entwerfen; gestalten II U2, 31

detail [ˈdiːteɪl] Detail; Einzelheit °II U3, 59

private detective [ˌpraɪvət dɪˈtektɪv] Privatdetektiv/-in II AC3, 130

diagram [ˈdaɪəɡræm] Diagramm I

dialect [ˈdaɪəlekt] Dialekt II U6, 115

dialogue [ˈdaɪəlɒɡ] Dialog; Gespräch I

diary entry [ˈdaɪəri entri] Tagebucheintrag II U6, 124

dice [daɪs] Würfel °II U2, 34
    Roll two dice. [ˌrəʊl tuː ˈdaɪs] Würfle/Würfelt mit zwei Würfeln. I
    throw the dice twice [ˌθrəʊ ðə daɪs ˈtwaɪs] würfle zweimal °II U2, 34

dictionary [ˈdɪkʃnri] Wörterbuch I

difference [ˈdɪfrəns] Unterschied I

different [ˈdɪfrnt] anders; unterschiedlich; verschieden I

difficult [ˈdɪfɪklt] schwierig II U4, 77

*to dig [dɪɡ] graben II U2, 33

dinner [ˈdɪnə] Abendessen I

dinosaur [ˈdaɪnəsɔː] Dinosaurier II U2, 40

direction [dɪˈrekʃn] Richtung I

dirty [ˈdɜːti] dreckig; schmutzig II U2, 40

disappointed [ˌdɪsəˈpɔɪntɪd] enttäuscht I

disaster [dɪˈzɑːstə] Desaster; Katastrophe; Unglück II U5, 102

to discover [dɪˈskʌvə] entdecken II U2, 28

to discuss [dɪˈskʌs] diskutieren I

discussion [dɪˈskʌʃn] Diskussion II U5, 90

display [dɪˈspleɪ] Ausstellung II U3, 59
    class display [ˈklɑːs dɪˌspleɪ] Ausstellung in der Klasse I

distance [ˈdɪstns] Distanz; Entfernung II U3, 60

*to do [duː] machen; tun I
    *to do about [ˈduː ˌəbaʊt] unternehmen wegen II U5, 100
    *to do our hair [ˌduː ˌaʊə ˈheə] uns frisieren; unsere Haare machen I

Don't translate … [ˌdəʊnt trænz'leɪt] Übersetze/Übersetzt nicht … I

Don't worry! [ˌdəʊnt 'wʌri] Keine Sorge! I

We **did** it! [wi: 'dɪdˌɪt] Wir haben es geschafft! II U4, 81

doctor ['dɒktə] Arzt/Ärztin II U4, 72

dog [dɒg] Hund I

to walk the **dog** [wɔːk ðə 'dɒg] den Hund ausführen; mit dem Hund spazieren gehen I

I'm **dog-tired**. [aɪm ˌdɒg'taɪəd] Ich bin hundemüde. I

door [dɔː] Tür I

front **door** [ˌfrʌnt 'dɔː] Haustür II U5, 102

down [daʊn] nach unten; herunter; hinunter II U3, 62

*to come **down** [kʌm 'daʊn] herunterkommen I

*to go **down** [gəʊ 'daʊn] hinuntergehen; nach unten gehen; entlanggehen I

to note **down** [ˌnəʊt 'daʊn] notieren; aufschreiben °II U2, 37

*to sit **down** [sɪt 'daʊn] sich hinsetzen; sich setzen I

*to write **down** [raɪt 'daʊn] aufschreiben I

to **download** [daʊn'ləʊd] herunterladen (aus dem Internet) II U5, 97

downstairs [daʊn'steəz] nach unten; im Untergeschoss; unten II U5, 102

draft [drɑːft] Entwurf; Konzept I

drama ['drɑːmə] Theater; Drama II U2, 28

dramatic [drə'mætɪk] dramatisch II U3, 63

*to **draw** [drɔː] zeichnen I; ziehen °II U6, 121

drawing ['drɔːɪŋ] Zeichnung I

dream [driːm] Traum II U1, 15

fancy **dress** ['fænsi dres] Verkleidung; Kostüm II U4, 80

drink [drɪŋk] Getränk I

*to **drink** [drɪŋk] trinken I

driver ['draɪvə] Fahrer/-in II U1, 13

to **drop** [drɒp] fallen (lassen) II U3, 62

during + noun ['djʊərɪŋ] während (+ Nomen) II U1, 9

DVD [ˌdiːviː'diː] DVD I

E

e.g. (= for example) [ˌiː'dʒiː] z.B. (= zum Beispiel) I

each [iːtʃ] jede/-r/-s I

each other [iːtʃ'ʌðə] einander; sich; sich gegenseitig I

each [iːtʃ] pro Person; pro Stück I

early ['ɜːli] früh I

to **earn** [ɜːn] verdienen I

earth [ɜːθ] Erdboden; Erde; die Erde II U2, 40

What on **earth** …? [ˌwɒtˌɒnˌ'ɜːθ] Was um alles in der Welt …? II U5, 95

east [iːst] Osten; Ost- I

Easter ['iːstə] Ostern I

easy ['iːzi] einfach; leicht I

*to **eat** [iːt] essen; fressen I

Eco [ikəʊ] Öko- II U2, 33

audio-visual **effect** [ˌɔːdiəʊvɪʒuəl ɪ'fekt] audiovisueller Effekt °II U1, 24

egg [eg] Ei I

eight [eɪt] acht I

electrician [ˌelɪk'trɪʃn] Elektriker/-in II U6, 123

electricity [ˌelɪk'trɪsəti] Elektrizität; Strom II U6, 122

electrics [ɪ'lektrɪks] Elektrik II U6, 123

electronic [ˌelek'trɒnɪk] elektronisch II U1, 21

element ['elɪmənt] Element °II U6, 119

eleven [ɪ'levn] elf I

nobody **else** ['nəʊbədi els] niemand anderes II U6, 124

what **else** [ˌwɒtˌ'els] was sonst; was noch I

e-mail ['iːmeɪl] E-Mail I

to **e-mail** ['iːmeɪl] mailen; per E-Mail schicken II U5, 97

embarrassed [ɪm'bærəst] verlegen II U1, 9

embarrassing [ɪm'bærəsɪŋ] peinlich II U1, 8

end [end] Ende; Schluss I

in the **end** [ɪnˌðiˌ'end] schließlich; zum Schluss II U1, 10

to **end** [end] enden; beenden II U4, 79

to **end** up [endˌ'ʌp] enden; landen II U1, 8

ending ['endɪŋ] Ende; Schluss (einer Geschichte) I

English ['ɪŋglɪʃ] englisch; Englisch; aus England; Engländer/-in I

English-speaking ['ɪŋglɪʃˌspiːkɪŋ] englischsprachig I

I'm **English**. [aɪmˌ'ɪŋglɪʃ] Ich bin Engländer/-in. I

to **enjoy** [ɪn'dʒɔɪ] genießen; sich freuen an II U1, 12

enough [ɪ'nʌf] genug; genügend I

to **enter** ['entə] hineingehen; betreten; eintreten; hier: mitmachen II U2, 40

diary **entry** ['daɪəri entri] Tagebucheintrag II U6, 124

environment [ɪn'vaɪrnmənt] Umwelt; Umgebung II U6, 114

equipment [ɪ'kwɪpmənt] Ausstattung; Ausrüstung II U4, 69

er [ɜː] äh I

escalator ['eskəleɪtə] Rolltreppe I

etc. (= et cetera) [ɪt'setrə] usw. (= und so weiter) °II U5, 101

euro ['jʊərəʊ] Euro (Währung) I

even ['iːvn] sogar; selbst I

evening ['iːvnɪŋ] Abend I

in the **evenings** [ɪnˌðiˌ'iːvnɪŋz] abends I

event [ɪ'vent] Ereignis; Veranstaltung I

ever ['evə] jemals II U2, 33

every ['evri] jede/-r/-s I

everybody ['evribɒdi] jeder; alle II U3, 54

everyone ['evriwʌn] jeder; alle I

everything ['evriθɪŋ] alles I

everywhere ['evriweə] überall I

exactly [ɪg'zæktli] genau II AC2, 88

exam [ɪg'zæm] Examen; Prüfung II U2, 28

example [ɪg'zɑːmpl] Beispiel I

for **example** [fərˌɪg'zɑːmpl] zum Beispiel II AC2, 89

to **exchange** [ɪks'tʃeɪndʒ] austauschen °II U2, 35

excited [ɪk'saɪtɪd] aufgeregt; begeistert I

exciting [ɪk'saɪtɪŋ] spannend; aufregend I

Excuse me … [ɪk'skjuːz mi] Entschuldigung!; Entschuldigen Sie! I

exercise ['eksəsaɪz] Übung; Aufgabe I

exercise book ['eksəsaɪzˌbʊk] Übungsheft I

expensive [ɪk'spensɪv] teuer I

experience [ɪk'spɪəriəns] Erfahrung II U4, 69

expert ['ekspɜːt] Experte/Expertin °II U4, 79

to **explain** [ɪk'spleɪn] erklären I

to **explore** [ɪk'splɔː] auf Entdeckungsreise gehen; sich umschauen; erkunden; erforschen I

to **express** [ɪk'spres] ausdrücken °II U4, 82

expression [ɪk'spreʃn] Ausdruck; Wendung; Äußerung II AC2, 89

extra ['ekstrə] extra; zusätzlich I

eye [aɪ] Auge II U1, 9

He couldn't believe his **eyes**. [hi ˌkʊdnt bɪˌliːv hɪzˌ'aɪz] Er traute seinen Augen nicht. II U2, 40

eyewitness ['aɪwɪtnəs] Augenzeuge/Augenzeugin II U4, 77

F

face [feɪs] Gesicht I

Put … **face** down. [pʊtˌfeɪs 'daʊn] Lege/Legt … umgedreht hin. I

face-to-face [ˌfeɪstə'feɪs] hier: persönlich; von Angesicht zu Angesicht II U5, 93

fact [fækt] Fakt; Tatsache II U2, 37

fair [feə] gerecht; fair I

to **fake** [feɪk] vortäuschen; fälschen II U4, 76

*to **fall** [fɔːl] fallen; hinfallen I

*to **fall** asleep [ˌfɔːlˌə'sliːp] einschlafen I

*to **fall** off [ˌfɔːlˌ'ɒf] herunterfallen; hinunterfallen II U2, 34

*to **fall** over [ˌfɔːlˌ'əʊvə] hinfallen; umkippen I

family ['fæməli] Familie I

family tree ['fæməliˌtriː] Stammbaum I

famous ['feɪməs] berühmt I

fan [fæn] Fan; Anhänger/-in II U4, 83

fancy dress ['fænsi dres] Verkleidung; Kostüm II U4, 80

fantastic [fæn'tæstɪk] fantastisch; großartig II U2, 29

fantasy ['fæntəsi] Fantasie; Traum- I

fanzine [fæn'ziːn] Fanzeitschrift II U2, 38

in the **far** west [ɪn ðə fɑːˈwest] im äußersten Westen II U6, 114

far [fɑː] weit II U3, 55

so **far** [səʊ 'fɑː] bis jetzt II U4, 75

fare [feə] Fahrpreis **II U6**, 112

farm [fɑːm] Farm; Bauernhof **I**

farmer ['fɑːmə] Farmer/-in; Landwirt/-in **II U1**, 13

fashion ['fæʃn] Mode **II U2**, 28

fast [fɑːst] schnell **I**

father ['fɑːðə] Vater **I**

favourite ['feɪvrɪt] Lieblings- **I**

My **favourite** … [maɪ 'feɪvrɪt] Mein/e Lieblings … **I**

What's your **favourite** …? ['wɒts jə ˌfeɪvrɪt] Was ist dein/-e Lieblings…? **I**

fear [fɪə] Angst; Furcht; Befürchtung **II U4**, 82

February ['februri] Februar **I**

fee [fiː] Gebühr **II U6**, 112

*to feed [fiːd] füttern; ernähren **II U6**, 119

feedback ['fiːdbæk] Feedback; Rückmeldung **II U2**, 29

*to feel [fiːl] fühlen; sich fühlen **I**

*to **feel** left out [ˌfiːl left ˈaʊt] sich ausgeschlossen fühlen **II U5**, 104

*to **feel** sick [ˌfiːl 'sɪk] Übelkeit verspüren; sich schlecht fühlen **II U4**, 73

feeling ['fiːlɪŋ] Gefühl **II U1**, 9

festival ['festɪvl] Festival; Fest **I**

fever ['fiːvə] Fieber **II U4**, 73

few [fjuː] wenige **II U1**, 18

a **few** [ə ˈfjuː] ein paar; wenige; einige **I**

science fiction [ˌsaɪəns ˈfɪkʃn] Science-Fiction (Zukunftsdichtung) **II U1**, 22

field [fiːld] Feld; Spielfeld; Wiese; Weide; Acker **II U1**, 18

fifteen [ˌfɪfˈtiːn] fünfzehn **I**

fight [faɪt] Kampf; Streit **II U2**, 41

*to fight [faɪt] kämpfen; (sich) streiten **II U5**, 102

figure ['fɪgə] Figur; Gestalt **II U3**, 51

wax **figure** ['wæks ˌfɪgə] Wachsfigur **II U3**, 51

to fill in [fɪl ˈɪn] ausfüllen °**II U5**, 96

film [fɪlm] Film **I**

to film [fɪlm] filmen; drehen °**II U6**, 119

filmmaker ['fɪlmˌmeɪkə] Filmemacher/-in **II U1**, 24

final ['faɪnl] endgültig °**II U4**, 79

finally ['faɪnli] schließlich; endlich; zum Schluss; letztlich **II U2**, 31

*to find [faɪnd] finden; herausfinden **I**

*to **find** out [ˌfaɪnd ˈaʊt] herausfinden **I**

fine [faɪn] gut; in Ordnung; schön **I**

I'm **fine**. [ˌaɪm ˈfaɪn] Mir geht's gut. **I**

finger ['fɪŋgə] Finger **I**

*to keep your **fingers** crossed [ˌkiːp jɔː ˌfɪŋgəz ˈkrɒst] die Daumen drücken **I**

finish line ['fɪnɪʃ ˌlaɪn] Ziellinie **II U4**, 81

to finish ['fɪnɪʃ] beenden; enden; fertigstellen; aufhören **I**

finished ['fɪnɪʃt] fertig °**II U5**, 99

fireworks (pl) ['faɪəwɜːks] Feuerwerk **I**

first [fɜːst] zuerst; als Erstes; erste/-r/-s **I**

at **first** [ət ˈfɜːst] zuerst; zunächst **II U3**, 63

first language [ˌfɜːst ˈlæŋgwɪdʒ] Muttersprache **II AC2**, 89

fish, fish (pl) [fɪʃ] Fisch **I**

fishing ['fɪʃɪŋ] Angeln; Fischen; Fischerei **II U6**, 114

to fit [fɪt] passen °**II U5**, 101

*to get fit [ˌget ˈfɪt] in Form kommen; fit werden **I**

five [faɪv] fünf **I**

to fix [fɪks] reparieren; befestigen **II U5**, 95

flair [fleə] Flair; Atmosphäre **II U3**, 51

flat [flæt] Wohnung **I**

flea market ['fliː ˌmɑːkɪt] Flohmarkt **I**

floor [flɔː] Fußboden **I**

to flow out [fləʊ ˈaʊt] hinausfließen **II U3**, 62

flower ['flaʊə] Blume **II U2**, 41

flyer ['flaɪə] Flyer **I**

to focus (on) ['fəʊkəs ˌɒn] sich konzentrieren (auf) °**II U2**, 37

folder ['fəʊldə] Ordner; Mappe **I**

to follow ['fɒləʊ] folgen; hinterhergehen; befolgen **II U3**, 54

the following [ðə ˈfɒləʊɪŋ] folgende/-r/-s °**II U6**, 109

food [fuːd] Essen; Lebensmittel **I**

foot, feet (pl) [fʊt; fiːt] Fuß **I**

on **foot** [ɒn ˈfʊt] zu Fuß **II U3**, 60

football ['fʊtbɔːl] Fußball **I**

for [fɔː; fə] wegen **II U5**, 91

for example [fər ɪgˈzɑːmpl] zum Beispiel **II AC2**, 89

for … [fɔː; fə] … lang **II U1**, 12

weather forecast ['weðə ˌfɔːkɑːst] Wettervorhersage **II U6**, 112

foreign language [ˌfɒrɪn ˈlæŋgwɪdʒ] Fremdsprache **II U2**, 38

forest ['fɒrɪst] Wald **II U1**, 16

forever [fəˈrevə] für immer; ewig **II U5**, 93

*to forget [fəˈget] vergessen **I**

*to forgive [fəˈgɪv] vergeben; verzeihen **II U4**, 81

form [fɔːm] Form **I**; Formular **II U6**, 112

negative **form** ['negətɪv ˌfɔːm] verneinte Form **I**

past **form** ['pɑːst fɔːm] Vergangenheitsform °**II U1**, 10

possessive **form** [pəˌsesɪv ˈfɔːm] Possessivform **I**

short **form** ['ʃɔːt fɔːm] Kurzform **I**

to form [fɔːm] formen; bilden °**II U4**, 79

formal ['fɔːml] formal; formell; förmlich °**II U4**, 77

forum ['fɔːrəm] Forum **II U5**, 90

to look forward to [ˌlʊk ˈfɔːwəd tə] sich freuen auf **II U2**, 33

four [fɔː] vier **I**

Four and six is ten. [ˌfɔːr ənd ˌsɪks ɪz 'ten] Vier plus sechs ist zehn. **I**

fox [fɒks] Fuchs **II U2**, 34

free [friː] frei; kostenlos **I**

free time [ˌfriː ˈtaɪm] Freizeit **I**

French [frenʃ] französisch; Französisch **II U2**, 32

frequently asked [ˌfriːkwəntli ˈɑːskt] häufig gefragt **I**

fresh [freʃ] frisch **I**

Friday ['fraɪdeɪ] Freitag **I**

fridge [frɪdʒ] Kühlschrank **I**

friend [frend] Freund/-in **I**

*to make friends [ˌmeɪk ˈfrendz] Freundschaft schließen **II U2**, 43

That's what **friends** are for. [ˌðæts wɒt ˈfrendz ɑː ˌfɔː] Dafür sind Freunde da. **I**

friendly ['frendli] freundlich; nett **II U1**, 14

friendship ['frendʃɪp] Freundschaft **II U5**, 94

from [frɒm; frəm] aus; von **I**

from … to [frəm … tə] von … bis **I**

from around the world [frəm əˌraʊnd ðə ˈwɜːld] aus aller Welt **II U6**, 114

Where … from? [ˌweə … ˈfrɒm] Woher …? **I**

front [frʌnt] Vorderseite; Front-; Vorder- °**II U6**, 120

front door [frʌnt ˈdɔː] Haustür **II U5**, 102

in front of [ɪn ˈfrʌnt əv] vor **I**

fruit [fruːt] Frucht; Obst **I**

full (of) [fʊl əv] voll (von) **I**

fun [fʌn] Freude; Spaß **I**

*to have fun [ˌhæv ˈfʌn] Spaß haben; sich amüsieren **I**

It's fun. [ɪts ˈfʌn] Es macht Spaß. **I**

fun [fʌn] lustig; witzig; fröhlich **I**

funny ['fʌni] lustig; witzig **I**

future ['fjuːtʃə] Zukunft **II U6**, 109

G

Gaelic ['geɪlɪk] gälisch; Gälisch **II U6**, 114

gallery walk ['gælri ˌwɔːk] Museumsrundgang; Vernissage **I**

game [geɪm] Spiel **I**

guessing game ['gesɪŋ ˌgeɪm] Ratespiel °**II U1**, 13

gap [gæp] Lücke; Spalt; Abstand **I**

garage ['gærɑːʒ] Garage **I**

garden ['gɑːdn] Garten **I**

genius ['dʒiːniəs] Genie **II U5**, 95

geocaching ['dʒiːəʊkæʃɪŋ] Geocaching **II U6**, 119

geography [dʒiˈɒgrəfi] Geografie; Erdkunde **II U6**, 114

German ['dʒɜːmən] deutsch; Deutsch; aus Deutschland; Deutsche/-r **I**

*to get [get] holen; bringen; bekommen; besorgen; kaufen **I**; werden **II U6**, 122

*to get around [ˌget əˈraʊnd] hier: sich fortbewegen **II U3**, 53

*to get away with [ˌget əˈweɪ wɪð] davonkommen mit **II U4**, 76

*to get fit [ˌget ˈfɪt] in Form kommen; fit werden **I**

*to get in the way [ˌget ɪn ðə ˈweɪ] stören; im Weg stehen **II U4**, 80 *to **get** into [ˌget ˈɪntə] einsteigen; hinein-gelangen I

*to **get** lost [ˌget ˈlɒst] verloren gehen; sich verirren II U6, 119

*to **get** off (a bus/train) [ˌget ˈɒf] aus-steigen (aus einem Bus/Zug) II U3, 53

*to **get** on (the bus) [ˌget ˈɒn] einsteigen (in den Bus) II U6, 112

*to **get** on people's nerves [ˌget ɒn ˈsʌmbɒdiz ˈnɜːvz] jemandem auf die Nerven gehen I

*to **get** organised [get ˈɔːgənaɪzd] sich organisieren °II U6, 120

*to **get** out of [get ˌaʊt ˌəv] aussteigen II U5, 102

*to **get** right [get ˈraɪt] richtig beantwor-ten °II U6, 121

*to **get** started [get ˈstɑːtɪd] anfangen II U2, 33

*to **get** there [ˈget ðeə] hinkommen I

*to **get** to [ˈget tə] kommen zu; kommen nach; erreichen I

*to **get** to know [ˌget tə ˈnəʊ] kennen lernen II U6, 114

*to **get** up [ˌget ˈʌp] aufstehen *(aus dem Bett)* I

Time to **get** up! [ˌtaɪm tə ˌget ˈʌp] Es ist Zeit aufzustehen! I

ghost [gəʊst] Geist II U2, 30

girl [gɜːl] Mädchen I

a **girl** from Germany [ə ˌgɜːl frəm ˈdʒɜːməni] ein Mädchen aus Deutsch-land I

girlfriend [ˈgɜːlfrend] Freundin *(in einer Paarbeziehung)* II U3, 54

gist [dʒɪst] das Wesentliche °II U3, 56

*to **give** [gɪv] geben; schenken I

*to **give** the bumps [ˌgɪv ðə ˈbʌmps] hoch-leben lassen I

glass [glɑːs] Glas I

glasses (pl) [ˈglɑːsɪz] Brille II U4, 80

glove [glʌv] Handschuh I

*to **go** [gəʊ] gehen; fahren I

*to **go** black [ˌgəʊ ˈblæk] schwarz werden II U5, 102

*to **go** crazy [ˌgəʊ ˈkreɪzi] ausflippen; durchdrehen; verrückt werden II U5, 95

*to **go** down [ˌgəʊ ˈdaʊn] hinuntergehen; nach unten gehen; entlanggehen I

*to **go** for a walk [ˌgəʊ fər ə ˈwɔːk] spa-zieren gehen II U1, 18

*to **go** on [ˌgəʊ ˈɒn] weitergehen; weiter-machen; weiterführen; fortfahren I

*to **go** out [ˌgəʊ ˈaʊt] ausgehen; hinaus-gehen II U6, 122

*to **go** over to [ˌgəʊ ˈəʊvə tə] hinüberge-hen zu; zu jmdm. nach Hause gehen II U5, 95

*to **go** right back to [ˌgəʊ raɪt ˈbæk tə] zurückgehen auf II U6, 122

*to **go** shopping [ˌgəʊ ˈʃɒpɪŋ] einkaufen gehen I

*to **go** swimming [ˌgəʊ ˈswɪmɪŋ] Schwim-men gehen I

*to **go** to bed [ˌgəʊ tə ˈbed] ins Bett gehen I

*to **go** together [ˌgəʊ təˈgeðə] zueinander passen; zueinander gehören I

*to **go** with [ˈgəʊ wɪð] passen zu; gehö-ren zu I

*to **go** wrong [ˌgəʊ ˈrɒŋ] schiefgehen I

*to let **go** (of) [ˌlet ˈgəʊ (əv)] loslassen II U4, 80

It's **gone**. [ɪts ˈgɒn] Es ist weg. II U3, 62

goal [gəʊl] Tor; Ziel I

golf [gɒlf] Golf II U6, 114

*to be **gone** [bi: ˈgɒn] verschwunden sein; weg sein II U4, 81

good [gʊd] gut I

*to be **good** at [bi: ˈgʊd ˌət] gut sein in I

Good morning. [gʊd ˈmɔːnɪŋ] Guten Morgen. I

goodbye [gʊdˈbaɪ] auf Wiedersehen I

gorge scrambling [ˈgɔːdʒ ˌskræmblɪŋ] Schluchtenklettern II U1, 16

to **grab** [græb] greifen; ergreifen; schnap-pen II U3, 62

grammar [ˈgræmə] Grammatik °II U2, 33

grammar school [ˈgræmə ˌskuːl] Gymnasi-um II U6, 113

grandad [ˈgrændæd] Opa I

grandma [ˈgrænmɑː] Oma I

grandparents (pl) [ˈgrænˌpeərənts] Groß-eltern I

granny [ˈgræni] Oma I

great [greɪt] großartig; toll; super I

It's **great** for … [ɪts ˈgreɪt fə] Es ist super zum/für … I

… is a **great** sport. [ɪz ə ˈgreɪt ˌspɔːt] … ist ein toller Sport. I

green [griːn] grün I

Greenwich Mean Time (= GMT) [ˌgrenɪdʒ ˈmiːn ˌtaɪm] westeuropäische Zeit I

greeting [ˈgriːtɪŋ] Gruß I

grey [greɪ] grau I

grid [grɪd] Gitter; Tabelle; Raster I

group [gruːp] Gruppe; Klasse I

a **group** of three [ə ˌgruːp əv ˈθriː] eine Dreiergruppe I

tutor **group** [ˈtjuːtə ˌgruːp] Klasse *(in einer englischen Schule)* I

*to **grow** [grəʊ] wachsen II U6, 109

guard [gɑːd] Wache; Wächter/-in II AC1, 49

to **guess** [ges] raten; erraten; vermuten I

guessing game [ˈgesɪŋ ˌgeɪm] Ratespiel °II U1, 13

guide [gaɪd] Führer/-in; Reiseführer II U3, 56

guinea pig [ˈgɪni: ˌpɪg] Meerschweinchen I

guy [gaɪ] Typ; Kerl; *(Pl.)* Leute II U1, 9

H

*to do our **hair** [ˌduː ˌaʊə ˈheə] uns frisieren; unsere Haare machen I

half, halves (pl) (of) [hɑːf; hɑːvz] die Hälfte I

half [hɑːf] halb I

half past [ˌhɑːf ˈpɑːst] halb *(bei Uhrzeit-angaben)* I

half-sister [ˈhɑːfˌsɪstə] Halbschwester I

half-term break [ˌhɑːftɜːm ˈbreɪk] Halb-jahresferien I

hall [hɔːl] Halle; Saal II U2, 29; Flur; Diele; Korridor II U6, 122

hammer [ˈhæmə] Hammer II U2, 34

hand [hænd] Hand I

Clap your **hands**. [ˌklæp jɔː ˈhændz] Klatsch/Klatscht in die Hände. I

On the one **hand** …, (but) on the other **hand** … [ɒn ðə ˌwʌn ˌhænd … (bʌt) ɒn ðiˌʌðə ˌhænd …] Einerseits …, (aber) andererseits … II U4, 82

*to **hang** up [ˌhæŋ ˈʌp] aufhängen II U2, 33

to **happen** [ˈhæpn] geschehen; passieren I

happy [ˈhæpi] glücklich; froh; fröhlich I

Happy Birthday! [ˌhæpi ˈbɜːθdeɪ] Alles Gute zum Geburtstag!; Herzlichen Glückwunsch zum Geburtstag! I

harbour [ˈhɑːbə] Hafen II U6, 109

hard [hɑːd] hart; schwer; schwierig II U1, 12; *hier:* stark II U3, 56

hat [hæt] Hut I

to **hate** [heɪt] hassen; nicht mögen II U2, 42

*to **have** [hæv] haben I

*to **have** a look (at) [ˌhæv ə ˈlʊk] anschau-en II U4, 73

*to **have** breakfast [ˌhæv ˈbrekfəst] früh-stücken I

*to **have** fun [ˌhæv ˈfʌn] Spaß haben; sich amüsieren I

*to **have** got [hæv ˈgɒt] besitzen; haben I

*to **have** to [ˈhæv tə] müssen II U2, 40

*to **have** (a sweet) [hæv] (ein Bonbon) nehmen; (ein Bonbon) essen I

he [hiː] er I

head [hed] Kopf I

head of state [ˌhed əv ˈsteɪt] Staatsober-haupt II AC2, 89

With a very big **head**! [ˌwɪð ə ˌveri big ˈhed] Und ein Angeber! II U5, 95

headache (no pl) [ˈhedeɪk] Kopfschmerzen; Kopfweh II U4, 73

heading [ˈhedɪŋ] Überschrift; Titel I

headphones (pl) [ˈhedfəʊnz] Kopfhörer II U5, 102

health [helθ] Gesundheit II U4, 69

healthy [ˈhelθi] gesund I

*to **hear** [hɪə] hören I

I **hear** … [aɪ ˈhɪə] Ich habe gehört, dass … I

heart [hɑːt] Herz; *hier:* Zentrum II U3, 62

*to learn … by **heart** [ˌlɜːn baɪ ˈhɑːt] auswendig lernen I

Hello. [heˈləʊ] Hallo. I
  *to say **hello** (to) [seɪ helˈəʊ tə] grüßen; Grüße ausrichten (an) I
help [help] Hilfe I
to **help** [help] helfen I
helpful [ˈhelpfl] hilfsbereit; hilfreich I
helpless [ˈhelpləs] hilflos I
her [hɜː] ihr/-e; sie I
here [hɪə] hier I
  right **here** [raɪt ˈhɪə] genau hier II U4, 70
  Here you are. [ˈhɪə juˈɑː] Bitte schön. I
  Here's … [ˈhɪəz] Hier ist … I
hero, **heroes** (pl) [ˈhɪərəʊ, ˈhɪərəʊz] Held II AC3, 130
heroine [ˈherəʊɪn] Heldin II AC3, 130
Hey! [heɪ] Hi.; He!; Hallo. I
Hi. [haɪ] Hi.; Hallo. I
*to **hide** [haɪd] (sich) verstecken II AC3, 130
high [haɪ] hoch; groß II U1, 17
  high tide [ˈhaɪ ˌtaɪd] Flut II U3, 62
highlight [ˈhaɪlaɪt] Highlight; Höhepunkt II U1, 9
hiking [ˈhaɪkɪŋ] Wandern II U6, 109
hill [hɪl] Berg; Hügel II U6, 122
him [hɪm] ihn; ihm I
himself [hɪmˈself] er/sich (selbst); selber II U1, 8
his [hɪz] sein/-e I
historical [hɪˈstɒrɪkl] historisch; geschichtlich I
history [ˈhɪstri] Geschichte II U2, 30
  living **history** show [ˌlɪvɪŋ ˈhɪstəri ˌʃəʊ] Show, in der historischer Alltag nachgespielt wird II U6, 108
*to **hit** [hɪt] schlagen; treffen I
hobby, **hobbies** (pl) [ˈhɒbi; ˈhɒbiz] Hobby I
hockey [ˈhɒki] Hockey II U6, 69
*to **hold** [həʊld] halten; festhalten I
hole [həʊl] Loch II U2, 33
holiday [ˈhɒlədeɪ] Urlaub; Feiertag I
  holidays (pl) [ˈhɒlədeɪz] Ferien I
home [həʊm] Zuhause; Heim I
  at **home** [ət ˈhəʊm] zu Hause I
home [həʊm] nach Hause I
homepage [ˈhəʊmpeɪdʒ] Homepage I
homework [ˈhəʊmwɜːk] Hausaufgabe(n) I
hope [həʊp] Hoffnung II U4, 82
to **hope** [həʊp] hoffen I
hopeful [ˈhəʊpfl] hoffnungsvoll I
horrified [ˈhɒrɪfaɪd] entsetzt I
horse [hɔːs] Pferd I
hospital [ˈhɒspɪtl] Hospital; Krankenhaus II U2, 30
hotel [həʊˈtel] Hotel II U2, 33
hour [aʊə] Stunde II U3, 63
house [haʊs] Haus I
  to move (**house**) [muːv (haʊs)] umziehen II U6, 110
how [haʊ] wie I
  How many …? [ˌhaʊ ˈmeni] Wie viele …? I

How are you? [ˌhaʊ ˈɑː jə] Wie geht es dir?; Wie geht es euch?; Wie geht es Ihnen? I
How much (is/are) …? [ˌhaʊ ˈmʌtʃ ɪz/ɑː] Wie viel (kostet/kosten) …? I
How old are you? [haʊ ˈəʊld ə juː] Wie alt bist du?; Wie alt sind Sie? I
How to … [ˈhaʊ tə] Wie man … I
  Is this **how** you (do) …? [ɪz ˈðɪs haʊ jʊ ˌduː] Machst du so …? I
  that's **how** [ðæts ˈhaʊ] so II U1, 10
to **hug** [hʌg] umarmen I
huge [hjuːdʒ] riesig; riesengroß; gewaltig II AC1, 48
to **hum** [hʌm] summen II U2, 33
human body [ˌhjuːmən ˈbɒdi] menschlicher Körper II U3, 62
Humanities (pl) [hjuːˈmænətiz] Sozialwissenschaften II U2, 32
hungry [ˈhʌŋgri] hungrig I
to **hurry** [ˈhʌri] eilen; sich beeilen I
*to **hurt** [hɜːt] verletzen; weh tun II U4, 72
hurt [hɜːt] verletzt II U1, 24
husband [ˈhʌzbənd] Ehemann II U2, 30

I

I [aɪ] ich I
  I don't know! [aɪ ˌdəʊnt ˈnəʊ] Ich weiß (es) nicht! I
  I don't like … [aɪ ˈdəʊnt laɪk] Ich mag … nicht.; Ich mache … nicht gern. I
  I hear … [aɪ ˈhɪə] Ich habe gehört, dass … I
  I like … [aɪ ˈlaɪk] Mir gefällt …; Ich mag … I
  I love you. [aɪ ˈlʌv juː] Ich liebe dich.; Ich mag dich. I
  I love … [aɪ ˈlʌv] Ich liebe …; Ich mag … total gern. I
  I'd like to … (= I would like to) [aɪd ˈlaɪk tə] Ich möchte …; Ich würde gern … I
  I'm (not) scared of … [aɪm (nɒt) ˈskeəd ˌəv] Ich habe (keine) Angst vor … I
  I'm dog-tired. [aɪm ˈdɒgˈtaɪəd] Ich bin hundemüde. I
  I'm English. [aɪmˈɪŋglɪʃ] Ich bin Engländer/-in. I
  I'm fine. [ˌaɪm ˈfaɪn] Mir geht's gut. I
  I'm from … [ˌaɪm frɒm] Ich bin aus … I
  I'm sorry! [ˌaɪm ˈsɒri] Tut mir leid! I
  I'm … [aɪm] Ich bin … I
ice [aɪs] Eis I
  ice cream [aɪs ˈkriːm] Eis; Eiscreme I
  ice rink [ˈaɪs ˌrɪŋk] Eisbahn; Schlittschuhbahn I
idea [aɪˈdɪə] Idee; Einfall I
  no **idea** [ˌnəʊ aɪˈdɪə] keine Ahnung II U1, 19
identity [aɪˈdentəti] Identität II AC1, 49
idiot [ˈɪdiət] Idiot/-in II U2, 41
if [ɪf] wenn; falls; ob I

if-clause [ˈɪf klɔːz] if-Satz °II U6, 114
to **imagine** [ɪˈmædʒɪn] sich (etwas) vorstellen I
important [ɪmˈpɔːtnt] wichtig I
impressed [ɪmˈprest] beeindruckt II U2, 36
to **improve** [ɪmˈpruːv] sich verbessern; verbessern I
in [ɪn] in; im; rein; herein I
  in front of [ɪn ˈfrʌnt ˌəv] vor I
  in need [ɪn ˈniːd] bedürftig; in Not II U1, 10
  in secret [ɪn ˈsiːkrət] heimlich II U4, 81
  in the end [ˌɪn ðiˈend] schließlich; zum Schluss II U1, 10
  in the evenings [ɪn ðiˈiːvnɪŋz] abends I
  in the mornings [ˌɪn ðə ˈmɔːnɪŋz] morgens; vormittags I
  in the photo(s) [ˌɪn ðə ˈfəʊtəʊ(z)] auf dem Foto/den Fotos I
  in the street [ˌɪn ðə ˈstriːt] in der Straße; auf der Straße I
to **include** [ɪnˈkluːd] einschließen; beinhalten II U6, 108
Indian [ˈɪndiən] Inder/-in; indisch I
individual [ˌɪndɪˈvɪdʒuəl] individuell; einzeln II U4, 69
infinitive [ɪnˈfɪnətɪv] Infinitiv I
to **influence** [ˈɪnfluəns] beeinflussen II AC2, 89
information (no pl) [ˌɪnfəˈmeɪʃn] Information; Informationen I
ingredient [ɪnˈgriːdiənt] Zutat II AC3, 130
injury [ˈɪndʒəri] Verletzung II U4, 76
inline skating [ˈɪnlaɪn ˌskeɪtɪŋ] Inlineskatefahren I
inside [ɪnˈsaɪd] innen; im Innern; hinein; nach drinnen; in; drin I
instruction [ɪnˈstrʌkʃn] Instruktion; Anweisung I
instructor [ɪnˈstrʌktə] Lehrer/-in; Betreuer/-in II U1, 18
interest [ˈɪntrəst] Interesse II U5, 90
to **interest** [ˈɪntrəst] (sich) interessieren °II U2, 38
*to be **interested** in [bɪˈɪntrəstɪd ˌɪn] interessiert sein an; sich interessieren für II U2, 31
interesting [ˈɪntrəstɪŋ] interessant I
international [ˌɪntəˈnæʃnl] international I
internet [ˈɪntənet] Internet I
interview [ˈɪntəvjuː] Interview; Befragung I
to **interview** [ˈɪntəvjuː] interviewen; befragen I
into [ˈɪntə] in; in … hinein I
*to be **into** [biːˈɪntə] mögen; stehen auf I
  You're **into** … [ˈjɔːrˌɪntə] Du magst …; Du stehst auf … I
Introduce … [ˌɪntrəˈdjuːs] Stelle/Stellt … vor. I
introduction [ˌɪntrəˈdʌkʃn] Einführung; Einleitung; Vorstellung II U2, 29
invitation [ˌɪnvɪˈteɪʃn] Einladung I

to **invite** [ɪn'vaɪt] einladen I
inward ['ɪnwəd] ankommend II U6, 112
Irish ['aɪrɪʃ] irisch; Irisch II U6, 114
irregular [ɪ'regjələ] unregelmäßig I
Is this how you (do) …? [ɪz 'ðɪs haʊ jʊ ˌduː] Machst du so …? I
island ['aɪlənd] Insel II U6, 109
it [ɪt] es I
  It's fun. [ɪts 'fʌn] Es macht Spaß. I
  It's great for … [ɪts 'greɪt fə] Es ist super zum/für … I
  It's your turn. [ˌɪts 'jɔː tɜːn] Du bist dran. I
  It's …/They're … [ɪts/ðeə] Es kostet …/ Sie kosten … I
its [ɪts] sein/-e; ihr/-e I

J

January ['dʒænjuri] Januar I
*to be **jealous** (of) [biː 'dʒeləs] eifersüchtig sein (auf); neidisch sein (auf) I
jelly ['dʒeli] Tortenguss; Götterspeise; Wackelpudding; Gelee I
crown **jewels** [ˌkraʊn 'dʒuːəlz] Kronjuwelen II U3, 56
jewellery ['dʒuːəlri] Schmuck I
job [dʒɒb] Arbeit; Aufgabe; Job I
mouth **jogging** ['maʊθ ˌdʒɒgɪŋ] Training für den Mund I
to **join** [dʒɔɪn] beitreten; sich anschließen; verbinden II U2, 33
joke [dʒəʊk] Witz I
to **joke** [dʒəʊk] scherzen II U5, 102
journey ['dʒɜːni] Reise; Fahrt II U6, 109
juggling ['dʒʌɡlɪŋ] Jonglieren II U2, 38
juice [dʒuːs] Saft I
July [dʒʊ'laɪ] Juli I
to **jump** [dʒʌmp] springen I
  to **jump** back [dʒʌmp ˌbæk] zurückspringen; hier: zurückschrecken II U3, 57
  to **jump** the queue [ˌdʒʌmp ðə 'kjuː] sich vordrängeln I
June [dʒuːn] Juni I
just [dʒʌst] gerade; nur; einfach I

K

*to **keep** [kiːp] behalten; aufbewahren; halten I
  *to **keep** away from [ˌkiːp ə'weɪ frəm] (sich) fernhalten von II U6, 122
  *to **keep** going [kiːp 'gɔɪŋ] aufrechterhalten II U1, 12
  *to **keep** up (with) [kiːp 'ʌp (wɪð)] mithalten (mit); Schritt halten (mit) II U4, 80
  *to **keep** your fingers crossed [ˌkiːp jɔː ˌfɪŋɡəz 'krɒst] die Daumen drücken I
key [kiː] Schlüssel II U3, 63
  key word ['kiː ˌwɜːd] Stichwort; Schlüsselbegriff I
to **kick** [kɪk] schießen; treten II U4, 68
kind [kaɪnd] Art; Sorte I

king [kɪŋ] König I
kitchen ['kɪtʃɪn] Küche I
knight [naɪt] Ritter II AC3, 130
knob [nɒb] Griff II U5, 95
*to **know** [nəʊ] kennen; wissen I
  *to get to **know** [ˌget tə 'nəʊ] kennen lernen II U6, 114
  I don't **know**! [aɪ ˌdəʊnt 'nəʊ] Ich weiß (es) nicht! I
  You **know** how to … [juː 'nəʊ ˌhaʊ tə] Du weißt, wie man …; Ihr wisst, wie man … I
Korean [kə'riːən] koreanisch; Koreanisch; Koreaner/-in II U4, 76
  South **Korean** [ˌsaʊθ kə'riːən] Südkoreaner/-in; südkoreanisch; Südkoreanisch II AC2, 88

L

ladder ['lædə] Leiter II U2, 34
lake [leɪk] See I
  boating **lake** ['bəʊtɪŋ ˌleɪk] See zum Rudern I
lamb [læm] Lamm; Lämmchen I
land [lænd] Land I
to **land** [lænd] landen II U4, 78
landscape ['lændskeɪp] Landschaft II U6, 108
language ['læŋgwɪdʒ] Sprache I
  first **language** [ˌfɜːst 'læŋgwɪdʒ] Muttersprache II AC2, 89
  foreign **language** [ˌfɒrɪn 'læŋgwɪdʒ] Fremdsprache II U2, 38
  official **language** [ə'fɪʃl 'læŋgwɪdʒ] Amtssprache II AC2, 89
laptop ['læptɒp] Laptop II U5, 97
large [lɑːdʒ] groß; riesig II AC1, 48
lassi ['lʌsi] Lassi I
last [lɑːst] letzte/-r/-s I
  at **last** [ət 'lɑːst] endlich; schließlich I
late [leɪt] spät; zu spät I
  *to be **late** [biː 'leɪt] zu spät dran sein; zu spät kommen I
later ['leɪtə] später I
to **laugh** [lɑːf] lachen I
*to **learn** [lɜːn] lernen I
  *to **learn** … by heart [ˌlɜːn baɪ 'hɑːt] auswendig lernen I
  a lot to **learn** [ə ˌlɒt tə 'lɜːn] viel zu lernen I
at **least** [ət 'liːst] mindestens; wenigstens °II U3, 63
*to **leave** [liːv] verlassen; lassen; abfahren II U2, 30; losgehen II U4, 72
  *to **leave** a message [ˌliːv ə 'mesɪdʒ] eine Nachricht hinterlassen I
  *to **leave** it to cool [ˌliːv ɪt tə 'kuːl] kalt stellen I
  *to **leave** space [liːv 'speɪs] Platz lassen I
left [left] linke/-r/-s; links I

on the **left** [ɒn ðə 'left] auf der linken Seite; links I
left [left] übrig I
leg [leg] Bein II U4, 71
legend ['ledʒənd] Legende; Sage II AC3, 130
leisure ['leʒə] Freizeit; Freizeit- I
  leisure centre ['leʒə ˌsentə] Freizeitzentrum I
lemon ['lemən] Zitrone II U1, 24
lemonade [ˌlemə'neɪd] Limonade I
lesson ['lesn] Unterrichtsstunde; Schulstunde; Unterricht I
*to **let** [let] lassen I
  *to **let** go (of) [ˌlet 'gəʊ (əv)] loslassen II U4, 80
  Let's … [lets] Lass/Lasst uns … I
letter ['letə] Buchstabe I; Brief II U5, 91
  capital **letter** [ˌkæpɪtl 'letə] Großbuchstabe I
to **lie** [laɪ] lügen II U1, 9
*to **lie** [laɪ] liegen II U2, 40
life, **lives** (pl) [laɪf, laɪvz] Leben II U2, 39
lifeboat ['laɪfbəʊt] Rettungsboot I
lifebuoy ['laɪfbɔɪ] Rettungsring I
light [laɪt] Licht; Lampe II U5, 102
lightning (no pl) ['laɪtnɪŋ] Blitz II U5, 102
to **like** [laɪk] mögen; gern haben I
  would **like** [wʊd 'laɪk] würde/-st/-n/-t gern; hätte/-st/-n/-t gern I
  I don't **like** … [aɪ 'dəʊnt laɪk] Ich mag … nicht.; Ich mache … nicht gern. I
  I **like** singing and dancing. [aɪ laɪk ˌsɪŋɪŋ ənd 'dɑːnsɪŋ] Ich singe und tanze gern. I
  I **like** … [aɪ 'laɪk] Mir gefällt …; Ich mag … I
  I'd **like** to … (= I would like to) [aɪd 'laɪk tə] Ich möchte …; Ich würde gern … I
  Would you **like** …? [ˌwʊd jʊ 'laɪk] Möchtest du …?; Möchten Sie …?; Möchtet ihr …? °II U4, 70
like [laɪk] wie I
  like that [laɪk 'ðæt] so I
  like this [laɪk 'ðɪs] so I
line [laɪn] Zeile; Linie I
  finish **line** ['fɪnɪʃ ˌlaɪn] Ziellinie II U4, 81
  time **line** ['taɪm ˌlaɪn] Zeitstrahl I
link [lɪŋk] Link; Verbindung II U3, 59
to **link** [lɪŋk] verbinden II U5, 104
  linking word ['lɪŋkɪŋ ˌwɜːd] Bindewort I
lion [laɪən] Löwe II U3, 56
list [lɪst] Liste I
to **listen** (to) ['lɪsn] zuhören; anhören I
  Listen again. [ˌlɪsn ə'gen] Hör/Hört noch einmal zu. I
  to **listen** for ['lɪsn fə] horchen auf I
listener ['lɪsənə] Zuhörer/-in II U4, 77
listening ['lɪsnɪŋ] Hören I
little ['lɪtl] klein I
a **little** [ə 'lɪtl] ein wenig; etwas I
to **live** [lɪv] wohnen; leben I
lively ['laɪvli] lebendig II U2, 29
living room ['lɪvɪŋ rʊm] Wohnzimmer I

living history show [ˌlɪvɪŋ ˈhɪstəri ˌʃəʊ] *Show, in der historischer Alltag nachgespielt wird* II **U6**, 108
local [ˈləʊkl] örtlich; lokal II **U6**, 115
location [ləʊˈkeɪʃn] Handlungsort; Lage; Standort II **U3**, 58
locked [lɒkt] abgeschlossen II **U1**, 19
locker [ˈlɒkə] Schließfach; Spind I
loft [lɒft] Dachboden I
LOL (= laughing out loud) [lɒl] LOL II **U1**, 8
Londoner [ˈlʌndənə] Londoner/-in I
lonely [ˈləʊnli] einsam I
long [lɒŋ] lang I
  (not) any **longer** [nɒtˌeni ˈlɒŋgə] (nicht) mehr; (nicht) länger II **U6**, 110
look [lʊk] Blick I
  *to have a **look** (at) [ˌhævˌə ˈlʊk] anschauen II **U4**, 73
  *to take a **look** at [ˌteɪkˌə ˈlʊk æt] einen Blick werfen auf II **U2**, 37
to look [lʊk] schauen; sehen; aussehen I
  Look! [lʊk] Schau/Schaut mal! I
  to **look** after [lʊkˌˈɑːftə] aufpassen auf; hüten; sich kümmern um I
  to **look** at [ˈlʊkˌət] anschauen; ansehen I
  to **look** for [ˈlʊk fɔː] suchen nach I
  to **look** forward to [ˌlʊk ˈfɔːwəd tə] sich freuen auf II **U2**, 33
  to **look** out [lʊkˌˈaʊt] aufpassen II **U4**, 70
  to **look** up [lʊkˌˈʌp] nachschlagen; nachschauen I
  Look closely … [lʊk ˈkləʊsli] Schau(t) genau … °II **U4**, 78
  what the man **looked** like [ˌwɒt ðə mæn ˈlʊkt laɪk] wie der Mann aussah II **U1**, 13
*to lose [luːz] verlieren II **U4**, 68
*to get lost [get ˈlɒst] verloren gehen; sich verirren II **U6**, 119
a lot [ə ˈlɒt] viel I
  a **lot** of [ə ˈlɒtˌəv] viel/-e; eine Menge I
  lots (of) [ˈlɒtsˌəv] viel/-e; jede Menge I
loud [laʊd] laut I
love [lʌv] Liebe II **U6**, 119
Love … [lʌv] Liebe Grüße *(am Briefende)*; Herzliche Grüße *(am Briefende)* I
to love [lʌv] lieben; gern mögen I
  would **love** [wʊd ˈlʌv] würde/-st/-n/-t sehr gern; hätte/-st/-n/-t sehr gern I
  I **love** you. [aɪ ˈlʌv ju] Ich liebe dich.; Ich mag dich. I
  I **love** … [aɪ ˈlʌv] Ich liebe …; Ich mag … total gern. I
lovebirds *(pl)* [ˈlʌvˌbɜːdz] Turteltauben II **U1**, 9
low [ləʊ] niedrig II **U1**, 17
  low tide [ˈləʊ ˌtaɪd] Ebbe II **U3**, 62
lucky … [ˈlʌki] … der/die Glückliche I
  *to be **lucky** [biˌˈlʌki] Glück haben II **U3**, 62
  lucky charm [ˌlʌki ˈtʃɑːm] Glücksbringer; Talisman I
  … is/are **lucky.** [ɪz/ɑː ˈlʌki] … hat/haben Glück. I

lunch [lʌnʃ] Mittagessen I
  lunch break [ˈlʌnʃbreɪk] Mittagspause I

M

machine [məˈʃiːn] Automat; Maschine; Apparat; Gerät I
  answering **machine** [ˈɑːnsrɪŋ məˌʃiːn] Anrufbeantworter I
  washing **machine** [ˈwɒʃɪŋ məˌʃiːn] Waschmaschine II **U5**, 95
mad [mæd] verrückt II **U5**, 97
Dear Sir or **Madam** [dɪə ˌsɜːrˌɔː ˈmædəm] Sehr geehrte Dame, sehr geehrter Herr II **U6**, 113
magazine [ˌmægəˈziːn] Zeitschrift I
magical [ˈmædʒɪkəl] magisch; Zauber- II **AC3**, 130
to mail [ˈiːmeɪl] mailen; per E-Mail schicken II **U5**, 97
main [meɪn] Haupt- I
  main clause [ˈmeɪn ˌklɔːz] Hauptsatz °II **U6**, 114
*to make [meɪk] machen; tun; bilden; *hier:* ergeben I
  *to **make** a decision [ˌmeɪkˌə dɪˈsɪʒn] eine Entscheidung treffen °II **U3**, 61
  *to **make** a wish [ˌmeɪkˌə ˈwɪʃ] sich etwas wünschen I
  *to **make** friends [ˌmeɪk ˈfrendz] Freundschaft schließen II **U2**, 43
  *to **make** money [ˌmeɪk ˈmʌni] Geld verdienen I
  *to **make** notes [ˌmeɪk ˈnəʊts] Notizen machen I
  *to **make** somebody do something [meɪk] jmdn. dazu bringen, etw. zu tun II **U5**, 92
  *to **make** sure [ˌmeɪk ˈʃɔː] sich versichern I
  *to **make** trouble [ˌmeɪk ˈtrʌbl] Ärger machen; in Schwierigkeiten bringen I
man, men *(pl)* [mæn; men] Mann I
  what the **man** looked like [ˌwɒt ðə mæn ˈlʊkt laɪk] wie der Mann aussah II **U1**, 13
manga [ˈmæŋgə] Manga *(japanischer Comic)* II **U2**, 38
mango [ˈmæŋgəʊ] Mango I
many [ˈmeni] viele I
  How **many** …? [ˌhaʊ ˈmeni] Wie viele …? I
map [mæp] Stadtplan; Landkarte I
  mind **map** [ˈmaɪnd mæp] Wörternetz *(eine Art Schaubild)* I
marathon [ˈmærəθn] Marathon II **U4**, 68
March [mɑːtʃ] März I
to mark [mɑːk] markieren; kennzeichnen °II **U6**, 121
market [ˈmɑːkɪt] Markt I
  flea **market** [ˈfliː ˌmɑːkɪt] Flohmarkt I
raven **master** [ˈreɪvn ˌmɑːstə] Herr der Raben II **U3**, 56
match [mætʃ] Spiel; Match II **U4**, 68

to match [mætʃ] zuordnen; passen zu; entsprechen I
mate [meɪt] Schiffsoffizier; Maat I
material [məˈtɪəriəl] Material II **U3**, 61
Maths [mæθs] Mathematik; Mathe II **U2**, 32
What's the **matter?** [ˌwɒts ðə ˈmætə] Was ist los?; Was hast du? II **U6**, 122
May [meɪ] Mai I
may [meɪ] (vielleicht) können; dürfen II **U5**, 95
maybe [ˈmeɪbi] vielleicht I
me [miː] ich; mich; mir I
meal [miːl] Mahlzeit; Essen II **U1**, 18
  ready **meal** [ˌredi ˈmiːl] Fertiggericht I
*to mean [miːn] bedeuten; meinen II **U3**, 54
meaning [ˈmiːnɪŋ] Bedeutung; Sinn II **U1**, 21
mechanic [məˈkænɪk] Mechaniker/-in; Kfz-Mechaniker/-in II **U1**, 13
media [ˈmiːdiə] Medien II **U5**, 91
mediation [ˌmiːdiˈeɪʃn] Sprachmittlung I
medieval [ˌmediˈiːvl] mittelalterlich II **U6**, 108
*to meet [miːt] treffen; sich treffen I
member [ˈmembə] Mitglied II **U2**, 33
memory [ˈmemri] Erinnerung; Gedächtnis II **U1**, 19
to mention [ˈmenʃn] erwähnen II **AC2**, 88
merchant [ˈmɜːtʃənt] Kaufmann; Händler II **AC2**, 89
message [ˈmesɪdʒ] Botschaft; Nachricht I
  *to leave a **message** [ˌliːvˌə ˈmesɪdʒ] eine Nachricht hinterlassen I
  *to take a **message** [ˌteɪkˌə ˈmesɪdʒ] eine Nachricht entgegennehmen; jmdm. etw. ausrichten I
  text (**message**) [ˈtekst ˌmesɪdʒ] SMS; Kurznachricht I
metre [ˈmiːtə] Meter II **U3**, 62
middle [ˈmɪdl] Mitte I
mile [maɪl] Meile *(brit. Längenmaß)* II **U4**, 72
milk [mɪlk] Milch I
to milk [mɪlk] melken II **U6**, 119
million [ˈmɪljən] Million II **AC1**, 48
  I've done this a **million** times before. [ˌaɪv dʌn ðɪs ə ˌmɪljən taɪmz bɪˈfɔː] Ich habe das schon eine Million Mal gemacht. II **U5**, 95
mind map [ˈmaɪnd mæp] Wörternetz *(eine Art Schaubild)* I
mine [maɪn] Mine II **U6**, 122
mine [maɪn] mein/-er/-e/-es II **U2**, 41
mini [ˈmɪni] Mini- II **U4**, 70
mining [ˈmaɪnɪŋ] Bergbau II **U6**, 114
minute [ˈmɪnɪt] Minute I
to miss [mɪs] verpassen; versäumen II **U5**, 99; vermissen II **U6**, 110
missing [ˈmɪsɪŋ] fehlend; verschwunden II **U1**, 13
  What is **missing?** [ˌwɒt ɪz ˈmɪsɪŋ] Was fehlt? I
mistake [mɪˈsteɪk] Fehler I

mobile ['məʊbaɪl] Handy; Mobiltelefon
II U5, 91
modal ['məʊdl] Modalverb °II U5, 91
model ['mɒdl] Modell; Tonmodell; Model I
modern ['mɒdn] modern II U3, 64
moment ['məʊmənt] Moment; Augenblick
II U2, 40
at the moment [ət ðə 'məʊmənt] im
Moment; gerade I
Monday ['mʌndeɪ] Montag I
on Mondays [ɒn 'mʌndeɪz] montags I
money ['mʌni] Geld I
*to make money [ˌmeɪk 'mʌni] Geld
verdienen I
pocket money ['pɒkɪt ˌmʌni] Taschengeld I
to raise money [ˌreɪz 'mʌni] Geld sammeln II U1, 10
monster ['mɒnstə] Monster; Ungeheuer I
month [mʌnθ] Monat II U1, 10
monument ['mɒnjəmənt] Monument;
Denkmal II U6, 114
mood [muːd] Stimmung; Laune II U1, 24
more [mɔː] mehr; weitere I
more … than ['mɔː ðən] mehr … als I
not any more [ˌnɒt eni 'mɔː] nicht mehr I
morning ['mɔːnɪŋ] Morgen; Vormittag I
in the mornings [ɪn ðə 'mɔːnɪŋz] morgens; vormittags I
Good morning. [gʊd 'mɔːnɪŋ] Guten
Morgen. I
(the) most [ðə 'məʊst] der/die/das meiste;
die meisten I
mother ['mʌðə] Mutter I
to motivate ['məʊtɪveɪt] motivieren I
bicycle motocross [ˌbaɪsɪkl 'məʊtəʊkrɒs]
Fahrradmotocross II U4, 83
mountain ['maʊntɪn] Berg II U1, 16
mountain biking ['maʊntɪn ˌbaɪkɪŋ]
Mountainbikefahren II U6, 109
mouse (sg), mice (pl) [maʊs; maɪs] Maus/
Mäuse I
mouth [maʊθ] Mund I
mouth jogging ['maʊθ ˌdʒɒgɪŋ] Training
für den Mund I
move [muːv] Bewegung I
to move [muːv] (sich) bewegen I
to move in/into [ˌmuːv ˌɪn/'ɪntə] einziehen
in II U6, 122
to move (house) [muːv (haʊs)] umziehen
II U6, 110
Mr ['mɪstə] Herr (Anrede) I
Mrs ['mɪsɪz] Frau (Anrede) I
much [mʌtʃ] viel I
mud [mʌd] Schlamm II U3, 62
muddy ['mʌdi] schlammig II U3, 62
mudlark ['mʌdlɑːk] jemand, der im
Schlamm nach Sachen sucht, die er dann
verkaufen kann II U3, 62
multi-ethnic [ˌmʌlti'eθnɪk] Vielvölker-;
international II AC1, 48
mum [mʌm] Mama I

museum [mjuː'ziːəm] Museum I
music ['mjuːzɪk] Musik I
musician [mjuː'zɪʃn] Musiker/-in II U3, 53
must [mʌst] müssen I
mustn't ['mʌsnt] nicht dürfen I
my [maɪ] mein/-e I
My favourite … [maɪ 'feɪvrɪt] Mein/e
Lieblings … I
My name is … [maɪ 'neɪm ˌɪz] Ich heiße … I
myself [maɪ'self] ich/mir/mich (selbst);
selber II U5, 93
mysterious [mɪ'stɪəriəs] mysteriös; geheimnisvoll II AC3, 130

N

name [neɪm] Name I
name day ['neɪm ˌdeɪ] Namenstag I
My name is … [maɪ 'neɪm ˌɪz] Ich heiße … I
What's your name? [ˌwɒts jə 'neɪm] Wie
heißt du?; Wie heißen Sie? I
to name [neɪm] nennen; benennen I
Can you name …? ['kæn jʊ ˌneɪm] Kannst
du … nennen? I
nasty ['nɑːsti] garstig; gemein II U5, 91
national ['næʃnl] national; landesweit I
nature ['neɪtʃə] Natur II U2, 43
near [nɪə] nahe; in der Nähe von I
nearly ['nɪəli] fast; annähernd II U2, 41
with special needs [wɪð ˌspeʃl 'niːdz] behindert II U2, 29
in need [ɪn 'niːd] bedürftig; in Not II U1, 10
to need (to do) [niːd] (tun) müssen I
to need (to) [niːd] brauchen; benötigen I
needn't ['niːdnt] nicht brauchen; nicht
müssen I
negative ['negətɪv] negativ; verneint
II U6, 108
negative form ['negətɪv ˌfɔːm] verneinte
Form I
neighbour (BE) ['neɪbə] Nachbar/-in I
*to get on people's nerves [ˌget ɒn
sʌmbɒdiz 'nɜːvz] jemandem auf die
Nerven gehen I
nervous ['nɜːvəs] nervös; aufgeregt II U1, 12
net [net] Netz II U4, 68
netball ['netbɔːl] Korbball I
social network [ˌsəʊʃl 'netwɜːk] soziales
Netzwerk II U5, 91
never ['nevə] nie; niemals I
new [njuː] neu I
news (sg) [njuːz] Nachrichten; Neuigkeiten
II U2, 40
next [nekst] nächste/-r/-s; der/die
Nächste(n); als Nächstes I
next to ['nekst tə] neben I
the next day [ðə ˌnekst 'deɪ] am nächsten
Tag II U1, 11
nice [naɪs] nett; schön; lieb I
night [naɪt] Nacht I

all night [ɔːl 'naɪt] die ganze Nacht I
night walk ['naɪt wɔːk] Nachtwanderung
II U1, 18
nine [naɪn] neun I
2nite (= tonight) [tə'naɪt] heute Abend I
no [nəʊ] kein/-e I
no idea [ˌnəʊ aɪ'dɪə] keine Ahnung
II U1, 19
no [nəʊ] nein I
nobody ['nəʊbɒdi] niemand II U2, 41
nobody else ['nəʊbɒdi els] niemand
anderes II U6, 124
noise [nɔɪz] Lärm; Geräusch II U1, 18
non- [nɒn] nicht- II U1, 10
normal ['nɔːml] normal II U3, 58
north [nɔːθ] Norden; Nord- II U3, 53
nose [nəʊz] Nase II U1, 8
not [nɒt] nicht I
not any more [ˌnɒt eni 'mɔː] nicht mehr I
not … any [nɒt … eni] kein/-e I
not … anything [ˌnɒt 'eniθɪŋ] nichts I
not … yet [nɒt 'jet] noch nicht II U4, 72
note [nəʊt] Notiz; Anmerkung I
*to make notes [ˌmeɪk 'nəʊts] Notizen
machen I
*to take notes [ˌteɪk 'nəʊts] sich Notizen
machen I
to note down [ˌnəʊt 'daʊn] notieren; aufschreiben °II U2, 37
nothing ['nʌθɪŋ] nichts I
to notice ['nəʊtɪs] bemerken; wahrnehmen
II U2, 40
noticeboard ['nəʊtɪsbɔːd] schwarzes Brett
II U1, 10
noun [naʊn] Nomen; Hauptwort I
November [nə'vembə] November I
now [naʊ] jetzt; nun I
right now [ˌraɪt 'naʊ] jetzt gleich; sofort;
gerade II U5, 103
nowhere ['nəʊweə] nirgendwo; nirgendwohin II U6, 110
number ['nʌmbə] Zahl, Nummer I
nut [nʌt] Nuss I

O

o'clock [ə'klɒk] Uhr (Zeitangabe bei vollen
Stunden) I
object ['ɒbdʒɪkt] Objekt °II U2, 31
October [ɒk'təʊbə] Oktober I
of [ɒv; əv] von I
of course [əv 'kɔːs] natürlich; selbstverständlich I
*to take off [ˌteɪk 'ɒf] abnehmen; herunter-
nehmen; ausziehen I
to turn off [ˌtɜːn 'ɒf] abschalten; ausschalten II U1, 12
special offer [ˌspeʃl 'ɒfə] Sonderangebot I
to offer ['ɒfə] anbieten II U2, 28
office ['ɒfɪs] Büro I
police officer [pə'liːs ˌɒfɪsə] Polizeibeamter
II U2, 36

official [əˈfɪʃl] Schiedsrichter/-in II U4, 81

official language [əˈfɪʃl ˈlæŋgwɪdʒ] Amtssprache II AC2, 89

offline [ˈɒflaɪn] offline II U5, 103

often [ˈɒfn] oft; häufig I

oh [əʊ] null (bei Telefonnummern und
Uhrzeitangaben) I

Oh! [əʊ] O! I
Oh dear! [əʊ ˈdɪə] Oje! II U6, 122

ointment [ˈɔɪntmənt] Salbe II U4, 73

OK [əʊˈkeɪ] o.k.; in Ordnung I

old [əʊld] alt I
How old are you? [haʊ ˌəʊld ə ˈjuː] Wie alt
bist du?; Wie alt sind Sie? I

11-year-old [ɪˌlevnˈjɪərəʊld] 11-Jährige/-r
II U4, 70

on [ɒn] auf; an; am; in; im I
*to be on [bi ˈɒn] an sein; laufen II U5, 102
on Mondays [ɒn ˈmʌndeɪz] montags I
on my own [ɒn maɪ ˈəʊn] allein; für mich
II U2, 40
on the left [ɒn ðə ˈleft] auf der linken
Seite; links I
on the right [ɒn ðə ˈraɪt] auf der rechten Seite; rechts I
on time [ɒn ˈtaɪm] pünktlich II U2, 37
on top [ɒn ˈtɒp] oben; obendrauf I
Come on! [kʌm ˈɒn] Komm schon!;
Komm jetzt! I

once [wʌns] einmal; einst I

one [wʌn] eins I

one (sg)/ones (pl) [wʌn/wʌnz] eine/-r/-s
II U3, 54

one-way ticket [ˈwʌnweɪ ˌtɪkɪt] einfache
Fahrkarte II U6, 112

online [ɒnˈlaɪn] online II U1, 21

only [ˈəʊnli] einzige/-r/-s II U5, 103

only [ˈəʊnli] erst; bloß; nur I
only child [ˈəʊnli ˌtʃaɪld] Einzelkind I

Oops! [uːps] Hoppla!; Huch! I

to open [ˈəʊpn] öffnen; aufmachen I

open [ˈəʊpn] offen; geöffnet; aufgeschlagen I

opinion [əˈpɪnjən] Meinung II U5, 92

opposite [ˈɒpəzɪt] gegenüber; auf der
anderen Seite von I

or [ɔː] oder I

orange [ˈɒrɪndʒ] Orange I

orange [ˈɒrɪndʒ] orange I

order [ˈɔːdə] Reihenfolge; Ordnung I
word order [ˈwɜːd ˌɔːdə] Wortstellung;
Satzstellung I

organisation [ˌɔːgnaɪˈzeɪʃn] Organisation
°II U6, 113

to organise [ˈɔːgənaɪz] organisieren I

*to get organised [get ˈɔːgənaɪzd] sich
organisieren °II U6, 120

originally [əˈrɪdʒnli] ursprünglich II AC1, 48

other [ˈʌðə] anders; andere/-r/-s; weitere I
each other [iːtʃ ˈʌðə] einander; sich; sich
gegenseitig I
the others [ðiˈʌðəz] die anderen I

Ouch! [aʊtʃ] Aua! II U1, 8

our [aʊə; ɑː] unser/-e I

out [aʊt] außerhalb; heraus; hinaus; nach
draußen I
out and about [ˌaʊt ən əˈbaʊt] unterwegs
II U3, 58
a day out in … [ə ˌdeɪ ˈaʊt ɪn] ein Tag
in … II U3, 58
to clear out [klɪər ˈaʊt] ausräumen;
entrümpeln I

outdoor [aʊtˈdɔː] Freiluft-; Outdoor- II U1, 16

outfit [ˈaʊtfɪt] Outfit; Kleidung II U1, 8

outlaw [ˈaʊtlɔː] Geächtete/-r; Gesetzlose/-r
II AC3, 130

outline [ˈaʊtlaɪn] Skizze; Umriss °II U6, 121

outside [aʊtˈsaɪd] nach draußen; draußen;
außerhalb I

outward [ˈaʊtwəd] abfahrend II U6, 112

over [ˈəʊvə] hinüber; über I; vorüber; vorbei
II U4, 79
*to go over to [gəʊ ˈəʊvə tə] hinüberge-
hen zu; zu jmdm. nach Hause gehen
II U5, 95

to overreact [ˌəʊvəriˈækt] überreagieren
II U5, 92

own [əʊn] eigene/-r/-s I
on my own [ɒn maɪ ˈəʊn] allein; für mich
II U2, 40

P

p.m. [ˌpiːˈem] nachmittags (Uhrzeit);
abends (Uhrzeit) I

packet [ˈpækɪt] Päckchen; Paket; Packung I

page [peɪdʒ] Seite I

pain [peɪn] Schmerz II U4, 72

to paint [peɪnt] anmalen; malen I

painting [ˈpeɪntɪŋ] Malerei; Gemälde
II U2, 28

pair [peə] Paar I
pair work [ˈpeə wɜːk] Partnerarbeit
°II U5, 100

palm tree [ˈpɑːm ˌtriː] Palme II U6, 109

to panic [ˈpænɪk] panisch werden II U2, 36

piece of paper [ˌpiːs əv ˈpeɪpə] Stück
Papier I

paper [ˈpeɪpə] Papier I

paradise [ˈpærədaɪs] Paradies II U5, 90

parcel [ˈpɑːsl] Paket; Päckchen I

parents (pl) [ˈpeərənts] Eltern I

park [pɑːk] Park I

part [pɑːt] Teil; Stadtteil I
*to take part (in) [teɪk ˈpɑːt (ɪn)] teilneh-
men (an) II U5, 90

partially sighted [ˌpɑːʃəli ˈsaɪtɪd] sehbehindert II U2, 32

to participate [pɑːˈtɪsɪpeɪt] teilnehmen
°II U2, 29

past participle [ˌpɑːst pɑːˈtɪsɪpl] Partizip
°II U4, 71

partner [ˈpɑːtnə] Partner/-in I

party [ˈpɑːti] Party; Feier I

to pass [pɑːs] zupassen; zuspielen II U4, 68
to pass (on) [pɑːs ˈɒn] weitergeben I

past [pɑːst] Vergangenheit II U1, 9
past form [ˈpɑːst fɔːm] Vergangenheitsform °II U1, 10
past participle [ˌpɑːst pɑːˈtɪsɪpl] Partizip
°II U4, 71
past progressive [ˌpɑːst prəˈgresɪv] Verlaufsform der Vergangenheit °II U2, 29
simple past [ˌsɪmpl ˈpɑːst] Vergangenheitsform °II U1, 9

past [pɑːst] nach (bei Uhrzeitangaben);
vorbei (an); vorüber (an) I
half past [hɑːf ˈpɑːst] halb (bei Uhrzeitangaben) I
quarter past/to [ˈkwɔːtə pɑːst/tə] Viertel
nach/vor I

pasta [ˈpæstə] Pasta; Nudeln I

coastal path [ˌkəʊstl ˈpɑːθ] Küstenweg
II U6, 122

pattern [ˈpætn] Muster °II U6, 114

*to pay (for) [peɪ] bezahlen I

PC (= Personal Computer) [piːˈsiː] PC
II AC2, 89

PE (= Physical Education) [piːˈiː; ˌfɪzɪkl
edʒʊˈkeɪʃn] Sportunterricht II U2, 32

to peer-edit [ˈpɪərˌedɪt] gegenseitig kontrollieren °II U2, 35

pen [pen] Füller I

penny, pence (pl) [ˈpeni; pens] Penny;
Pence (brit. Währungseinheit) I

pencil [ˈpensl] Bleistift; Buntstift I
pencil-case [ˈpensl ˌkeɪs] Federmäppchen;
Mäppchen I

penny, pence (pl) [ˈpeni; pens] Penny;
Pence (brit. Währungseinheit) I

people (pl) [ˈpiːpl] Leute; Menschen I

per [pɜː; pə] pro II U6, 111

present perfect [ˌpreznt ˈpɜːfɪkt] das Perfekt
°II U4, 69

perfect [ˈpɜːfɪkt] perfekt; vollkommen I

person, people (pl) [ˈpɜːsn; ˈpiːpl] Person;
Mensch I

personal [ˈpɜːsnl] persönlich I

perspective [pəˈspektɪv] Perspektive; Blick-
winkel °II U3, 63

to persuade [pəˈsweɪd] überreden II U3, 52

pet [pet] Haustier I

phone [fəʊn] Telefon; Handy I
to answer the phone [ɑːnsə ðə ˈfəʊn]
einen Anruf entgegennehmen I
phone call [ˈfəʊn ˌkɔːl] Anruf; Telefonanruf I

photo [ˈfəʊtəʊ] Foto; Fotografie I
in the photo(s) [ˌɪn ðə ˈfəʊtəʊ(z)] auf
dem Foto/den Fotos I
photo story [ˈfəʊtəʊ ˌstɔːri] Fotostory;
Bildgeschichte I
*to take photos [teɪk ˈfəʊtəʊz] fotografie-
ren; Fotos machen I

phrase [freɪz] Redewendung; Ausdruck;
Satz I

Useful **phrases** [ˈjuːsfl ˈfreɪsɪz] nützliche Ausdrücke I

to **pick** [pɪk] auswählen; aussuchen °II U5, 101

pick-up [ˈpɪkʌp] Pick-up; Wiederaufnehmen I

picnic [ˈpɪknɪk] Picknick I

picture [ˈpɪktʃə] Bild; Foto I

pie [paɪ] Kuchen; Pastete I

piece [piːs] Stück I

piece of paper [ˌpiːs əv ˈpeɪpə] Stück Papier I

pier [pɪə] Pier; Hafendamm I

pig [pɪg] Schwein I

guinea **pig** [ˈgɪni ˌpɪg] Meerschweinchen I

pill [pɪl] Pille; Tablette II U4, 73

pilot [ˈpaɪlət] Pilot/-in II U2, 36

pink [pɪŋk] pink; rosa I

pipe [paɪp] Rohr; Rohrleitung II U2, 34

clay **pipe** [ˈkleɪ paɪp] Tonpfeife II U3, 63

pitch [pɪtʃ] Spielfeld; Platz II U4, 68

pizza [ˈpiːtsə] Pizza I

place [pleɪs] Ort; Stelle; Platz I

starting **place** [ˈstɑːtɪŋ pleɪs] Startpunkt II U6, 112

*to take **place** [teɪk ˈpleɪs] stattfinden I

to **place** [pleɪs] legen °II U6, 121

placemat [ˈpleɪsmæt] Placemat; Platzdeckchen I

plan [plæn] Plan; Entwurf I

to **plan** [plæn] planen I

planet [ˈplænɪt] Planet II U1, 18

planner [ˈplænə] Handbuch; Kalender I

plant [plɑːnt] Pflanze II U6, 114

to **plant** [plɑːnt] pflanzen; anpflanzen II U2, 41

platform [ˈplætfɔːm] Plattform; Bahnsteig II U6, 112

role **play** [ˈrəʊl ˌpleɪ] Rollenspiel I

to **play** [pleɪ] spielen I

to **play** a trick (on) [ˌpleɪ ə ˈtrɪk ˌɒn] einen Streich spielen I

player [ˈpleɪə] Spieler/-in; Mitspieler/-in II U4, 75

Please. [pliːz] Bitte. I

plumber [ˈplʌmə] Installateur/-in; Klempner/-in II U6, 122

plumbing [ˈplʌmɪŋ] Sanitärarbeit II U6, 123

plural [ˈplʊərəl] Plural; Mehrzahl I

pocket money [ˈpɒkɪt ˌmʌni] Taschengeld I

poem [ˈpəʊɪm] Gedicht I

point [pɔɪnt] Punkt II U4, 68; Zeitpunkt °II U5, 104

point of view [ˌpɔɪnt əv ˈvjuː] Standpunkt; Ansicht; Perspektive II U4, 76

Point to … [ˈpɔɪnt tə] Zeige/Zeigt auf … I

Point. [pɔɪnt] Zeige/Zeigt darauf. I

police [pəˈliːs] Polizei II U1, 13

police officer [pəˈliːs ˌɒfɪsə] Polizeibeamter II U2, 36

polite [pəˈlaɪt] höflich I

Be **polite.** [bi pəˈlaɪt] Sei/Seid höflich. I

pollution [pəˈluːʃn] Verschmutzung II U3, 62

pond [pɒnd] Teich II U2, 33

pony [ˈpəʊni] Pony I

pony trekking [ˈpəʊni ˌtrekɪŋ] Ponyreiten im Gelände II U6, 109

the **poor** [ðə pʊə] die Armen II AC3, 131

popular [ˈpɒpjələ] beliebt; populär I

positive [ˈpɒzətɪv] positiv II U2, 29

possessive form [pəˌsesɪv ˈfɔːm] Possessivform I

possibility [ˌpɒsəˈbɪləti] Möglichkeit °II U6, 114

possible [ˈpɒsəbl] möglich I

post [pəʊst] Post (Eintrag im Internet) I

to **post** [pəʊst] online stellen; posten II U5, 90

postcard [ˈpəʊstkɑːd] Postkarte II U6, 124

poster [ˈpəʊstə] Poster I

class **poster** [ˈklɑːs ˌpəʊstə] Klassenposter I

postman [ˈpəʊstmən] Briefträger II U1, 13

pound (£) [paʊnd] Pfund (brit. Währungseinheit) I

to **pour** [pɔː] einschenken; eingießen; schütten I

power [paʊə] Kraft; Macht; Stärke II AC3, 130

power cut [ˈpaʊə ˌkʌt] Stromausfall II U5, 103

Word **power** [ˈwɜːd ˌpaʊə] die Kraft der Wörter (Wortschatzübung) I

powerful [ˈpaʊəfl] stark; mächtig II AC3, 130

practical [ˈpræktɪkl] praktisch II U5, 91

to **practise** [ˈpræktɪs] üben; trainieren I

practising [ˈpræktɪsɪŋ] Üben I

prediction [prɪˈdɪkʃn] Vorhersage; Voraussage °II U6, 111

prehistoric [ˌpriːhɪˈstɒrɪk] vorgeschichtlich II U6, 114

to **prepare** [prɪˈpeə] vorbereiten; zubereiten I

preposition [ˌprepəˈzɪʃn] Präposition I

pre-reading [ˌpriːˈriːdɪŋ] vor dem Lesen I

prescription [prɪˈskrɪpʃn] Rezept (für Arzneimittel) II U4, 73

present [ˈpreznt] Geschenk I; Gegenwart; Präsens °II U1, 14

present perfect [ˌpreznt ˈpɜːfɪkt] das Perfekt °II U4, 69

present progressive [ˌpreznt prəˈgresɪv] Verlaufsform des Präsens/der Gegenwart I

simple **present** [ˌsɪmpl ˈpreznt] Gegenwart; Präsens I

to **present** [prɪˈzent] präsentieren; vorstellen I

presentation [ˌpreznˈteɪʃn] Präsentation; Vortrag I

presenter [prɪˈzentə] Moderator/-in I

to **press** [pres] drücken; pressen II U5, 102

price [praɪs] Preis I

primary school [ˈpraɪmri ˌskuːl] Grundschule I

print [prɪnt] gedruckt; Druck- II U5, 91

prison [ˈprɪzn] Gefängnis II U3, 56

private detective [ˌpraɪvət dɪˈtektɪv] Privatdetektiv/-in II AC3, 130

prize [praɪz] Preis; Gewinn I

pro [prəʊ] Argument dafür II U3, 55

probably [ˈprɒbəbli] möglicherweise; wahrscheinlich II U3, 52

problem [ˈprɒbləm] Problem; Schwierigkeit I

profile [ˈprəʊfaɪl] Profil; Porträt I

programme [ˈprəʊgræm] Programm; Sendung II U4, 68

progress [ˈprəʊgres] Fortschritt °II U2, 33

past **progressive** [ˌpɑːst prəˈgresɪv] Verlaufsform der Vergangenheit °II U2, 29

present **progressive** [ˌpreznt prəˈgresɪv] Verlaufsform des Präsens/der Gegenwart I

project [ˈprɒdʒekt] Projekt I

to **promise** [ˈprɒmɪs] versprechen II U6, 111

prompt card [ˈprɒmpt kɑːd] Stichwortkarte; Rollenkarte °II U2, 32

relative **pronoun** [ˌrelətɪv ˈprəʊnaʊn] Relativpronomen °II U2, 31

pronunciation [prəˌnʌnsiˈeɪʃn] Aussprache I

prop [prɒp] Requisite II AC3, 131

proud (of) [ˈpraʊd ˌɒv] stolz (auf) II U1, 9

public [ˈpʌblɪk] öffentlich II U3, 52

public transport (no pl) [ˌpʌblɪk ˈtrænspɔːt] öffentliche Verkehrsmittel II U3, 52

pudding [ˈpʊdɪŋ] Pudding; Nachtisch I

to **pull** [pʊl] ziehen I

purple [ˈpɜːpl] violett; lila I

to **push** [pʊʃ] stoßen; schieben; schubsen II U2, 41

*to **put** [pʊt] setzen; stellen; legen I

Put in … [pʊt ˈɪn] Setze/Setzt ein … I

Put it in … [ˌpʊt ɪt ˈɪn] Lege/Legt es in …; Stelle/Stellt es in … I

*to **put** through [pʊt ˈθruː] verbinden I

*to **put** up [pʊt ˈʌp] aufstellen; aufhängen; errichten II U2, 33

Put … face down. [pʊt ˌfeɪs ˈdaʊn] Lege/Legt … umgedreht hin. I

puzzle [ˈpʌzl] Rätsel; Puzzle I

pyjamas [pɪˈdʒɑːməz] Schlafanzug; Pyjama II U1, 12

Q

quality [ˈkwɒləti] Qualität I

quarter past/to [ˈkwɔːtə pɑːst/tə] Viertel nach/vor I

queen [kwiːn] Königin II U2, 30

question [ˈkwestʃən] Frage I

question tag [ˈkwestʃən ˌtæg] Frageanhängsel; Bestätigungsfrage °II U5, 94

queue [kjuː] Schlange; Warteschlange I

to jump the **queue** [ˌdʒʌmp ðə ˈkjuː] sich vordrängeln I

quick [kwɪk] schnell I

quickly [ˈkwɪkli] schnell II **U2**, 40

quiet [kwaɪət] still; ruhig; leise I

quiz [kwɪz] Quiz; Rätsel I

quote [kwəʊt] Zitat °II **U2**, 28

R

rabbit [ˈræbɪt] Kaninchen I

race [reɪs] Wettlauf; Rennen II **U4**, 68

camel **racing** [ˈkæml ˌreɪsɪŋ] Kamelrennen II **U4**, 68

racquet [ˈrækɪt] Schläger II **U4**, 68

radio [ˈreɪdiəʊ] Radio II **U4**, 68

raffle [ˈræfl] Tombola I

to **rain** [reɪn] regnen II **U5**, 102

to **raise** money [reɪz ˈmʌni] Geld sammeln II **U1**, 10

rap [ræp] Rap I

to **rap** [ræp] rappen I

rat [ræt] Ratte I

raven [ˈreɪvn] Rabe II **U3**, 56
  raven master [ˈreɪvn ˌmɑːstə] Herr der Raben II **U3**, 56

RE (= Religious Education) [ɑːˈriː; rɪˌlɪdʒəs ˌedʒʊˈkeɪʃn] Religion (Schulfach) II **U2**, 32

to **reach** [riːtʃ] erreichen; dran kommen II **U5**, 95

reaction [riˈækʃn] Reaktion II **U2**, 29

*to **read** [riːd] lesen I

reader [ˈriːdə] Leser/-in I

reading [ˈriːdɪŋ] Lesen I

ready [ˈredi] fertig; bereit II **U2**, 41
  ready meal [ˌredi ˈmiːl] Fertiggericht I

real [rɪəl] echt; richtig; wirklich II **U1**, 10

realistic [ˌrɪəˈlɪstɪk] realistisch II **U3**, 61

really [ˈrɪəli] wirklich I

reason [ˈriːzn] Grund II **U4**, 82

to **receive** [rɪˈsiːv] empfangen; erhalten; bekommen II **U4**, 77

to **record** [rɪˈkɔːd] aufnehmen; aufzeichnen II **U4**, 78

recording [rɪˈkɔːdɪŋ] Aufnahme; Aufzeichnung I
  recording studio [rɪˈkɔːdɪŋ ˌstjuːdiəʊ] Aufnahmestudio; Tonstudio I

recycling [ˌriːˈsaɪklɪŋ] Recycling; Wiederaufbereitung II **U2**, 40

red [red] rot I

to **reef** the sails [ˌriːf ðə ˈseɪlz] die Segel einholen I

region [ˈriːdʒn] Region; Gegend II **AC2**, 89

registration [ˌredʒɪsˈtreɪʃn] Anwesenheitskontrolle II **U2**, 32

regular [ˈregjələ] regelmäßig; gleichmäßig I

relationship [rɪˈleɪʃnʃɪp] Beziehung II **U4**, 82

defining **relative** clause [dɪˌfaɪnɪŋ ˈrelətɪv ˌklɔːz] notwendiger Relativsatz °II **U2**, 30
  relative pronoun [ˌrelətɪv ˈprəʊnaʊn] Relativpronomen °II **U2**, 31

to **relax** [rɪˈlæks] sich entspannen; sich ausruhen; sich beruhigen II **U2**, 36

religious [rɪˈlɪdʒəs] religiös; gläubig I

to **remember** [rɪˈmembə] sich erinnern (an); sich merken; denken an I
  Remember? [rɪˈmembə] Erinnerst du dich?; Erinnert ihr euch? I

to **repeat** [rɪˈpiːt] wiederholen °II **U5**, 94

reply [rɪˈplaɪ] Antwort; Erwiderung; Entgegnung I

to **reply** [rɪˈplaɪ] antworten; erwidern; entgegnen I

report [rɪˈpɔːt] Bericht; Meldung II **U1**, 9
  travel **report** [ˌtrævl rɪˈpɔːt] Reisebericht II **U1**, 20

reporter [rɪˈpɔːtə] Reporter/-in II **U4**, 75

rescue [ˈreskjuː] Rettung II **U4**, 77

the **rest** [rest] der Rest I

restaurant [ˈrestrɒnt] Restaurant; Gaststätte I

result [rɪˈzʌlt] Ergebnis; Resultat II **U5**, 97

*to **retell** [riːˈtel] nacherzählen; nochmals erzählen I

return ticket [rɪˈtɜːn ˌtɪkɪt] Hin- und Rückfahrkarte II **U6**, 112

to **return** [rɪˈtɜːn] zurückkehren; zurückfahren II **U6**, 112

revision [rɪˈvɪʒn] Wiederholung °II **U1**, 15

rhyme [raɪm] Reim I

rhythm [ˈrɪðm] Rhythmus I

the **rich** [ðə rɪtʃ] die Reichen II **AC3**, 131

rigging [ˈrɪgɪŋ] Takelage I

right [raɪt] richtig; korrekt; rechts; rechte/-r/-s I
  *to be **right** [bi ˈraɪt] recht haben I
  *to get **right** [get ˈraɪt] richtig beantworten °II **U6**, 121
  on the **right** [ɒn ðə ˈraɪt] auf der rechten Seite; rechts I
  right away [raɪt əˈweɪ] sofort; gleich I
  right here [ˌraɪt ˈhɪə] genau hier II **U4**, 70
  right now [raɪt ˈnaʊ] jetzt gleich; sofort; gerade II **U5**, 103

*to **ring** [rɪŋ] klingeln; läuten I

ice **rink** [ˈaɪs ˌrɪŋk] Eisbahn; Schlittschuhbahn I

river [ˈrɪvə] Fluss I
  by the **river** [baɪ ðə ˈrɪvə] am Fluss II **U2**, 31

road [rəʊd] Straße II **U1**, 18

robber [ˈrɒbə] Räuber/-in II **AC3**, 130

rock 'n' roll [ˌrɒk ən ˈrəʊl] Rock 'n' Roll II **AC2**, 89

rocky [ˈrɒki] felsig; steinig II **U6**, 109

role [rəʊl] Rolle I
  role play [ˈrəʊl ˌpleɪ] Rollenspiel I
  to swap **roles** [ˌswɒp ˈrəʊlz] Rollen tauschen I

rock 'n' **roll** [ˌrɒk ən ˈrəʊl] Rock 'n' Roll II **AC2**, 89

to **roll** off [rəʊl] hinunterrollen; herunterrollen II **U3**, 62

Roll two dice. [ˌrəʊl ˌtuː ˈdaɪs] Würfle/Würfelt mit zwei Würfeln. I

Roman [ˈrəʊmən] Römer/-in; römisch II **AC1**, 48

Romanian [rʊˈmeɪniən] Rumäne/Rumänin; rumänisch; Rumänisch II **AC2**, 88

roof [ruːf] Dach II **U6**, 122

room [ruːm; rʊm] Zimmer; Raum I
  chat **room** [ˈtʃæt rʊm] Chatroom II **AC2**, 88
  living **room** [ˈlɪvɪŋ rʊm] Wohnzimmer I

roommate [ˈruːmmeɪt] Zimmergenosse/ Zimmergenossin I

round [raʊnd] Runde II **U1**, 8
  round of boxing [ˌraʊnd əv ˈbɒksɪŋ] Boxrunde II **U1**, 8

the **Round** Table [ðə ˌraʊnd ˈteɪbl] die Tafelrunde II **AC3**, 131

to turn **round** [ˌtɜːn (ə)ˈraʊnd] (sich) umdrehen; wenden II **U2**, 41

round [raʊnd] um … herum II **U5**, 103

route [ruːt] Strecke; Route II **U1**, 16

royal [ˈrɔɪəl] königlich I

rubber [ˈrʌbə] Radiergummi I

rubbish [ˈrʌbɪʃ] Müll; Gerümpel I

rude [ruːd] unhöflich; unverschämt I

rugby [ˈrʌgbi] Rugby II **U4**, 68

to **ruin** [ˈruːɪn] ruinieren; zerstören II **U4**, 81

rule [ruːl] Regel I
  What's the **rule** for …? [wɒts ðə ˈruːl fə] Was ist die Regel für …? I

to **rule** [ruːl] herrschen; regieren II **U6**, 116

ruler [ˈruːlə] Lineal I

run [rʌn] Rennen; Lauf II **U4**, 70

*to **run** [rʌn] rennen; laufen I
  *to **run** away [ˌrʌn əˈweɪ] wegrennen I

runner [ˈrʌnə] Läufer/-in II **U4**, 68

running [ˈrʌnɪŋ] Laufen; Rennen II **U4**, 70

S

sad [sæd] traurig I

safe [seɪf] sicher; ungefährlich II **U3**, 56

to **reef** the **sails** [ˌriːf ðə ˈseɪlz] die Segel einholen I

sailboat [ˈseɪlbəʊt] Segelboot II **U6**, 124

sailor [ˈseɪlə] Seemann; Matrose I

salad [ˈsæləd] Salat I

sale [seɪl] Verkauf II **U1**, 12

the **same** [ðə ˈseɪm] der-/die-/dasselbe; der/die/das gleiche I
  the **same** way as [ðə seɪm ˈweɪ æz] genauso wie °II **U1**, 24

sandwich [ˈsænwɪdʒ] Sandwich; belegtes Brot I

sandy [ˈsændi] sandig; Sand- II **U6**, 109

Saturday [ˈsætədeɪ] Samstag I

to **save** [seɪv] retten; bergen I

sax [ˈsæks] Saxofon I

saxophone [ˈsæksəfəʊn] Saxofon I

*to **say** [seɪ] sagen; aufsagen; sprechen I
  *to **say** hello (to) [ˌseɪ helˈəʊ tə] grüßen; Grüße ausrichten (an) I

to **scan** [skæn] scannen; nach Details durchsuchen °II U3, 59

*to be **scared** (of) [bi: 'skeəd əv] Angst haben (vor) I
I'm (not) **scared** of … [aɪm (nɒt) 'skeəd əv] Ich habe (keine) Angst vor … I

scary ['skeəri] unheimlich; gruselig; beängstigend II U1, 24

scene [si:n] Szene I; Schauplatz II U4, 77
acting a **scene** [ˌæktɪŋ ə 'si:n] eine Theaterszene spielen I

school [sku:l] Schule I
grammar **school** ['græmə ˌsku:l] Gymnasium II U6, 113
primary **school** ['praɪmri ˌsku:l] Grundschule I

schoolbag ['sku:lbæg] Schultasche I

Science [saɪəns] Naturwissenschaften II U2, 32

science fiction [ˌsaɪəns 'fɪkʃn] Science-Fiction (Zukunftsdichtung) II U1, 22

score [skɔ:] Punktestand; Spielstand II U4, 68

Scottish ['skɒtɪʃ] schottisch II U6, 108

gorge **scrambling** ['gɔ:dʒ ˌskræmblɪŋ] Schluchtenklettern II U1, 16

to **scream** [skri:m] schreien; kreischen II U3, 63

sea [si:] Meer I

search [sɜ:tʃ] Suche; Such- II U1, 21

second ['seknd] zweite/-r/-s I

secret ['si:krət] Geheimnis II U1, 19
in **secret** [ɪn 'si:krət] heimlich II U4, 81

section ['sekʃn] Abschnitt; Paragraf °II U1, 22

*to **see** [si:] sehen I
See you! ['si: jə] Bis dann!; Bis … I
Wait and **see**! [weɪt ənd 'si:] Warte ab! I

self-critical ['self̩krɪtɪkl] selbstkritisch II U5, 92

self-evaluation [ˌselfɪˌvælju'eɪʃn] Selbsteinschatzung I

selfie ['selfi] Selfie II U4, 81

*to **sell** [sel] verkaufen I

seller ['selə] Verkäufer/-in (auf einem Flohmarkt) I

*to **send** [send] schicken; senden I
*to **send** off [send ˌɒf] abschicken II U6, 113

sentence ['sentəns] Satz I
conditional **sentence** [kənˌdɪʃnl 'sentəns] Bedingungssatz °II U6, 109

separate ['seprət] separat; getrennt; verschieden II U1, 16

September [sep'tembə] September I

serious ['sɪəriəs] ernsthaft; ernst I

set [set] Umgebung; Rahmen II AC3, 131

*to **set** up [set ˌʌp] einrichten; aufbauen I

setting ['setɪŋ] Schauplatz; Rahmen °II U3, 58

seven ['sevn] sieben I

---

several ['sevrl] einige; mehrere; verschiedene °II U2, 37

to **share** [ʃeə] teilen II U2, 40

she [ʃi:] sie I

sheep, **sheep** (pl) [ʃi:p] Schaf II U1, 18

*to **shine** [ʃaɪn] scheinen; glänzen II U2, 33

ship [ʃɪp] Schiff I

shock [ʃɒk] Schock II U4, 79

shoe [ʃu:] Schuh I

shop [ʃɒp] Geschäft; Laden I
charity **shop** ['tʃæriti ʃɒp] Second-Hand-Laden I

shopping ['ʃɒpɪŋ] Einkaufen; Einkäufe I
*to go **shopping** [gəʊ 'ʃɒpɪŋ] einkaufen gehen I

shore [ʃɔ:] Ufer; Küste II U3, 62

short [ʃɔ:t] kurz I
short answer [ˌʃɔ:t 'ɑ:nsə] Kurzantwort I
short form ['ʃɔ:t fɔ:m] Kurzform I

shorts (pl) [ʃɔ:ts] Shorts; kurze Hose II U4, 75

shot [ʃɒt] Einstellung; Kameraeinstellung °II U5, 98

should [ʃʊd] sollte; solltest; sollten; solltet II U4, 74
shouldn't ['ʃʊdnt] sollte(n) nicht II U4, 73

shoulder ['ʃəʊldə] Schulter II U4, 73

to **shout** [ʃaʊt] schreien; rufen I

show [ʃəʊ] Show; Schau; Aufführung II U4, 75
comedy **show** ['kɒmədi ˌʃəʊ] Comedy Show II U1, 10
living history **show** [ˌlɪvɪŋ 'hɪstəri ˌʃəʊ] Show, in der historischer Alltag nachgespielt wird II U6, 108
talent **show** ['tælənt ˌʃəʊ] Talentwettbewerb I
to **show** [ʃəʊ] zeigen I
to **show** off [ʃəʊ ˌɒf] angeben II U5, 103

shower ['ʃaʊə] Dusche I

to **shuffle** ['ʃʌfl] mischen °II U6, 109

shy [ʃaɪ] schüchtern II U1, 9

sick [sɪk] krank, unwohl II U4, 73
*to feel **sick** [ˌfi:l 'sɪk] Übelkeit verspüren; sich schlecht fühlen II U4, 73

side [saɪd] Seite II U2, 40

sight [saɪt] Sehenswürdigkeit; Anblick II AC1, 48

sightseeing ['saɪtsi:ɪŋ] Sightseeing-; Besichtigungs- II U3, 58

sign [saɪn] Zeichen; Schild II U1, 18

signal word ['sɪgnəl ˌwɜ:d] Signalwort I

silly ['sɪli] Dummkopf II U4, 80

silly ['sɪli] dumm; doof; albern I

silver ['sɪlvə] Silber II U3, 62

similar ['sɪmɪlə] ähnlich °II AC1, 49

simple past [ˌsɪmpl 'pɑ:st] Vergangenheitsform °II U1, 9
simple present [ˌsɪmpl 'preznt] Gegenwart; Präsens I

*to **sing** [sɪŋ] singen I
I like **singing** and dancing. [aɪ laɪk ˌsɪŋɪŋ ənd 'dɑ:nsɪŋ] Ich singe und tanze gern. I

---

singer ['sɪŋə] Sänger/-in II U1, 15

single ticket [ˌsɪŋl ˌtɪkɪt] einfache Fahrkarte II U6, 112

Dear **Sir** or Madam [dɪə ˌsɜ:r ɔ: 'mædəm] Sehr geehrte Dame, sehr geehrter Herr II U6, 113

sister ['sɪstə] Schwester I
half-**sister** ['hɑ:f̩sɪstə] Halbschwester I

*to **sit** [sɪt] sitzen I
Sit! [sɪt] Sitz! (Befehl für Hunde); Platz! (Befehl für Hunde) I
*to **sit** down [ˌsɪt 'daʊn] sich hinsetzen; sich setzen I
*to **sit** face to face [sɪt feɪs tə ˌfeɪs] sich gegenüber sitzen I

site [saɪt] Webseite II U5, 92

situation [ˌsɪtju'eɪʃn] Situation I

six [sɪks] sechs I
Four and **six** is ten. [ˌfɔ:r ənd ˌsɪks ɪz 'ten] Vier plus sechs ist zehn. I

size [saɪz] Größe; Kleidergröße I

to **skate** [skeɪt] Inlineskates fahren; Schlittschuh laufen I

skateboard ['skeɪtbɔ:d] Skateboard II U1, 11

skateboarding ['skeɪtbɔ:dɪŋ] Skateboardfahren I

skates (pl) [skeɪts] Inlineskates; Rollschuhe; Schlittschuhe I

(inline) **skating** ['ɪnlaɪn ˌskeɪtɪŋ] Inlineskatefahren I

skill [skɪl] Fertigkeit; Geschick I

to **skim** [skɪm] überfliegen °II U3, 59

skirt [skɜ:t] Rock II U6, 122

*to **sleep** [sli:p] schlafen I

sleepover ['sli:p̩əʊvə] Übernachtung I

to **slice** [slaɪs] in Scheiben schneiden I

slide [slaɪd] Rutschbahn I
water **slide** ['wɔ:tə ˌslaɪd] Wasserrutsche I

slogan ['sləʊgən] Slogan; Werbespruch II U2, 35

time **slot** ['taɪm slɒt] Zeitfenster °II U2, 38

slow [sləʊ] langsam I

small [smɔ:l] klein I

smartcard ['smɑ:tkɑ:d] Chipkarte II U3, 52

smartphone ['smɑ:tfəʊn] Smartphone II U4, 79

smile [smaɪl] Lächeln I

to **smile** [smaɪl] lächeln I

snack [snæk] Snack; Imbiss I
snack bar ['snæk ˌbɑ:] Café; Imbissstube I

word **snake** ['wɜ:d ˌsneɪk] Wortschlange I

to **sneak** around [ˌsni:k ə'raʊnd] herumschleichen II U1, 24

to **snore** [snɔ:] schnarchen I

so [səʊ] so; also I
so far [ˌsəʊ 'fɑ:] bis jetzt II U4, 75

social network [ˌsəʊʃl 'netwɜ:k] soziales Netzwerk II U5, 91

society [sə'saɪəti] Verein; Gesellschaft II U6, 123

sofa ['səʊfə] Sofa; Couch I

solution [sə'lu:ʃn] Lösung II U1, 13

to **solve** [sɒlv] lösen **II U6**, 122
some [sʌm; səm] einige; ein paar; etwas **I**
somebody ['sʌmbədi] jemand **I**
someone ['sʌmwʌn] jemand **II U1**, 13
something ['sʌmθɪŋ] etwas **I**
sometimes ['sʌmtaɪmz] manchmal **I**
somewhere ['sʌmweə] irgendwo **II U3**, 65
song [sɒŋ] Song; Lied **I**
soon [suːn] bald **II U1**, 18
 as **soon** as [əz 'suːn ˌəz] sobald **II U5**, 92
*to be **sorry** [biː 'sɒri] leid tun **I**
 Sorry! ['sɒri] Entschuldigung!; Tut mir
 leid! **I**
 I'm **sorry**! [ˌaɪm 'sɒri] Tut mir leid! **I**
sound [saʊnd] Ton; Geräusch; Klang **I**
to **sound** [saʊnd] klingen **I**
source [sɔːs] Quelle °**II U6**, 120
south [saʊθ] Süden; Süd- **II U3**, 53
 South Korean [ˌsaʊθ kə'riːən]
 Südkoreaner/-in; südkoreanisch; Südkoreanisch **II AC2**, 88
souvenir [ˌsuːvn'ɪə] Souvenir; Andenken
 II U3, 54
space [speɪs] Raum; Fläche; Platz; Ort
 II U2, 30
 *to leave **space** [liːv 'speɪs] Platz lassen **I**
spaceship ['speɪsʃɪp] Raumschiff **II U1**, 22
*to **speak** [spiːk] sprechen **I**
speaker ['spiːkə] Redner/-in; Sprecher/-in **I**
speaking ['spiːkɪŋ] Sprechen **I**
spear [spɪə] Speer **II U6**, 122
special ['speʃl] besonders; speziell **I**
 special offer [ˌspeʃl 'ɒfə] Sonderangebot **I**
 with **special** needs [wɪð speʃl 'niːdz]
 behindert **II U2**, 29
speech bubble ['spiːtʃ ˌbʌbl] Sprechblase **I**
*to **spell** [spel] buchstabieren **I**
spelling ['spelɪŋ] Rechtschreibung **I**
*to **spend** [spend] ausgeben (Geld) **I**; verbringen (Zeit) **II U5**, 92
spoken ['spəʊkn] gesprochen °**II U4**, 82
sponge [spʌndʒ] Rühr-; Biskuit- **I**
spontaneous [spɒn'teɪniəs] spontan
 °**II U6**, 111
sport [spɔːt] Sport; Sportart **I**
 … is a great **sport**. [ɪz ˌə 'greɪt ˌspɔːt] … ist
 ein toller Sport. **I**
squirrel ['skwɪrəl] Eichhörnchen **I**
stadium ['steɪdiəm] Stadion **II U4**, 68
*to **stand** [stænd] stehen **I**
 *to **stand** up [ˌstænd ˈʌp] aufstehen (von
 einer Sitzgelegenheit) **I**
star [stɑː] Star; Stern **I**
to **stare** [steə] starren; anstarren **I**
to **start** [stɑːt] anfangen; beginnen;
 starten **I**
 *to get **started** [get 'stɑːtɪd] anfangen
 II U2, 33
 starting place ['stɑːtɪŋ pleɪs] Startpunkt
 II U6, 112
head of **state** [ˌhed əv 'steɪt] Staatsober-
 haupt **II AC2**, 89

statement ['steɪtmənt] Aussage; Behauptung; Erklärung **II AC2**, 88
station ['steɪʃn] Haltestelle; Bahnhof; Station **I**; Sender **II U4**, 77
 bus **station** ['bʌs ˌsteɪʃn] Busbahnhof **I**
to **stay** [steɪ] bleiben **I**; übernachten
 II U6, 110
 to **stay** away from [ˌsteɪ ə'weɪ frəm] fernbleiben von; meiden **II U5**, 97
 to **stay** in touch (with) [ˌsteɪ ɪn 'tʌtʃ (wɪð)]
 in Kontakt bleiben (mit) **II U5**, 90
 to **stay** with ['steɪ wɪð] wohnen bei
 II U3, 52
steak [steɪk] Steak **I**
*to **steal** [stiːl] stehlen **II U2**, 34
step [step] Stufe; Schritt **I**
 step-by-**step** [ˌstepbaɪ'step] Schritt-für-
 Schritt- **II U5**, 95
stepmum ['stepmʌm] Stiefmutter **I**
still [stɪl] Standbild °**II U2**, 36
still [stɪl] still **I**
still [stɪl] noch; immer noch **I**; dennoch
 II U5, 95
stomach ['stʌmək] Magen; Bauch **II U4**, 80
stomachache ['stʌməkeɪk] Bauchschmerzen; Bauchweh **II U4**, 73
stop [stɒp] Haltestelle; Halt **II U3**, 53
to **stop** [stɒp] aufhören (mit); anhalten;
 stoppen **I**
 Stop and think [ˌstɒp ˌənd 'θɪŋk] Warte/
 Wartet und denk/denkt nach. **I**
 Stop it! ['stɒp ˌɪt] Mach/Macht das aus!;
 Hör/Hört auf! **I**
storm [stɔːm] Sturm **I**
story, **stories** (pl) ['stɔːri; 'stɔːriz] Story;
 Geschichte; Erzählung **I**
 photo **story** ['fəʊtəʊ ˌstɔːri] Fotostory;
 Bildgeschichte **I**
straight on [streɪt ˈɒn] geradeaus **I**
strange [streɪndʒ] fremd; seltsam; merkwürdig **I**
street [striːt] Straße (in der Stadt) **I**
 in the **street** [ˌɪn ðə 'striːt] in der Straße;
 auf der Straße **I**
strong [strɒŋ] stark **II U2**, 42
student ['stjuːdnt] Schüler/-in; Student/-in **I**
studies (pl) ['stʌdiz] Studium; Lernen;
 Arbeit für die Schule **II U2**, 28
recording **studio** [rɪ'kɔːdɪŋ ˌstjuːdiəʊ] Aufnahmestudio; Tonstudio **I**
stuff [stʌf] Zeug **I**
stupid ['stjuːpɪd] dumm; blöd **II U4**, 81
subject ['sʌbdʒɪkt] Schulfach **II U2**, 28; Subjekt; Satzgegenstand °**II U2**, 31
substitute ['sʌbstɪtjuːt] Ersatz; Ersatz-
 °**II U5**, 91
such [sʌtʃ] solch; solche/-r/-s **II U2**, 36
suddenly ['sʌdnli] plötzlich; auf einmal **I**
suggestion [sə'dʒestʃn] Vorschlag; Anregung **I**
to **sum** up [ˌsʌm ˈʌp] zusammenfassen
 °**II U2**, 42

summer ['sʌmə] Sommer **II AC2**, 88
 summer camp [ˌsʌmə kæmp] Sommerferienlager **II AC2**, 88
sun [sʌn] Sonne **II U2**, 33
Sunday ['sʌndeɪ] Sonntag **I**
superlative [suː'pɜːlətɪv] Superlativ °**II U1**, 16
supermarket ['suːpəˌmɑːkɪt] Supermarkt **I**
superpower ['suːpəˌpaʊə] Supermacht
 II AC2, 89
to **supply** [sə'plaɪ] versorgen **II U6**, 116
sure [ʃʊə; ʃɔː] sicher **I**
 *to make **sure** [ˌmeɪk 'ʃɔː] sich versichern **I**
surfing ['sɜːfɪŋ] Surfen **II U6**, 109
surgery ['sɜːdʒəri] Arztpraxis; Praxis;
 Praxisräume **I**
surprise [sə'praɪz] Überraschung **I**
to **surprise** [sə'praɪz] überraschen **II U4**, 81
*to be **surprised** [bi sə'praɪzd] überrascht
 sein **II U3**, 63
surprising [sə'praɪzɪŋ] überraschend
 II U1, 24
survey ['sɜːveɪ] Umfrage; Studie **I**
suspense [sə'spens] Spannung °**II U6**, 119
to **swap** roles [ˌswɒp 'rəʊlz] Rollen
 tauschen **I**
sweet [swiːt] süß **I**
sweets (pl) [swiːts] Süßigkeiten; Bonbons **I**
*to **swim** [swɪm] schwimmen **I**
swimming ['swɪmɪŋ] Schwimmen **I**
 *to go **swimming** [ˌgəʊ 'swɪmɪŋ] Schwimmen gehen **I**
symbol ['sɪmbl] Symbol °**II U3**, 58

T

table ['teɪbl] Tisch **I**
 the Round **Table** [ðə ˌraʊnd 'teɪbl] die
 Tafelrunde **II AC3**, 131
tablet ['tæblət] Tablet **II U5**, 95
taekwondo [ˌtækwʌn'duː] Taekwondo
 II U2, 38
question **tag** ['kwestʃən ˌtæg] Frageanhängsel; Bestätigungsfrage °**II U5**, 94
tail [teɪl] Schwanz; Schweif **I**
*to **take** [teɪk] nehmen; mitnehmen; wegnehmen; bringen; mitbringen **I**; dauern;
 (Zeit) brauchen **II U5**, 95
*to **take** a look at [ˌteɪk ə 'lʊk æt] einen Blick
 werfen auf **II U2**, 37
 *to **take** a message [ˌteɪk ə 'mesɪdʒ] eine
 Nachricht entgegennehmen; jmdm. etw.
 ausrichten **I**
 *to **take** a test [ˌteɪk ə 'test] einen Test
 machen °**II U5**, 97
 *to **take** a vote [ˌteɪk ə 'vəʊt] abstimmen **I**
 *to **take** notes [ˌteɪk 'nəʊts] sich Notizen
 machen **I**
 *to **take** off [ˌteɪk 'ɒf] abnehmen; herunternehmen; ausziehen **I**
 *to **take** part (in) [teɪk 'pɑːt (ɪn)] teilnehmen (an) **II U5**, 90

*to **take** photos [ˌteɪk 'fəʊtəʊz] fotografieren; Fotos machen I

*to **take** place [teɪk 'pleɪs] stattfinden I

Take turns. [ˌteɪk 'tɜːnz] Wechselt euch ab. I

Take a deep breath. [teɪk ə ˌdiːp 'breθ] Atme(t) tief ein. II U2, 36

talent show ['tælənt ˌʃəʊ] Talentwettbewerb I

to **talk** [tɔːk] sprechen; reden I

to **talk** about ['tɔːk əˌbaʊt] sprechen über; erzählen von I

to **talk** to ['tɔːk tə] reden mit I

talking ['tɔːkɪŋ] Sprechen I

tall [tɔːl] groß; hoch II U1, 17

to **tap** [tæp] antippen II U5, 102

task [tɑːsk] Aufgabe; Auftrag I

taxi ['tæksi] Taxi II U1, 13

tea [tiː] Tee I

*to **teach** [tiːtʃ] unterrichten; lehren; beibringen II U4, 76

*to **teach** somebody a lesson [ˌtiːtʃ ə 'lesn] jmdm. eine Lehre/Lektion erteilen II U4, 76

teacher ['tiːtʃə] Lehrer/-in I

team [tiːm] Team; Gruppe II U1, 8

Technology [tek'nɒlədʒi] Technik; Computerunterricht II U2, 32

technology [tek'nɒlədʒi] Technologie II AC2, 89

teen [tiːn] Jugend- II U5, 92

teenager ['tiːnˌeɪdʒə] Teenager; Jugendliche/-r I

telephone ['telɪfəʊn] Telefon I

*to **tell** [tel] erzählen; sagen; mitteilen I

Tell me about … ['tel miː əˌbaʊt] Erzähle mir von … I

ten [ten] zehn I

ten times [ten 'taɪmz] zehnmal I

Four and six is **ten.** [ˌfɔːr ənd ˌsɪks ɪz 'ten] Vier plus sechs ist zehn. I

tennis ['tenɪs] Tennis I

tense [tens] Zeit; Zeitform (grammatisch) °II U4, 71

test [test] Test; Klassenarbeit; Prüfung I

*to take a **test** [ˌteɪk ə 'test] einen Test machen °II U5, 97

to **test** [test] testen; prüfen °II U6, 121

text [tekst] Text I

text (message) ['tekst ˌmesɪdʒ] SMS; Kurznachricht I

to **text** [tekst] eine SMS schicken II U5, 90

than [ðæn] als (bei Vergleichen) II U1, 16

more … **than** ['mɔː ðən] mehr … als I

to **thank** [θæŋk] danken II U2, 36

Thank you. ['θæŋk ju] Danke. I

thankful ['θæŋkfl] dankbar I

Thanks. [θæŋks] Danke. I

that [ðæt; ðət] dass I

that [ðæt] das; jenes I

after **that** [ˌɑːftə 'ðæt] danach I

like **that** [laɪk 'ðæt] so I

That was close! [ˌðæt wəz 'kləʊs] Das war knapp! I

that's how [ðæts 'haʊ] so II U1, 10

That's what friends are for. [ˌðæts wɒt 'frendz ˌɑː ˌfɔː] Dafür sind Freunde da. I

that's why [ðæts 'waɪ] deshalb II U2, 30

That's … [ðæts] Das macht … I

that [ðæt] der; dem; den; die; das (Relativpronomen) II U1, 9

the [ðə; ðɪ] der; die (auch Pl.); das I

the others [ðɪ 'ʌðəz] die anderen I

the same [ðə 'seɪm] der-/die-/dasselbe; der/die/das gleiche I

the … the [ðə … ðə] je … desto II U4, 68

theatre ['θɪətə] Theater I

their [ðeə] ihr/-e (Pl.) I

them [ðem] sie (Pl.); ihnen I

theme [θiːm] Thema; Motto I

then [ðen] dann; danach I

there [ðeə] da; dort; dahin; dorthin I

there is/are [ðər 'ɪz/'ɑː] da ist/sind; es gibt I

these [ðiːz] diese (hier) I

they [ðeɪ] sie (Pl.) I

It's …/**They**'re … [ɪts/ðeə] Es kostet …/ Sie kosten … I

thing [θɪŋ] Ding; Sache I

*to **think** [θɪŋk] denken; nachdenken; glauben I

Stop and **think** [ˌstɒp ənd 'θɪŋk] Warte/ Wartet und denk/denkt nach. I

*to **think** of ['θɪŋk əv] halten von; denken über I; ausdenken; sich etwas einfallen lassen II U1, 12

Think of … ['θɪŋk əv] Denke/Denkt an … I

third [θɜːd] dritte/-r/-s I

thirteen [ˌθɜː'tiːn] dreizehn I

this [ðɪs] dies; diese/-r/-s I

this afternoon [ðɪs ˌɑːftənuːn] heute Nachmittag II U3, 52

This is … [ˌðɪs ˌɪz] Das (hier) ist … I

those [ðəʊz] diese dort; jene I

thought [θɔːt] Gedanke °II U4, 82

thousands of ['θaʊzndz əv] tausende (von) I

three [θriː] drei I

through [θruː] durch I

*to **throw** (at) [θrəʊ] werfen (nach) I

*to **throw** away [ˌθrəʊ əˈweɪ] wegwerfen I

throw the dice twice [ˌθrəʊ ðə daɪs 'twaɪs] würfle zweimal °II U2, 34

thumb [θʌm] Daumen II U2, 34

thunder (no pl) ['θʌndə] Donner II U5, 102

Thursday ['θɜːzdeɪ] Donnerstag I

to **tick** [tɪk] abhaken °II U3, 60

ticket ['tɪkɪt] Los; Ticket; Eintrittskarte I; Fahrschein II U6, 111

one-way ticket ['wʌnweɪ ˌtɪkɪt] einfache Fahrkarte II U6, 112

return ticket [rɪ'tɜːn ˌtɪkɪt] Hin- und Rückfahrkarte II U6, 112

single ticket [ˌsɪŋgl ˌtɪkɪt] einfache Fahrkarte II U6, 112

high tide ['haɪ ˌtaɪd] Flut II U3, 62

low tide ['ləʊ ˌtaɪd] Ebbe II U3, 62

to **tidy** (a room) ['taɪdi] aufräumen; in Ordnung bringen I

till [tɪl] bis I

time [taɪm] Zeit I; Mal II U1, 10

all the time [ˌɔːl ðə 'taɪm] die ganze Zeit II U3, 62

at the same time [ət ðə ˌseɪm 'taɪm] zur selben Zeit; gleichzeitig I

free time [ˌfriː 'taɪm] Freizeit I

on time [ɒn 'taɪm] pünktlich II U2, 37

ten times [ten 'taɪmz] zehnmal I

time line ['taɪm ˌlaɪn] Zeitstrahl I

time slot ['taɪm slɒt] Zeitfenster °II U2, 38

I can't wait till next time. [aɪ kɑːnt ˌweɪt tɪl nekst 'taɪm] Ich kann es bis zum nächsten Mal kaum erwarten. II U1, 10

Time to get up! [ˌtaɪm tə ˌget 'ʌp] Es ist Zeit aufzustehen! I

What time? [wɒt 'taɪm] Um wie viel Uhr? I

What's the time? [ˌwɒts ðə 'taɪm] Wie spät ist es?; Wie viel Uhr ist es? I

timetable ['taɪmˌteɪbl] Stundenplan; Fahrplan I

tin [tɪn] Zinn II U6, 122

tinned [tɪnd] Dosen-; aus der Dose I

tip [tɪp] Tipp; Ratschlag I

to **tiptoe** ['tɪptəʊ] auf Zehenspitzen gehen II U1, 19

tired ['taɪəd] müde I

title ['taɪtl] Titel; Überschrift °II U5, 104

to [tʊ; tə] zu; nach; auf; in; vor (bei Uhrzeitangaben) I

from … **to** [frəm … tə] von … bis I

quarter past/to ['kwɔːtə pɑːst/tə] Viertel nach/vor I

toast [təʊst] Toast I

today [tə'deɪ] heute I

together [tə'geðə] zusammen; miteinander; gemeinsam I

toilet ['tɔɪlət] Toilette I

tomato, tomatoes (pl) [tə'mɑːtəʊ; tə'mɑːtəʊz] Tomate I

tomorrow [tə'mɒrəʊ] morgen I

too [tuː] auch; zu I

Too bad! [ˌtuː 'bæd] Zu dumm!; Schade! I

You too? [ju 'tuː] Du auch? I

tool [tuːl] Werkzeug; Gerät II U6, 123

top [tɒp] Spitze; oberer Teil; oberes Ende I

on top [ɒn 'tɒp] oben; obendrauf I

to **top up** [tɒp'ʌp] aufladen II U3, 52

topic ['tɒpɪk] Thema II U2, 37

torch [tɔːtʃ] Fackel; Taschenlampe II U1, 18

to stay in touch (with) [ˌsteɪ ɪn 'tʌtʃ (wɪð)] in Kontakt bleiben (mit) II U5, 90

tour [tʊə] Tour; Fahrt; Rundgang II U3, 56

audio tour ['ɔːdiəʊ ˌtʊə] Audioführung II U3, 56

tourism ['tʊərɪzm] Tourismus II U6, 114

tourist ['tʊərɪst] Tourist/-in I
  tourist board ['tʊərɪst bɔːd] Touristeninformation II U6, 113
  tourist information centre [ˌtʊərɪst ɪnfəˈmeɪʃn ˌsentə] Touristeninformation I
towards [təˈwɔːdz] in Richtung; auf … zu; darauf zu II U3, 62
town [taʊn] Stadt I
toy [tɔɪ] Spielzeug I
to **trace** [treɪs] verfolgen; nachspüren I
to **trade** [treɪd] austauschen °II U4, 79
tradition [trəˈdɪʃn] Tradition I
walking **trail** ['wɔːkɪŋ treɪl] Wanderweg II U6, 114
train [treɪn] Zug I
to **train** [treɪn] trainieren II U4, 72
training ['treɪnɪŋ] Training II U4, 80
to **translate** [trænzˈleɪt] übersetzen I
  Don't **translate** … [ˌdəʊnt trænzˈleɪt] Übersetze/Übersetzt nicht … I
translation [trænzˈleɪʃn] Übersetzung I
transport ['trænspɔːt] Verkehrsmittel; Transport II U6, 110
  public **transport** (no pl) [ˌpʌblɪk 'trænspɔːt] öffentliche Verkehrsmittel II U3, 52
travel ['trævl] (das) Reisen; Reise II U1, 20
  travel agent's ['trævl ˌeɪdʒnts] Reisebüro II U6, 111
  travel report [ˌtrævl rɪˈpɔːt] Reisebericht II U1, 20
to **travel** ['trævl] fahren; reisen II U3, 52
treasure ['treʒə] Schatz II U3, 56
tree [triː] Baum I
  family **tree** ['fæməli ˌtriː] Stammbaum I
  palm **tree** ['pɑːm ˌtriː] Palme II U6, 109
pony **trekking** ['pəʊni ˌtrekɪŋ] Ponyreiten im Gelände II U6, 109
trial ['traɪəl] Qualifikation II U4, 70
trick [trɪk] Trick; Streich I
  to play a **trick** (on) [ˌpleɪ ə 'trɪk ɒn] einen Streich spielen I
trifle ['traɪfl] Trifle (englischer Nachtisch) I
trip [trɪp] Trip; Reise; Ausflug; Fahrt II U1, 9
trouble ['trʌbl] Ärger; Probleme; Schwierigkeiten II U1, 19
  *to make **trouble** [ˌmeɪk 'trʌbl] Ärger machen; in Schwierigkeiten bringen I
trousers (pl) ['traʊzəz] Hose II U6, 122
trowel ['traʊəl] kleiner Spaten II U3, 62
true [truː] wahr °II U2, 34
to **try** [traɪ] versuchen; probieren I
  to **try** on [traɪ ˈɒn] anprobieren II U2, 31
  Try … [traɪ] Versuch es mal mit …; Probier mal … I
T-shirt ['tiːʃɜːt] T-Shirt I
the **Tube** [ðə 'tjuːb] die Londoner U-Bahn II AC1, 48
Tuesday ['tjuːzdeɪ] Dienstag I
tunnel ['tʌnl] Tunnel I
It's your **turn**. [ˌɪts 'jɔː tɜːn] Du bist dran. I

Take **turns**. [ˌteɪk 'tɜːnz] Wechselt euch ab. I
Your **turn**. ['jɔː tɜːn] Du bist dran. I
to **turn** [tɜːn] einbiegen; abbiegen I
  to **turn** (a)round [tɜːn ˌ(ə)ˈraʊnd] (sich) umdrehen; wenden II U2, 41
  to **turn** back [tɜːn ˈbæk] umkehren; zurückgehen II U2, 41
  to **turn** off [tɜːn ˈɒf] abschalten; ausschalten II U1, 12
  to **turn** to ['tɜːn tə] sich wenden an; sich zuwenden II U6, 123
tutor ['tjuːtə] Klassenlehrer/-in I
  tutor group ['tjuːtə ˌgruːp] Klasse (in einer englischen Schule) I
TV [ˌtiːˈviː] Fernsehen; Fernseher I
  to watch **TV** [ˌwɒtʃ tiːˈviː] fernsehen I
twelve [twelv] zwölf I
twin [twɪn] Zwilling; Zwillings- II U6, 123
to **twist** your ankle [ˌtwɪst jɔːr ˈæŋkl] sich den Knöchel verrenken II U4, 72
two [tuː] zwei I
  the **two** of them [ðə 'tuː əv ðəm] beide II U5, 92
  two of which ['tuː əv wɪtʃ] zwei von ihnen °II U6, 120
typical ['tɪpɪkl] typisch I

U

u (= you) [juː; jə] du; Sie; ihr I
UFO [ˌjuːefˈəʊ] UFO II U4, 78
uncle ['ʌŋkl] Onkel I
under ['ʌndə] unter I
underground ['ʌndəgraʊnd] U-Bahn II AC1, 48
*to **understand** [ˌʌndəˈstænd] verstehen I
understanding [ˌʌndəˈstændɪŋ] Verständnis II U5, 93
unfair [ʌnˈfeə] unfair II U4, 72
unfriendly [ʌnˈfrendli] unfreundlich II U1, 24
uniform ['juːnɪfɔːm] Uniform I
unit ['juːnɪt] Lektion; Kapitel; Einheit I
*to be **unlucky** [biː ʌnˈlʌki] Pech haben I
until [ʌnˈtɪl] bis; erst wenn II U4, 70
to **unwrap** [ʌnˈræp] auswickeln; auspacken I
up [ʌp] hinauf; nach oben II U5, 94
  to end **up** [ˌend ˈʌp] enden; landen II U1, 8
  *to get **up** [ˌget ˈʌp] aufstehen (aus dem Bett) I
  to look **up** [ˌlʊk ˈʌp] nachschlagen; nachschauen I
upset [ʌpˈset] aufgebracht; bestürzt II U2, 30
upstairs [ʌpˈsteəz] nach oben; im Obergeschoss; oben II U5, 102
us [ʌs] uns I
to **use** [juːz] benutzen; verwenden; gebrauchen I
useful ['juːsfl] nützlich; hilfreich I

Useful phrases [ˌjuːsfl 'freɪsɪz] nützliche Ausdrücke I
usually ['juːʒli] normalerweise; gewöhnlich; meistens I

V

verb [vɜːb] Verb I
very ['veri] sehr I
  very much [ˌveri 'mʌtʃ] sehr I
vet [vet] Tierarzt/Tierärztin I
video ['vɪdiəʊ] Video II U5, 91
  video chat ['vɪdiəʊ ˌtʃæt] Videochat II U3, 50
view [vjuː] Aussicht; Sicht; Ausblick; Blick II U2, 30
  point of **view** [ˌpɔɪnt əv 'vjuː] Standpunkt; Ansicht; Perspektive II U4, 76
viewer ['vjuːə] Zuschauer/-in °II U3, 58
viewing ['vjuːɪŋ] Hör-/Sehverstehen I
village ['vɪlɪdʒ] Dorf I
villain ['vɪlən] Bösewicht II AC3, 130
visit ['vɪzɪt] Besuch I
to **visit** ['vɪzɪt] besichtigen; besuchen I
visitor ['vɪzɪtə] Besucher/-in I
vocabulary [vəˈkæbjəlri] Vokabular; Wortschatz I
voice [vɔɪs] Stimme I
volleyball ['vɒlibɔːl] Volleyball I
*to take a **vote** [ˌteɪk ə 'vəʊt] abstimmen I
to **vote** [vəʊt] abstimmen; wählen I

W

to **wait** (for) [weɪt] warten (auf) I
  I can't **wait** till next time. [aɪ kɑːnt ˌweɪt tɪl nekst 'taɪm] Ich kann es bis zum nächsten Mal kaum erwarten. II U1, 10
  Wait and see! [ˌweɪt ənd 'siː] Warte ab! I
*to go for a **walk** [ˌgəʊ fər ə 'wɔːk] spazieren gehen II U1, 18
  gallery **walk** ['gælri ˌwɔːk] Museumsrundgang; Vernissage I
  night **walk** ['naɪt wɔːk] Nachtwanderung II U1, 18
to **walk** [wɔːk] gehen; laufen I
  to **walk** the dog [ˌwɔːk ðə 'dɒg] den Hund ausführen; mit dem Hund spazieren gehen I
walking ['wɔːkɪŋ] Wandern II U1, 16
  walking trail ['wɔːkɪŋ treɪl] Wanderweg II U6, 114
wall [wɔːl] Wand; Mauer I
to **want** (to) ['wɒnt tə] wollen; mögen I
wardrobe ['wɔːdrəʊb] Kleiderschrank I
to **warm** up [ˌwɔːm ˈʌp] aufwärmen; sich aufwärmen I
warm-up [ˌwɔːmˈʌp] Aufwärmübung I
warrior ['wɒriə] Krieger II U6, 123
to **wash** [wɒʃ] waschen; sich waschen I
  to **wash** up [ˌwɒʃ ˈʌp] angespült werden II U3, 62

washing machine [ˈwɒʃɪŋ məˌʃiːn] Waschmaschine II **U5**, 95

to **waste** [weɪst] verschwenden II **U5**, 95

to **watch** [wɒtʃ] beobachten; (sich) ansehen; zuschauen I

to **watch** TV [ˌwɒtʃ tiːˈviː] fernsehen I

water [ˈwɔːtə] Wasser I

water slide [ˈwɔːtə ˌslaɪd] Wasserrutsche I

wave [weɪv] Welle I

wax [wæks] Wachs II **U3**, 51

wax figure [ˈwæks ˌfɪɡə] Wachsfigur II **U3**, 51

way [weɪ] Weg; Art und Weise I

*to be in the **way** [biːˌɪn ðə ˈweɪ] im Weg sein/stehen I

*to get in the **way** [getˌɪn ðə ˈweɪ] stören; im Weg stehen II **U4**, 80

in other **ways** [ɪnˌʌðə weɪz] auf andere Weise II **U5**, 97

the same **way** as [ˌðə seɪm ˈweɪ æz] genauso wie °II **U1**, 24

we [wiː; wi] wir I

We're from … [ˈwɪə frəm] Wir sind aus … I

*to **wear** [weə] anhaben; tragen (Kleidung) I

weather [ˈweðə] Wetter I

weather forecast [ˈweðə ˌfɔːkɑːst] Wettervorhersage II **U6**, 112

website [ˈwebsaɪt] Website; Internetauftritt I

wedding [ˈwedɪŋ] Hochzeit I

Wednesday [ˈwenzdeɪ] Mittwoch I

week [wiːk] Woche I

weekday [ˈwiːkdeɪ] Wochentag II **U5**, 100

weekend [ˌwiːkˈend] Wochenende I

at the **weekend** [ət ðə ˌwiːkˈend] am Wochenende I

weird [wɪəd] merkwürdig; seltsam; sonderbar II **U5**, 99

Welcome! [ˈwelkəm] Willkommen! II **U1**, 18

to **welcome** [ˈwelkəm] willkommen heißen II **U2**, 35

You're **welcome**. [jɔː ˈwelkəm] Bitte schön.; Nichts zu danken.; Gern geschehen. I

well [wel] tja; nun I

Welsh [welʃ] walisisch; Walisisch; Waliser/-in II **U1**, 16

west [west] Westen; West- I

in the far **west** [ɪn ðə fɑːˈwest] im äußersten Westen II **U6**, 114

wet [wet] nass II **U3**, 62

what [wɒt] was; welche/-r/-s; was für ein I

What about … ? [ˈwɒt əˌbaʊt] Wie wär's mit …?; Was ist mit …? I

What are …? [ˈwɒt ˌɑː] Welche … sind es? I

What colour is …? [ˌwɒt ˈkʌlər ɪz] Welche Farbe hat …? I

what else [ˌwɒt ˈels] was sonst; was noch I

What is missing? [ˌwɒt ɪz ˈmɪsɪŋ] Was fehlt? I

What is … about? [ˌwɒt ɪz …əˈbaʊt] Worum geht es in/im …? I

what it's like [ˌwɒt ɪts ˈlaɪk] wie das ist II **U4**, 74

What on earth …? [ˌwɒtː ɒn ˈɜːθ] Was um alles in der Welt …? II **U5**, 95

what the man looked like [ˌwɒt ðə mæn ˈlʊkt laɪk] wie der Mann aussah II **U1**, 13

What time? [wɒt ˈtaɪm] Um wie viel Uhr? I

what to … [ˈwɒt tə] was man … I

What's that? [wɒts ˈðæt] Was ist das? I

What's the matter? [ˌwɒts ðə ˈmætə] Was ist los?; Was hast du? II **U6**, 122

What's the rule for …? [ˌwɒts ðə ˈruːl fə] Was ist die Regel für …? I

What's your favourite …? [ˌwɒts jə ˌfeɪvrɪt] Was ist dein/-e Lieblings…? I

What's your name? [ˌwɒts jə ˈneɪm] Wie heißt du?; Wie heißen Sie? I

What's the time? [ˌwɒts ðə ˈtaɪm] Wie spät ist es?; Wie viel Uhr ist es? I

… **what** to do. [ˈwɒt tə duː] … was ich tun soll. II **U5**, 92

wheel [wiːl] Rad; Steuerrad; Steuer I

wheelchair [ˈwiːltʃeə] Rollstuhl II **U3**, 53

when [wen] wenn; wann; als I

whenever [wenˈevə] wann immer; jedes Mal, wenn; so oft II **U5**, 92

where [weə] wo; wohin I

Where … from? [ˌweə … ˈfrɒm] Woher …? I

… **where** to go. [ˌweə tə ˈɡəʊ] … wohin ich gehen kann. II **U3**, 54

which [wɪtʃ] welche/-r/-s I

which [wɪtʃ] der; die; das; dem; den (Relativpronomen) II **U2**, 30

a **while** [ə ˈwaɪl] eine Weile II **U3**, 54

while [waɪl] während I

to **whip** [wɪp] schlagen I

to **whisper** [ˈwɪspə] flüstern I

white [waɪt] weiß I

who [huː] wer; wem; wen I

Who … for? [ˌhuː ˈfɔː] Für wen …? I

Who is it? [ˌhuː ˈɪz ɪt] Wer ist es? I

Who's in? [ˌhuːz ˈɪn] Wer macht mit?; Wer ist dabei? II **U4**, 70

who [huː] der; den; die (Relativpronomen) II **U2**, 30

whole [həʊl] ganz I

whoosh [wʊʃ] wusch I

whose [huːz] dessen; deren (Relativpronomen) II **U2**, 30

why [waɪ] warum I

that's **why** [ðæts ˈwaɪ] deshalb II **U2**, 30

wide [waɪd] breit; weit; ausgedehnt II **U6**, 109

wife, **wives** (pl) [waɪf, waɪvz] Ehefrau II **U2**, 31

wild [waɪld] wild II **U6**, 114

wildlife [ˈwaɪldlaɪf] Tierwelt (in freier Wildbahn) II **U2**, 33

*to **win** [wɪn] gewinnen; siegen I

wind [wɪnd] Wind II **U6**, 122

window [ˈwɪndəʊ] Fenster I

windsurfing [ˈwɪndsɜːfɪŋ] Windsurfen II **U6**, 109

wine [waɪn] Wein I

winner [ˈwɪnə] Gewinner/-in; Sieger/-in I

wish [wɪʃ] Wunsch I

*to make a **wish** [ˌmeɪk ə ˈwɪʃ] sich etwas wünschen I

Best **wishes** [ˌbest ˈwɪʃɪz] Viele Grüße; Herzliche Grüße II **U6**, 113

with [wɪð] mit; bei I

without [wɪˈðaʊt] ohne I

witness [ˈwɪtnəs] Zeuge/Zeugin II **U4**, 77

wizard [ˈwɪzəd] Zauberer II **AC3**, 130

wobbly [ˈwɒbli] wackelig II **U3**, 62

woman, **women** (pl) [ˈwʊmən; ˈwɪmɪn] Frau I

wonderful [ˈwʌndəfl] wunderbar II **U2**, 40

Woof! [wʊf] Wau! I

word [wɜːd] Wort I

compound **word** [ˈkɒmpaʊnd wɜːd] Kompositum (zusammengesetztes Wort) °II **U3**, 55

key **word** [ˈkiː wɜːd] Stichwort; Schlüsselbegriff I

linking **word** [ˈlɪŋkɪŋ ˌwɜːd] Bindewort I

signal **word** [ˈsɪɡnəl ˌwɜːd] Signalwort I

word cloud [ˈwɜːd ˌklaʊd] Wörterwolke °II **U4**, 68

word order [ˈwɜːdˌɔːdə] Wortstellung; Satzstellung I

Word power [ˈwɜːd ˌpaʊə] die Kraft der Wörter (Wortschatzübung) I

word snake [ˈwɜːd ˌsneɪk] Wortschlange I

word-building [ˈwɜːdˌbɪldɪŋ] Wortbildung °II **U3**, 51

work [wɜːk] Arbeit I

pair **work** [ˈpeə wɜːk] Partnerarbeit °II **U5**, 100

to **work** [wɜːk] arbeiten I; funktionieren II **U5**, 95

to **work** out [ˌwɜːkˈaʊt] herausfinden; ausarbeiten °II **U3**, 61

workshop [ˈwɜːkʃɒp] Workshop I

world [wɜːld] Erde; Welt I

from around the **world** [frɒm əˌraʊnd ðə ˈwɜːld] aus aller Welt II **U6**, 114

worm [wɜːm] Wurm I

*to be **worried** [bi ˈwʌrid] beunruhigt sein; besorgt sein II **U4**, 80

to **worry** [ˈwʌri] sich Sorgen machen II **U5**, 93

Don't **worry**! [ˌdəʊnt ˈwʌri] Keine Sorge! I

the **worst** [ðə ˈwɜːst] der/die/das schlimmste; der/die/das schlechteste II **U1**, 16

*to be **worth** [bi ˈwɜːθ] wert sein I

would like [wʊd ˈlaɪk] würde/-st/-n/-t gern; hätte/-st/-n/-t gern I

would love [wʊd ˈlʌv] würde/-st/-n/-t sehr gern; hätte/-st/-n/-t sehr gern I

Would you like …? [ˌwʊd jʊ ˈlaɪk]
Möchtest du …?; Möchten Sie …?;
Möchtet ihr …? °**II U4**, 70
Wow! [waʊ] Wow! **I**
to **wrap** [ræp] einwickeln; einpacken **I**
wrapping [ˈræpɪŋ] Verpackung; Hülle **I**
wrist [rɪst] Handgelenk **II U3**, 62
*to **write** [raɪt] schreiben **I**
  *to **write** down [ˌraɪt ˈdaʊn] aufschreiben **I**
writing [ˈraɪtɪŋ] Schreiben **I**
wrong [rɒŋ] falsch **I**
  *to be **wrong** [bi: ˈrɒŋ] unrecht haben;
  sich irren **I**
  *to go **wrong** [ˌɡəʊ ˈrɒŋ] schiefgehen **I**

X

XOXO [ˌhʌɡzˌən ˈkɪsɪz] Umarmungen und
  Küsse *(am Ende von E-Mails und SMS)* **I**

Y

yeah *(infml)* [jeə] ja **I**
year [jɪə] Jahr; Schuljahr **I**
11-year-old [ɪˌlevnˈjɪərəʊld] 11-Jährige/-r
  II U4, 70
18-year-old [ˌeɪtiːn ˈjɪərˌəʊld] 18-jährig
  II U3, 52
yearbook [ˈjɪəbʊk] Jahrbuch **II U1**, 8
yellow [ˈjeləʊ] gelb **I**
yes [jes] ja **I**
yesterday [ˈjestədeɪ] gestern **II U1**, 11
yet [jet] schon; noch **II U4**, 72
  not … **yet** [nɒt ˈjet] noch nicht **II U4**, 72
yoghurt [ˈjɒɡət] Joghurt **I**
you [juː; jə] du; ihr; Sie **I**
  You know how to … [juː ˈnəʊ ˌhaʊ tə]
  Du weißt, wie man …; Ihr wisst, wie
  man … **I**
  You too? [juː ˈtuː] Du auch? **I**
  You're into … [ˈjɔːrˌɪntə] Du magst …; Du
  stehst auf … **I**
  You're welcome. [jɔː ˈwelkəm] Bitte
  schön.; Nichts zu danken.; Gern geschehen. **I**
  You're … [jɔːr] Sie sind …; Du bist … **I**
young [jʌŋ] jung **I**
your [jɔː; jə] dein/-e; euer/eure; Ihr/-e **I**
  What's **your** name? [ˌwɒts jə ˈneɪm] Wie
  heißt du?; Wie heißen Sie? **I**
  Your turn. [ˈjɔː ˈtɜːn] Du bist dran. **I**
yours [jɔːz] dein/-er/-e/-es; eure/-r/-s; Ihr/-e
  II U2, 41
  Yours … [jɔːz] Viele Grüße … *(am Ende von
  Briefen und Mails)* **II U5**, 99
yourself [jɔːˈself] du/dir/dich/Sie/sich
  (selbst); selber **I**
yourselves [jɔːˈselvz] selber; ihr/euch/Sie/
  sich (selbst) **II U6**, 113

Z

zero [ˈzɪərəʊ] null **I**
zoo [zuː] Zoo; Tierpark **II U3**, 53

Boys' names

Amir [ˌɑːˈmiːr] **II U3**, 50
Ben [ben] **I**
Bob [bɒb] **I**
Damian [ˈdeɪmiən] **I**
Dave [deɪv] **I**
David [ˈdeɪvɪd] **I**
Desmond [ˈdezmənd] **I**
Ed [ed] **II U5**, 94
Filip [ˈfɪlɪp] **I**
Frank [fræŋk] **II U5**, 102
Fumio [ˈfjuːmɪəʊ] **II U2**, 41
Henry [ˈhenri] **I**
Jack [dʒæk] **I**
Jago [ˈdʒeɪɡəʊ] **II U6**, 123
Jahangir [dʒəˈhʌŋɡɪə] **I**
James [dʒeɪmz] **II U2**, 30
Jamie [ˈdʒeɪmi] **I**
Jay [dʒeɪ] **I**
Jinsoo [ˈdʒɪnzuː] **II U3**, 58
John [dʒɒn] **II U1**, 13
Jon [dʒɒn] **II U5**, 90
Luke [luːk] **I**
Marley [ˈmɑːli] **II U3**, 58
Mick [mɪk] **II U5**, 100
Mike [maɪk] **II U3**, 62
Nathan [ˈneɪθn] **II U5**, 98
Nick [nɪk] **II U3**, 58
Peter [ˈpiːtə] **II U1**, 13
Rokuro [rəˈkuːrəʊ] **II U2**, 40
Satoshi [səˈtɒʃi] **II U2**, 40
Shahid [ʃɑːˈhiːd] **I**
Steve [stiːv] **I**
Tony [ˈtəʊni] **I**
Tyler [ˈtaɪlə] **I**
Will [wɪl] **II U1**, 18

Girls' names

Alice [ˈælɪs] **II U2**, 33
Alicia [əˈlɪsiə; əˈlɪʃə] **I**
Amber [ˈæmbə] **I**
Anna [ˈænə] **I**
Anne [æn] **I**
Ayla [ˈeɪlə] **II U4**, 74
Beata [biˈɑːtə] **I**
Bunko [ˈbʌŋkəʊ] **II U2**, 41
Carol [ˈkærəl] **I**
Ceri [ˈkeri] **II U1**, 18
Claire [ˈkleə] **I**
Emily [ˈemɪli] **I**
Frances [ˈfrɑːnsɪs] **I**
Gwen [ɡwen] **II U2**, 32
Helen [ˈhelɪn] **II U6**, 123
Holly [ˈhɒli] **I**
Irina [ɪˈriːnə] **I**

Judith [ˈdʒuːdɪθ] **II U6**, 116
Julie [ˈdʒuːli] **I**
Kate [keɪt] **II U2**, 33
Laura [ˈlɔːrə] **I**
Lauren [ˈlɔːrən] **II U5**, 92
Lou [luː] **I**
Lucy [ˈluːsi] **I**
Maisie [ˈmeɪzi] **II U5**, 98
Mary [ˈmeəri] **II U2**, 30
Megan [ˈmeɡən] **II U6**, 124
Mila [ˈmiːlə] **I**
Mina [ˈmiːnə] **II U3**, 58
Olivia [ɒˈlɪviə] **I**
Pia [ˈpiːə] **I**
Polly [ˈpɒli] **II U2**, 36
Rose [rəʊz] **I**
Ruby [ˈruːbi] **II U5**, 92
Sally [ˈsæli] **I**
Seeta [ˈsiːtə] **I**
Tamara [təˈmɑːrə] **II U6**, 123
Tomoko [təˈmɒkəʊ] **II U2**, 40
Vivien [ˈvɪvjən] **II AC3**, 131

Surnames

Ashton [ˈæʃtən] **II U4**, 75
Azad [əˈzɑːd] **I**
Bayram [ˈbeɪrəm] **II U4**, 74
Elliot [ˈeliət] **I**
Fraser [ˈfreɪzə] **I**
Green [ɡriːn] **I**
Nicholls [ˈnɪkəlz] **II U6**, 116
Parker [ˈpɑːkə] **II U4**, 81
Preston [ˈprestən] **I**
Richardson [ˈrɪtʃədsn] **I**
Swindon [ˈswɪndən] **I**
Thompson [ˈtɒmsən] **II U4**, 76
Walker [ˈwɔːkə] **I**
Wright [raɪt] **II U2**, 30
Zajac [ˈzeɪdʒæk] **I**

Place names

Baker Street [ˈbeɪkə ˌstriːt] **II AC3**, 131
Begbie Road [ˌbeɡbi ˈrəʊd] **II U5**, 102
Bradford [ˈbrædfəd] **II U3**, 50
Brick Lane [brɪk ˈleɪn] **II U3**, 51
Brook Lane [brʊk ˈleɪn] **I**
Caerphilly [keəˈfɪli] *walisische Stadt*
  II U6, 108
Camden Market [ˈkæmdən ˌmɑːkɪt] **II U3**, 58
College Way [ˌkɒlɪdʒ ˈweɪ] **I**
Cologne [kəˈləʊn] Köln **I**
Covent Garden [ˌkɒvnt ˈɡɑːdn] **II U3**, 51
Cracow [ˈkrækɒv; ˈkrɑːkaʊ] Krakau **I**
Edinburgh [ˈedɪnbrə] **II U6**, 109
Enfield [en'fiːld] **I**
Greenwich Park [ˌɡrenɪdʒ ˈpɑːk] **I**
Greenwich Pier [ˌɡrenɪdʒ ˈpɪə] **I**
Hollywood [ˈhɒliwʊd] **II AC2**, 89
Hyde Park [ˌhaɪd ˈpɑːk] **II AC1**, 48
Isle of Man [ˌaɪlˌəv ˈmæn] **II U6**, 115

Kidbrooke Gardens [ˌkɪdbrʊk ˈgɑːdnz] I
King William Walk [ˌkɪŋ ˈwɪljəm ˌwɔːk] I
Leicester Square [ˌlestə ˈskweə] II U3, 65
London [ˈlʌndən] I
Nelson Road [ˌnelsn ˈrəʊd] I
Nottingham [ˈnɒtɪŋəm] II AC3, 131
Oxford Street [ˈɒksfəd ˌstriːt] II AC1, 48
Paddington [ˈpædɪŋtən] II U6, 111
South Street [ˈsaʊθ striːt] I
Southend [saʊθˈend] II U1, 25
St Agnes [ˌseɪnt ˈægnəs] II U6, 110
St Austell [ˌseɪnt ˈɔstel] II U6, 114
Tintagel [tɪnˈtædʒl] II AC3, 131
Tower Hill [ˌtaʊə ˈhɪl] II U3, 53
Ty'n y Berth [tiːnˌə ˈbɜːθ] II U1, 16
Victoria Park [vɪktɔːriə ˈpɑːk] I
Village Way [ˈvɪlɪdʒ ˌweɪ] I
Wimbledon [ˈwɪmbldən] I

Geographical names

America [əˈmerɪkə] II AC2, 89
Atlantic Ocean [ətˌlæntɪk ˈəʊʃn] Atlantischer Ozean II U6, 114
Australia [ɒsˈtreɪliə] Australien II AC2, 89
Austria [ˈɔːstriə] Österreich II U4, 71
Bodmin Moor [ˌbɒdmɪn ˈmɔː] Hochmoorlandschaft im nordöstlichen Cornwall II U6, 114
Britain [ˈbrɪtn] Großbritannien I
British Empire [ˌbrɪtɪʃ ˈempaɪə] britisches Königreich II AC2, 89
British Isles [ˌbrɪtɪʃ ˈaɪlz] Britische Inseln II U6, 109
Canada [ˈkænədə] Kanada I
China [ˈtʃaɪnə] China I
Cornwall [ˈkɔːnwɔːl] II U6, 108
England [ˈɪŋglənd] England I
Europe [ˈjʊərəp] Europa II AC1, 48
France [frɑːns] Frankreich II U3, 56
Germany [ˈdʒɜːməni] Deutschland I
Great Britain (GB) [ˌgreɪt ˈbrɪtn] Großbritannien II U6, 108
India [ˈɪndiə] Indien II AC2, 88
Isle of Dogs [ˌaɪl əv ˈdɒgz] I
Italy [ˈɪtəli] Italien II U5, 96
Kent [kent] Grafschaft im Südosten Englands II U4, 76
Normandy [ˈnɔːməndi] die Normandie II U3, 56
North Sea [ˌnɔːθ ˈsiː] Nordsee II U6, 109
Northern Ireland [ˌnɔːðn ˈaɪələnd] Nordirland II U6, 108
Pakistan [ˌpɑːkɪˈstɑːn] I
Poland [ˈpəʊlənd] Polen I
Republic of Ireland [rɪˌpʌblɪk əvˈaɪələnd] Republik Irland II U6, 108
Riviera [rɪvˈjeɪrə] Landschaft in Italien II U6, 109
Scotland [ˈskɒtlənd] Schottland II U6, 113
Sherwood Forest [ˌʃɜːwʊd ˈfɒrɪst] II AC3, 131

Snowdonia National Park [snəʊˌdəʊniə ˌnæʃnl ˈpɑːk] II U1, 16
South Africa [ˌsaʊθ ˈæfrɪkə] Südafrika II AC2, 89
Spain [speɪn] Spanien II U5, 99
Thames [temz] I
United Kingdom (UK) [juːˈkeɪ] Vereinigtes Königreich von Großbritannien und Nordirland I
USA (United States of America) [ˌjuːesˈeɪ (juːˌnaɪtɪd ˌsteɪts əvəˈmerɪkə)] USA (Vereinigte Staaten von Amerika) II AC2, 89
Wales [weɪlz] II U1, 16

Other names

Arches Leisure Centre [ˌɑːtʃɪz ˈleʒə ˌsentə] I
Ben Briggs [ben ˈbrɪgz] I
Big Ben [bɪg ˈben] II AC1, 48
British Museum [ˌbrɪtɪʃ mjuːˈziːəm] II U3, 50
Buckingham Palace [ˌbʌkɪŋəm ˈpæləs] II AC1, 48
Changing of the Guards [ˌtʃeɪndʒɪŋ əv ðə ˈgɑːdz] Wachwechsel vor dem Buckingham Palace II AC1, 49
Comic Relief [ˌkɒmɪk rɪˈliːf] wohltätige Organisation II U1, 10
2Cool Performing Academy [ˌtuːkuːl pəˌfɔːmɪŋ əˈkædəmi] I
Croeso i Gymru [ˌkrɔɪsəʊ iː ˈgʌmri] II U1, 18
Crossharbour [ˈkrɒsˌhɑːbə] II U3, 53
Cutty Sark [ˌkʌti ˈsɑːk] I
Diwali [dɪˈwɑːli] I
Docklands Light Railway (DLR) [ˌdɒklændz ˌlaɪt ˈreɪlweɪ] Regionalbahn im Osten Londons I
Eden [ˈiːdn] (der Garten) Eden II U6, 114
Eid [iːd] I
Elephant & Castle [ˈelɪfənt ənd kɑːsl] II U3, 53
Excalibur [ekˈskælɪbə] II AC3, 131
Fan Museum [ˌfæn mjuːˈziːəm] I
For he's a jolly good fellow [fə ˌhiːz ə ˌdʒɒli gʊd ˈfeləʊ] Volkslied I
Greenwich Foot Tunnel [ˌgrenɪdʒ ˈfʊt ˌtʌnl] I
Guy Fawkes Night [ˌgaɪ fɔːks ˈnaɪt] I
Halloween [ˌhæləʊˈiːn] Tag vor Allerheiligen I
Hanukkah [ˈhɑːnəkə] I
Honey [ˈhʌni] I
the Houses of Parliament [ðə ˌhaʊzɪz əv ˈpɑːləmənt] britisches Parlamentsgebäude II U3, 50
London Eye [ˌlʌndən ˈaɪ] II AC1, 48
London Wall [ˌlʌndən ˈwɔːl] II U3, 50
London Zoo [ˌlʌndən ˈzuː] II U3, 53
Madame Tussauds [ˌmædəm tʊˈsɔːdz] II U3, 51
Manchester City [ˌmæntʃɪstə ˈsɪti] englischer Fußballclub II U5, 94
Meridian Line [məˌrɪdiən ˈlaɪn] Nullmeridian I
Mickey Mouse [ˌmɪki ˈmaʊs] I

Millennium Footbridge [mɪˌleniəm ˈfʊtbrɪdʒ] II U3, 62
Mother's Day [ˈmʌðəz ˌdeɪ] I
Mousebook [ˈmaʊsbʊk] II U5, 90
Mr Fluff [ˌmɪstə ˈflʌf] I
Mudchute Farm [ˌmʌdʃuːt ˈfɑːm] I
Natural History Museum [ˌnætʃrl ˈhɪstri mjuːˌziːəm] II U2, 40
Notting Hill Carnival [ˌnɒtɪŋ hɪl ˈkɑːnɪvl] I
Oyster card [ˈɔɪstə ˌkɑːd] II U3, 52
Pancake Day [ˈpænkeɪk ˌdeɪ] I
Pets Corner [pets ˈkɔːnə] I
Red Nose Day [ˌred nəʊz ˈdeɪ] II U1, 8
Rocky [ˈrɒki] II U3, 56
Royal Observatory [ˌrɔɪəl əbˈzɜːvətri] I
Rugby Football Club (RFC) [ˌrʌgbi ˌfʊtbɔːl ˈklʌb (ɑːr ef ˈsiː)] II U4, 75
Sherlock [ˈʃɜːlɒk] I
Shrove Tuesday [ˌʃrəʊv ˈtjuːzdeɪ] Fastnachtsdienstag I
Sid [sɪd] I
star4ever [ˌstɑːfəˈrevə] I
Tandoori [tænˈdʊəri] I
Thomas Tallis School (= TTS) [ˌtɒməs ˈtælɪs ˌskuːl] I
the Tower of London [ðə ˌtaʊər əv ˈlʌndən] II AC1, 49
Transport Museum [ˈtrænspɔːt mjuːˈziːəm] II U3, 53
TTS planner [ˌtiːtiːˈes ˈplænə] Handbuch für TTS-Schülerinnen und -Schüler I
Valentine's Day [ˈvæləntaɪnz ˌdeɪ] I
Victoria [vɪkˈtɔːriə] II U3, 53
Whitehall [ˈwaɪthɔːl] Straße in London II U3, 51
World War II [ˌwɜːld ˌwɔː ˈtuː] Zweiter Weltkrieg II AC2, 89

Famous names

Agatha Christie [ˌægəθə ˈkrɪsti] II AC3, 131
Boudicca [ˈbuːdɪkə] II AC3, 131
Christopher Wren [ˌkrɪstəfə ˈren] II U2, 30
Daniel Craig [ˌdænjəl ˈkreɪg] II U1, 15
Dr Watson [ˌdɒktə ˈwɒtsən] II AC3, 131
Elizabeth I [ɪˌlɪzəbəθ ðə ˈfɜːst] II U2, 31
James Bond [ˌdʒeɪmz ˈbɒnd] II U1, 15
King Arthur [ˌkɪŋ ˈɑːθə] König Artus II AC3, 131
Lenny Harry [ˌleni ˈhæri] britischer Comedian II U1, 10
Louis Armstrong [ˌluːi ˈɑːmstrɒŋ] II U2, 35
Maid Marian [ˌmeɪd ˈmæriən] II AC3, 131
Miss Marple [mɪs ˈmɑːpl] II AC3, 131
Prince Albert [ˌprɪns ˈælbət] II AC1, 49
Queen Victoria [ˌkwiːn vɪkˈtɔːriə] II AC1, 49
Robin Hood [ˌrɒbɪn ˈhʊd] II AC3, 131
Sherlock Holmes [ˌʃɜːlɒk ˈhəʊmz] II AC3, 130
William the Conqueror [ˌwɪljəm ðə ˈkɒŋkrə] II U3, 56;

A

abbiegen to turn **I**
abblocken to block **II U5**, 93
Abend evening **I**
  heute **Abend** 2nite (= tonight) **I**
Abendessen dinner **I**
abends in the evenings **I**
abends (Uhrzeit) p.m. **I**
Abenteuer adventure **II U1**, 16
aber but **I**
abfahren *to leave **II U2**, 30; to depart **II U6**, 112
abfahrend outward **II U6**, 112
abgeschlossen locked **II U1**, 19
abhängen von to depend (on) **II U6**, 111
abnehmen *to take off **I**
abschalten to turn off **I**; to turn off **II U1**, 12
  Schalt/Schaltet es ab! Turn it off! **I**
abschicken *to send off **II U6**, 113
abschneiden *to cut (off) **II U2**, 30
abschreiben to copy **I**
absolut absolutely **II U2**, 42
Abstand gap **I**
abstimmen *to take a vote; to vote **I**
abstürzen to crash **II U5**, 103
acht eight **I**
Acker field **II U1**, 18
Action action **I**
Adresse address **I**
AG club **I**
aggressiv aggressive **II U1**, 24
äh er **I**
keine **Ahnung** no idea **II U1**, 19
Akku battery **II U1**, 19
Aktion action **I**
Aktivität activity **I**
Akzent accent **II U6**, 115
albern silly **I**
alle all of them; everyone **I**; everybody **II U3**, 54
alle/-s all **I**
  wir **alle** all of us **II U6**, 110
allein alone **I**; on my own **II U2**, 40
alles everything **I**
Alphabet alphabet **I**
als as **II U2**, 30
als (bei Vergleichen) than **II U1**, 16
als when **I**
also so **I**
alt old **I**
  Wie **alt** bist du? How old are you? **I**
  Wie **alt** sind Sie? How old are you? **I**
am on **I**
  am besten best **I**
  am Fluss by the river **II U2**, 31
  am Wochenende at the weekend **I**
aus **Amerika** American **II U1**, 9
Amerikaner/-in American **II U1**, 9
amerikanisch American **II U1**, 9
Amtssprache official language **II AC2**, 89
sich **amüsieren** *to have fun **I**

an on; at **I**; by **II U6**, 122
  an Bord aboard **I**
  an sein *to be on **II U5**, 102
anbieten to offer **II U2**, 28
Anblick sight **II AC1**, 48
Andenken souvenir **II U3**, 54
die **anderen** the others **I**
andere/-r/-s other **I**
  ein/-e **andere/-r/-s** another **I**
Einerseits …, (aber) **andererseits** … On the one hand …, (but) on the other hand … **II U4**, 82
(sich) **ändern** to change **II U5**, 90
anders different; other **I**
Änderung change **II U6**, 123
Anfang beginning **II U1**, 22
anfangen to start **I**; *to get started **II U2**, 33; *to begin **II U5**, 99
anfeuern to cheer **II U4**, 72
angeben to show off **II U5**, 103
Und ein **Angeber**! With a very big head! **II U5**, 95
Angeln fishing **II U6**, 114
von **Angesicht** zu **Angesicht** face-to-face **II U5**, 93
angespült werden to wash up **II U3**, 62
Angst fear **II U4**, 82
  Angst haben (vor) *to be scared (of) **I**
  Ich habe (keine) **Angst** vor … I'm (not) scared of … **I**
anhaben *to wear **I**
anhalten to stop **I**
Anhänger/-in fan **II U4**, 83
anhören to listen (to) **I**
anklicken to click on **II U6**, 112
ankommen to arrive **II U6**, 112
ankommend inward **II U6**, 112
Ankündigung announcement **II U6**, 115
anmalen to paint **I**
Anmerkung note **I**
annähernd nearly **II U2**, 41
anonym anonymous **II U1**, 13
anpflanzen to plant **II U2**, 41
anprobieren to try on **II U2**, 31
Anregung suggestion **I**
Anruf phone call **I**
  einen **Anruf** entgegennehmen to answer the phone **I**
Anrufbeantworter answering machine **I**
anrufen to call **I**
Anrufer/-in caller **I**
anschauen to look at **I**; *to have a look (at) **II U4**, 73
sich **anschließen** to join **II U2**, 33
ansehen to look at **I**
(sich) **ansehen** to watch **I**
Ansicht point of view **II U4**, 76
anstarren to stare **I**
antippen to tap **II U5**, 102
Antwort answer; reply **I**
antworten to answer; to reply **I**
Anweisung instruction **I**

Anwesenheitskontrolle registration **II U2**, 32
Apfel apple **I**
App app **II U5**, 97
Apparat machine **I**
April April **I**
Arbeit job; work **I**
Arbeit für die Schule studies (pl) **II U2**, 28
arbeiten to work **I**
Architekt/-in architect **II U2**, 30
Areal area **II U4**, 70
Ärger trouble **II U1**, 19
  Ärger machen *to make trouble **I**
Argument dafür pro **II U3**, 55
  Argument dagegen con **II U3**, 55
Arm arm **II U2**, 41
die **Armen** the poor **II AC3**, 131
Art kind **I**
  Art und Weise way **I**
Artikel article **II U2**, 33
Arzt/Ärztin doctor **II U4**, 72
Arztpraxis surgery **I**
Assistent/-in assistant **II U4**, 78
Atlantischer Ozean Atlantic Ocean **II U6**, 114
Atlas atlas **II AC2**, 88
atmen to breathe **II U4**, 80
Atmosphäre flair **II U3**, 51
Attraktion attraction **II U3**, 59
Aua! Ouch! **II U1**, 8
auch too **I**; also **II U1**, 10
  Du **auch**? You too? **I**
Audio- audio **I**
Audioführung audio tour **II U3**, 56
auf on; at; to **I**
  auf dem Foto/den Fotos in the photo(s) **I**
  auf der anderen Seite von across; opposite **I**
  auf der Straße in the street **I**
  auf einmal suddenly **I**
  auf Wiedersehen goodbye **I**
  auf … zu towards **II U3**, 62
aufbauen *to set up **I**
aufbewahren *to keep **I**
Aufführung show **II U4**, 75
Aufgabe task; exercise; job **I**
aufgebracht upset **II U2**, 30
aufgeregt excited **I**; nervous **II U1**, 12
aufgeschlagen open **I**
aufhängen *to hang up; to put up **II U2**, 33
aufhören to finish **I**
aufhören (mit) to stop **I**
  Hör/Hört auf! Stop it! **I**
aufladen to top up **II U3**, 52
aufmachen to open **I**
Aufmerksamkeit attention **II U5**, 93
Aufnahme recording **I**
Aufnahmestudio recording studio **I**
aufnehmen to record **II U4**, 78
aufpassen to look out **II U4**, 70
  aufpassen auf to look after **I**
  Pass/Passt auf! Be careful! **I**
aufräumen to tidy (a room) **I**

aufrechterhalten *to keep going **II U1**, 12
aufregend exciting **I**
aufsagen *to say **I**
aufschreiben *to write down **I**
aufstehen *(aus dem Bett)* *to get up **I**
  Es ist Zeit **aufzustehen**! Time to get up! **I**
aufstehen *(von einer Sitzgelegenheit)* *to stand up **I**
aufstellen *to put up **II U2**, 33
Auftrag task **I**
aufwärmen to warm up **I**
  sich **aufwärmen** to warm up **I**
Aufwärmübung warm-up **I**
aufzeichnen to record **II U4**, 78
Aufzeichnung recording **I**
Auge eye **II U1**, 9
  Er traute seinen **Augen** nicht. He couldn't believe his eyes. **II U2**, 40
Augenblick moment **II U2**, 40
Augenzeuge/Augenzeugin eyewitness **II U4**, 77
August August **I**
aus from **I**
  aus Cornwall Cornish **II U6**, 110
  aus aller Welt from around the world **II U6**, 114
ausblasen *to blow out **I**
Ausblick view **II U2**, 30
Auschecken Check-out **I**
(sich) **ausdenken** *to think of **II U1**, 12
Ausdruck phrase **I**; expression **II AC2**, 89
  nützliche **Ausdrücke** Useful phrases **I**
ausflippen *to go crazy **II U5**, 95
Ausflug trip **II U1**, 9
den Hund **ausführen** to walk the dog **I**
ausgeben *(Geld)* *to spend **I**
ausgedehnt wide **II U6**, 109
ausgehen *to go out **II U6**, 122
sich **ausgeschlossen** fühlen *to feel left out **II U5**, 104
(sich) **ausleihen** to borrow **II U5**, 103
Mach/Macht das aus! Stop it! **I**
auspacken to unwrap **I**
auspusten *to blow out **I**
ausräumen to clear out **I**
jmdm. etw. **ausrichten** *to take a message **I**
sich **ausruhen** to relax **II U2**, 36
Ausrüstung equipment **II U4**, 69
Aussage statement **II AC2**, 88
ausschalten to turn off **I**; to turn off **II U1**, 12
  Schalt/Schaltet es aus! Turn it off! **I**
aussehen to look **I**
  wie der Mann **aussah** what the man looked like **II U1**, 13
im **äußersten** Westen in the far west **II U6**, 114
außerhalb outside; out **I**
Außerirdische/-r alien **I**
Äußerung expression **II AC2**, 89
Aussicht view **II U2**, 30
Aussprache pronunciation **I**
Ausstattung equipment **II U4**, 69

aussteigen *to get out of **II U5**, 102
aussteigen (aus einem Bus/Zug) *to get off (a bus/train) **II U3**, 53
Ausstellung display **II U3**, 59
  Ausstellung in der Klasse class display **I**
Australien Australia **II AC2**, 89
Auswahl choice **II U3**, 58
auswählen *to choose **II U2**, 30
Wähle/Wählt … aus. Choose … **I**
auswendig lernen *to learn … by heart **I**
auswickeln to unwrap **I**
Auszeichnung award **II U4**, 74
ausziehen *to take off **I**
Auto car **I**
Automat machine **I**

B

Baby baby **I**
Bad bath **I**
Badewanne bath **I**
Badezimmer bathroom **I**
Badminton badminton **I**
Bahnhof station **I**
Bahnsteig platform **II U6**, 112
bald soon **II U1**, 18
Ball ball **I**
Banane banana **I**
Bär bear **II U3**, 56
Basketball basketball **I**
Batterie battery **II U1**, 19
Bauch stomach **II U4**, 80
Bauchschmerzen stomachache **II U4**, 73
Bauchweh stomachache **II U4**, 73
bauen *to build **II U2**, 30
Bauernhof farm **I**
Baum tree **I**
Beachtung attention **II U5**, 93
beängstigend scary **II U1**, 24
beantworten to answer **I**
bedeckt cloudy **II U1**, 19
bedeuten *to mean **II U3**, 54
Bedeutung meaning **II U1**, 21
bedürftig in need **II U1**, 10
sich **beeilen** to hurry **I**
beeindruckt impressed **II U2**, 36
beeinflussen to influence **II AC2**, 89
beenden to finish **I**; to end **II U4**, 79
sich **befassen** mit *to deal (with) **II U3**, 54
befestigen to fix **II U5**, 95
befolgen to follow **II U3**, 54
befragen to interview **I**
Befragung interview **I**
Befürchtung fear **II U4**, 82
begeistert excited **I**
Beginn beginning **II U1**, 22
beginnen to start **I**; *to begin **II U5**, 99
behalten *to keep **I**
Behauptung statement **II AC2**, 88
behindert with special needs **II U2**, 29
bei with; at **I**; by **II U6**, 122
beibringen *to teach **II U4**, 76

beide both **II U4**, 81
beide the two of them **II U5**, 92
Bein leg **II U4**, 71
beinahe almost **II U4**, 75
beinhalten to include **II U6**, 108
Beispiel example **I**
zum **Beispiel** for example **II AC2**, 89
beißen *to bite **II U3**, 56
beitreten to join **II U2**, 33
bekommen *to get **I**; to receive **II U4**, 77
belebt busy **I**
beliebt popular **I**
bellen to bark **I**
bemerken to notice **II U2**, 40
benötigen to need (to) **I**
benutzen to use **I**
beobachten to watch **I**
bequem comfortable **II U3**, 65
bereit ready **II U2**, 41
bereits already **I**
Berg mountain **II U1**, 16; hill **II U6**, 122
Bergbau mining **II U6**, 114
bergen to save **I**
Bericht report **II U1**, 9
Bericht (in einer Zeitschrift, Zeitung) article **II U2**, 33
sich **beruhigen** to relax **II U2**, 36; to calm down **II U2**, 41
berühmt famous **I**
beschäftigt busy **I**
beschreiben to describe **I**
besichtigen to visit **I**
Besichtigungs- sightseeing **II U3**, 58
besiegen *to beat **II U3**, 54
besitzen *to have got **I**
besonders special **I**
besorgen *to get **I**
besorgt sein *to be worried **II U4**, 80
besser better **I**
(der/die/das) **Beste** (the) best **II U1**, 10
besteigen to climb **I**
beste/-r/-s best **I**
  am **besten** best **I**
bestürzt upset **II U2**, 30
Besuch visit **I**
besuchen to visit **I**
Besucher/-in visitor **I**
betreten to enter **II U2**, 40
Betreuer/-in instructor **II U1**, 18
Bett bed **I**
  ins **Bett** gehen *to go to bed **I**
beunruhigt sein *to be worried **II U4**, 80
bevor before **I**
(sich) **bewegen** to move **I**
Bewegung move **I**
bewölkt cloudy **II U1**, 19
bezahlen *to pay (for) **I**
Beziehung relationship **II U4**, 82
Biene bee **II U2**, 33
Bild picture **I**
bilden *to make **I**
Bildgeschichte photo story **I**

billig cheap I
Bindewort linking word I
Bis … CU (= See you); See you! I
  Bis dann! CU (= See you); See you! I
  bis jetzt so far II U4, 75
  von … **bis** from … to I
bis till I; until II U4, 70
Biskuit- sponge I
ein **bisschen** a bit II U1, 18
Bitte. Please. I
  Bitte schön. Here you are.; You're welcome. I
bitten to ask I
  bitten um to ask for I
blau blue I
bleiben to stay I
Bleistift pencil I
Blick look I; view II U2, 30
  einen **Blick** werfen auf *to take a look at II U2, 37
Blitz lightning (no pl) II U5, 102
blockieren to block II U5, 93
blöd stupid II U4, 81
bloß only I
Blume flower II U2, 41
BMX BMX II U4, 68
weiße **Bohnen** in Tomatensoße baked beans (pl) I
Bonbons sweets (pl) I
Boot boat I
an **Bord** aboard I
böse angry; bad I
Bösewicht villain II AC3, 130
Botschaft message I
Bowlingbahn bowling alley I
Box box I
Boxen boxing II U1, 8
Boxrunde round of boxing II U1, 8
brauchen to need (to) I
  nicht **brauchen** needn't I
  (Zeit) **brauchen** *to take II U5, 95
braun brown I
brechen *to break I
breit wide II U6, 109
schwarzes **Brett** noticeboard II U1, 10
Brief letter II U5, 91
Briefträger postman II U1, 13
Brille glasses (pl) II U4, 80
bringen *to bring; *to get; *to take I
  in Schwierigkeiten **bringen** *to make trouble I
  jmdn. dazu **bringen**, etw. zu tun *to make somebody do something II U5, 92
Brite/Britin British I
britisch British I
Bronzezeit (ca. 2200–800 v. Chr.) Bronze Age II U6, 114
Broschüre brochure I
Brot bread I
  belegtes **Brot** sandwich I
Brücke bridge II U3, 62
Bruder brother I

Buch book I
buchen to book II U6, 112
Büchse can I
Buchstabe letter I
buchstabieren *to spell I
bunt colourful I
Buntstift pencil I
Burg castle II U3, 56
Büro office I
Bus bus I
Busbahnhof bus station I

C

Cache cache II U6, 122
Café café; snack bar I
Cafeteria cafeteria I
campen to camp II U6, 124
Camping camping II U5, 99
Cent (Währung) cent I
Center centre I
Chance chance II U5, 100
Charakter character I
Chatroom chat room II AC2, 88
chatten (sich online unterhalten) to chat I
China China I
Chipkarte smartcard II U3, 52
circa about I
Clown clown II U4, 80
Cola coke I
Comedian comedian II U1, 10
Comedy Show comedy show II U1, 10
Comic comic II U4, 82
Comicheft comic II U4, 82
Computer computer I
Computerunterricht Technology II U2, 32
cool cool I
aus **Cornwall** Cornish II U6, 110
Couch sofa I
Cousin/Cousine cousin I
Creme cream I
Cricket cricket II U4, 69
Curry (Gewürz oder Gericht) curry I

D

da because I
da there I
  da ist/sind there is/are I
dabei sein *to be in II U4, 70
Dach roof II U6, 122
Dachboden loft I; attic II U4, 76
dahin there I
Sehr geehrte **Dame**, sehr geehrter Herr Dear Sir or Madam II U6, 113
danach then; after that I
dankbar thankful I
Danke. Thank you.; Thanks. I
danken to thank II U2, 36
  Nichts zu **danken.** You're welcome. I
dann then I
darauf zu towards II U3, 62

das the I
das that I
  Das (hier) ist … This is … I
  Das macht … That's … I
  Das war knapp! That was close! I
das (Relativpronomen) which II U2, 30
dass that I
Datum date I
dauern *to take II U5, 95
Daumen thumb II U2, 34
  die **Daumen** drücken *to keep your fingers crossed I
davonkommen mit *to get away with II U4, 76
Deck deck I
dein/-e your I
dein/-er/-e/-es yours II U2, 41
Dekoration decorations (pl) I
dekorieren to decorate I
dem (Relativpronomen) who; which II U2, 30
den (Relativpronomen) who; which II U2, 30
denken *to think I
  Denke/Denkt an … Think of … I
  denken an to remember I
  denken über *to think of I
Denkmal monument II U6, 114
dennoch still II U5, 95
der the I
der; **dem**; **den**; **die**; **das** (Relativpronomen) that II U1, 9
der (Relativpronomen) who; which II U2, 30
deren (Relativpronomen) whose II U2, 30
der-/die-/dasselbe the same I
Desaster disaster II U5, 102
deshalb that's why II U2, 30
Design design II U2, 30
dessen (Relativpronomen) whose II U2, 30
deutlich clear I
Deutsch German I
deutsch German I
Deutsche/-r German I
aus **Deutschland** German I
Deutschland Germany I
Dezember December I
Diagramm diagram I
Dialekt dialect II U6, 115
Dialog dialogue I
dich (selbst) yourself I
die (auch Pl.) the I
die (Relativpronomen) who; which II U2, 30
Diele hall II U6, 122
Dienstag Tuesday I
dies this I
diese (hier) these I
  diese dort those I
diese/-r/-s this I
Ding thing I
Dinosaurier dinosaur II U2, 40
dir (selbst) yourself I
Diskussion discussion II U5, 90
diskutieren to discuss I

Distanz distance **II U3**, 60
doch after all **I**
Donner thunder *(no pl)* **II U5**, 102
Donnerstag Thursday **I**
doof silly **I**
Dorf village **I**
dort there **I**
dorthin there **I**
Dose can **I**
  aus der **Dose** tinned **I**
Dosen- tinned **I**
Drama drama **II U2**, 28
dramatisch dramatic **II U3**, 63
dran kommen to reach **II U5**, 95
  Du bist **dran**. Your turn.; It's your turn. **I**
draußen outside **I**
nach **draußen** out **I**
dreckig dirty **II U2**, 40
drei three **I**
eine **Dreiergruppe** a group of three **I**
dreizehn thirteen **I**
drin inside **I**
dritte/-r/-s third **I**
dröhnen to boom **II U6**, 122
Druck- print **II U5**, 91
drücken to press **II U5**, 102
  die Daumen **drücken** *to keep your
  fingers crossed **I**
du you; u *(= you)* **I**
  du (selbst) yourself **I**
  Du auch? You too? **I**
  Du bist dran. Your turn.; It's your turn. **I**
  Du bist … You're … **I**
  Du weißt, wie man … You know how
  to … **I**
dumm silly **I**; stupid **II U4**, 81
  Zu **dumm**! Too bad! **I**
Dummkopf silly **II U4**, 80
dunkel dark **II U1**, 18
Dunkelheit the dark **II U1**, 18; darkness
  II U6, 119
durch through **I**
durchdrehen *to go crazy **II U5**, 95
Durchsage announcement **II U6**, 115
dürfen can **I**; *to be allowed to (do sth); *to
  be able to (do sth); may **II U5**, 95
  nicht **dürfen** mustn't **I**
Dusche shower **I**
DVD DVD **I**

E

Ebbe low tide **II U3**, 62
echt real **II U1**, 10
Ecke corner **II U2**, 34
(der Garten) Eden Eden **II U6**, 114
Ehefrau wife, wives *(pl)* **II U2**, 31
Ehemann husband **II U2**, 30
Ei egg **I**
Eichhörnchen squirrel **I**
eifersüchtig sein (auf) *to be jealous (of) **I**
eigene/-r/-s own **I**

eilen to hurry **I**
Eimer bucket **II U3**, 62
ein/-e a; an **I**
  ein paar a couple of **I**
  ein wenig a little **I**
  ein/-e andere/-r/-s another **I**
  noch **ein/-e** another **I**
einander each other **I**
Atme(t) tief ein. Take a deep breath.
  II U2, 36
einbiegen to turn **I**
Einchecken Check-in **I**
eine/-r/-s one *(sg)*/ones *(pl)* **II U3**, 54
Einerseits …, (aber) andererseits … On the
  one hand …, (but) on the other hand …
  II U4, 82
einfach easy **I**
  einfache Fahrkarte one-way ticket; single
  ticket **II U6**, 112
einfach just **I**
Einfall idea **I**
sich etwas **einfallen** lassen *to think of
  II U1, 12
Einführung introduction **II U2**, 29
eingießen to pour **I**
Einheit unit **I**
die Segel **einholen** to reef the sails **I**
einige some; a few **I**
Einkäufe shopping **I**
Einkaufen shopping **I**
einkaufen gehen *to go shopping **I**
einladen to invite **I**
Einladung invitation **I**
Einleitung introduction **II U2**, 29
einmal once **I**
einpacken to wrap **I**
einrichten *to set up **I**
eins one **I**
einsam lonely **I**
einschenken to pour **I**
einschlafen *to fall asleep **I**
einschließen to include **II U6**, 108
Setze/Setzt ein … Put in … **I**
einst once **I**
einsteigen *to get into **I**
einsteigen (in den Bus) *to get on (the bus)
  II U6, 112
eintreten to enter **II U2**, 40
Eintrittskarte ticket **I**
einwickeln to wrap **I**
Einzelkind only child **I**
einzeln individual **II U4**, 69
einziehen in to move in/into **II U6**, 122
einzige/-r/-s only **II U5**, 103
Eis ice; ice cream **I**
Eisbahn ice rink **I**
Eiscreme ice cream **I**
Elektrik electrics **II U6**, 123
Elektriker/-in electrician **II U6**, 123
Elektrizität electricity **II U6**, 122
elektronisch electronic **II U1**, 21
elf eleven **I**

Eltern parents *(pl)* **I**
E-Mail e-mail **I**
  per **E-Mail** schicken to mail **II U5**, 97
empfangen to receive **II U4**, 77
Ende ending; end **I**
enden to finish **I**; to end up **II U1**, 8; to end
  II U4, 79
endlich at last **I**; finally **II U2**, 31
eng close **I**
aus **England** English **I**
England England **I**
Engländer/-in English **I**
  Ich bin **Engländer/-in**. I'm English. **I**
Englisch English **I**
englisch English **I**
englischsprachig English-speaking **I**
entdecken to discover **II U2**, 28
auf **Entdeckungsreise** gehen to explore **I**
Entfernung distance **II U3**, 60
eine Nachricht **entgegennehmen** *to take a
  message **I**
  einen Anruf **entgegennehmen** to answer
  the phone **I**
entgegnen to reply **I**
Entgegnung reply **I**
entlang along **I**
entlanggehen *to go down **I**
entrümpeln to clear out **I**
(sich) **entscheiden** to decide **I**
Entschuldigen Sie! Excuse me … **I**
Entschuldigung! Sorry!; Excuse me … **I**
entsetzt horrified **I**
sich **entspannen** to relax **II U2**, 36
entsprechen to match **I**
enttäuscht disappointed **I**
entwerfen to design **II U2**, 31
Entwurf plan; draft **I**; design **II U2**, 30
er he **I**
Erdboden earth **II U2**, 40
Erde world **I**; earth **II U2**, 40
  die **Erde** earth **II U2**, 40
Erdkunde geography **II U4**, 114
Ereignis event **I**
Erfahrung experience **II U4**, 69
erfinden to create **I**
erforschen to explore **I**
ergänzen to add **I**
Ergebnis result **II U5**, 97
ergreifen to grab **II U3**, 62
erhalten to receive **II U4**, 77
sich **erinnern** (an) to remember **I**
  Erinnerst du dich? Remember? **I**
  Erinnert ihr euch? Remember? **I**
Erinnerung memory **II U1**, 19
Erkältung cold **II U4**, 73
erklären to explain **I**
Erklärung statement **II AC2**, 88
erkunden to explore **I**
ernähren *to feed **II U6**, 119
ernst serious **I**
ernsthaft serious **I**
erraten to guess **I**

erreichen *to get to I; to reach II U5, 95
errichten *to put up II U2, 33
erschaffen to create I
erst only I
    erst wenn until II U4, 70
erstaunlich amazing II U1, 18
erste/-r/-s first I
    als Erstes first I
ertappt caught on camera II U1, 8
Erwachsene/-r adult II U3, 58
erwähnen to mention II AC2, 88
Ich kann es bis zum nächsten Mal kaum erwarten. I can't wait till next time. II U1, 10
erwidern to reply I
Erwiderung reply I
erzählen *to tell I
    erzählen von to talk about I
    nochmals erzählen *to retell I
    Erzähle mir von … Tell me about … I
Erzählung story, stories (pl) I
es it I
    Es ist super zum/für … It's great for … I
Essen food I; meal II U1, 18
(ein Bonbon) essen *to have (a sweet) I
essen *to eat I
etwa about I
etwas some; something; a little I
euer/eure your I
eure/-r/-s yours II U2, 41
Euro (Währung) euro I
Europa Europe II AC1, 48
ewig forever II U5, 93
Examen exam II U2, 28
extra extra I

F

Fackel torch II U1, 18
fähig sein zu *to be able to (do sth) II U5, 95
fahren *to go I; to travel II U3, 52
Fahrer/-in driver II U1, 13
einfache Fahrkarte one-way ticket; single ticket II U6, 112
Fahrplan timetable I
Fahrpreis fare II U6, 112
Fahrrad bike I
Fahrradmotocross bicycle motocross II U4, 83
Fahrschein ticket II U6, 111
Fahrt trip II U1, 9; tour II U3, 56; journey II U6, 109
fair fair I
Fakt fact II U2, 37
fallen *to fall I
    fallen (lassen) to drop II U3, 62
falls if I
falsch wrong I
fälschen to fake II U4, 76
Familie family I
Fan fan II U4, 83
fangen *to catch II U4, 68
Fantasie fantasy I

fantastisch fantastic II U2, 29
Fanzeitschrift fanzine II U2, 38
Farbe colour I
    Welche Farbe hat …? What colour is …? I
farbenfroh colourful I
Farm farm I
Farmer/-in farmer II U1, 13
fast nearly II U2, 41; almost II U4, 75
Fastnachtsdienstag Shrove Tuesday I
Februar February I
Federmäppchen pencil-case I
Feedback feedback II U2, 29
Was fehlt? What is missing? I
fehlend missing II U1, 13
Fehler mistake I
Feier party I
feiern to celebrate I
Feiertag holiday I
Feld field II U1, 18
felsig rocky II U6, 109
Fenster window I
Ferien holidays (pl) I
fernbleiben von to stay away from II U5, 97
(sich) fernhalten von *to keep away from II U6, 122
Fernsehen TV I
fernsehen to watch TV I
Fernseher TV I
fertig ready II U2, 41
Fertiggericht ready meal I
Fertigkeit skill I
fertigstellen to finish I
Fest festival I
festhalten *to hold I
Festival festival I
festnehmen to arrest II U1, 13
Feuerwerk fireworks (pl) I
Fieber fever II U4, 73
Figur character I; figure II U3, 51
Film film I
Filmemacher/-in filmmaker II U1, 24
finden *to find I
Finger finger I
Fisch fish, fish (pl) I
Fischen fishing II U6, 114
Fischerei fishing II U6, 114
fit werden *to get fit I
Fläche space II U2, 30; area II U4, 70
Flair flair II U3, 51
Flasche bottle I
Flohmarkt flea market I
Flughafen airport II AC1, 48
Flur hall II U6, 122
Fluss river I
    am Fluss by the river II U2, 31
flüstern to whisper I
Flut high tide II U3, 62
Flyer flyer I
folgen to follow II U3, 54
Form form I
    in Form kommen *to get fit I

verneinte Form negative form I
Formular form II U6, 112
hier: sich fortbewegen *to get around II U3, 53
fortfahren *to go on I
Forum forum II U5, 90
Foto photo; picture I
    auf dem Foto/den Fotos in the photo(s) I
    Fotos machen *to take photos I
Fotoapparat camera II U1, 8
Fotografie photo I
fotografieren *to take photos I
Fotostory photo story I
Frage question I
fragen to ask I
    Frage/Fragt nach … Ask about … I
    fragen nach to ask for I
Französisch French II U2, 32
französisch French II U2, 32
Frau woman, women (pl) I
Frau (Anrede) Mrs I
frei free I
Freiluft- outdoor II U1, 16
Freitag Friday I
Freizeit free time; leisure I
Freizeitzentrum leisure centre I
fremd strange I
Fremdsprache foreign language II U2, 38
fressen *to eat I
Freude fun I
Freudenfeuer bonfire I
sich freuen auf to look forward to II U2, 33
    sich freuen an to enjoy II U1, 12
Freund/-in friend I
    Dafür sind Freunde da. That's what friends are for. I
Freundin (in einer Paarbeziehung) girlfriend II U3, 54
freundlich friendly II U1, 14
Freundschaft friendship II U5, 94
    Freundschaft schließen *to make friends II U2, 43
frisch fresh I
uns frisieren *to do our hair I
froh happy I
fröhlich happy; fun I
Frucht fruit I
früh early I
Frühstück breakfast I
frühstücken *to have breakfast I
Frühstückszerealie cereal (no pl) I
Fuchs fox II U2, 34
fühlen *to feel I
    sich fühlen *to feel I
    sich ausgeschlossen fühlen *to feel left out II U5, 104
    sich schlecht fühlen *to feel sick II U4, 73
Führer/-in guide II U3, 56
Füller pen I
fünf five I
fünfzehn fifteen I
funktionieren to work II U5, 95

für mich on my own **II U2**, 40
    Für wen …? Who … for? **I**
Furcht fear **II U4**, 82
furchtbar awful **I**
Fuß foot, feet *(pl)* **I**
    zu **Fuß** on foot **II U3**, 60
Fußball football **I**
Fußboden floor **I**
Fußgelenk ankle **II U4**, 72
Fußknöchel ankle **II U4**, 72
füttern *to feed **II U6**, 119

G

Gälisch Gaelic **II U6**, 114
gälisch Gaelic **II U6**, 114
ganz all **I**
    den **ganzen** Tag all day **II U1**, 14
ganz whole **I**
Garage garage **I**
garstig nasty **II U5**, 91
Garten garden **I**
Gaststätte restaurant **I**
Geächtete/-r outlaw **II AC3**, 130
Gebäude building **I**
geben *to give **I**
    es **gibt** there is/are **I**
Gebiet area **II U4**, 70
gebrauchen to use **I**
gebrochen broken **I**
Gebühr fee **II U6**, 112
Geburtstag birthday **I**
    Alles Gute zum **Geburtstag**! Happy
    Birthday! **I**
    Herzlichen Glückwunsch zum **Geburtstag**!
    Happy Birthday! **I**
Gedächtnis memory **II U1**, 19
Gedicht poem **I**
gedruckt print **II U5**, 91
Sehr **geehrte** Dame, sehr **geehrter** Herr
    Dear Sir or Madam **II U6**, 113
gefährlich dangerous **I**
Mir **gefällt** … I like … **I**
Gefängnis prison **II U3**, 56
Gefühl feeling **II U1**, 9
gegen against **II U1**, 19
Gegend region **II AC2**, 89
sich **gegenseitig** each other **I**
gegenüber opposite **I**
Geheimnis secret **II U1**, 19
geheimnisvoll mysterious **II AC3**, 130
gehen *to go; to walk **I**
    ins Bett **gehen** *to go to bed **I**
    nach unten **gehen** *to go down **I**
    zu jmdm. nach Hause **gehen** *to go over
    to **II U5**, 95
    Wie **geht** es dir? How are you? **I**
    Wie **geht** es euch? How are you? **I**
    Wie **geht** es Ihnen? How are you? **I**
gehören (zu) to belong (to) **II U2**, 29
    gehören zu *to go with **I**
    zueinander **gehören** *to go together **I**

Geist ghost **II U2**, 30
gelangweilt bored **I**
gelb yellow **I**
Geld money **I**
    Geld sammeln to raise money **II U1**, 10
    Geld verdienen *to make money **I**
Gelee jelly **I**
Gelegenheit chance **II U5**, 100
Gemälde painting **II U2**, 28
gemein nasty **II U5**, 91
Gemeindezentrum community centre **I**
gemeinsam together **I**
genau exactly **II AC2**, 88
    genau hier right here **II U4**, 70
Genie genius **II U5**, 95
genießen to enjoy **II U1**, 12
genug enough **I**
genügend enough **I**
Geocaching geocaching **II U6**, 119
geöffnet open **I**
Geografie geography **II U6**, 114
gerade just; at the moment **I**; right now
    II U5, 103
geradeaus straight on **I**
Gerät machine **I**; tool **II U6**, 123
Geräusch sound **I**; noise **II U1**, 18
gerecht fair **I**
Gern geschehen. You're welcome. **I**
    gern haben to like **I**
    gern mögen to love **I**
    hätte/-st/-n/-t **gern** would like **I**
    hätte/-st-/-n/-t sehr **gern** would love **I**
    würde/-st/-n/-t **gern** would like **I**
    würde/-st/-n/-t sehr **gern** would love **I**
Gerümpel rubbish **I**
Geschäft shop **I**
geschehen to happen **I**
Geschenk present **I**
Geschichte story, stories *(pl)* **I**; history
    II U2, 30
geschichtlich historical **I**
Geschick skill **I**
Gesellschaft society **II U6**, 123
Gesetzlose/-r outlaw **II AC3**, 130
Gesicht face **I**
Gespräch dialogue; conversation **I**
Gestalt figure **II U3**, 51
gestalten to design **II U2**, 31
Gestaltung design **II U2**, 30
gestern yesterday **II U1**, 11
gesund healthy **I**
Gesundheit health **II U4**, 69
Getränk drink **I**
getrennt separate **II U1**, 16
gewaltig huge **II AC1**, 48
Gewinn prize **I**
gewinnen *to win **I**
Gewinner/-in winner **I**
gewöhnlich usually **I**
Gitter grid **I**
glänzen *to shine **II U2**, 33
Glas glass **I**

glauben *to think; to believe **I**
gläubig religious **I**
der/die/das **gleiche** the same **I**
gleich right away **I**
    jetzt **gleich** right now **II U5**, 103
gleichmäßig regular **I**
gleichzeitig at the same time **I**
Glocke bell **II AC1**, 48
Glück haben *to be lucky **II U3**, 62
    … hat/haben **Glück**. … is/are lucky. **I**
glücklich happy **I**
Glücksbringer lucky charm **I**
Golf golf **II U6**, 114
Götterspeise jelly **I**
graben *to dig **II U2**, 33
grau grey **I**
grausam cruel **II AC3**, 130
greifen to grab **II U3**, 62
Griff knob **II U5**, 95
groß big **I**; tall; high **II U1**, 17; large **II AC1**, 48
großartig great **I**; fantastic **II U2**, 29
Großbritannien Britain **I**
Großbuchstabe capital letter **I**
Größe size **I**
Großeltern grandparents *(pl)* **I**
Großstadt city **I**
grün green **I**
Grund reason **II U4**, 82
Grund- basic **II U3**, 59
grundlegend basic **II U3**, 59
Grundschule primary school **I**
Gruppe group **I**; team **II U1**, 8
gruselig scary **II U1**, 24
Gruß greeting **I**
    Grüße ausrichten (an) *to say hello (to) **I**
    Herzliche **Grüße** Best wishes **II U6**, 113
    Herzliche **Grüße** (am Briefende) Love … **I**
    Liebe **Grüße** (am Briefende) Love … **I**
    Viele **Grüße** Best wishes **II U6**, 113
    Viele **Grüße** … (am Ende von Briefen und
    Mails) Yours … **II U5**, 99
grüßen *to say hello (to) **I**
gut good; fine **I**
    gut sein in *to be good at **I**
    Guten Morgen. Good morning. **I**
    Mir geht's **gut**. I'm fine. **I**
Guthaben credit **II U3**, 52
Gymnasium grammar school **II U6**, 113

H

unsere **Haare** machen *to do our hair **I**
haben *to have got; *to have **I**
    hätte/-st/-n/-t gern would like **I**
    hätte/-st-/-n/-t sehr gern would love **I**
Hafen harbour **II U6**, 109
Hafendamm pier **I**
Hähnchen chicken **I**
halb (bei Uhrzeitangaben) half past **I**
halb half **I**
Halbjahresferien half-term break **I**
Halbschwester half-sister **I**

die **Hälfte** half, halves *(pl)* (of) **I**
Halle hall **II U2**, 29
Hallo. Hello.; Hi.; Hey! **I**
Halt stop **II U3**, 53
halten *to hold; *to keep **I**
   halten von *to think of **I**
Haltestelle station **I**; stop **II U3**, 53
Hamburger burger **I**
Hammer hammer **II U2**, 34
Hand hand **I**
   Klatsch/Klatscht in die **Hände**. Clap your hands. **I**
Handbuch planner **I**
   Handbuch für TTS-Schülerinnen und -Schüler TTS planner **I**
sich **handeln** um *to be about **I**
Handgelenk wrist **II U3**, 62
Händler merchant **II AC2**, 89
Handlung action **I**
Handlungsort location **II U3**, 58
Handschuh glove **I**
Handy phone **I**; mobile **II U5**, 91
hart hard **II U1**, 12
hassen to hate **II U2**, 42
häufig often **I**
   häufig gefragt frequently asked **I**
Haupt- main **I**
Hauptstadt capital **II AC1**, 48
Hauptwort noun **I**
Haus house **I**
   nach **Hause** home **I**
   zu **Hause** at home **I**
   zu jmdm. nach **Hause** gehen *to go over to **II U5**, 95
Hausaufgabe(n) homework **I**
Haustier pet **I**
Haustür front door **II U5**, 102
He! Hey! **I**
Heim home **I**
heimlich in secret **II U4**, 81
Ich **heiße** … My name is … **I**
   Wie **heißen** Sie? What's your name? **I**
   Wie **heißt** du? What's your name? **I**
Held hero, heroes *(pl)* **II AC3**, 130
Heldin heroine **II AC3**, 130
helfen to help **I**
heraus out **I**
herausfinden *to find; *to find out **I**
Herausforderung challenge **II U1**, 16
Herd cooker **I**
herein in **I**
hereinkommen *to come in **II U6**, 122
Herr *(Anrede)* Mr **I**
   Herr der Raben raven master **II U3**, 56
Sehr geehrte Dame, sehr geehrter **Herr** Dear Sir or Madam **II U6**, 113
herrschen to rule **II U6**, 116
um … **herum** around **I**
herumschleichen to sneak around **II U1**, 24
herunter down **II U3**, 62
herunterfallen *to fall off **II U2**, 34
herunterkommen *to come down **I**

herunterladen *(aus dem Internet)* to download **II U5**, 97
herunternehmen *to take off **I**
herunterrollen to roll off **II U3**, 62
Herz heart **II U3**, 62
Herzliche Grüße Best wishes **II U6**, 113
   Herzliche Grüße *(am Briefende)* Love … **I**
heute today **I**
   heute Abend 2nite *(= tonight)* **I**
   heute Nachmittag this afternoon **II U3**, 52
Hi. Hi.; Hey! **I**
hier here **I**
   genau **hier** right here **II U4**, 70
   Hier ist … Here's … **I**
Highlight highlight **II U1**, 9
Hilfe help **I**
   ohne fremde **Hilfe** alone **I**
hilflos helpless **I**
hilfreich useful; helpful **I**
hilfsbereit helpful **I**
hinauf up **II U5**, 94
hinaus out **I**
hinausfließen to flow out **II U3**, 62
hinausgehen *to go out **II U6**, 122
hinein inside **I**
hineingehen to enter **II U2**, 40
hineingelangen *to get into **I**
Hin- und Rückfahrkarte return ticket **II U6**, 112
hinfallen *to fall over; *to fall **I**
hinkommen *to get there **I**
Lege/Legt … umgedreht **hin**. Put … face down. **I**
sich **hinsetzen** *to sit down **I**
hinter behind **I**
Hintergrund background **I**
hinterhergehen to follow **II U3**, 54
hinüber over; across **I**
hinübergehen zu *to go over to **II U5**, 95
hinunter down **II U3**, 62
hinunterfallen *to fall off **II U2**, 34
hinuntergehen *to go down **I**
hinunterrollen to roll off **II U3**, 62
Hinweis clue **II U1**, 13
hinzufügen to add **I**
historisch historical **I**
Hobby hobby, hobbies *(pl)* **I**
hoch tall; high **II U1**, 17
hochleben lassen *to give the bumps **I**
Hochzeit wedding **I**
Hockey hockey **II U4**, 69
hoffen to hope **I**
Hoffnung hope **II U4**, 82
hoffnungsvoll hopeful **I**
höflich polite **I**
   Sei/Seid **höflich**. Be polite. **I**
Höhepunkt highlight **II U1**, 9
Höhle cave **II U6**, 119
holen *to get **I**
Homepage homepage **I**
Hoppla! Oops! **I**
Hör- audio **I**

horchen auf to listen for **I**
Hören listening **I**
hören *to hear **I**
   Ich habe **gehört**, dass … I hear … **I**
Hör-/Sehverstehen viewing **I**
Hose trousers *(pl)* **II U6**, 122
   kurze **Hose** shorts *(pl)* **II U4**, 75
Hospital hospital **II U2**, 30
Hotel hotel **II U2**, 33
hübsch beautiful **II U2**, 30
Huch! Oops! **I**
Hügel hill **II U6**, 122
Huhn chicken **I**
Hülle wrapping **I**
Hund dog **I**
   den **Hund** ausführen to walk the dog **I**
   mit dem **Hund** spazieren gehen to walk the dog **I**
Ich bin **hundemüde**. I'm dog-tired. **I**
hungrig hungry **I**
Husten cough **II U4**, 73
Hut hat **I**
hüten to look after **I**

I

ich I; me **I**
   Ich bin aus … I'm from … **I**
   Ich bin Engländer/-in. I'm English. **I**
   Ich bin … I'm … **I**
   Ich heiße … My name is … **I**
   Ich mache … nicht gern. I don't like … **I**
   Ich mag … nicht. I don't like … **I**
   Ich möchte … I'd like to … *(= I would like to)* **I**
   Ich weiß (es) nicht! I don't know! **I**
   Ich würde gern … I'd like to … *(= I would like to)* **I**
Idee idea **I**
Identität identity **II AC1**, 49
Idiot/-in idiot **II U2**, 41
ihm him **I**
ihn him **I**
ihnen them **I**
ihr you; u *(= you)* **I**
Ihr/-e your **I**; yours **II U2**, 41
ihr/-e her; its **I**
ihr/-e *(Pl.)* their **I**
   Ihr wisst, wie man … You know how to … **I**
im in; on **I**
   im Innern inside **I**
   im Moment at the moment **I**
   im Weg sein/stehen *to be in the way **I**
Imbiss snack **I**
Imbissstube snack bar **I**
immer always **I**
   für **immer** forever **II U5**, 93
   immer noch still **I**
immerhin after all **I**
in in; on; at; to; into; inside **I**
   in Cornwall Cornish **II U6**, 110

in der Nähe von near I
in der Straße in the street I
in Not in need II U1, 10
in … hinein into I
in Ordnung OK; fine I
indem as I
Inder/-in Indian I
indisch Indian I
individuell individual II U4, 69
Infinitiv infinitive I
Information information *(no pl)* I
Informationen information *(no pl)* I
Inlineskates fahren to skate I
Inlineskatefahren inline skating I
Inlineskates skates *(pl)* I
innen inside I
Insel island II U6, 109
Installateur/-in plumber II U6, 122
Instruktion instruction I
interessant interesting I
Interesse interest II U5, 90
sich **interessieren** (für) to care (about)
II U5, 93
sich **interessieren** für *to be interested in
II U2, 31
interessiert sein an *to be interested in
II U2, 31
Interkulturelles Across cultures I
international international I; multi-ethnic
II AC1, 48
Internet internet I
Internetauftritt website I
Interview interview I
interviewen to interview I
irgendein/-e/-er any I
irgendwelche any I
irgendwo anywhere II U3, 54; somewhere
II U3, 65
Irisch Irish II U6, 114
irisch Irish II U6, 114
sich **irren** *to be wrong I
Italien Italy II U5, 96

J

ja yes; yeah *(infml)* I
jagen to chase I
Jahr year I
Jahrbuch yearbook II U1, 8
Jahrhundert century II U3, 62
18-jährig 18-year-old II U3, 52
11-Jährige/-r 11-year-old II U4, 70
Januar January I
je … desto the … the II U4, 68
jedenfalls anyway II U3, 62
jede/-r/-s every; each I
jeder everyone I; everybody II U3, 54
jede Menge lots (of) I
jedes Mal, wenn whenever II U5, 92
jemals ever II U2, 33
jemand somebody I; someone II U1, 13
jemand anderes anyone else II U2, 40

jene those I
jenes that I
jetzt now I
jetzt gleich right now II U5, 103
Job job I
Joghurt yoghurt I
Jonglieren juggling II U2, 38
jubeln to cheer II U4, 72
Jugend- teen II U5, 92
Jugendliche/-r teenager I
Juli July I
jung young I
Junge boy I
Juni June I

K

Kaffee coffee I
Kalender planner I
kalt cold II U1, 18
kalt stellen *to leave it to cool I
Kamelrennen camel racing II U4, 68
Kamera camera II U1, 8
mit der Kamera festgehalten caught on
camera II U1, 8
Kamin chimney II U6, 122
Kampf fight II U2, 41
kämpfen *to fight II U5, 102
Kanada Canada I
Kaninchen rabbit I
Kapitän/-in captain I
Kapitel unit I
kaputt broken I
Karneval carnival II AC1, 48
Karotte carrot I
Karte card I
Kartoffelchip crisp *(BE)* I
Käse cheese I
Kasten box I
Katastrophe disaster II U5, 102
Katze cat I
kaufen *to buy; *to get I
Käufer/-in buyer I
Kaufmann merchant II AC2, 89
keine Ahnung no idea II U1, 19
Keine Sorge! Don't worry! I
kein/-e no; not … any I
Keks biscuit I
keltisch Celtic II U1, 16
kennen *to know I
kennen lernen *to get to know II U6, 114
Kerl guy II U1, 9
Kerze candle I
Kerzenlicht candlelight *(no pl)* II U5, 103
Kfz-Mechaniker/-in mechanic II U1, 13
Kind child, children *(pl)* I
Kino cinema I
Kirche church I
Kiste box I
Klang sound I
klar clear I
Klasse group; class I

Ausstellung in der Klasse class display I
Klasse *(in einer englischen Schule)* tutor
group I
Klassenarbeit test I
Klassenkamerad/-in classmate I
Klassenlehrer/-in tutor I
Klassenposter class poster I
Klassenzimmer classroom I
klatschen to clap I
Klatsch/Klatscht in die Hände. Clap your
hands. I
Kleider clothes *(pl)* I
Kleidergröße size I
Kleiderschrank wardrobe I
Kleidung clothes *(pl)* I; outfit II U1, 8
klein small; little I
Klempner/-in plumber II U6, 122
Klettern climbing II U1, 16
klettern to climb I
Klick click II U5, 103
Klicken click II U5, 103
klingeln *to ring I
klingen to sound I
Klub club I
klug clever II U2, 41
knapp close I
Das war knapp! That was close! I
sich den Knöchel verrenken to twist your
ankle II U4, 72
Koch-AG Cooking Club I
Kochen cooking I
kochen to cook II U5, 103
Kokosnuss coconut II U3, 63
Kollektion collection II U1, 10
Köln Cologne I
Kolonie colony II AC2, 89
komfortabel comfortable II U3, 65
Komiker/-in comedian II U1, 10
kommen *to come I
kommen nach *to get to I
kommen zu *to get to I
Komm jetzt! Come on! I
Komm schon! Come on! I
Kommentar comment II U1, 12
kommentieren to comment (on) II U5, 97
kommunizieren to communicate II AC2, 89
Kompromiss compromise II U5, 93
König king I
Königin queen II U2, 30
königlich royal I
königlicher Leibgardist Beefeater
II U3, 56
können can I; *to be able to (do sth)
II U5, 95
kann nicht can't I; cannot II U5, 95
können nicht can't I; cannot II U5, 95
könnte/-n could II U2, 40
(vielleicht) können may II U5, 95
Kannst du … nennen? Can you
name …? I
konnte/-n could II U5, 95
Kontakt contact II U2, 37

in **Kontakt** bleiben (mit) to stay in touch (with) II **U5**, 90
kontrollieren to check I
Konversation conversation I
Konzept draft I
Kopf head I
Kopfhörer headphones *(pl)* II **U5**, 102
Kopfschmerzen headache *(no pl)* II **U4**, 73
Kopfweh headache *(no pl)* II **U4**, 73
kopieren to copy I
Korbball netball I
Koreaner/-in Korean II **U4**, 76
Koreanisch Korean II **U4**, 76
koreanisch Korean II **U4**, 76
menschlicher **Körper** human body II **U3**, 62
korrekt correct; right I
Korridor hall II **U6**, 122
Korrigiere/**Korrigiert** … Correct … I
kosten *to cost I
Es **kostet** …/Sie **kosten** … It's …/ They're … I
Wie viel **kostet**/**kosten** …? How much is/ are …? I
kostenlos free I
Kostüm costume I; fancy dress II **U4**, 80
Kraft power II **AC3**, 130
die **Kraft** der Wörter *(Wortschatzübung)* Word power I
Krakau Cracow I
Krampf cramp II **U4**, 74
krank sick II **U4**, 73
Krankenhaus hospital II **U2**, 30
kreativ creative I
Kreis circle I
kreischen to scream II **U3**, 63
Kreuz cross II **U6**, 114
kreuzen to cross II **AC2**, 89
Krieger warrior II **U6**, 123
Kriminalität crime II **AC3**, 130
Kriminelle/-r criminal II **AC3**, 130
Kronjuwelen crown jewels II **U3**, 56
Küche kitchen I
Kuchen cake; pie I
Küchenschrank cupboard I
Kuh cow II **U6**, 119
Kühlschrank fridge I
Kultur culture I
Kummerkastentante agony aunt II **U5**, 92
sich **kümmern** (um) to care (about) II **U5**, 93
sich **kümmern** um to look after I
Kunde/**Kundin** customer II **U6**, 116
Kunst art II **U2**, 29
Kunstunterricht Art I
Kurs course II **U1**, 16
kurz short I
Kurzantwort short answer I
Kurzform short form I
Kurznachricht text (message) I
Küste shore II **U3**, 62; coastline II **U6**, 114
Küstenverlauf coastline II **U6**, 114
Küstenweg coastal path II **U6**, 122

L

Lächeln smile I
lächeln to smile I
lachen to laugh I
Laden shop I
Lage location II **U3**, 58
Lagerfeuer bonfire I
Lamm lamb I
Lämmchen lamb I
Lampe light II **U5**, 102
Land country, countries *(pl)*; land I; countryside II **U6**, 110
landen to end up II **U1**, 8; to land II **U4**, 78
landesweit national I
Landkarte map I
Landschaft landscape II **U6**, 108
Landwirt/-in farmer II **U1**, 13
lang long I
(nicht) **länger** (not) any longer II **U6**, 110
… **lang** for … II **U1**, 12
langsam slow I
langweilig boring I
Laptop laptop II **U5**, 97
Lärm noise II **U1**, 18
lassen *to let I; *to leave II **U2**, 30
Lass/**Lasst** uns … Let's … I
Lassi lassi I
Lauf run II **U4**, 70
Laufen running II **U4**, 70
laufen *to run; to walk I; *to be on II **U5**, 102
Läufer/-in runner II **U4**, 68
Laune mood II **U1**, 24
laut loud I
läuten *to ring I
Leben life, lives *(pl)* II **U2**, 39
leben to live I
lebendig lively II **U2**, 29
Lebensmittel food I
legen *to put I
Lege/**Legt** es in … Put it in … I
Legende legend II **AC3**, 130
jmdm. eine **Lehre**/**Lektion** erteilen *to teach somebody a lesson II **U4**, 76
lehren *to teach II **U4**, 76
Lehrer/-in teacher I; instructor II **U1**, 18
königlicher **Leibgardist** Beefeater II **U3**, 56
leicht easy I
leid tun *to be sorry I
Tut mir **leid**! Sorry!; I'm sorry! I
leise quiet I
Leiter ladder II **U2**, 34
Lektion unit I
jmdm. eine Lehre/**Lektion** erteilen *to teach somebody a lesson II **U4**, 76
Lernen studies *(pl)* II **U2**, 28
lernen *to learn I
viel zu **lernen** a lot to learn I
auswendig **lernen** *to learn … by heart I
Lesen reading I
vor dem **Lesen** pre-reading I
lesen *to read I

Leser/-in reader I
letzte/-r/-s last I
letztlich finally II **U2**, 31
Leute people *(pl)* I
Licht light II **U5**, 102
lieb nice I
Lieber … Dear … I
Liebe … *(Anrede in Briefen)* Dear … I
Liebe Grüße *(am Briefende)* Love … I
Liebe love II **U6**, 119
lieben to love I
Ich **liebe** dich. I love you. I
Ich **liebe** … I love … I
lieber better I
Lieblings- favourite I
Mein/e **Lieblings** … My favourite … I
Was ist dein/-e **Lieblings**…? What's your favourite …? I
Lied song I
liegen *to lie II **U2**, 40
lila purple I
Limonade lemonade I
Lineal ruler I
Linie line I
Link link II **U3**, 59
linke/-r/-s left I
links on the left; left I
auf der **linken** Seite on the left I
Liste list I
Loch hole II **U2**, 33
lokal local II **U6**, 115
LOL LOL (= laughing out loud) II **U1**, 8
Londoner/-in Londoner I
Los ticket I
lösen to solve II **U6**, 122
losgehen *to leave II **U4**, 72
loslassen *to let go (of) II **U4**, 80
Lösung solution II **U1**, 13
Löwe lion II **U3**, 56
Lücke gap I
lügen to lie II **U1**, 9
lustig funny; fun I

M

Maat mate I
machen *to do; *to make I
Fotos **machen** *to take photos I
sich Notizen **machen** *to take notes I
Machst du so …? Is this how you (do) …? I
Macht power II **AC3**, 130
mächtig powerful II **AC3**, 130
Mädchen girl I
ein **Mädchen** aus Deutschland a girl from Germany I
Magen stomach II **U4**, 80
magisch magical II **AC3**, 130
Mahlzeit meal II **U1**, 18
Mai May I
mailen to mail II **U5**, 97
Mal time II **U1**, 10

malen to paint I
Malerei painting II U2, 28
Mama mum I
manchmal sometimes I
Manga (japanischer Comic) manga II U2, 38
Mango mango I
Mann man, men (pl) I
   wie der **Mann** aussah what the man
   looked like II U1, 13
Mannschaftsführer/-in captain I
Mäppchen pencil-case I
Mappe folder I
Marathon marathon II U4, 68
Markt market I
März March I
Maschine machine I
Match match II U4, 68
Material material II U3, 61
Mathe Maths II U2, 32
Mathematik Maths II U2, 32
Matrose sailor I
Mauer wall I
Maus/Mäuse mouse (sg), mice (pl) I
Mechaniker/-in mechanic II U1, 13
Medien media II U5, 91
Meer sea I
Meerschweinchen guinea pig I
mehr more I
   (nicht) **mehr** (not) any longer II U6, 110
   mehr … als more … than I
Mehrzahl plural I
meiden to stay away from II U5, 97
Meile (brit. Längenmaß) mile II U4, 72
mein/-e my I
   Mein/e Lieblings… My favourite … I
mein/-er/-e/-es mine II U2, 41
meinen *to mean II U3, 54
Meinung opinion II U5, 92
die **meisten** (the) most I
   der/die/das **meiste** (the) most I
meistens usually I
Meldung report II U1, 9
melken to milk II U6, 119
eine **Menge** a lot of I
   jede **Menge** lots (of) I
Mensch person, people (pl) I
Menschen people (pl) I
Menschenmenge crowd II U3, 58
menschlicher Körper human body II U3, 62
sich **merken** to remember I
merkwürdig strange I; weird II U5, 99
Meter metre II U3, 62
mich me I
Milch milk I
Million million II AC1, 48
   Ich habe das schon eine **Million** Mal
   gemacht. I've done this a million times
   before. II U5, 95
Mine mine II U6, 122
Mini- mini II U4, 70
Minute minute I
mir me I

Mir geht's gut. I'm fine. I
mit with I
mit (dem Fahrrad) by (bike) I
mitbringen *to bring; *to take I
miteinander together I
Mitglied member II U2, 33
mithalten (mit) *to keep up (with) II U4, 80
hier: **mitmachen** to enter II U2, 40
mitmachen *to be in II U4, 70
mitnehmen *to take I
Mitschüler/-in classmate I
Mitspieler/-in player II U4, 75
Mittagessen lunch I
Mittagspause lunch break I
Mitte middle I
mitteilen *to tell I
mittelalterlich medieval II U6, 108
Mittwoch Wednesday I
Mobiltelefon mobile II U5, 91
Mode fashion II U2, 28
Model model I
Modell model I
Moderator/-in presenter I
modern modern II U3, 64
mögen to like; *to be into; to want (to) I
   gern **mögen** to love I
   nicht **mögen** to hate II U2, 42
   Du **magst** … You're into … I
   Ich **mag** dich. I love you. I
   Ich **mag** … I like … I
   Ich **mag** … nicht. I don't like … I
   Ich **mag** … total gern. I love … I
   Ich **möchte** … I'd like to … (= I would
   like to) I
möglich possible I
möglicherweise probably II U3, 52
Möglichkeit chance II U5, 100
Möhre carrot I
Moment moment II U2, 40
   im **Moment** at the moment I
Monat month II U1, 10
Monster monster I
Montag Monday I
montags on Mondays I
Monument monument II U6, 114
Morgen morning I
   Guten **Morgen**. Good morning. I
morgen tomorrow I
morgens in the mornings I
motivieren to motivate I
Motto theme I
Mountainbikefahren mountain biking
   II U6, 109
müde tired I
Müll rubbish I
Mund mouth I
Training für den **Mund** mouth jogging I
Münze coin I
Museum museum I
Museumsrundgang gallery walk I
Musik music I
Musiker/-in musician II U3, 53

müssen must I; *to have to II U2, 40
(**tun**) **müssen** to need (to do) I
   nicht **müssen** needn't I
mutig brave I
Mutter mother I
Muttersprache first language II AC2, 89
mysteriös mysterious II AC3, 130

N

nach unten down II U3, 62
nach to I
   nach draußen outside; out I
   nach drinnen inside I
   nach Hause home I
   nach oben up II U5, 94; upstairs II U5, 102
   nach unten downstairs II U5, 102
nach (bei Uhrzeitangaben) past I
nach (zeitlich) after I
Nachbar/-in neighbour (BE) I
nachdenken *to think I
   Warte/Wartet und **denk/denkt nach**. Stop
   and think I
nacherzählen *to retell I
nachjagen to chase I
Nachmittag afternoon I
   heute **Nachmittag** this afternoon II U3, 52
nachmittags (Uhrzeit) p.m. I
Nachricht message I
   eine **Nachricht** entgegennehmen *to take
   a message I
   eine **Nachricht** hinterlassen *to leave a
   message I
Nachrichten news (sg) II U2, 40
nachschauen to look up I
nachschlagen to look up I
nachspüren to trace I
nächste/-r/-s next I
   der/die **Nächste(n)** next I
   als **Nächstes** next I
   am **nächsten** Tag the next day II U1, 11
Nacht night I
   die ganze **Nacht** all night I
Nachtisch pudding I
Nachtwanderung night walk II U1, 18
in der **Nähe** von near I
nahe near I; close II U3, 56
Name name I
Namenstag name day I
Nase nose II U1, 8
nass wet II U3, 62
national national I
Natur nature II U2, 43
natürlich of course I
Naturwissenschaften Science II U2, 32
neben next to I; besides II U6, 114; by
   II U6, 122
negativ negative II U6, 108
(ein Bonbon) **nehmen** *to have (a sweet) I
nehmen *to take I
neidisch sein (auf) *to be jealous (of) I
nein no I

benennen to name I
  Kannst du … nennen? Can you name …? I
nennen to name; to call I
jemandem auf die Nerven gehen *to get on
  people's nerves I
nervös nervous II U1, 12
nett nice I; friendly II U1, 14
Netz net II U4, 68
soziales Netzwerk social network II U5, 91
neu new I
Neuigkeiten news (sg) II U2, 40
neun nine I
nicht not I
  nicht mehr not any more I
  nicht mögen to hate II U2, 42
  noch nicht not … yet II U4, 72
nicht- non- II U1, 10
nichts nothing; not … anything I
  Nichts zu danken. You're welcome. I
nie never I
niedlich cute I
niedrig low II U1, 17
niemals never I
niemand nobody II U2, 41
  niemand anderes nobody else II U6, 124
nirgendwo nowhere II U6, 110
nirgendwohin nowhere II U6, 110
noch still I; yet II U4, 72
  noch ein/-e another I
  noch einmal again I
  noch mal again I
  noch nicht not … yet II U4, 72
Nomen noun I
Nord- north II U3, 53
Norden north II U3, 53
Nordsee North Sea II U6, 109
normal normal II U3, 58
normalerweise usually I
in Not in need II U1, 10
Notiz note I
  Notizen machen *to make notes I
  sich Notizen machen *to take notes I
November November I
Nudeln pasta I
null zero I
null (bei Telefonnummern und Uhrzeitangaben) oh I
Nullmeridian Meridian Line I
Nummer number I
nun now I
nun well I
nur only; just I
Nuss nut I
nützlich useful I
  nützliche Ausdrücke Useful phrases I

O

O! Oh! I
o.k. OK I
ob if I
oben on top I; upstairs II U5, 102

nach oben up II U5, 94
obendrauf on top I
oberer Teil top I
  oberes Ende top I
im Obergeschoss upstairs II U5, 102
Obst fruit I
oder or I
offen open I
öffentlich public II U3, 52
offline offline II U5, 103
öffnen to open I
oft often I
  so oft whenever II U5, 92
ohne without I
  ohne fremde Hilfe alone I
Oje! Oh dear! II U6, 122
Öko- Eco II U2, 33
Oktober October I
Oma grandma; granny I
Onkel uncle I
online stellen to post II U5, 90
online online II U1, 21
Opa grandad I
Orange orange I
orange orange I
Ordner folder I
Ordnung order I
  in Ordnung fine I
  in Ordnung bringen to tidy (a room) I
organisieren to organise I
Ort place I; space II U2, 30
örtlich local II U6, 115
Ost- east I
Osten east I
Ostern Easter I
Österreich Austria II U4, 71
Outdoor- outdoor II U1, 16
Outfit outfit II U1, 8

P

Paar pair I; couple II U6, 116
ein paar some; a few; a couple of I
Päckchen packet; parcel I
Packung packet I
Paket packet; parcel I
Palme palm tree II U6, 109
panisch werden to panic II U2, 36
Papa dad I
Papier paper I
  Stück Papier piece of paper I
Paradies paradise II U5, 90
Park park I
Partner/-in partner I
Party party I
passen zu *to go with; to match I
  zueinander passen *to go together I
passieren to happen I
Pasta pasta I
Pastete pie I
Pause break II U2, 40
PC PC (= Personal Computer) II AC2, 89

Pech haben *to be unlucky I
peinlich embarrassing II U1, 8
Pence (brit. Währungseinheit) penny, pence
  (pl) I
Peng! Bang! II U5, 102
Penny (brit. Währungseinheit) penny, pence
  (pl) I
perfekt perfect I
Person person, people (pl) I
  pro Person each I
hier: persönlich face-to-face II U5, 93
persönlich personal I
Perspektive point of view II U4, 76
Pferd horse I
Pflanze plant II U6, 114
pflanzen to plant II U2, 41
Pfund (brit. Währungseinheit) pound (£) I
Picknick picnic I
Pick-up pick-up I
Pier pier I
Pille pill II U4, 73
Pilot/-in pilot II U2, 36
pink pink I
Pizza pizza I
Placemat placemat I
Platzdeckchen placemat I
Plan plan I
planen to plan I
Planet planet II U1, 18
Plattform platform II U6, 112
Platz place I; space II U2, 30; pitch II U4, 68
Platz! (Befehl für Hunde) Sit! I
plaudern to chat I
plötzlich suddenly I
Plural plural I
Polen Poland I
Polizei police II U1, 13
Polizeibeamter police officer II U2, 36
Pommes frites chips (pl) (BE) I
Pony pony I
Ponyreiten im Gelände pony trekking
  II U6, 109
populär popular I
Porträt profile I
positiv positive II U2, 29
Possessivform possessive form I
Post (Eintrag im Internet) post I
Poster poster I
Postkarte postcard II U6, 124
praktisch practical II U5, 91
Präposition preposition I
Präsentation presentation I
präsentieren to present I
Praxis surgery I
Praxisräume surgery I
Preis price; prize I; award II U4, 74
preiswert cheap I
pressen to press II U5, 102
Privatdetektiv/-in private detective
  II AC3, 130
pro per II U6, 111
  pro Person each I

pro Stück each I
probieren to try I
   Probier mal … Try … I
Problem problem I
Probleme trouble II U1, 19
Profil profile I
Programm programme II U4, 68
Projekt project I
Prospekt brochure I
prüfen to check I
Prüfung test I; exam II U2, 28
Publikum audience II U2, 37
Pudding pudding I
Punkt point II U4, 68
Punktestand score II U4, 68
pünktlich on time II U2, 37
Puzzle puzzle I
Pyjama pyjamas II U1, 12

Q

Qualifikation trial II U4, 70
Qualität quality I
quer durch across I
Quiz quiz I

R

Rabe raven II U3, 56
   Herr der **Raben** raven master II U3, 56
Rad wheel I
Radfahren cycling I
Radiergummi rubber I
Radio radio II U4, 68
Rahmen set II AC3, 131
Rap rap I
rappen to rap I
Raster grid I
Rat advice II U2, 36
raten to guess I
Ratschlag tip I; advice II U2, 36
Rätsel puzzle; quiz I
Ratte rat I
Räuber/-in robber II AC3, 130
Raum room I; space II U2, 30
Raumschiff spaceship II U1, 22
Reaktion reaction II U2, 29
realistisch realistic II U3, 61
recht haben *to be right I
rechte/-r/-s right I
rechts on the right; right I
   auf der **rechten** Seite on the right I
Rechtschreibung spelling I
Recycling recycling II U2, 40
reden to talk I
   reden mit to talk to I
Redewendung phrase I
Redner/-in speaker I
Regel rule I
   Was ist die **Regel** für …? What's the rule for …? I
regelmäßig regular I

regieren to rule II U6, 116
Region region II AC2, 89
regnen to rain II U5, 102
die **Reichen** the rich II AC3, 131
Reihenfolge order I
Reim rhyme I
rein in I
reinigen to clean I
Reise trip II U1, 9; travel II U1, 20; journey II U6, 109
Reisebericht travel report II U1, 20
Reisebüro travel agent's II U6, 111
Reisebus coach II U1, 13
Reiseführer guide II U3, 56
(das) **Reisen** travel II U1, 20
reisen to travel II U3, 52
Religion (Schulfach) RE (= Religious Education) II U2, 32
religiös religious I
Rennen race II U4, 68; running; run II U4, 70
rennen *to run I
reparieren to fix II U5, 95
Reporter/-in reporter II U4, 75
Requisite prop II AC3, 131
reservieren to book II U6, 112
der **Rest** the rest I
Restaurant restaurant I
Resultat result II U5, 97
retten to save I
Rettung rescue II U4, 77
Rettungsboot lifeboat I
Rettungsring lifebuoy I
Rezept (für Arzneimittel) prescription II U4, 73
Rhythmus rhythm I
richtig correct; right I; real II U1, 10
Richtung direction I
   in **Richtung** towards II U3, 62
riesengroß huge II AC1, 48
riesig huge; large II AC1, 48
Ring circle I
Ritter knight II AC3, 130
Rock skirt II U6, 122
Rock 'n' Roll rock 'n' roll II AC2, 89
Rohr pipe II U2, 34
Rohrleitung pipe II U2, 34
Rolle role I
   Rollen tauschen to swap roles I
Rollenspiel role play I
Rollschuhe skates (pl) I
Rollstuhl wheelchair II U3, 53
Rolltreppe escalator I
Römer/-in Roman II AC1, 48
römisch Roman II AC1, 48
rosa pink I
rot red I
Route route II U1, 16
Rücken an **Rücken** back to back I
Rückenschmerzen backache II U4, 73
Rückenweh backache II U4, 73
Hin- und **Rückfahrkarte** return ticket II U6, 112

Rückmeldung feedback II U2, 29
rufen to shout; to call I; to cry II U5, 102
Rugby rugby II U4, 68
ruhig quiet I
Rühr- sponge I
ruinieren to ruin II U4, 81
Rumäne/Rumänin Romanian II AC2, 88
Rumänisch Romanian II AC2, 88
rumänisch Romanian II AC2, 88
Runde round II U1, 8
Rundgang tour II U3, 56
Rutschbahn slide I

S

Saal hall II U2, 29
Sache thing I
Saft juice I
Sage legend II AC3, 130
sagen *to say; *to tell I
Sahne cream I
Salat salad I
Salbe ointment II U4, 73
sammeln to collect I
   Geld **sammeln** to raise money II U1, 10
Sammlung collection II U1, 10
Samstag Saturday I
Sand- sandy II U6, 109
sandig sandy II U6, 109
Sandwich sandwich I
Sänger/-in singer II U1, 15
Sanitärarbeit plumbing II U6, 123
Satz phrase; sentence I
Satzstellung word order I
säubern to clean I
Säugling baby I
Saxofon saxophone; sax I
Schach chess II U2, 28
Schachtel box I
Schade! Too bad! I
Schaf sheep, sheep (pl) II U1, 18
schaffen to create I
   Wir haben es **geschafft**! We did it! II U4, 81
Schälchen bowl I
Schale bowl I
Schatz treasure II U3, 56
Schau show II U4, 75
schauen to look I
   Schau/Schaut mal! Look! I
Schauplatz scene II U4, 77
Schauspieler actor II U2, 36
in **Scheiben** schneiden to slice I
scheinen *to shine II U2, 33
schenken *to give I
scherzen to joke II U5, 102
schicken *to send I
schieben to push II U2, 41
Schiedsrichter/-in official II U4, 81
schiefgehen *to go wrong I
schießen to kick II U4, 68
Schiff ship I

Schiffsjunge cabin boy I
Schiffsoffizier mate I
Schild sign II U1, 18
Schinkenspeck bacon I
Schlafanzug pyjamas II U1, 12
schlafen *to sleep I; *to be asleep II U1, 19
Schlafzimmer bedroom I
schlagen *to hit; to whip I; *to beat II U3, 54
Schläger racquet II U4, 68
Schlamm mud II U3, 62
schlammig muddy II U3, 62
Schlange queue I
schlau clever II U2, 41
der/die/das **schlechteste** the worst II U1, 16
 sich **schlecht** fühlen *to feel sick II U4, 73
schlecht bad I
schließen to close I
Schließfach locker I
schließlich at last; after all I; in the end
 II U1, 10; finally II U2, 31
der/die/das **schlimmste** the worst II U1, 16
schlimm *(ugs.)* bad I
Schlittschuh laufen to skate I
Schlittschuhbahn ice rink I
Schlittschuhe skates *(pl)* I
Schloss castle II U3, 56
Schluchtenklettern gorge scrambling
 II U1, 16
Schluss end I
 zum **Schluss** in the end II U1, 10; finally
 II U2, 31
Schluss *(einer Geschichte)* ending I
Schlüssel key II U3, 63
Schlüsselbegriff key word I
Schmerz pain II U4, 72
Schmuck jewellery; decorations *(pl)* I
schmücken to decorate I
schmutzig dirty II U2, 40
Schnäppchen bargain I
schnappen to grab II U3, 62
schnarchen to snore I
schneiden *to cut (off) II U2, 30
 in Scheiben **schneiden** to slice I
schnell fast; quick I
schnell quickly II U2, 40
Schock shock II U4, 79
Schokolade chocolate I
schön nice; fine I; beautiful II U2, 30
schon already I; yet II U4, 72
 schon einmal before II U4, 71
Schornstein chimney II U6, 122
schottisch Scottish II U6, 108
Schottland Scotland II U6, 113
Schrank cupboard I
schrecklich awful I
Schreiben writing I
schreiben *to write I
schreien to shout I; to scream II U3, 63; to
 cry II U5, 102
Schritt step I
 Schritt halten (mit) *to keep up (with)
 II U4, 80

Schritt-für-**Schritt**- step-by-step II U5, 95
schubsen to push II U2, 41
schüchtern shy II U1, 9
Schuh shoe I
Schule school I
Schüler/-in student I
Schulfach subject II U2, 28
Schuljahr year I
Schulklasse class I
Schulstunde lesson I
Schultasche schoolbag I
Schulter shoulder II U4, 73
Schüssel bowl I
schütten to pour I
Schwanz tail I
schwarz black I
 schwarz werden *to go black II U5, 102
 schwarzes Brett noticeboard II U1, 10
Schweif tail I
Schwein pig I
schwer hard II U1, 12
Schwester sister I
schwierig hard II U1, 12; difficult II U4, 77
Schwierigkeit problem I
Schwierigkeiten trouble II U1, 19
 in **Schwierigkeiten** bringen *to make
 trouble I
Schwimmen swimming I
 Schwimmen gehen *to go swimming I
schwimmen *to swim I
Science-Fiction *(Zukunftsdichtung)* science
 fiction II U1, 22
sechs six I
 Vier plus **sechs** ist zehn. Four and six is
 ten. I
Second-Hand-Laden charity shop I
See lake I
 See zum Rudern boating lake I
Seemann sailor I
die **Segel** einholen to reef the sails I
Segelboot sailboat II U6, 124
sehbehindert partially sighted II U2, 32
sehen *to see; to look I
Sehenswürdigkeit sight II AC1, 48; attraction II U3, 59
sehr very; very much I
 Sehr geehrte Dame, **sehr** geehrter Herr
 Dear Sir or Madam II U6, 113
Hör-/**Sehverstehen** viewing I
sein *to be I
 Sei/Seid höflich. Be polite. I
sein/-e his; its I
Seite page I; side II U2, 40
 auf der anderen **Seite** von across; opposite I
selber yourself I; himself II U1, 8; myself
 II U5, 93; yourselves II U6, 113
selbst even I
er/sich (**selbst**) himself II U1, 8
 du/dich/dir/die/sich (**selbst**) yourself I
 ihr/euch/Sie/sich (**selbst**) yourselves
 II U6, 113

ich/mir/mich (**selbst**) myself II U5, 93
selbstbewusst confident II U1, 16
Selbsteinschätzung self-evaluation I
selbstkritisch self-critical II U5, 92
selbstsicher confident II U1, 16
selbstverständlich of course I
Selfie selfie II U4, 81
seltsam strange I; weird II U5, 99
senden *to send I
Sender station II U4, 77
Sendung programme II U4, 68
separat separate II U1, 16
September September I
Sessel chair I
setzen *to put I
 sich **setzen** *to sit down I
Shorts shorts *(pl)* II U4, 75
Show show II U4, 75
 Comedy **Show** comedy show II U1, 10
sich each other I
sicher sure I; safe II U3, 56
Sicht view II U2, 30
Sie you; u *(= you)* I
sie her; she I
sie *(Pl.)* them; they I
sieben seven I
siegen *to win I
Sieger/-in winner I
Sightseeing- sightseeing II U3, 58
Signalwort signal word I
Silber silver II U3, 62
singen *to sing I
 Ich **singe** und tanze gern. I like singing
 and dancing. I
Sinn meaning II U1, 21
Situation situation I
Sitz! *(Befehl für Hunde)* Sit! I
sitzen *to sit I
 sich gegenüber **sitzen** *to sit face to face I
Skateboard skateboard II U1, 11
Skateboardfahren skateboarding I
Slogan slogan II U2, 35
Smartphone smartphone II U4, 79
SMS text (message) I
 eine **SMS** schicken to text II U5, 90
Snack snack I
so like this; so; like that I; that's how
 II U1, 10
 so oft whenever II U5, 92
 so … wie as … as I
sobald as soon as II U5, 92
Sofa sofa I
sofort right away I; right now II U5, 103
sogar even I
solch such II U2, 36
solche/-r/-s such II U2, 36
sollte should II U4, 74
 sollte(n) nicht shouldn't II U4, 73
sollten should II U4, 74
solltest should II U4, 74
solltet should II U4, 74
Sommer summer II AC2, 88

Sommerferienlager summer camp **II AC2**, 88
Sonderangebot special offer **I**
sonderbar weird **II U5**, 99
Song song **I**
Sonne sun **II U2**, 33
Sonntag Sunday **I**
Sonst noch etwas? Anything else? **I**
Keine Sorge! Don't worry! **I**
   sich **Sorgen** machen to worry **II U5**, 93
sorgfältig careful **II U3**, 56
Sorte kind **I**
Souvenir souvenir **II U3**, 54
sowieso anyway **II U3**, 62
soziales Netzwerk social network **II U5**, 91
Sozialwissenschaften Humanities (pl)
   II U2, 32
Spalt gap **I**
Spanien Spain **II U5**, 99
spannend exciting **I**
Spaß fun **I**
   Spaß haben *to have fun **I**
   Es macht **Spaß**. It's fun. **I**
spät late **I**
   zu **spät** late **I**
   zu **spät** kommen *to be late **I**
   Wie **spät** ist es? What's the time? **I**
   zu **spät** dran sein *to be late **I**
kleiner Spaten trowel **II U3**, 62
später later **I**
spazieren gehen *to go for a walk **II U1**, 18
   mit dem Hund **spazieren** gehen to walk
   the dog **I**
Speck bacon **I**
Speer spear **II U6**, 122
speziell special **I**
Spiel game **I**; match **II U4**, 68
spielen to play **I**
   eine Theaterszene **spielen** acting a
   scene **I**
   einen Streich **spielen** to play a trick (on) **I**
spielen (Theater) to act **I**
Spieler/-in player **II U4**, **75**
Spielfeld field **II U1**, 18; court; pitch **II U4**, 68
Spielkarte card **I**
Spielstand score **II U4**, 68
Spielzeug toy **I**
Spind locker **I**
Spitze top **I**
Sport sport **I**
   … ist ein toller **Sport**. … is a great sport. **I**
Sportart sport **I**
Sportunterricht PE (= Physical Education)
   II U2, 32
Sprache language **I**
Sprachmittlung mediation **I**
Sprechblase speech bubble **I**
Sprechen speaking; talking **I**
sprechen *to say; to talk; *to speak **I**
   sprechen über to talk about **I**
Sprecher/-in speaker **I**
Sprechgesang chant **II U4**, 72
springen to jump **I**

Spur clue **II U1**, 13
Staatsoberhaupt head of state **II AC2**, 89
Stadion stadium **II U4**, 68
Stadt city; town **I**
Stadtplan map **I**
Stadtteil part **I**
Stammbaum family tree **I**
ständig always **I**
Standort location **II U3**, 58
Standpunkt point of view **II U4**, 76
Star star **I**
hier: stark hard **II U3**, 56
stark strong **II U2**, 42; powerful **II AC3**, 130
Stärke power **II AC3**, 130
starren to stare **I**
starten to start **I**
Startpunkt starting place **II U6**, 112
Station station **I**
stattfinden *to take place **I**
Steak steak **I**
stehen *to stand **I**
   stehen auf *to be into **I**
   Du **stehst** auf … You're into … **I**
stehlen *to steal **II U2**, 34
steigen to climb **I**
steinig rocky **II U6**, 109
Stelle place **I**
stellen *to put **I**
   online **stellen** to post **II U5**, 90
   Stelle/Stellt es in … Put it in … **I**
Stern star **I**
Steuer wheel **I**
Steuerrad wheel **I**
Stichwort key word **I**
Stiefmutter stepmum **I**
still quiet; still **I**
Stimme voice **I**
Stimmung mood **II U1**, 24
stolz (auf) proud (of) **II U1**, 9
stoppen to stop **I**
stören *to get in the way **II U4**, 80
Story story, stories (pl) **I**
stoßen to push **II U2**, 41
Strand beach **II U5**, 99
Straße road **II U1**, 18
Straße (in der Stadt) street **I**
   auf der **Straße** in the street **I**
   in der **Straße** in the street **I**
Strecke route **II U1**, 16
Streich trick **I**
   einen **Streich** spielen to play a trick (on) **I**
Streit fight **II U2**, 41
(sich) streiten *to fight **II U5**, 102
Strom electricity **II U6**, 122
Stromausfall power cut **II U5**, 103
Stück piece **I**
   pro **Stück** each **I**
   Stück Papier piece of paper **I**
Student/-in student **I**
Studie survey **I**
Studium studies (pl) **II U2**, 28
Stufe step **I**

Stuhl chair **I**
Stunde hour **II U3**, 63
Stundenplan timetable **I**
Sturm storm **I**
Such- search **II U1**, 21
Suche search **II U1**, 21
suchen nach to look for **I**
Süd- south **II U3**, 53
Südafrika South Africa **II AC2**, 89
Süden south **II U3**, 53
Südkoreaner/-in South Korean **II AC2**, 88
Südkoreanisch South Korean **II AC2**, 88
südkoreanisch South Korean **II AC2**, 88
summen to hum **II U2**, 33
super great; cool **I**
   Es ist **super** zum/für … It's great for … **I**
Supermacht superpower **II AC2**, 89
Supermarkt supermarket **I**
Surfen surfing **II U6**, 109
süß cute; sweet **I**
Süßigkeiten sweets (pl) **I**
Szene scene **I**

T

Tabelle grid **I**
Tablet tablet **II U5**, 95
Tablette pill **II U4**, 73
Taekwondo taekwondo **II U2**, 38
die Tafelrunde the Round Table **II AC3**, 131
Tag day **I**
   am nächsten **Tag** the next day **II U1**, 11
   den ganzen **Tag** all day **II U1**, 14
   ein **Tag** in … a day out in … **II U3**, 58
   eines **Tages** one day **II U2**, 36
Tagebucheintrag diary entry **II U6**, 124
Takelage rigging **I**
Talentwettbewerb talent show **I**
Talisman lucky charm **I**
Tante aunt **I**
tanzen to dance **I**
   Ich singe und **tanze** gern. I like singing
   and dancing. **I**
Tänzer/-in dancer **II U2**, 36
tapfer brave **I**
Tasche bag **I**
Taschengeld pocket money **I**
Taschenlampe torch **II U1**, 18
Tatsache fact **II U2**, 37
Rollen tauschen to swap roles **I**
tausende (von) thousands of **I**
Taxi taxi **II U1**, 13
Team team **II U1**, 8
Technik Technology **II U2**, 32
Technologie technology **II AC2**, 89
Tee tea **I**
Teenager teenager **I**
Teich pond **II U2**, 33
Teil part **I**
teilen to share **II U2**, 40
teilnehmen (an) *to take part (in) **II U5**, 90
Telefon phone; telephone **I**

Telefonanruf phone call I
Tennis tennis I
Teppich carpet II U3, 65
Test test I
teuer expensive I
Text text I
Theater theatre I; drama II U2, 28
eine **Theaterszene** spielen acting a scene I
Thema theme I; topic II U2, 37
Ticket ticket I
tief deep II U6, 109
Tier animal I
Tierarzt/Tierärztin vet I
Tierpark zoo II U3, 53
Tierwelt (in freier Wildbahn) wildlife II U2, 33
Tipp tip I
Tisch table I
Titel heading I
tja well I
Toast toast I
Toilette toilet I
toll great I; amazing II U1, 18
… ist ein **toller** Sport. … is a great sport. I
Tomate tomato, tomatoes (pl) I
Tombola raffle I
Ton sound I
Tonmodell model I
Tonpfeife clay pipe II U3, 63
Tonstudio recording studio I
Tor goal I
Torte cake I
Tortenguss jelly I
tot dead II U3, 62
Tour tour II U3, 56
Tourismus tourism II U6, 114
Tourist/-in tourist I
Touristeninformation tourist information centre I; tourist board II U6, 113
Tradition tradition I
tragen to carry II AC3, 131
tragen (Kleidung) *to wear I
Trainer/-in coach I
trainieren to practise I; to train II U4, 72
Training training II U4, 80
Training für den Mund mouth jogging I
Transport transport II U6, 110
Er **traute** seinen Augen nicht. He couldn't believe his eyes. II U2, 40
Traum dream II U1, 15
Traum- fantasy I
traurig sad I
treffen *to meet; *to hit I
sich **treffen** *to meet I
treten to kick II U4, 68
Trick trick I
Trifle (englischer Nachtisch) trifle I
trinken *to drink I
Trip trip II U1, 9
trotzdem anyway II U3, 62
Tschüss! Bye! II U4, 72
T-Shirt T-shirt I

tun *to do; *to make I
tun als ob to act like II U5, 92
Tunnel tunnel I
Tür door I
Turnier competition II U2, 29
Turteltauben lovebirds (pl) II U1, 9
Tüte bag I
Typ guy II U1, 9
typisch typical I

U

U-Bahn underground II AC1, 48
die Londoner **U-Bahn** the Tube II AC1, 48
Übelkeit verspüren *to feel sick II U4, 73
Üben practising I
üben to practise I
über about; over; across I
überall everywhere I
überall (in) all over I
überall (egal, wo) anywhere II U3, 54
überhaupt at all I
übernachten to stay II U6, 110
Übernachtung sleepover I
überprüfen to check I
überqueren to cross II AC2, 89
überraschen to surprise II U4, 81
überraschend surprising II U1, 24
überrascht sein *to be surprised II U3, 63
Überraschung surprise I
überreagieren to overreact II U5, 92
überreden to persuade II U3, 52
Überschrift heading I
übersetzen to translate I
Übersetze/Übersetzt nicht … Don't translate … I
Übersetzung translation I
übrig left I
Übung exercise I
Übungsheft exercise book I
Ufer bank; shore II U3, 62
UFO UFO II U4, 78
Uhr clock I
Uhr (Zeitangabe bei vollen Stunden) o'clock I
Um wie viel **Uhr**? What time? I
Wie viel **Uhr** ist es? What's the time? I
um (bei Uhrzeitangaben) at I
um halb acht at 7:30 I
um … herum around I; round II U5, 103
Um wie viel Uhr? What time? I
umarmen to hug I
(sich) **umdrehen** to turn round II U2, 41
Umfrage survey I
Umgebung environment II U6, 114; set II AC3, 131
Lege/Legt … **umgedreht** hin. Put … face down. I
umgehen mit *to deal (with) II U3, 54
umher around I
umkehren to turn back II U2, 41
umkippen *to fall over I

sich **umschauen** to explore I
umsteigen (in) to change (onto) II U3, 53
Umwelt environment II U6, 114
umziehen to move (house) II U6, 110
und and I
unfair unfair II U4, 72
Unfall accident II U4, 69
unfreundlich unfriendly II U1, 24
ungefähr about I
ungefährlich safe II U3, 56
Ungeheuer monster I
unglaublich amazing II U1, 18
Unglück disaster II U5, 102
unheimlich scary II U1, 24
unhöflich rude I
Uniform uniform I
unrecht haben *to be wrong I
unregelmäßig irregular I
uns us I
unser/-e our I
unten downstairs II U5, 102
nach **unten** down II U3, 62
nach **unten** gehen *to go down I
unten below I
unter under I
im **Untergeschoss** downstairs II U5, 102
unterhalb below I
Unterhaltung conversation I
unternehmen wegen *to do about II U5, 100
Unterricht lesson I; class II U2, 40
unterrichten *to teach II U4, 76
Unterrichtsstunde lesson I
Unterschied difference I
unterschiedlich different I
unterwegs out and about II U3, 58
unverschämt rude I
unwohl sick II U4, 73
Urlaub holiday I
Seid ihr im **Urlaub**? Are you on holiday? I
Sind Sie im **Urlaub**? Are you on holiday? I
ursprünglich originally II AC1, 48

V

Vanillepudding custard I
Vanillesoße custard I
Vater father I
Veränderung change II U6, 123
Veranstaltung event I
verärgert angry I
Verb verb I
verbessern to improve I
sich **verbessern** to improve I
verbinden *to put through I; to join II U2, 33; to link II U5, 104
Verbindung link II U3, 59; connection II U6, 112
Verbrechen crime II AC3, 130
Verbrecher/-in criminal II AC3, 130
verbringen (Zeit) *to spend II U5, 92
verdienen to earn I; to deserve II U4, 76
Geld **verdienen** *to make money I

Verein club I; society II U6, 123
verfolgen to trace I
Vergangenheit past II U1, 9
vergeben *to forgive II U4, 81
vergessen *to forget I
vergleichen (mit) to compare (with/to) I
sich **verirren** *to get lost II U6, 119
Verkauf sale II U1, 12
verkaufen *to sell I
Verkäufer/-in assistant II U4, 78
Verkäufer/-in (auf einem Flohmarkt) seller I
Verkehrsmittel transport II U6, 110
    öffentliche **Verkehrsmittel** public transport (no pl) II U3, 52
Verkleidung fancy dress II U4, 80
verlassen *to leave II U2, 30
verlegen embarrassed II U1, 9
verletzen *to hurt II U4, 72
verletzt hurt II U1, 24
Verletzung injury II U4, 76
verlieren *to lose II U4, 68
verloren gehen *to get lost II U6, 119
vermissen to miss II U6, 110
vermuten to guess I
verneint negative II U6, 108
    verneinte Form negative form I
Vernissage gallery walk I
Verpackung wrapping I
verpassen to miss II U5, 99
sich den Knöchel **verrenken** to twist your ankle II U4, 72
verrückt crazy I; mad II U5, 97
    verrückt werden *to go crazy II U5, 95
Versammlung assembly II U2, 29
versäumen to miss II U5, 99
verschieden different I; separate II U1, 16
Verschmutzung pollution II U3, 62
verschwenden to waste II U5, 95
verschwunden missing II U1, 13
    verschwunden sein *to be gone II U4, 81
sich **versichern** *to make sure I
versorgen to supply II U6, 116
versprechen to promise II U6, 111
sich **verständigen** to communicate II AC2, 89
Verständnis understanding II U5, 93
(sich) **verstecken** *to hide II AC3, 130
verstehen *to understand I
versuchen to try I
    Versuch es mal mit … Try … I
verursachen to cause II U4, 82
Vervollständige/Vervollständigt … Complete … I
verwenden to use I
verzeihen *to forgive II U4, 81
verzieren to decorate I
Video video II U5, 91
Videochat video chat II U3, 50
viel much I
    Viele Grüße Best wishes II U6, 113
viel/-e lots (of); a lot of I

viel a lot I
    viel zu lernen a lot to learn I
viele many I
vielleicht maybe I
Vielvölker- multi-ethnic II AC1, 48
vier four I
    Vier plus sechs ist zehn. Four and six is ten. I
Viertel nach/vor quarter past/to I
violett purple I
Vogel bird II U2, 33
Vogelbeobachtung birdwatching II U2, 28
Vokabular vocabulary I
voll (von) full (of) I
Volleyball volleyball I
völlig absolutely II U2, 42; completely II AC3, 130
vollkommen perfect I
von from; about; of I
    von … bis from … to I
vor in front of I
vor (bei Uhrzeitangaben) to I
vor (zeitlich) before I; ago II U1, 10
    vor dem Lesen pre-reading I
vorbei over II U4, 79
vorbei (an) past I
vorbereiten to prepare I
sich **vordrängeln** to jump the queue I
vorgeschichtlich prehistoric II U6, 114
vorher before II U4, 71
Vormittag morning I
vormittags in the mornings I
vormittags (Uhrzeit) a.m. I
Vorschlag suggestion I
Vorsicht! Be careful! I
vorsichtig careful II U3, 56
vorstellen to present I
    sich (etwas) **vorstellen** to imagine I
    Stelle/Stellt … **vor**. Introduce … I
Vorstellung introduction II U2, 29
vortäuschen to fake II U4, 76
Vortrag presentation I
vorüber over II U4, 79
vorüber (an) past I

W

Wache guard II AC1, 49
Wachs wax II U3, 51
wachsen *to grow II U6, 109
Wachsfigur wax figure II U3, 51
Wächter/-in guard II AC1, 49
wackelig wobbly II U3, 62
Wackelpudding jelly I
Wahl choice II U3, 58
wählen to vote I; *to choose II U2, 30
während (+ Nomen) during + noun II U1, 9
während while; as I
wahrnehmen to notice II U2, 40
wahrscheinlich probably II U3, 52
Wald forest II U1, 16
Waliser/-in Welsh II U1, 16

Walisisch Welsh II U1, 16
walisisch Welsh II U1, 16
Wand wall I
Wandern walking II U1, 16; hiking II U6, 109
Wanderweg walking trail II U6, 114
wann when I
    wann immer whenever II U5, 92
warten (auf) to wait (for) I
    Warte/Wartet und denk/denkt nach. Stop and think I
Warte ab! Wait and see! I
Warteschlange queue I
warum why I
was what I
    was für ein what I
    Was fehlt? What is missing? I
    Was hast du? What's the matter? II U6, 122
    Was ist das? What's that? I
    Was ist dein/-e Lieblings…? What's your favourite …? I
    Was ist die Regel für …? What's the rule for …? I
    Was ist los? What's the matter? II U6, 122
    Was ist mit …? What about …? I
    was man … what to … I
    was noch what else I
    was sonst what else I
    Was um alles in der Welt …? What on earth …? II U5, 95
    … **was** ich tun soll. … what to do. II U5, 92
waschen to wash I
    sich **waschen** to wash I
Waschmaschine washing machine II U5, 95
Wasser water I
Wasserrutsche water slide I
Wau! Woof! I
Webseite site II U5, 92
Website website I
Wechsel change II U6, 123
wechseln to change II U5, 90
Wechselt euch **ab.** Take turns. I
Wecker alarm clock II U2, 43
Weg way I
    im **Weg** sein/stehen *to be in the way I
    im **Weg** stehen *to get in the way II U4, 80
weg away I
    weg sein *to be gone II U4, 81
    Es ist **weg**. It's gone. II U3, 62
wegen because of II U4, 81; for II U5, 91
wegnehmen *to take I
wegrennen *to run away I
wegwerfen *to throw away I
weh tun *to hurt II U4, 72
Weide field II U1, 18
Weihnachten Christmas I
weil because I
eine **Weile** a while II U3, 54
Wein wine I
auf andere **Weise** in other ways II U5, 97
weiß white I

weit far **II U3**, 55; wide **II U6**, 109
weitere more; other **I**
weiterführen *to go on **I**
weitergeben to pass (on) **I**
weitergehen *to go on **I**
weitermachen *to go on **I**
welche/-r/-s what; which **I**
    Welche Farbe hat …? What colour is …? **I**
    Welche … sind es? What are …? **I**
Welle wave **I**
Welt world **I**
    aus aller **Welt** from around the world **II U6**, 114
    Was um alles in der **Welt** …? What on earth …? **II U5**, 95
wem who **I**
wen who **I**
    Für **wen** …? Who … for? **I**
wenden to turn round **II U2**, 41
    sich **wenden** an to turn to **II U6**, 123
Wendung expression **II AC3**, 89
ein wenig a little **I**; a bit **II U1**, 18
wenige a few **I**; few **II U1**, 18
wenn when; if **I**
wer who **I**
    Wer ist dabei? Who's in? **II U4**, 70
    Wer ist es? Who is it? **I**
    Wer macht mit? Who's in? **II U4**, 70
Werbespruch slogan **II U2**, 35
werden *to become **II U3**, 56; *to get **II U6**, 122
werfen (nach) *to throw (at) **I**
Werkzeug tool **II U6**, 123
wert sein *to be worth **I**
West- west **I**
Westen west **I**
    im äußersten **Westen** in the far west **II U6**, 114
westeuropäische Zeit Greenwich Mean Time (= GMT) **I**
Wettbewerb contest **I**; competition **II U2**, 29
ich wette **I** bet **II U3**, 54
Wetter weather **I**
Wettervorhersage weather forecast **II U6**, 112
Wettkampf contest **I**
Wettlauf race **II U4**, 68
wichtig important **I**
    wichtig nehmen to care (about) **II U5**, 93
wie like **I**
wie as **II AC2**, 88
wie how **I**
    Wie viele …? How many …? **I**
    Wie alt bist du? How old are you? **I**
    Wie alt sind Sie? How old are you? **I**
    wie das ist what it's like **II U4**, 74
    wie der Mann aussah what the man looked like **II U1**, 13
    Wie geht es dir? How are you? **I**
    Wie geht es euch? How are you? **I**
    Wie geht es Ihnen? How are you? **I**
    Wie heißen Sie? What's your name? **I**

    Wie heißt du? What's your name? **I**
    Wie man … How to … **I**
    Wie spät ist es? What's the time? **I**
    Wie viel (kostet/kosten) …? How much is/are …? **I**
    Wie viel Uhr ist es? What's the time? **I**
    Wie wär's mit …? What about …? **I**
wieder again **I**
Wiederaufbereitung recycling **II U2**, 40
Wiederaufnehmen pick-up **I**
auf **Wiedersehen** goodbye **I**
Wiese field **II U1**, 18
wild wild **II U6**, 114
Willkommen! Welcome! **II U1**, 18
willkommen heißen to welcome **II U2**, 35
Wind wind **II U6**, 122
Windsurfen windsurfing **II U6**, 109
wir we **I**
    Wir sind aus … We're from … **I**
wirklich real **II U1**, 10
wirklich really **I**
wissen *to know **I**
    Du **weißt**, wie man … You know how to … **I**
    Ich **weiß** (es) nicht! I don't know! **I**
    Ihr **wisst**, wie man … You know how to … **I**
Witz joke **I**
witzig funny; fun **I**
wo where **I**
Woche week **I**
Wochenende weekend **I**
    am **Wochenende** at the weekend **I**
Wochentag weekday **II U5**, 100
Woher …? Where … from? **I**
wohin where **I**
    … **wohin** ich gehen kann. … where to go. **II U3**, 54
Wohlfahrt charity **I**
wohltätige Zwecke charity **I**
Wohltätigkeitsverein charity **I**
wohnen to live **I**
    wohnen bei to stay with **II U3**, 52
Wohnung flat **I**
Wohnzimmer living room **I**
Wolke cloud **II U6**, 122
wollen to want (to) **I**
Workshop workshop **I**
Wort word **I**
    die Kraft der **Wörter** (Wortschatzübung) Word power **I**
Wörterbuch dictionary **I**
Wörternetz (eine Art Schaubild) mind map **I**
Wortschatz vocabulary **I**
Wortschlange word snake **I**
Wortstellung word order **I**
Worum geht es in/im …? What is … about? **I**
Wow! Wow! **I**
wunderbar beautiful **II U2**, 30; wonderful **II U2**, 40
Wunsch wish **I**

sich etwas wünschen *to make a wish **I**
würde/-st/-n/-t gern would like **I**
    Ich **würde** gern … I'd like to … (= I would like to) **I**
    würde/-st/-n/-t sehr gern would love **I**
Würfle/Würfelt mit zwei Würfeln. Roll two dice. **I**
Wurm worm **I**
wusch whoosh **I**
wütend angry **I**

Z

z.B. (= zum Beispiel) e.g. (= for example) **I**
Zahl number **I**
zählen (auf) to count (on) **I**
Zauber- magical **II AC3**, 130
Zauberer wizard **II AC3**, 130
auf Zehenspitzen gehen to tiptoe **II U1**, 19
zehn ten **I**
    Vier plus sechs ist **zehn**. Four and six is ten. **I**
zehnmal ten times **I**
Zeichen sign **II U1**, 18
zeichnen *to draw **I**
Zeichnung drawing **I**
zeigen to show **I**
    Zeige/Zeigt auf … Point to … **I**
    Zeige/Zeigt darauf. Point. **I**
Zeile line **I**
Zeit time **I**
    (**Zeit**) brauchen *to take **II U5**, 95
    zur selben **Zeit** at the same time **I**
    die ganze **Zeit** all the time **II U3**, 62
    Es ist **Zeit** aufzustehen! Time to get up! **I**
Zeitschrift magazine **I**
Zeitstrahl time line **I**
Zelten camping **II U5**, 99
zelten to camp **II U6**, 124
zentral central **II U3**, 62
Zentral- central **II U3**, 62
Zentrum centre **I**
zerbrechen *to break **I**
zerstören to ruin **II U4**, 81
Zeug stuff **I**
Zeuge/Zeugin witness **II U4**, 77
ziehen to pull **I**
Ziel goal **I**
Ziellinie finish line **II U4**, 81
Zimmer room **I**
Zimmergenosse/Zimmergenossin roommate **I**
Zinn tin **II U6**, 122
Zitrone lemon **II U1**, 24
Zoo zoo **II U3**, 53
zornig angry **I**
zu too **I**
    Zu dumm! Too bad! **I**
zu to **I**
    zu Hause at home **I**
zubereiten to prepare **I**
zuerst first **I**; at first **II U3**, 63

In the classroom

Die Wörter und Ausdrücke auf diesen Seiten musst du nicht auswendig lernen. Aber in vielen Situationen im Klassenzimmer wirst du sie nützlich finden!

Asking for help and information

Can you help me, please?	Kannst du / Können Sie mir bitte helfen?
How do you do this exercise?	Wie macht man diese Übung?
How do you spell … , please?	Wie schreibt man … , bitte?
Is this right? I'm not sure.	Ist das richtig? Ich bin mir nicht sicher.
Is it OK to …?	Ist es in Ordnung, wenn ich / wir …?
Is it true or false?	Ist das richtig oder falsch?
Sorry, I don't know. Ask …	Tut mir leid, das weiß ich nicht. Frag …
Sorry. Can you say that again, please?	Wie bitte? Können Sie das bitte wiederholen?
What does that mean?	Was bedeutet das?
What's for homework?	Was haben wir als Hausaufgabe auf?
What's that in English / German?	Was heißt das auf Englisch / Deutsch?

Vocabulary for instructions and activities

Act (out) one of the scenes. / Act (out) the dialogues.	Spiele eine der Szenen. / Spiele die Dialoge.
Add more words / ideas.	Füge weitere Wörter / Ideen hinzu.
Ask your partner questions.	Stelle deinem Partner / deiner Partnerin Fragen.
Answer your partner's questions.	Beantworte die Fragen deines Partners / deiner Partnerin.
Check your partner's text.	Überprüfe den Text deines Partners / deiner Partnerin.
Collect ideas.	Sammle Ideen.
Compare English and German.	Vergleiche das Englische und Deutsche.
Complete the answers.	Vervollständige die Antworten.
Copy the grid / the mind map.	Schreibe die Tabelle / das Wörternetz ab.
Correct the wrong sentences.	Korrigiere die falschen Sätze.

Describe your room.	Beschreibe dein Zimmer.
Decide who writes which part.	Entscheidet, wer welchen Teil schreibt.
Discuss different ideas.	Diskutiert verschiedene Ideen.
Draw a picture.	Zeichne ein Bild.
Exchange your flyers / questions.	Tauscht eure Flyer / Fragen untereinander aus.
Explain your answer. / Explain why.	Erkläre deine Antwort. / Erkläre warum.
Fill in your grid / the form.	Fülle deine Tabelle / das Formular aus.
Find the rule / the right word order.	Finde die Regel / die richtige Wortstellung.
Finish your brochure.	Stelle deine Broschüre fertig.
Form expert groups.	Bildet Expertengruppen.
Get organised.	Organisiert euch.
Go back to your home group.	Gehe zurück zu deiner ersten Gruppe.
Guess the new words.	Errate die neuen Wörter.
Imagine you're one of the people in the story.	Stelle dir vor, du bist eine der Personen in der Geschichte.
Improve your text / part of the report.	Verbessere deinen Text / Teil des Berichts.
Learn your text by heart.	Lerne deinen Text auswendig.
Listen to the sentences / the dialogue.	Höre dir die Sätze / den Dialog an.
Look at the picture / the examples.	Schau dir das Bild / die Beispiele an.
Look up the words.	Schlage die Wörter nach.
Make a poster / a grid / a mind map.	Fertige ein Poster / eine Tabelle / ein Wörternetz an.
Match the sentence parts.	Ordne die Satzteile einander zu.
Name more sports.	Nenne mehr Sportarten.
Note down what is missing.	Notiere, was fehlt.
Peer-edit each other's work.	Kontrolliert eure Arbeiten gegenseitig.
Plan the scenes.	Plane die Szenen.
Record your final report / dialogue.	Nehmt euren fertigen Bericht / Dialog auf.
Scan the text for details.	Suche den Text nach Details ab.
Share the information with your partner.	Teile die Informationen mit deinem Partner / deiner Partnerin.
Skim the text for the gist.	Überfliege den Text und finde die wichtigsten Aussagen.
Sum up what happens in the story.	Fasse zusammen, was in der Geschichte passiert.
Practise your scenes / the dialogues.	Übe deine Szenen / die Dialoge.
Present the information from your text.	Präsentiere die Informationen aus deinem Text.
Put in the correct forms.	Setze die richtigen Formen ein.
Read your text aloud.	Lies deinen Text laut vor.
Repeat the sentences / the dialogues.	Wiederhole die Sätze / die Dialoge.
Say the words / the sounds.	Sage die Wörter / die Laute.
Show your brochure.	Zeige deine Broschüre.
Swap roles.	Tauscht die Rollen.
Take a card.	Nimm eine Karte.

Take notes.	Mache dir Notizen.
Take turns.	Wechselt euch ab.
Talk with your partner.	Sprich mit deinem Partner / deiner Partnerin.
Tell your partner about your hobby.	Erzähle deinem Partner / deiner Partnerin von deinem Hobby.
Think of ideas for …	Überlege dir Ideen für …
Trade your part with somebody else.	Tausche deinen Teil mit jemandem.
Translate the words / sentences.	Übersetze die Wörter / Sätze.
Use the ideas / the vocabulary.	Verwende die Ideen / die Vokabeln.
Work with a partner or in a group.	Arbeite mit einem Partner / einer Partnerin oder in einer Gruppe.
Write dialogues / a short text / a reply.	Schreibe Dialoge / einen kurzen Text / eine Antwort.
Write about your friends.	Schreibe über deine Freunde.
Write down school words.	Schreibe Wörter zum Thema „Schule" auf.

Useful words

activity – Aktivität	presentation – Präsentation; Vortrag
answer – Antwort	prompt card – Rollenkarte
class display – Ausstellung in der Klasse	puzzle – Rätsel; Puzzle
collocation – Wortverbindung	pros and cons – Vor- und Nachteile
description – Beschreibung	question – Frage
dialogue – Dialog	quiz – Quiz; Rätsel
dice – Würfel	quote – Zitat
draft – Entwurf; Konzept	report – Bericht
drawing – Zeichnung	revision – Wiederholung
example – Beispiel	rhyme – Reim
fact – Tatsache; Fakt	role play – Rollenspiel
folder – Ordner; Mappe	rule – Regel
game – Spiel	scene – Szene
grid – Gitter; Tabelle; Raster	signal word – Signalwort
heading – Überschrift	slogan – Slogan; Werbespruch
information – Information(en)	speech bubble – Sprechblase
key word – Schlüsselwort	story – Geschichte; Erzählung
list – Liste	task – Aufgabe
mind map – Wörternetz	theme – Thema
order – Reihenfolge	title – Titel; Überschrift
perspective – Perspektive	unit – Lektion; Kapitel
phrase – Redewendung; Ausdruck	useful phrases – nützliche Ausdrücke
picture story – Bildergeschichte	vocabulary – Vokabular; Wortschatz
point of view – Standpunkt; Ansicht	word cloud – Wörterwolke

Find more online:
u693kn

Irregular verbs

- ■ ■ ■ Grundform, *simple past* und *past participle* sind identisch
- ■ ● ● Grundform unterscheidet sich vom *simple past* und *past participle*
- ■ ● ■ Grundform und *past participle* sind identisch, nur das *simple past* hat eine andere Form
- ■ ● ▲ Grundform, *simple past* und *past participle* haben alle eine andere Form

■ Grundform	■ simple past	■ past participle	Deutsch
cost [kɒst]	cost [kɒst]	cost [kɒst]	kosten
cut [kʌt]	cut [kʌt]	cut [kʌt]	schneiden
hit [hɪt]	hit [hɪt]	hit [hɪt]	schlagen, treffen
hurt [hɜ:t]	hurt [hɜ:t]	hurt [hɜ:t]	verletzen, sich weh tun
let [let]	let [let]	let [let]	lassen
put [pʊt]	put [pʊt]	put [pʊt]	legen, setzen, stellen
set up [ˈset ˌʌp]	set up [ˈset ˌʌp]	set up [ˈset ˌʌp]	erbauen, errichten

■ Grundform	● simple past	● past participle	Deutsch
bring [brɪŋ]	brought [brɔ:t]	brought [brɔ:t]	(mit)bringen
build [bɪld]	built [bɪlt]	built [bɪlt]	bauen
buy [baɪ]	bought [bɔ:t]	bought [bɔ:t]	kaufen
feel [fi:l]	felt [felt]	felt [felt]	fühlen
find [faɪnd]	found [faʊnd]	found [faʊnd]	finden
get [get]	got [gɒt]	got [gɒt]	bekommen, erhalten
have [hæv]	had [hæd]	had [hæd]	haben
hear [hɪə]	heard [hɜ:d]	heard [hɜ:d]	hören
hold [həʊld]	held [held]	held [held]	halten
keep [ki:p]	kept [kept]	kept [kept]	(auf)bewahren, behalten
learn [lɜ:n]	learned [lɜ:nd] / learnt [lɜ:nt]	learned [lɜ:nd] / learnt [lɜ:nt]	lernen
leave [li:v]	left [left]	left [left]	(ver)lassen
make [meɪk]	made [meɪd]	made [meɪd]	machen, tun
meet [mi:t]	met [met]	met [met]	treffen
pay [peɪ]	paid [peɪd]	paid [peɪd]	(be)zahlen
read [ri:d]	read [red]	read [red]	lesen
retell [ˌri:ˈtel]	retold [ˌri:ˈtəʊld]	retold [ˌri:ˈtəʊld]	nacherzählen
say [seɪ]	said [sed]	said [sed]	sagen
sell [sel]	sold [səʊld]	sold [səʊld]	verkaufen
send [send]	sent [sent]	sent [sent]	senden, verschicken
sit [sɪt]	sat [sæt]	sat [sæt]	sitzen
sleep [sli:p]	slept [slept]	slept [slept]	schlafen
spell [spel]	spelt [spelt]	spelt [spelt]	buchstabieren

spend [spend]	spent [spent]	spent [spent]	ausgeben, verbringen
stand (up) [stænd]	stood (up) [stʊd]	stood (up) [stʊd]	(auf)stehen
tell [tel]	told [təʊld]	told [təʊld]	erzählen
think [θɪŋk]	thought [θɔːt]	thought [θɔːt]	(nach)denken, glauben
understand [ˌʌndəˈstænd]	understood [ˌʌndəˈstʊd]	understood [ˌʌndəˈstʊd]	verstehen
win [wɪn]	won [wʌn]	won [wʌn]	gewinnen, siegen

■ Grundform	● simple past	■ past participle	Deutsch
become [bɪˈkʌm]	became [bɪˈkeɪm]	become [bɪˈkʌm]	werden
come [kʌm]	came [keɪm]	come [kʌm]	kommen
run [rʌn]	ran [ræn]	run [rʌn]	laufen, rennen

■ Grundform	● simple past	▲ past participle	Deutsch
be [biː]	was / were [wɒz / wɜː]	been [biːn]	sein
blow (out) [bləʊ]	blew [bluː]	blown [bləʊn]	(aus)blasen, (aus)pusten
break [breɪk]	broke [brəʊk]	broken [ˈbrəʊkn]	(zer)brechen, kaputt machen
choose [tʃuːz]	chose [tʃəʊz]	chosen [tʃəʊzn]	(aus)wählen
do [duː]	did [dɪd]	done [dʌn]	machen, tun
draw [drɔː]	drew [druː]	drawn [drɔːn]	zeichnen
drink [drɪŋk]	drank [dræŋk]	drunk [drʌŋk]	trinken
eat [iːt]	ate [et]	eaten [iːtn]	essen
fall [fɔːl]	fell [fel]	fallen [ˈfɔːlən]	fallen
fly [flaɪ]	flew [fluː]	flown [fləʊn]	fliegen
forget [fəˈget]	forgot [fəˈgɒt]	forgotten [fəˈgɒtn]	vergessen
give [gɪv]	gave [geɪv]	given [ˈgɪvn]	geben
go [gəʊ]	went [went]	gone [gɒn]	gehen, fahren
know [nəʊ]	knew [njuː]	known [nəʊn]	kennen, wissen
see [siː]	saw [sɔː]	seen [siːn]	sehen
show [ʃəʊ]	showed [ʃəʊd]	shown [ʃəʊn]	zeigen
sing [sɪŋ]	sang [sæŋ]	sung [sʌŋ]	singen
speak [spiːk]	spoke [spəʊk]	spoken [ˈspəʊkn]	sprechen
swim [swɪm]	swam [swæm]	swum [swʌm]	schwimmen
take [teɪk]	took [tʊk]	taken [ˈteɪkn]	nehmen
throw [θrəʊ]	threw [θruː]	thrown [θrəʊn]	werfen
wear [weə]	wore [wɔː]	worn [wɔːn]	anhaben, tragen
write [raɪt]	wrote [rəʊt]	written [ˈrɪtn]	schreiben

Check-out solutions

Unit 1   Page 25

Exercise 1
They talked about the 'dreams' page. / They put the sports pages together. / They looked at Jay's ideas for the music pages. / They collected ideas for the puzzles page. / They took a photo of the yearbook team. / They made a list of jobs for next week.

Exercise 2
1. went
2. was
3. wasn't
4. invited
5. did you go
6. did
7. were
8. was
9. was
10. didn't stay

Exercise 3
1. When did you get up this morning?
2. Where did you go?
3. What did you see?
4. Why did your classmates laugh at you?

Exercise 4
1. Luke's dog Sherlock is **the craziest** animal in England. There's nothing **funnier** than when he chases his tail. It's always **faster** than he is!
2. The **cutest** pets for Holly are her two guinea pigs. Mr Fluff likes to explore. He thinks a trip in a bag is **more interesting** than a game on the floor! Honey isn't as **brave** as Mr Fluff.
3. Cats are **the most popular** pets in the class. Dave's cat Sid brings presents for the family. Some presents are **better** than others. The **worst** thing for Dave is a mouse in his bed!

Unit 2   Page 43

Exercise 1
a) 1. which / that
   2. which / that
   3. who / that
   4. whose
   5. who / that

b) Contact clause possible in sentence 1 and 3

Exercise 2
1. Dave was washing his face when Sid came into the bathroom.
2. He sent Jay a text while his mother was making breakfast.
3. He was getting his bike when his father left the house.
4. He arrived at school while Luke was still sleeping.

Exercise 3
a) 1. Geography
   2. Music
   3. Technology
   4. History
   5. Art

b) Phrases: I really like … / I like … best because … / … is interesting/great/so much fun because … / I like to learn about … / …

Unit 3   Page 65

Exercise 1
1. The Frasers are going to have a picnic. / The Frasers are going to go on a picnic.
2. Luke and Sherlock are going to play ball in the park. / Luke and Sherlock are going to play in the park.
3. Mr and Mrs Azad are going to visit / see / go to the Tower of London.
4. Holly is going to go (inline) skating. / Holly is going to have fun on her skates.
5. Amir is going to take (lots of) photos / pictures.
6. Shahid is going to meet someone / his girlfriend / a friend (somewhere).

Exercise 2
1. anybody
2. someone
3. everybody
4. something
5. somewhere
6. everything
7. anywhere
8. nothing

Exercise 3
1. fast
2. comfortably
3. excitedly
4. slowly
5. clearly
6. well
7. loudly
8. sadly

Unit 4   Page 83

Exercise 1
1 c)
2 e)
3 b)
4 a)
5 f)
6 d)

Exercise 2
1. Luke: Have you found any interesting information on the internet yet?
   Dave: Yes, I have. I found some (information) yesterday after school.
2. Luke: Has Jay drawn any mangas for his report (yet)?
   Dave: Yes, he has. He drew some cool new characters at lunch.
3. Dave: Have you seen the two new manga comics yet?
   Luke: Yes, I have. I've already finished one of them.
4. Luke: Have you seen Olivia today?
   Dave: No, I haven't. But she sent me a text an hour ago. / But I sent her a text an hour ago.
5. Dave: Has Holly written about guinea pigs?
   Luke: I hope not! She wrote about guinea pigs last year.

Exercise 3

The full name of BMX is 'bicycle motocross'. It is a sport that **has become** *very* popular with young people. It **started** with children in the USA in about 1970. At first, the children **used** normal bikes on mud roads; there **were** no special BMX bikes. But then a few bicycle companies **discovered** the sport, and the world **had** its first BMX bikes. It's a fast, dangerous sport, and there **have been** many serious accidents. That's why many parents are *not* big fans. In one survey with parents last year, BMX **wasn't** at the top of the list of 'favourite sports'. One mother said: "**I've seen** dirty football and rugby uniforms, but my children's BMX clothes after a race? They're the worst!"

Unit 5   Page 105

Exercise 1

1 e)   When my dad wants to relax, he watches football on TV.
2 d)   When I want to know the words of a song I've heard, I look it up on the internet.
3 b)   When my mum works away from home, she sends me text messages.
4 a)   When I want to tell all my friends how great my holiday is, I post it on my social network profile.
5 c)   When my sister wants to know about the coolest new clothes, she reads girls' magazines.

Exercise 2

1. Lösungsvorschlag:
   A: I really hurt my foot. I hope it isn't broken. / I think it could be broken.
   B: Does it really hurt?
   A: Yes, it does.
   B: Well, you should go to the doctor's. / Why don't you go to the doctor's?
   A: Yes, maybe you're right.

2. Lösungsvorschlag:
   A: I can't believe I missed my favourite show last night!
   B: Well, you could watch it on the internet. / Why don't you watch it on the internet?
   A: The interent doesn't always have everything.
   B: Have you tried looking yet?
   A: Well, no.

3. Lösungsvorschlag:
   A: Oh no, something is wrong with my bike!
   B: What's the problem?
   A: I don't know.
   B: Have you tried looking on the internet yet? / Have you asked Mum and Dad / Ben / … for help?

4. Lösungsvorschlag:
   A: I can't believe she posted those photos – they're really embarrassing.
   B: Have you talked to her yet?
   A: Yes, I have. She doesn't think they're embarrassing. And she thinks she looks really good in them.
   B: Well, why don't you tell her to cut you off the photos?
   A: OK, that's a good idea.

5. Lösungsvorschlag:
   A: I'm not allowed to use my phone for a week because my parents are really angry with me.
   B: Well, maybe you should tell them that you're sorry.
   A: I've already told them, but they still took my phone.
   B: Just use my phone when you need it.

Exercise 3

When I was young, we **weren't able to** make phone calls from everywhere because there were no mobile phones. Now you **can** use your smartphones nearly everywhere. But you **aren't allowed to** use them at school, are you? There **must** be rules for using them, right? 30 years ago you **had to** look for information in books. Today you **can** look things up on the internet. When we were young, we **were able to** watch TV only sometimes, but today you **can** watch videos online all day.

Unit 6   Page 125

Exercise 1

1. will be
2. will be
3. won't be
4. will be
5. will get
6. will be
7. won't rain
8. will be
9. will change
10. will move in
11. will start

Exercise 2

a) 1. If you like surfing, you will love Cornwall.
   2. If we run, we won't be late.
   3. If you don't do your homework, you won't be allowed to play with your computer.
   4. If it doesn't rain, we will go swimming.
   5. If we don't book the train tickets now, they will be more expensive.
   6. If Mum works late, we will cook dinner for her.

b) 1. If my dad found a good job, I would get more pocket money.
   2. If my granny had time, we could go to London.
   3. If I were you, I wouldn't eat so much chocolate.
   4. If we got lost, we could use my smartphone to find the way home.
   5. If the shops were open on Sundays, we could go shopping now.
   6. If I were you, I wouldn't post those photos!

Exercise 3

1. **When** I get up, I'll make breakfast. – **If** I get up before you, I'll make breakfast.
2. I won't do my homework today **if** my teacher doesn't want it tomorrow. – I'll do my homework **when** I'm at home after school.

Grammar solutions

Unit 1

G1 Two years ago we raised lots of money.

Dear Olivia,
Thank you for your e-mail and the photos. I like them a lot.
You **wanted** to know about our charity event. Well, last month we
organised an event in the park and we **planned** lots of activities.
First there **were** games for students, parents and teachers. After
that we **sold** cakes. In the afternoon the students in Year 7 **did**
some really cool tricks. And then it **was** the turn of the students
in Year 8. They **created** a comedy show. The girls **wanted** to look
funny so they **painted** their faces and **wore** some funny costumes
too. In the evening the school band **sang** in the park – lots of
people **came** to listen. Michael **was** the real star of their show.
He **did** some cool moves!
We **raised** 400 euros in just one day!
Write soon.
Pia

G2 How did they know?

Lösungsvorschlag:
How old was he? – He was about twenty years old.
When did you see him? – I saw him at 10 o'clock.
Where did you see him? – I saw him in front of the sports shop in
Trafalgar Road.
Did you see what he took from the shop? – Well, he had two bags
full of T-shirts and shoes.
Was he alone? – Yes, he was.

G3 The police didn't know what the man looked like.

Man arrested
Greenwich. On 4th September a young man **broke into** a sports
shop in Trafalgar Road. Yesterday the police **arrested** him. They
didn't know what he **looked** like at first. But then they **got**
an anonymous phone call. The caller **didn't give** them much
information, but she **gave** them an address in Greenwich. When
the police **got to** the house, two women **were** there but the man
wasn't. So they **waited** till he **came** home and then they **arrested**
him – he **didn't try** to run away. The police **found** the sports shoes
and the T-shirts in the loft, but they **didn't find** the bike.

G4 An adventure course helps students to be more confident.

a) big – bigger – the biggest
    bad – worse – the worst
    happy – happier – the happiest
    important – more important – the most important

b) 1. Luke is tall. Holly is taller. But Olivia is the tallest of the
        three.
    2. The red car is expensive. The blue car is more expensive.
        But the black car is the most expensive of the three.
    3. Hook Lane is a busy road. King's Street is busier. But
        London Road is the busiest of the three.

4. Luke has got a good idea. Holly's idea is better. But Dave
    has got the best idea of the three.

G5 Outdoor activities are as important as lessons in the classroom.

Lösungsvorschlag:
The Rhine is longer than the Spree/Oder.
The Spree is shorter than the Oder/Rhine.
Düsseldorf is as big as Stuttgart.
Cologne is bigger than Düsseldorf/Stuttgart.
The Feldberg is the highest mountain. It is higher than the
Brocken/the Großer Arber.
The Großer Arber is about as high as the Feldberg.
The Saarland is the smallest state/region. It is smaller than
Hesse/Saxony.
Hesse is bigger than Saxony.

Unit 2

G6 The queen who loved parties

a) 1. Dave: Have you got any music **which/that** people
                listened to at Anne's parties? You can use it in your
                presentation.
        Luke: Yes, I have. But I'm not sure. I don't like the songs
                which/that they played in the 17th century.
        Dave: Well, don't worry about that. Luke, what's that
                under the table?
        Luke: Oh, thanks, Dave. This is the photo of the Queen's
                House **which/that** I'm looking for.

    2. Jay: Who was Christopher Wren?
        Olivia: He was the famous architect **whose** designs you
                can see in London.
        Jay: Really?
        Olivia: Yes, he was the man **who/that** designed the Royal
                Naval College, the Royal Observatory, St Paul's
                Cathedral and many other buildings.
        Jay: Cool! Those are all buildings **which/that** I know.

b) 1. Have you got any music people listened to at Anne's
        parties?
        I don't like the songs they played in the 17th century.
        This the photo of the Queen's House I'm looking for.
    2. Those are all buildings I know.

G7 What were they doing when Sally fell into the pond?

Lösungsvorschlag:
B: What were Holly and Olivia doing?
A: While Holly was practicing / learning new signs, Olivia was
    playing netball.

Unit 3

G8 It's going to be fun.

Jay is going to go to Covent Garden. He's going to listen to the buskers there.
Amir is going to send / write a postcard home.
Olivia and Holly aren't going to see / visit Brick Lane with its street art / graffiti.
Shahid is going to go to a café with his girlfriend.
Mrs Azad isn't going to go shopping / to the supermarket.
Mr Azad is going to wash his car.

G9 It's something important.

Amir: Listen, **everybody**. I want to buy a little present for my aunt to say 'thank you'. Is there a good shop **anywhere**?
Olivia: What are you thinking of?
Amir: Well, it must be **something** special, but it mustn't be **anything** expensive.
Jay: **Everything** is expensive in London!
Holly: That's not true! I know a good shop where **nothing** costs more than £10.
Amir: OK. Let's go there and see if we can find **something** for her.

G10 Now we're going slowly past the Tower of London.

1. Buy an Oyster card and travel by public transport **cheaply** and **comfortably**.
2. Stand on Westminster Bridge and take **fantastic** photos of Big Ben.
3. On a **nice** day, take a picnic with you and have lunch in one of London's **great** parks.
4. Go to the British Museum and learn about money, animals and ships. It's **free**!
5. Visit Madame Tussauds. The museum shows famous people very **realistically**.
6. If you're in London for a day or two only, take a sightseeing bus. Most guides know London and its history **well**.

G11 You can see London faster and more easily with a guide.

Lösungsvorschlag:
A bear runs faster than a pig or a cat. A horse runs fastest.
A pig eats less than a bear. A cat eats least.
A bear sleeps longer than a horse. A cat sleeps longest.
A bear weighs more than a lion. A horse weighs most.

Unit 4

G12 Have you ever run in a marathon?

Lösungsvorschlag:
a) 1. Have you prepared for Sports Day yet?
   2. Have you bought new sports shoes yet?
   3. Have you already started eating healthy food?
   4. Have you ever hurt your foot while you were playing sports?
   5. Have you found a name for your team yet?

b) 2. Have you bought new sports shoes yet?
   - No, I haven't. I don't need any new shoes. My old ones/ shoes are OK.
   - Yes, I have. I've just bought some new shoes. Look, they are in this bag.
   - Yes, I have. I bought them last week.
   3. Have you already started eating healthy food?
   - Yes, I have. I've already eaten two apples today.
   4. Have you ever hurt your foot while you were playing sports?
   - Yes, I have. I've hurt my leg twice/two times. When I was little, I broke my leg at the ice rink. And last year I twisted my ankle while I was playing basketball.
   - No, I haven't.
   5. Have you found a name for your team yet?
   - Yes, I have. But I'm not going to tell you.
   - No, I haven't found a nice name yet.

Unit 5

G13 I'm writing to you because I need your advice.

Joe: I like your magazine **because** it's always got the interesting news on my favourite stars in it.
Ginny: I buy *TeenLife* **as soon as/when** I get my pocket money from my parents. I love it!
Michael: The concert photos are fantastic. When I look at them, it's **like** I'm there.
Lisa: **Whenever/When** I read Ruby's advice, I think she really understands our problems.
Sheila: **After** I tried the make-up which came with the magazine last week, I'm not going to buy *TeenLife* again! It looked awful on my face.

G14 You watched the match last night, didn't you?

1. Olivia: Miss Brown played an interesting song in class today, **didn't she**?
   Holly: Its title was *Life before media technology*, **wasn't it**?
   Jay: Yes, and it's a really cool song, **isn't it**?
   Holly: Well, yeah. I liked it.

2. Luke: We're going to work on our media project this afternoon, **aren't we**?
   Dave: Of course. Let's meet in front of the school after lessons and go to my house.
   Luke: Good idea. With Jamie and Irina it's always very noisy at our house, **isn't it**?
   Dave: That's true! If we concentrate, perhaps we can finish the project today.
   Luke: I'm not sure. We haven't worked on this kind of project before, **have we**? So we don't really know how long it's going to take us, **do we**?
   Dave: That's right. But you've already collected some ideas, **haven't you**?
   Luke: Well, erm …

two hundred and eighty-nine **289**

G15 I wasn't allowed to go over to Jay's house yesterday.

Hi,
Guess what. When I came home from school, there was water everywhere on the kitchen floor. Something was wrong with the washing machine and Dad **had to** fix it before Mum came home. Dad had no idea what he was doing … But I **was allowed to** use his tablet and check for advice in a forum. I **was able to** find a great website quickly. It was very helpful. All we **had to** do was turn the knob off. So we **were able to** solve the problem in 20 minutes and Mum **was able to** use the washing machine when she came home.
See you at school on Monday.
Luke

G16 You could look at a forum for help.

Lösungsvorschlag:
1. You should say sorry (to her). / You could ask if she needs help. / You should be more careful when you play netball.
2. You should tell Dave. / You could buy him a new book. / You could ask how much the book was and give him the money.
3. You shouldn't pull him out from under the bed. / You could put some food in front of the bed. / You could leave a gap between the bed and the wall. Then it's easier to pick him up.
4. You should say sorry (to her). / You could buy her new flowers for her garden. / Next time if you are not sure, you should ask her first.

Unit 6

G17 I'll miss you so much!

1. Olivia: I hope Dave **will love** his new school.
2. Holly: I'm sure the Prestons **will visit** Granny Rose and Aunt Frances in London soon.
3. Luke: I don't think the new home **will be** a problem for Sid. There **are** lots of fields and he **will be able to run around**. He **will make** new cat friends quickly. He **won't get bored**!
4. Gwen: I hope Dave **won't forget** us.

G18 If you look at a map of Great Britain, you'll find Cornwall in the far west.

Lösungsvorschlag:
If you visit Hamburg, you should see the harbour and try a fish burger.
If you go to Cologne, climb to the top of the Dome.
If you're interested in cars, you could go to Stuttgart and visit the Porsche Museum/Mercedes Museum.
If you go to Eisenach, you should visit the Wartburg and try Thüringer Bratwurst/sausages there. You could also visit the Bachhaus/Lutherhaus.

<G19 If I were an adult, I could choose where I wanted to live.>

Lösungsvorschlag:
1. If I were an adult, I could choose what I wanted to learn.
2. My mum/dad would do anything if my brother and I didn't argue all the time.
3. If I got more pocket money, I would buy new shoes.
4. If I didn't live in a town, I could have a big dog.
   If I didn't live in a village, I could walk to school.

Bildquellennachweis:

U1.1 February Films (Andrew Kemp), London; **U1.2** Alamy stock photo, Abingdon/robertharding, Berlin; **2ff** *(Union Jack)* shutterstock (suicidecrew), New York, NY; **2.1** February Films (Andrew Kemp), London; **2.2** February Films (Andrew Kemp), London; **2.3** February Films (Andrew Kemp), London; **3.1** February Films (Andrew Kemp), London; **3.2** February Films (Andrew Kemp), London; **3.3** February Films (Andrew Kemp), London; **4.1** February Films (Andrew Kemp), London; **4.2** iStockphoto (andrearoad), Calgary, Alberta; **4.3** February Films (Andrew Kemp), London; **5.1** February Films (Andrew Kemp), London; **5.2** Thinkstock (Salah Malkawi), München; **5.3** February Films (Andrew Kemp), London; **6.1** Fotolia.com (visoook), New York; **6.2** iStockphoto (MattStansfield), Calgary, Alberta; **6.3** February Films (Andrew Kemp), London; **7.1** February Films (Andrew Kemp), London; **7.2** Alamy Images (Melissa Gaskell), Abingdon, Oxon; **7.3** Alamy Images (Jeff Morgan 06), Abingdon, Oxon; **8.1** February Films (Andrew Kemp), London; **8.2** February Films (Andrew Kemp), London; **9.1** February Films (Andrew Kemp), London; **9.2** February Films (Andrew Kemp), London; **10.2** Getty Images (Stuart Wilson), München; **12.1** shutterstock (Studio 37), New York, NY; **16.1** Fotolia.com (Jakub Cejpek), New York; **16.2** Thinkstock (Ammit), München; **16.3** Dream Maker Software (RF), Colorado; **19.1** February Films (Andrew Kemp), London; **20.1** Hath, Jessica Alice, Freiburg; **21.1** shutterstock (granata1111), New York, NY; **21.2** February Films (Andrew Kemp), London; **22.1** Fotolia.com (evron.info), New York; **22.2** ddp images GmbH (Newscom/UPI), Hamburg; **22.3** Fotolia.com (toolklickit), New York; **24.1** February Films, London; **28.1** February Films (Andrew Kemp), London; **28.2** February Films (Andrew Kemp), London; **28.3** February Films (Andrew Kemp), London; **28.4** February Films (Elke Bock), London; **29.1** February Films (Andrew Kemp), London; **30.1** laif (Pawel Libera/Loop Images), Köln; **31.1** February Films (Andrew Kemp), London; **32.1** February Films (Andrew Kemp), London; **34.1** Imago, Berlin; **35.1** Fotolia.com (caularatjada), New York; **35.2** shutterstock (dw1), New York, NY; **35.3** Thinkstock (Peter Elvidge), München; **35.4** Fotolia.com (Stephen Coburn), New York; **35.5** Thinkstock (Josh Rinehults), München; **35.6** shutterstock (Martijn Wisse), New York, NY; **36.1** February Films, London; **43.1** Thinkstock (Simon Greig), München; **43.2** Fotolia.com (matttilda), New York, NY; **43.4** akg-images, Berlin; **43.5** shutterstock (S-BELOV), New York, NY; **47.1** Getty Images (Blend Images), München; **48.1** Getty Images, München; **48.2** shutterstock (Bikeworldtravel), New York, NY; **48.3** shutterstock (Carsten Medom Madsen), New York, NY; **48.4** shutterstock (Francesco Carucci), New York, NY; **48.5** dreamstime.com (Emanuel Corso), Brentwood, TN; **48.6** Fotolia.com (geckospake), New York; **49.1** February Films, London; **50.1** February Films (Andrew Kemp), London; **51.1** iStockphoto (andrearoad), Calgary, Alberta; **51.2** laif (Polaris Images), Köln; **51.3** Corbis (Mike Kemp/In Pictures), Berlin; **51.4** February Films (Andrew Kemp), London; **54.1** February Films (Andrew Kemp), London; **54.2** February Films (Andrew Kemp), London; **54.3** February Films (Andrew Kemp), London; **54.4** February Films (Andrew Kemp), London; **54.5** February Films (Andrew Kemp), London; **54.6** February Films (Andrew Kemp), London; **56.1** Argus (Peter Frischmuth), Hamburg; **56.2** Corbis (Alison Wright), Berlin; **57.1** shutterstock (Arvydas Kniuksta), New York, NY; **57.2** shutterstock (Jacek Chabraszewski), New York, NY; **57.3** Fotolia.com (kateignatenko), New York; **57.4** BigStockPhoto.com (toxawww), Davis, CA; **57.5** Thinkstock (boggy22), München; **57.6** Thinkstock (Søren Sielemann), München; **58.1** February Films, London; **58.2** February Films, London; **60.1** Google Inc. (Kartendaten © 2014 Google), Mountain View, CA 94043; **62.1** Thinkstock (John Pavel),

München; **65.1** shutterstock (Four Oaks), New York, NY; **65.2** February Films (Andrew Kemp), London; **65.4** February Films (Andrew Kemp), London; **65.5** dreamstime.com (Woo Bing Siew), Brentwood, TN; **65.6** February Films (Andrew Kemp), London; **68.1** Thinkstock (Salah Malkawi), München; **68.2** shutterstock (Bikeworldtravel), New York, NY; **68.3** Klett-Archiv (Thomas Weccard), Stuttgart; **68.4** shutterstock (Eoghan McNally), New York, NY; **69.1** Picture-Alliance (Uli Gasper), Frankfurt; **71.1** Hath, Jessica Alice, Freiburg; **72.1** February Films (Andrew Kemp), London; **72.2** February Films (Andrew Kemp), London; **74.1** shutterstock (Glayan), New York, NY; **75.1** Thinkstock (AlbertoChagas), München; **76.1** February Films, London; **77.1** dreamstime.com (A1shutterbug), Brentwood, TN; **82.1** shutterstock (Michaelpuche), New York, NY; **82.2** February Films (Andrew Kemp), London; **83.1** Fotolia.com (José 16), New York; **86.1** Mauritius Images (Alamy), Mittenwald; **87.1** Alamy Images (David Robertson), Abingdon, Oxon; **88.1** February Films, London; **88.2** February Films, London; **89.1** Thinkstock (Ramon Purcell), München; **89.2** Ullstein Bild GmbH (ullstein - iT), Berlin; **90.1** February Films (Andrew Kemp), London; **91.1** Fotolia.com (visoook), New York; **91.2** Getty Images (Photodisc), München; **91.3** Thinkstock (Purestock), München; **91.4** February Films (Andrew Kemp), London; **92.1** iStockphoto (RF/Matt Ramos), Calgary, Alberta; **94.1** Picture-Alliance (PhotoAlto), Frankfurt; **98.1** February Films, London; **98.2** February Films, London; **98.3** February Films, London; **100.1** Getty Images (Photodisc), München; **104.1** www.CartoonStock.com (Cook, Gary), Bath; **105.1** Thinkstock (Elena Elisseeva), München; **108.1** Alamy Images (Melissa Gaskell), Abingdon, Oxon; **108.2** Alamy Images (Jeff Morgan 06), Abingdon, Oxon; **108.3** Alamy Images (Peter Horree), Abingdon, Oxon; **108.4** Thinkstock (versevend), München; **110.1** February Films (Andrew Kemp), London; **113.1** Klett-Archiv (Weccard), Stuttgart; **114.1** iStockphoto (MattStansfield), Calgary, Alberta; **115.1** Alamy Images (Kevin Britland), Abingdon, Oxon; **116.1** shutterstock (antb), New York, NY; **117.1** February Films (Andrew Kemp), London; **119.1** February Films, London; **120.1** iStockphoto (Deejpilot), Calgary, Alberta; **122.1** shutterstock (Helen Hotson), New York, NY; **124.1** Fotolia.com (acceleratorhams), New York; **125.1** shutterstock (Atlaspix), New York, NY; **129.1** Picture-Alliance (dpa/Armin Weigel), Frankfurt; **129.2** shutterstock (iurii), New York, NY; **129.3** Getty Images, München; **130.1** February Films, London; **130.2** February Films, London; **130.3** February Films, London; **132.1** dreamstime.com (Oleg Shipov), Brentwood, TN; **133.1** dreamstime.com (Ingrid Hogenbijl), Brentwood, TN; **133.2** Klett-Archiv (Simianer & Blühdorn), Stuttgart; **133.3** shutterstock (Michaelpuche), New York, NY; **133.4** shutterstock (criben), New York, NY; **136.1** Getty Images (LatitudeStock - Allan Hartley), München; **139.1** Getty Images (Sonya Hurtado), München; **139.2** Getty Images (Digital Vision), München; **143.1** Getty Images (E+), München; **143.2** Fotolia.com (Sophie James), New York; **144.1** Getty Images (Vetta), München; **145.1** Getty Images (Brand X Pictures), München; **146.1** February Films (Andrew Kemp), London; **146.2** February Films (Andrew Kemp), London; **149.1** Getty Images (E+), München; **150.1** February Films (Andrew Kemp), London; **153.41648** Fotolia.com (Kristina Afanasyeva), New York; **153.41648** shutterstock (yexelA), New York, NY; **154.1** shutterstock (M R), New York, NY; **155.1** iStockphoto (Stephen Rees), Calgary, Alberta; **155.2** Thinkstock (Robert Brown), München; **155.3** Avenue Images GmbH (StockDisc), Hamburg; **155.4** Klett-Archiv (Anke Bausch, Taucha), Stuttgart; **155.5** Klett-Archiv (Peter Nierhoff), Stuttgart; **161.1** shutterstock (Ferencz Teglas), New York, NY; **166.1** February Films, London; **166.2** February Films, London; **170.1** February Films (Andrew Kemp), London; **173.1** Thinkstock (RTimages), München; **174.1** February Films

Text- und Liedquellen:
S. 26 From *Middle School: How I Got Lost in London* by James Patterson. Published by Random House Children's Publishers. Reprinted by permission of the Random House Group Ltd.; **S. 44** Excerpt from *Horrid Henry Rules the World* by Francesca Simon, Orion Children's Books, an Imprint of The Orion Publishing Group Ltd, London, July 1, 2008 © Francesca Simon, 2008 (adapted); **S. 66** Excerpt from *The Copper Treasure* by Melvin Burgess, A & C Black Publishers Ltd, London, 1999/2002 © Melvin Burgess (adapted); **S. 73** Excerpt from the brochure *Erkennen – Bewerten – Handeln: Zur Gesundheit von Kindern und Jugendlichen in Deutschland*, Robert Koch-Institut, Bundeszentrale für gesundheitliche Aufklärung, p. 33, Berlin und Köln, 2008 © Robert Koch-Institut; **S. 84** „The Summer Table" from WONDER by R. J. Palacio, copyright © 2012 by R.J. Palacio. Reprinted by permission of R.J. Palacio and Alfred A. Knopf, an imprint of Random House Childrens's Books, a division of Random House LLC. All rights reserved; **S. 94** „Friends" Text: Armato, Antonina/Dione, Aura marie/James, Tim/Jost, David © Akashic Field Music/Antonina Songs/Good Songs Publishing A/S/ Universal/MCA Music Publishing GmbH, Berlin/Universal Music Publishing GmbH, Berlin/Rolf Budde Musikverlag GmbH, Berlin/Jost Music Publisching David Jost, Berlin; **S. 106** Excerpt from *Ratburger* by David Walliams, HarperCollins Children's Books, a division of HarperCollins Publishers Ltd, London, 2012 © David Walliams 2012 (adapted); **S. 116** From www.poetryarchive.org/poem/romans-britain, © Judith Nicholls; **S. 126** Excerpt from „A Harp on the Water" from *Welsh Legends and Folktales* by Gwyn Jones (ed.), Oxford University Press, 1955 (adapted); **S. 159** Excerpt from *Ratburger* by David Walliams, HarperCollins Children's Books, a division of HarperCollins Publishers Ltd, London, 2012 © David Walliams 2012 (adapted)

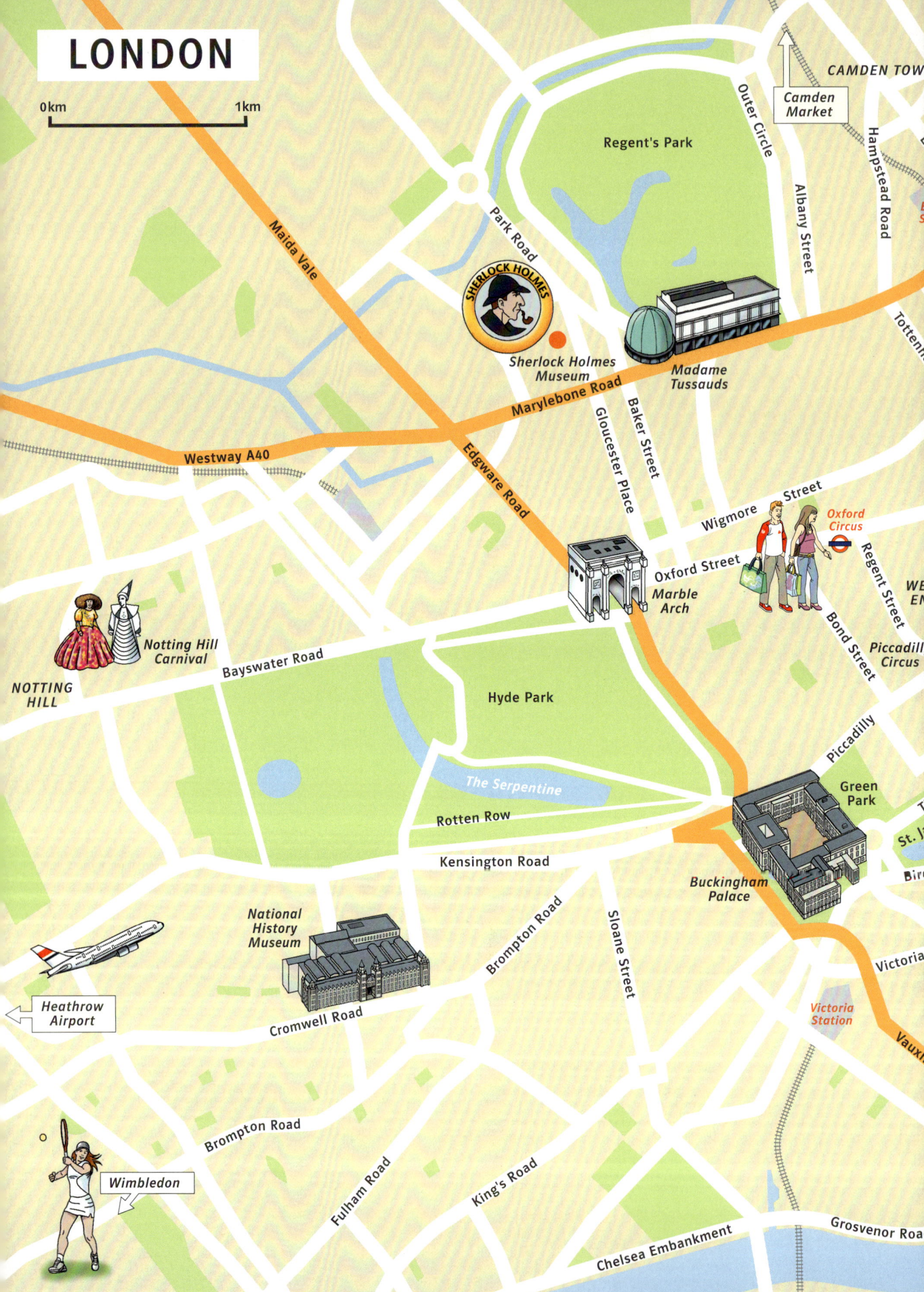

LONDON

0km 1km

Maida Vale

Regent's Park

Outer Circle

CAMDEN TOW

Camden Market

Albany Street

Hampstead Road

E
S

Park Road

Tottenha

SHERLOCK HOLMES

Sherlock Holmes Museum

Madame Tussauds

Marylebone Road

Edgware Road

Baker Street

Gloucester Place

Westway A40

Wigmore Street

Oxford Circus

WE
EN

Oxford Street

Marble Arch

Regent Street

Bond Street

Piccadilly Circus

Notting Hill Carnival

NOTTING HILL

Bayswater Road

Hyde Park

The Serpentine

Rotten Row

Kensington Road

Piccadilly

Green Park

St. Ja

Bird

Buckingham Palace

National History Museum

Brompton Road

Sloane Street

Victoria

Victoria Station

Heathrow Airport

Cromwell Road

Vauxh

Brompton Road

Fulham Road

King's Road

Wimbledon

Chelsea Embankment

Grosvenor Road

↑ Highbury

King's Cross Station

St. Pancras Station

City Road

Old Street

Great Eastern St.

Woburn Place

Gray's Inn Road

Clerkenwell Road

Farringdon Road

Bloomsbury St.

British Museum

City of London

Brick Lane

London Wall

High Holborn

St. Paul's Cathedral

Charing Cross Road

Avenue

Covent Garden

Covent Garden

Fleet Street

Tower of London

Shaftesbury Road

Strand

Embankment

Blackfriars Bridge

Millennium Bridge

Southwark Bridge

Trafalgar Square

Waterloo Bridge

Victoria

London Eye

Tate Modern

Southwark Street

Globe Theatre

The Shard

Tower Bridge

London Dungeon

the London Dungeon

Waterloo Station

Waterloo Road

Blackfriars Road

SOUTHWARK

Borough High Street

Docklands →

Thames Barrier →

Horse Guards

Houses of Parliament

Westminster Abbey

Westminster Bridge

WESTMINSTER

River Thames

Lambeth Bridge

Millbank

Albert Embankment

Vauxhall Bridge

Mudchute Farm

Trinity Hospital

Thames

Swimming Pool (Arches Leisure Centre)

Cutty Sark

Playground

Greenwich Market

Boating Lake

Vanbrugh Castle

Greenwich Station

Fan Museum

Planetarium

Royal Observatory

Deer Park

Tennis Court

Rose Garden

London

Greenwich

Thomas Tallis School

GREENWICH

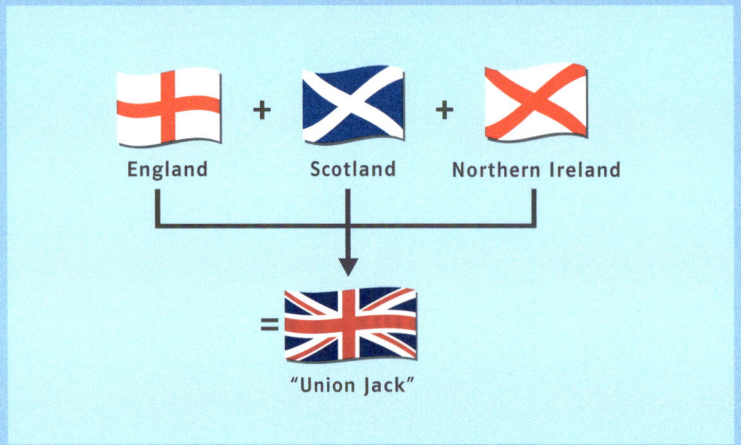

England + Scotland + Northern Ireland

= "Union Jack"

Atlantic Ocean

Galway

**REPUBLIC
OF IRELAND**

Cork